fP

To Jean —
one journalist
to another —
Best

Maureen Keller

MARVIN KALB

ONE SCANDALOUS STORY

CLINTON, LEWINSKY, AND THIRTEEN DAYS THAT TARNISHED AMERICAN JOURNALISM

THE FREE PRESS

New York   London   Toronto   Sydney   Singapore

THE FREE PRESS
A Division of Simon & Schuster, Inc.
1230 Avenue of the Americas
New York, NY 10020

For information about special discounts for bulk purchases,
please contact Simon & Schuster Special Sales:
1-800-456-6798 or business@simonandschuster.com

Designed by Brooke Koven

Manufactured in the United States of America

10 9 8 7 6 5 4 3 2 1

Library of Congress Cataloging-in-Publication Data

Kalb, Marvin L.
    One scandalous story : Clinton, Lewinsky, and thirteen days that tarnished American
journalism / Marvin Kalb.
        p. cm.
    Includes bibliographical references and index.
    ISBN 0-684-85939-4
    1. Clinton, Bill, 1946—Relations with journalists. 2. Clinton, Bill, 1946—Relations
with women. 3. Lewinsky, Monica S. (Monica Samille), 1973. 4. Press and politics—
United States—History—20th century. 5. Mass media—Political aspects—United
States—History—20th century. 6. Journalistic ethics—United States—History—
20th century. 7. Sensationalism in journalism—United States—History—20th century.
8. Privacy, Right of—United States—History—20th century. I. Title.

E886.2.K35 2001
973.929′092—dc21

                                                                                    2001033690

ISBN 0-684-85939-4

In memory of William P. Green, a very special father-in-law,
who set a model for elegant aging, political and literary engagement,
and
a love of family that I try to emulate.

CONTENTS

PREFACE AND
ACKNOWLEDGMENTS

Let me explain my motivation in writing *One Scandalous Story* and then acknowledge my gratitude to colleagues and family.

After twelve years as director of the Shorenstein Center on the Press, Politics and Public Policy, I wanted to write a book that would answer a number of questions. What had I, a veteran of thirty years as a broadcast journalist, learned about the practice of journalism? What impact had the press had on the fashioning of public policy? How had television affected our politics and politicians? What had I been able to pass on to my students? A number of ideas had been running through my mind, but none seemed quite right. None, that is, until January 21, 1998, when *The Washington Post* reported that President Clinton had been caught in an affair with a White House intern and that he had urged her to lie about it. Within hours, television pundits were on the air speculating about impeachment.

I had my subject. I decided to focus tightly on thirteen days of Washington coverage: the eight days leading up to the breaking of the story, the day it broke, and the next four days, when journalists focused on the scandal as if nothing else in the world mattered. In this way, through the lens of a breaking story, I could describe the revolutionary changes in contemporary journalism.

The first person I wish to thank is actually an institution—the Shorenstein Center itself, where students mix with faculty and practitioners to explore the press/politics issues of the day. My successor, Alex Jones, a Pulitzer Prize–winning reporter and author, is as excited and enthusiastic about the Center as I have been. Our principal benefactor, Walter Shorenstein, a businessman and friend from San Francisco, has supported the Center with exceptional dedication and concern.

Two of my students were particularly helpful: Kendra Proctor Goldbas, during the early months of the research, and Amy Sullivan, throughout the entire process of researching, writing, and editing the manuscript.

My Washington assistant, Michael Barre, also helped with the research. In addition, he collated and organized the chapters and maintained close liaison with the publisher.

I had two editors. Normally an author gets one; I was lucky. First Paul Golob, who helped shape the outline of the book before leaving for another publishing house. Then Rachel Klayman, who assumed Golob's responsibilities and threw herself into the project, reading the manuscript again and again with meticulous care. She made superb editorial suggestions, most of which I accepted with gratitude. Her assistant, Brian Selfon, was always available and helpful.

Among those who read and edited the manuscript were my brother Bernard Kalb and my friends Harry Schwartz and Andrew Glass. They offered gentle criticism.

My daughter Deborah Kalb, a journalist and writer, took time from her busy schedule to read and edit the manuscript. Her assistance was invaluable, best described as professional candor extended with loving concern.

My daughter Judith Kalb and her husband, Alexander Ogden, both professors of Russian language and literature at the University of South Carolina, provided a constant source of encouragement, advice, and good humor.

Finally, as always, I thank my wife, Madeleine G. Kalb, who is a scholar and writer and, without doubt, the best, toughest editor I've ever had. After more than forty-three years and ten books, I have learned to adapt to the sharpness of her pen and appreciate the clarity of her mind. We have had our editorial differences, but I find that she has always been right.

ONE SCANDALOUS STORY

INTRODUCTION

Scandal in the News, Then and Now

IT IS NOW ACCEPTED HISTORY THAT KENNEDY JUMPED CASU-
ALLY FROM BED TO BED WITH A WIDE VARIETY OF WOMEN. IT
WAS NOT ACCEPTED HISTORY THEN—DURING THE FIVE YEARS
THAT I KNEW HIM.

—Ben Bradlee, *A Good Life*

Late September in New York is a traffic and protocol nightmare. From all over the world, presidents and prime ministers, accompanied by foreign ministers and their many minions, arrive for the annual meeting of the United Nations General Assembly. Their limousines crisscross mid-Manhattan, adding to the usual, suffocating traffic. Aided by the FBI, the police provide the necessary protection. They are everywhere, standing in front of UN missions or sitting on horseback or in patrol cars looking at the passing parade for anyone or anything even slightly suspicious. Often, in triangular squadrons of motorcycles, they escort the VIPs from one corner of central Manhattan to another. It's an urban symphony of horns, sirens, and shrieking tires that, no matter the time of day, never seems to lose its urgency. The worst bottleneck, of course, is always near the United Nations, where cabs join the battle for every inch of maneuverable space. It's really quite a sight.

On September 20, 1963, two months before he was assassinated in Dallas, Texas, President John F. Kennedy decided that he would not stay at the Waldorf-Astoria, temporary home for so many of the other world leaders. For reasons of his own, he fancied the more fashionable Carlyle Hotel, farther north, which conveyed the comforting impression that it was situated on another planet, light-years removed from the midtown mess. During the president's visit, the usually elegant main entrance on

East 76th Street was—for reasons of security—flanked by wooden barricades, holding back television crews, reporters, onlookers eager for a glimpse of Kennedy. Around the corner on Madison Avenue, an unobtrusive side entrance was generally ignored.

For easy and quick identification, reporters who covered the president wore White House press badges. They were able to enter the Carlyle without much trouble. Some of us, with the help of the White House travel office, even managed to get lodging there. After filing our stories, a number of us in those years would usually gather late in the evening for some journalistic braggadocio—who got the better picture of the president? who got the better scoop? who wrote the best lead?—and a drink or two at the hotel bar off Madison Avenue.

After the president finished addressing the Eighteenth General Assembly, the principal purpose of his visit to New York, he returned to the Carlyle for a round of bilateral talks, a formal dinner, and, much later in the evening, a clandestine rendezvous with an unscheduled visitor. I, in the meantime, had returned to the headquarters of CBS News, which was then located on Madison Avenue at 52nd Street. Not too many months before, I had finished an absorbing, if somewhat exhausting, three-year assignment in Moscow, and—as a reward of sorts—I had been transferred to Washington and named diplomatic correspondent, the first ever appointed by a network. My assignment on this occasion was not so much Kennedy as his diplomacy, which focused on mending relations with the Soviet Union after the terrifying missile crisis in Cuba the year before. What I reported that evening in a couple of radio and television spots about Berlin and arms control has vanished, and deservedly so, into some distant archive; but what I remember about my brief encounter with the president's late night visitor underscores how dramatically American journalism has changed in the last thirty to forty years, particularly in its coverage of the private lives of public officials.

After dinner with a few CBS colleagues at a favorite restaurant, I jumped into a taxi for the ride up Madison Avenue to the Carlyle. I remember the ride and the time—just past 11 p.m.—because the driver was then listening to an hourly newscast featuring one of the spots I had taped earlier in the day at the United Nations. I got out at the side entrance and walked into the hotel. To my left was the bar, my ultimate destination, and diagonally to my right were two doors leading to the main lobby. Though I didn't see it on a recent visit to the Carlyle, I recall that there was also a private elevator just to the right of the entryway. Immediately, as I entered, I felt as if I had barged into a private party—the wrong person arriving at the wrong time.

I recognized two of the Secret Servicemen usually detailed to protect the president, one standing right in front of me and the other to my right. They knew me, and I knew them. We had been on a number of the same trips, and I had seen them around the White House. I smiled at one of them, but he not only did not return the smile—his face froze into a mask of sudden panic. He looked past me at someone who was just then being escorted into the small lobby. As I turned to see who had caught his eye, he pushed me and I fell hard against the door to the bar, ending up in a painful crouch on the floor. I looked up just long enough to see the back of a woman with stunningly attractive legs entering the elevator. I heard the clicking of her heels. I saw two other men from the president's Secret Service detail with her, one in front, the other behind, as the doors slowly closed. I looked up for an explanation, but the agent who had knocked me to the floor had by this time vanished. So too had his colleague. The entire episode took no more than ten seconds.

I joined a few reporters at the bar. I must have been more than just a bit shaken, but I didn't tell them anything. After a few minutes of stories about scoops and counterscoops, I looked back at the door and saw the agent beckoning to me. I excused myself and went back into the lobby. "I'm sorry," the agent whispered. "I'm really sorry." The agent, barely audible, said that he should never have pushed me, that he had made a terrible mistake, and he hoped that I would forgive him. "Of course," I muttered, "but, my God, what happened? Why did you push me? Who was that woman?" The agent did not answer. He looked up at the ceiling, as if appealing to higher, perhaps presidential, authority, and shook his head. He seemed totally flustered and embarrassed. Again, he said only, "I'm sorry," and left.

In my room a while later, still hurting from the fall, I thought about complaining to Pierre Salinger, the president's spokesman. The Secret Service's job, after all, was to protect the president, not to push or bully a reporter. I decided to do nothing. I thought it would be better for me and CBS News to store this grievance in a future file—one day, that agent might be able to help me with a story. He owed me.

As I write about this incident more than thirty-seven years later, I am amazed not by my decision to do nothing but by the fact, quite undeniable, that never for one moment did I even consider pursuing and reporting what I had seen and experienced that evening: that U.S. Secret Service agents, normally detailed to protect the president, had escorted an attractive woman into the Carlyle, presumably for a rendezvous with Kennedy (who else but the president would concern them?), and then, to protect their embarrassing secret, one of the agents had for a moment panicked and pushed a reporter to the floor only to apologize later for his inexcusable behavior.

It was my judgment at the time that such an incident was simply not "news." Although there has never been one commonly accepted definition of news, it has usually been defined broadly as what's new, what's relevant, what's interesting, what's timely, and what sells. In those days, the possibility of a presidential affair, while titillating, was not considered "news" by the mainstream press—not when the Cuban missile crisis was still a fresh and frightening memory of the nuclear dangers of the Cold War, not when racial tensions were again clawing at the soul of the nation. Though tabloids existed, those were not tabloid times; 1963 was not a year for stories about Kennedy's sex life, even if rumors persisted that he was engaging in "extracurricular screwing," as Ben Bradlee, the former editor of *The Washington Post*, spoke of it in his memoirs.

Many years later, my friend R. W. Apple, Jr., recalled a similar experience at the Carlyle Hotel in 1963. He was then a young reporter at *The New York Times*, and he was assigned to do "legwork" on a Kennedy visit to New York—meaning in this case that he went to the Carlyle to see what, if anything, was happening, and then to report back to his editor. A "legman" didn't write the story, he just observed and reported it. His information was then included in someone else's story or simply dropped. On this particular evening, Apple saw a "beautiful woman being escorted to Kennedy's suite." Excited by the implication, he returned to the *Times* office on West 43rd Street and told Sheldon Binn, the chief assignment editor of the Metro desk. Binn listened impatiently. "Apple," he said, "you're supposed to report on political and diplomatic policies, not girlfriends. No story." And so it was.

But even if I had decided to defy the conventional news standards of the day and tried to report that the president had a secret rendezvous at the Carlyle Hotel with a beautiful woman who was not his wife, what exactly would I have broadcast? Did I know for an absolute fact that the agents had escorted the woman to his suite? No. But I'd have bet the kitchen sink that they had. Did I see her face? Did I know her name? No. Was there, possibly, an innocent explanation? Could she have been just a friend, a relative? No. Friends and relatives were not secretly hustled into a back elevator late at night; they would have entered the main lobby at a proper time. Anything was theoretically possible, but at the time, given what I had seen and heard, I knew in my gut that the president was having an illicit affair and the Secret Service was complicit in arranging it and hushing it up.

Let's take the scenario one step further and assume for a moment that I actually had written and submitted the story to my CBS editors. Was there any chance that they would have cleared it for broadcast? I am certain that the answer would have been no. They would almost certainly have questioned my professional judgment. "What's happened to Kalb? He used to be a good reporter."

In other words, the story was not written, and it would not have been approved for broadcast, because it did not satisfy the accepted journalistic standards of the day. Between then and now, these standards have dramatically changed. Now, I suspect, my story would quickly dominate the Internet, provide fodder for radio and television talk shows, work its way into the mainstream media, and then assault the front page on the strength of an ensuing string of allegations, presidential denials, White House cover-ups, and journalistic investigations.

How is this change in journalistic standards to be explained? How could the press have ignored Kennedy's escapades but blasted Bill Clinton for his? The answer is that journalism has changed dramatically in this forty-year period, just as the nation has changed. The business of the news has been radically recast. The technology has been revolutionized. And many journalists have been transformed into national celebrities and political players—all in step with a succession of crises that jolted the nation beyond recognition. Kennedy was assassinated. African Americans went into the streets and demanded equal rights. Robert Kennedy and Martin Luther King, Jr., were both murdered. Richard Nixon won twice but still was forced to resign, one step ahead of almost certain impeachment after the Watergate scandal uncovered the lies and deception in his administration. In a small country called Vietnam, half a world away, the United States lost the first war in its history. These two factors in particular—Watergate and Vietnam—combined to sour popular attitudes toward the presidency. Trust in government (and other large institutions) declined in the public and in the press.

Reporters came to assume that officials lied routinely. Nixon once felt the need to tell the American people that he was not "a crook." Presidents were no longer held in especially high regard. They became more human, more accessible. By 1987, a reporter crossed a once uncrossable line by asking a presidential candidate if he had ever committed adultery. Within twenty-four hours, Gary Hart had to withdraw from the race. Only five years later, during the 1992 campaign, adultery blossomed into a major story when a tabloid disclosed that Clinton had had a long-running affair with a woman from Arkansas. And once the story was "out there," it was quickly everywhere. Even *Nightline* discussed it, an indication of changing public attitudes toward personal privacy.

By the mid-1990s, media mergers flowered in an expanding economy. Huge corporations continued to acquire news companies and networks and create global conglomerates more interested in the bottom line than in public service. By the turn of the century, AOL and Time Warner capped this trend by concluding a $182 billion deal, combining the older business of news with the new demands of cyberspace. The new news cycle was now a twenty-four-hour-a-day challenge. There was an endless demand for talk—filling time was the burning need. Accountability seemed nonexistent. Competition among the cable channels became ferocious. The maximization of profit drove the news business, and old worries about standards fell by the wayside. As a governing concept, journalistic integrity suddenly sounded quaint.

It could be argued, of course, that for most of American history, except for the decades of the Great Depression, World War II, and the Cold War, serious journalism was a rare happening. With a few notable exceptions, most reporters used to wallow happily in gossip, slander, and sensationalism. That was the norm. James Thomson Callender, a Virginia "newsmonger," to quote *New York Times* columnist William Safire, claimed that President Thomas Jefferson had several children with "the luscious Sally," one of his slaves. Grover Cleveland fathered an illegitimate daughter, and during his first presidential campaign the press gloried in a catchy political jingle: "Ma, ma, where's my pa? Gone to the White House, ha, ha, ha." During World War I, Warren Harding, then a senator with presidential ambitions, inspired some gossipy copy when he persuaded the Republican National Committee to send one of his lovers on an all-expenses-paid trip to Japan.

The post–Cold War period of the 1990s has seen a return to this earlier tradition. With old-fashioned abandon now buttressed by new technologies that make possible virtually instantaneous communication, many reporters seem to revel in the rebirth of scandal and sensational coverage. The O. J. Simpson trial, Princess Diana's life, loves, and death, and the Lewinsky scandal defined the news of the nineties. *New York Times* columnist Frank Rich labeled these "dramatic 24/7 TV miniseries" as "mediathons" or "total national immersions." He thought of these stories as being "played out in real time before a mass audience." In this way, a mediathon was seen as different from other big stories; it was all-consuming and inescapable, it affected the viewer just as the viewer's reaction fed back into the mediathon in a modern variation of the Heisenberg principle. A mediathon changed the flow of history.

When the story broke on January 21, 1998, that President Clinton had had an affair with White House intern Monica Lewinsky, the press plunged into the scandal, disclosing every tasteless detail. Its self-justifying explanation was that it had no choice: a criminal investigation had begun against the president of the United States and "the story" had to be covered.

How did this mediathon unfold? That is the central question in this book, which focuses on thirteen days of scandal coverage in January 1998. Many other books have examined the role of the independent counsel, the White House spin doctors, the president's friends, the combative lawyers, the "vast right-wing conspiracy," the Whitewater land deal in Little Rock, the tale of Monica Lewinsky, the congressional impeachment proceeding, and, no doubt, many more books will be written and published in the years ahead. The Lewinsky scandal stained the presidency, the country, and the Clinton legacy, which seriously damaged Vice President Gore's 2000 campaign. It is not a surprise that it has spawned a literary industry. Until now, though, the role of the journalist, a key player in this drama, has not yet been the subject of serious analysis. Whether it was Michael Isikoff or Susan Schmidt or Jackie Judd, the journalist was the indispensable messenger carrying the story from one side of the Washington battlefield to another. The journalist informed and inflamed the public. The journalist saw old standards fall and new ones created for the occasion. The Lewinsky scandal marks an important chapter in the history of American journalism.

I have chosen to examine the recent history of Washington journalism through a sharply focused lens: thirteen days in the life of a story that would preoccupy the nation for the next thirteen months. The thirteen days can be divided into three parts: the buildup from January 13 to January 20; the breaking of the story on January 21; and the aftermath from January 22 to January 25, 1998. I have basically devoted a chapter to each day, hoping in this way to X-ray the Washington press corps. Several questions emerge:

- How did the new economic changes in the news business affect copy?
- How has journalism been changed by the new technology, including the Internet?
- Was there a journalistic rush to judgment?
- Was there a surge in copy cat journalism?
- How could one explain the "blurring of the lines" between reporters and commentators? Between reporters and ex–political operatives?
- Were sources, generally recognized as the essential lubricant of a free press, used well or poorly during this period?
- Did many Washington reporters make special arrangements with government sources?

There are no easy answers to these questions, which cut to the very heart of contemporary American journalism. I have tried to answer them by taking the reader into the journalistic process during a hot and demanding story. I have read the literature, done the research often based on content and script analysis, and I have interviewed hundreds of Washington reporters who covered the scandal.

Journalism is too important, too crucial for our democracy, to be left unexamined. I know from personal experience that Washington reporters have notoriously thin skins. They don't take criticism easily. Who does? If they read my analysis as criticism, I hope they will understand that it is rendered with continuing admiration and affection.

For all other readers, concerned about the media's growing power and impact on society, wondering about its value system, its sense of responsibility and ethics, and genuinely baffled about how this eight-hundred-pound gorilla works, here is my report on one scandalous story.

CHAPTER I

WHITEWATER, WHERE IT
ALL BEGAN

"THERE IS NO REAL NEWS HERE."
—Cokie Roberts, ABC News

"LEN THINKS THIS IS HIS WATERGATE."
—Karen de Young, *The Washington Post*

"MY ZEAL WAS TO GET WHITEWATER, NOT ANOTHER WATER-
GATE."
—Leonard Downie, *The Washington Post*

For the journalists who lived or worked within the Washington Beltway, 1997 was a deceptively quiet year. Mark Jurkowitz, media critic of the *Boston Globe*, compared them to Maytag repairmen with no genuine emergency to occupy their time. There was no conflict, no crisis, no criminal indictment. There was prosperity at home, tranquility abroad. No longer were politicians trumpeting huge concepts aimed at transforming the nation and the world. Now they thought small and local, recommending, among other things, school uniforms, national testing of teachers, and a modest expansion of health care.

"Why is this happening on my watch?" lamented *USA Today* columnist Walter Shapiro. "It wasn't this bad for Walter Lippmann." "There is no real news here," concluded ABC News correspondent Cokie Roberts. "The country is bored, desperately bored," echoed *New York Times* columnist Frank Rich. "We have small ideas, small plans, small schemes." *Time*'s Margaret Carlson agreed: "There's no consensus for any big solutions." Kate O'Beirne, Washington editor of the *National Review*, complained about the vanishing distinctions between Republicans and Democrats. With both parties reaching for the comfortable center, she said, "the Washington bureau is less interesting."

Toward the end of the year, even President Clinton, often described as the master wonk of his era, totally dedicated to polls, proposals, and politics, surprised a number of his closest aides by lapsing into long reveries about . . . golf. Everyone knew Clinton loved golf, but in the past it had been nothing more than a relaxing distraction from politics. Now he seemed less than fully absorbed with the intricacies of public policy. In early December, Richard Berke and John Broder, two reporters in the Washington bureau of *The New York Times,* interviewed the president, as well as dozens of his colleagues, and emerged with the impression that he was "listless," "distracted," and "no longer consumed by big ideas." "It's golf, golf, golf—interspersed with politics," Senator John Breaux, Democrat of Louisiana, was quoted as saying. "He's willing to accept smaller, incremental victories." Dick Morris, who had helped engineer Clinton's 1996 reelection campaign until he got embroiled in a sex scandal of his own, provided a one-liner for an analysis, consistent with his new profession as a Fox TV pundit. "Everyone wondered after the election whether he'd go to the left or to the right," Morris joked. "Nobody thought he'd go to sleep."

The president, of course, denied that he was the slumbering custodian of a second-term philosophy of "don't rock the boat." He told Berke and Broder, "Presidents are the custodians of the time in which they live. We don't have a war, we don't have a depression." He stated, for the record, that his administration would advance very ambitious proposals, but he did not choose at that time to cite a single one as his overarching priority. The president's pollsters found no deep yearning in the American people for expansive social programs, such as Lyndon Johnson's "Great Society." The people seemed content with a bullish market and a booming economy and rewarded Clinton with a steady 60 percent job approval rating. In addition, they were soon to learn that the national budget, so wildly out of whack since the Reagan years, was on the verge of being balanced—an economic victory for the nation and a stupendous political triumph for the president and the Democrats. "As far as the public is concerned," crowed Mark Mellman, a Democratic pollster, "there aren't that many big things that need to be done."

Why shouldn't the president play golf? His staff was planning a January 1998 calendar full of calculated leaks and meticulously timed announcements of economic accomplishments, to be capped in the State of the

Union message on January 27 by the biggest bulletin of them all: for the first time in thirty years, a president would submit a balanced budget to Congress with a projected surplus of more than $660 billion over the next decade.

Presidents relish such moments; presidential advisers would kill for one. Paul Begala, one of Clinton's advisers, organized the press buildup with all the dedication of an experienced engineer constructing a thermonuclear bomb. Day after day, week after week, he and his colleagues leaked one story after another for maximum political effect. Begala explained their strategy, based on the notion that some newspapers were drawn to a certain type of story and others to another type. "This is a story that is a classic concern of *USA Today*. This is a story that's really built for the *Wall Street Journal*. This is a story that has particular interest for this reporter at *The New York Times*." As Begala told me, "Sequencing mattered," because this was "a very exciting time." Congress was out of session, meaning the president would stand alone on the national stage. "We decided to make the most of that."

Mike McCurry, the White House spokesman, injected the administration's top salesman, the president himself, into this public relations campaign. McCurry arranged three high-visibility interviews with Clinton for the afternoon of January 21, 1998, each designed to provide presidential quotes and images for the buildup. The reporters were carefully selected: Jim Lehrer, of PBS's *NewsHour with Jim Lehrer;* Mara Liasson and Robert Siegel of National Public Radio; and Mort Kondracke, executive editor of *Roll Call,* a newspaper that covers Capitol Hill. All were seasoned, serious journalists; if they could not fairly be described as "friendly" to the administration, they most certainly were not antagonistic.

No one could then have anticipated that the subject matter of these interviews would change so dramatically. At the start of 1998, the Clinton presidency seemed to be at the peak of its power and influence. The budget was being balanced. Unemployment was low. While problems persisted in parts of the world, the Cold War was history, American troops were not dying on distant battlefields, and nuclear war was widely regarded as inconceivable. As the American century—the twentieth—rushed to a close, the American people seemed like a fat, contented lot. But beneath this glow of popular satisfaction and national accomplishment there were problems rooted in the president's character and background that were about to explode into public view and challenge his right to remain in office.

For the Washington press corps, the story began in 1992 during Clinton's first presidential campaign, when tales of sexual adventures and financial irregularities surfaced, raising questions about his character. Clinton's tortured explanations about how he avoided the draft during the Vietnam War and how he tried marijuana but did not inhale suggested a lack of candor on matters large and small.

From the start, the mainstream press organizations were more comfortable digging into stories about Clinton's financial problems than about his sexual embarrassments, but there were times when sex clearly dominated the news. On January 23, 1992, in the midst of the New Hampshire primary campaign, a supermarket tabloid named *The Star* broke the Gennifer Flowers story, raising immediate political problems for Governor Clinton and ethical questions for journalists that would be discussed in editorial offices and academic seminars for years to come. One question was whether Ted Koppel's highly respected *Nightline* had violated an unwritten taboo by reporting Flowers's allegation of a twelve-year affair with Clinton, even though he reported it in the form of media criticism: how did the press cover the story?

For his part, Clinton used CBS's *60 Minutes,* the trailblazing paragon of network magazine programs, to state his case. A huge audience was assured, since on this Sunday *60 Minutes* followed the Super Bowl. With his wife sitting demurely at his side, candidate Clinton denied the Flowers allegation but conceded that he had not always behaved impeccably in his marriage. Many journalists assumed that Clinton was making a tacit promise to the American people: the past is the past; if you elect me, I'll behave myself as president. The voters were well aware of what had come to be called the "character issue," but they decided to give Clinton the benefit of the doubt. A strong plurality apparently believed that his personal failings were outweighed by his intelligence, his compassion, his obvious political skills, and the policies he advocated.

Considered more appropriate for the mainstream press was the subject of Clinton's financial entanglements. Arkansas provided a heady mix of crooked bankers, well-connected lawyers, and other characters out of a southern novel—all linked to a complicated land deal known as Whitewater. The first story about a questionable investment by the Clintons was reported by Jeff Gerth in *The New York Times* on March 8, 1992. For most of the next nine years, journalists and then prosecutors tried to get to the bottom of this story, which expanded from a land deal to lying about a sexual dalliance with a White House intern. Finally, on January 19, 2001, the last full day of the Clinton presidency, the president and prosecutor Robert W. Ray brought legal closure to the case. Ray abandoned the possibility of indicting Clinton for lying under oath and obstructing justice, and in exchange Clinton admitted that he had played games with the truth. "I tried to walk a line between acting lawfully and testifying falsely," Clinton said, "but I now recognize that I did not fully accomplish this goal and that certain of my responses to questions . . . were false."

Still, whether the early disclosures about Clinton were sexual or financial, they left a residue of mistrust among many reporters so that each new accusation, in Arkansas or at the White House, fell on fertile ground. The fact that the president and the first lady had to testify under oath at various times about their financial dealings and missing documents created the impression that all was not as it should be in the Clinton White House. In November 1993, the president felt the need to hire a personal lawyer, David Kendall, to deal with Whitewater.

By the time Clinton had been in office for only one year, Attorney General Janet Reno was forced to name a special prosecutor—an outsider with a very broad mandate—to investigate the Whitewater affair and all its tangled ramifications. She chose Robert Fiske, a moderate Republican who had served as a U.S. attorney in the Ford and Carter administrations and was regarded as both fair and tough. Ironically, on June 30, 1994, the same day that Fiske issued his first report, affirming that the death of high-ranking White House aide Vincent Foster really was a suicide, Clinton signed a law restoring the Independent Counsel Act, which had lapsed under Republican pressure and which he and the Democrats had championed.

It was assumed that the three-judge panel of the Circuit Court of Appeals responsible for naming the independent counsel would reappoint Fiske; in six months he had made considerable progress toward indictments in Little Rock. Instead, on August 5, 1994, the panel unexpectedly replaced him with Kenneth Starr, a former judge more sympathetic to their views. Although many observers—including Clinton's White House counsel Lloyd Cutler and his personal lawyer, Kendall—believed that Starr, as a former Circuit Court judge and Solicitor General, would be as fair-minded as Fiske, there were signs from the beginning that Starr was a partisan Republican with right-wing connections, and that the battle lines between him and Clinton would be sharply drawn.

No newspaper, no network, no magazine devoted more time, energy, and resources to the Whitewater scandal than *The Washington Post,* the most influential paper in the nation's capital. Editor Leonard Downie knew that *The New York Times* had beaten the *Post* to the initial story in March 1992, and now he wanted to beat the *Times* to the ultimate prize: the full story of the president's involvement. During the Watergate scandal—coverage of which the *Post* owned in the early 1970s—Howard Baker, then a Republican senator from Tennessee, asked two key questions: "What did the president know? And when did he know it?" Downie had his updated version of the Baker questions: Did Clinton benefit financially from the Whitewater land deal? And was Clinton engaged in a broad cover-up, characterized by lies, half-truths, and a steady stream of misleading statements, to protect his political flanks? Downie, like every other journalist in Washington interested in this story, wanted facts, documents, files. He was tired of evasions. He encouraged reporters Susan Schmidt and Michael Isikoff to "dig, dig, dig." "Look," Downie told me, "I was a land deal reporter years ago. Checking court records—that sort of thing. I loved the Whitewater story."

In late October and early November 1993, they began to hit pay dirt. Schmidt, a veteran investigative reporter who had labored for years in the Metro section of the *Post,* and Isikoff, whom Downie described as a "renegade," a "rebel" constantly at war with his editors, came up with a series of tantalizing stories. First, they discovered that the Resolution Trust Corporation (RTC), set up to deal with the rash of failed savings and loan banks in the 1980s, was investigating Madison Guaranty Trust, a defunct bank owned by the Clintons' Whitewater partners, James and Susan McDougal, that had cost the taxpayers an estimated $47 million. The RTC had asked federal prosecutors in Little Rock to open a criminal investigation, in part to determine whether the bank had used depositors' funds "to benefit local politicians, including a reelection campaign of then governor Bill Clinton."

Next, they reported that David Hale, a former municipal judge in Little Rock under indictment for defrauding the Small Business Administration (SBA), had charged that in the mid-1980s Clinton pressured him to make an illegal SBA loan to Susan McDougal which was used for Whitewater land purchases.

They followed up with a story that Webster Hubbell, associate attorney general and a former partner of Hillary Rodham Clinton at the Rose Law Firm in Little Rock, might have had a conflict of interest involving Madison Guaranty when he switched from defending the S&L to working for the Federal Deposit Insurance Corporation (FDIC), the government agency that was suing the failed bank, without informing the FDIC of his prior relationship.

And then, on November 10, the *Post* reported that the Justice Department was sending a three-man team of prosecutors to investigate Madison Guaranty after the local U.S. attorney, a Clinton appointee and campaign volunteer, finally agreed to recuse herself. Jeff Gerth of *The New York Times* also reported this development along with a story that the House Banking Committee would investigate Madison Guaranty.

None of these stories accused the Clintons of specific wrongdoing, but they all raised questions about issues that had dogged them since the campaign: the scope of Hillary Clinton's legal work for Madison Guaranty, the casual attitude of their business partners, the McDougals, toward other people's money deposited in their bank, the complicated relationships between politicians and questionable business people in Little Rock. The White House denied any wrongdoing, but the denials did not discourage other reporters from dipping more deeply into the Whitewater story or Republicans from demanding congressional hearings. *The Washington Post*'s requests to the White House for relevant documents got no response.

Enter David Gergen, who had mastered the art of political spinning for a succession of Republican White Houses from Nixon's to Reagan's. Gergen had joined the Clinton White House in May, primarily to improve the president's stormy relations with the press. By November, relations clearly had not improved, especially with *The Washington Post*. Gergen proposed a "peace conference" to Downie: Gergen would accompany two top White House aides—Mark Gearan and Bruce Lindsey—to the *Post*'s newsroom on 15th Street and Downie would produce his top editors and reporters. Together, they would try to find a way out of their growing confrontation. The meeting, which took place on December 6, lasted more than an hour. It proved to be a total disaster.

Downie pointed out that the *Post* had been asking for White House records about Whitewater for a year and a half and gotten nowhere. Why? Downie wanted to know. Gergen, trying to be helpful, asked for specifics. Did the *Post* mean all the records? What did it really want and need? Lindsey intervened. "First you tell us what story you want to write." Downie declined. First the records, the editor demanded; then we read and study them, and only then do we know what we are going to write. That's the way journalism works. Lindsey, irritated by this Journalism 101 lesson, snapped that the *Post*'s focus on Whitewater was typical of the "gotcha" journalism so prevalent in American political life. "Why should we give you any of this?" he asked. "You'll just use [it] to write more stories." Isikoff, watching this exchange, wondered about the White House people. "Why can't they ever give you straight answers? What are they hiding?" Downie concluded the unproductive meeting by again asking for documents. A few weeks later, he got his answer in a White House letter signed by Bruce Lindsey. The answer was no.

From November 1993 until early February 1994, *The Washington Post* published sixty-two articles on the Whitewater story. Sixteen were on the front page. It was, Gergen recalled, "a full court press." A special Whitewater team was established in the *Post* newsroom. Downie chaired the meetings. It was serious and exhilarating stuff, but, after a while, a number of reporters, including Isikoff, thought the *Post* might be "overdoing it a bit." One day Isikoff expressed his discomfort to a senior editor, Karen de Young, who confessed that she shared his sense of uneasiness. But, she added, Downie felt very strongly about the story. "Len thinks this is his Watergate," she said.

Downie, when questioned about de Young's comment, simply dismissed it as "not true." "My zeal," he told me, "was to get Whitewater, not another Watergate." Why zeal? I asked. "Because in my view government officials have to tell the truth, and it's our responsibility to tell people if they don't," he replied. Downie felt Clinton had lied during the 1992 campaign about avoiding the draft and had misled reporters about smoking marijuana. Clinton had also made an unwelcome pass at a *Post* reporter during a Gridiron dinner, an incident that especially upset the dean of political reporters, David Broder. Downie was not an ideologue, and he was not a prude; but Clinton offended him, and Downie's assessment of the president influenced the *Post*'s coverage of Whitewater and Clinton. He was, after all, editor.

The Clintons, shell-shocked by the unrelenting demands for more information, established a Whitewater response team in the White House to deal with the press and congressional investigators. Why was the atmosphere so hostile? they asked their friends. Why were reporters so determined to "get" them? Why didn't they understand that they were being manipulated by right-wing zealots who refused to accept the legitimacy of the president's victory? The Clintons had experienced the same sort of hostility in Arkansas campaign after campaign, and they had survived. They were determined to survive in Washington, the city they thought they had conquered in the 1992 election.

There were officials at the White House who urged the Clintons to provide the relevant documents to the *Post* and put the issue behind them, but Hillary Clinton argued that the press would never be satisfied. Once again enter Gergen, who was still determined to warm the "frosty" relations between the White House and the *Post*. He persuaded Mrs. Clinton to meet with Len Downie. An off-the-record summit was arranged in the Indian Treaty Room at the White House with no one present but Downie and Mrs. Clinton, joined by her press secretary Liz Caputo.

Like Gergen's first effort at reconciliation, this one too was a stunning flop. Mrs. Clinton was, Downie later recalled, "very lawyerlike." She represented "the Clintons, the White House," and she wanted to know why the *Post* was "going after the president." Downie replied, predictably, that the *Post* was not going after the president. He said this was a story about a land deal involving both Clintons; it was also a story about a failed savings and loan and a very secretive law firm, where Mrs. Clinton had once worked. All of these stories involved questions of possible conflicts of interest, Downie explained, and naturally he and his colleagues wanted to check them out. Again he repeated, "Let us have the documents." If there was nothing there, no story. He repeated that the *Post* had "no predisposition" to "go after President Clinton," emphasizing that "the *Post* treats Republicans the same way it treats Democrats."

Mrs. Clinton responded by blaming the whole Whitewater problem on Jim McDougal. "He got us into this deal," Mrs. Clinton said, according to Downie, "and he left us holding the bag. We made no money in this deal, we lost money." She then acknowledged, "I probably made a mistake in the way I handled it, but Bill had nothing to do with it. He wasn't involved at all." Downie seized the opportunity to request the documents.

Rather than either agree or disagree, Mrs. Clinton changed the subject. Unprompted, she raised the Troopergate story, which had just rocketed into national headlines. The story, first published by the right-wing *American Spectator* magazine in December 1993 and then in the *Los Angeles Times,* alleged that Arkansas state troopers had procured women for Governor Clinton and then covered up for him. Mrs. Clinton, having raised this embarrassing subject, did not deny the essence of the charge; she merely brushed it aside, saying at one point that she had repeatedly urged her husband to fire some of the troopers for incompetence. She charged that it was yet another illustration of a political conspiracy: right-wingers had raised money for these troopers, who revealed their embarrassing stories to the press.

Mrs. Clinton, sensing that she did not have a very strong hand, again switched subjects. She appealed to Downie's experience as a Washington insider and a doyen of Washington journalism. She earnestly asked for his advice on how the Clintons should deal with the press corps. She admitted that she was "mystified" by the "media culture" of the capital. Downie must have dramatically deflated her expectations. He responded coldly, "That's not my business." He made it clear that he spoke only for the *Post.* Any problems with the *Post,* call him. Any problems with other news organizations, call them.

A few days later, Ann Devroy, *The Washington Post*'s fiercely independent White House correspondent in those years, called Downie to report that the first lady was telling everyone that Downie "hated" her and that he was "jealous" of Ben Bradlee, his predecessor, who "got" Nixon with Watergate; now he, Downie, was trying to "get" Clinton with Whitewater. Downie acknowledged that others at the *Post* might have believed the same thing at the time, but he insisted to me that "never, not once" did the Watergate comparison influence his journalistic decisions.

Gergen saw that the Clintons' distrust of the Washington press corps and their repeated refusal to provide Whitewater documents would only inflame the situation. "It's not rocket science," he later told me. "By stonewalling, they put a red flag in front of a raging bull, and just as sure as day following night, *The Washington Post* then redoubled its efforts. It just spurred them on."

The small band of journalists who began looking into Whitewater in Arkansas during and after the 1992 campaign developed their own view of Clinton—and it was far from complimentary. In addition to Gerth, Schmidt, and Isikoff, the group included Jim Wooten, Jackie Judd, and producer Chris Vlasto of ABC News, investigative reporter Glenn Simpson of the *Wall Street Journal*, Sara Fritz and Bill Rempel of the *Los Angeles Times*, Bob Franken of CNN, David Shuster of Fox, and a few other hardy souls. A number of these reporters would play key roles in the coverage of the scandal of 1998.

Little Rock, Arkansas, proved to be a lonely and lengthy assignment, especially for reporters normally based in Washington, New York, or Los Angeles. During the day they would cover court proceedings, read endless legal documents, and try to cultivate local sources—a trooper, a lawyer, a local reporter, anyone who could provide a revealing glimpse into the president's past. Then they would pitch their stories to distant and usually uninterested editors. In the evening they would bond at the bar of the Capital Hotel, which they fondly nicknamed "Rick's Café," exchanging theories about Whitewater and Clinton.

In time, most of these reporters developed a portrait of Clinton as a wild, reckless womanizer accustomed to lying about what Isikoff called his "serial indiscretions" to protect his political career and his family. They saw him as unscrupulous and unprincipled, a cunning cad who kept slipping through their investigative net, evading responsibility for his immoral and possibly illegal activities and, whenever possible, laying the blame on others. Of course, this remained an essentially private portrait of the president, discussed among themselves and their editors but not yet reported. The reporters needed a hook on which they could hang this portrait, and at that time they didn't have one strong enough.

While Clinton had his enthusiastic supporters, there was no shortage of critics in a town where he was once known as "Slick Willie." Perhaps the most active was Cliff Jackson, a former friend of Clinton's who had been at Oxford with him but then turned into a virulent Clinton-hater, who rarely missed an opportunity to orchestrate press coverage damaging to the president. He was involved in everything from Gennifer Flowers to the state trooper story. But Jackson was not alone. There was a Little Rock–Washington axis of anti-Clinton zealots who kept stoking the flames of controversy about Clinton's personal life and spreading rumors suggesting, among other things, that Vincent Foster's death was not a suicide and that Clinton was responsible for his murder. The mainstream press rejected these poisonous tales, but they found a sympathetic audience among such writers as David Brock, who wrote the original Troopergate story. (Interestingly, Brock later changed his mind about the story and publicly apologized to the Clintons.) Once in print or on the air, some of these stories were picked up by the mainstream press but were then quickly dropped—often because the White House issued denials, but also because the sources seemed so biased and disreputable. Still, the stories lingered in the minds of many reporters, who believed that they might one day prove to be true.

Another set of sources arrived in Little Rock when the official Whitewater investigations got underway in 1994. Fiske, the special prosecutor, set up a highly professional operation, but six months later, when the newly appointed independent counsel, Starr, arrived on the scene, Fiske's prosecutors refused to stay and work with him. They thought Starr carried too much baggage. For one thing, Starr had been named by a panel headed by Judge David Sentelle, who had met shortly before the appointment with North Carolina senators Jesse Helms and Lauch Faircloth, sharp critics of Fiske. For another, Starr had offered advice and support to Paula Jones's lawyers when they were deciding how to proceed with their court case. Still, he hired a group of reputable prosecutors and started to follow up on Fiske's cases.

Starr believed at first that he "could have the thing wrapped up in six months or a year or so," but he had never been a prosecutor and was totally unrealistic. He reopened the question of Vincent Foster's suicide, and it took him three full years to reach the same conclusion Fiske had reached after six months: it really was a suicide. By that time, many of his best prosecutors had moved on to other jobs, and he was left with such critics of Clinton as Jackie Bennett, Jr., and Hickman Ewing, Jr., who were to play major roles in the Lewinsky saga. Bennett and Ewing were career prosecutors, brusque and resourceful legal street fighters, ready to subpoena the devil to win a case. In Texas back in 1993, Bennett had gone so far as to subpoena two reporters in his determined quest to prosecute former Democratic representative Albert Bustamante on racketeering and bribery charges. To defense attorneys in Texas, he was an overzealous bully, but the Justice Department had given him its top honor, the John Marshall Award.

It was inevitable in a town such as Little Rock that the prosecutors and the journalists would meet, as both groups examined the financial irregularities of the governor who had become president. CNN's Bob

Franken, an Arkansas native, recalled that whenever there was a trial, Starr and Ewing would appear on the courthouse steps once or even twice a day to give reporters their side of the story. They did not gush with information, but they were available. Occasionally, prosecutors would brief reporters "on background," though, like many other officials, they would often confuse "background" (meaning a reporter could use the information but not name the source) with "off the record" (a reporter could not use the information or name the source).

A few of the prosecutors would occasionally engage in surreptitious spinning. Bennett and Ewing, for example, briefed sympathetic writers. According to freelance journalist Dan E. Moldea, who tape-recorded his conversations with both prosecutors and then included the transcripts in an affidavit to the U.S. District Court on August 24, 1998, Ewing spoke "freely" with two authors whose books raised questions about whether Vincent Foster had committed suicide: Christopher Ruddy, author of *The Strange Death of Vincent Foster,* and Ambrose Evans-Pritchard, author of *The Secret Life of Bill Clinton.* Ewing told Moldea that he decided to disclose privileged information to the authors "when we heard where they're coming from"—in other words, when Ewing was sure that they were sympathetic to the goals of the Starr investigation or manifestly critical of Clinton. After talking with Bennett, who was also willing to disclose what he termed "substantive information" under certain conditions, Moldea concluded that the Office of the Independent Counsel (OIC) provided leaks to a "stable of selected reporters." Moldea did not identify the reporters in his affidavit.

The prosecutors used the press, but didn't enjoy the process. They worried incessantly about unauthorized leaks. In their universe of secrecy, journalists represented problems. Still, even if they were deeply suspicious of reporters, they did get to meet a number of them outside the courthouse, and these chance or arranged encounters served a practical purpose when the scene later shifted to Washington. Isikoff, Schmidt, and Vlasto became names with faces, just as Bennett and Ewing became sources for leaks. Were it not for their common experiences in Little Rock, they might not have engaged in the kind of unorthodox cooperation between press and prosecutor so typical of the early coverage of this scandal.

At the beginning of 1997, Starr's investigation into Whitewater was running out of steam. Once again, Clinton seemed to have outlasted his critics and prosecutors. In February, Starr announced he would retire and become the dean of the law school at Pepperdine University in California. A few days later, shamed by columnist William Safire and other conservatives, he reversed himself and agreed to stay on in the job as independent counsel.

Meanwhile, the sexual scandals—the ones the mainstream press generally avoided—hovered in the background of the Clinton presidency. The salacious allegations in the Troopergate articles in December 1993 were embarrassing, but the matter could have been contained if it had not been for Paula Jones, identified in the *American Spectator* article only as "Paula," who accused the president of demanding oral sex from her in an Arkansas hotel room. By May 1994, she was about to bring suit against Clinton, and he was obliged to add another personal lawyer, Robert Bennett, to his roster. Bennett's task was either to settle the suit—several attempts over the years failed—or to persuade the Supreme Court that a sitting president could not be a defendant in a civil suit. He managed to get the decision postponed until after the 1996 elections, but in May 1997 the Court in a surprising 9–0 decision announced that the case could proceed since the suit would not interfere with the president's duties. Subsequent events proved that it was an extraordinarily naive and unrealistic decision made by justices who were sheltered from the rough legal-political world of Clinton and his adversaries.

At this point, the plot thickened with the addition of three new characters so unlikely that only a director of grade-B movies could have imagined them.

Monica Lewinsky was a twenty-one-year-old graduate of Lewis and Clark University in Portland, Oregon, when she began her stint at the White House in 1995. First as an unpaid intern and then as a staffer in the legislative affairs office, she conducted a flirtatious and then sexual relationship with the president, starting in November 1995 and ending in May 1997. It lasted, amazingly, through the entire 1996 presidential campaign, and not a single reporter learned anything about it. In the spring of 1996, she was unceremoniously transferred to the Pentagon's press office after Evelyn Lieberman, then deputy chief of staff, and a number of other White House aides suspected that Monica spelled b-i-g t-r-o-u-b-l-e. They didn't realize quite how big.

Linda Tripp was a forty-seven-year-old civil servant, a divorced mother of two, who lived in Columbia, Maryland. She had worked in the

White House during both the Bush and Clinton administrations. Although she admired Bush, she had only disdain for Clinton and his staff, and she referred to White House counsel Bernard Nussbaum, her immediate supervisor, and two of his associates as "the three stooges." She was, colleagues said, a natural gossip, who tended to blow her own horn. She saw conspiracies behind every door and a sex scandal in every closet.

When Tripp was moved to the Pentagon in 1994, she started bad-mouthing the White House. In 1995, she testified in the Senate investigation of the Vincent Foster suicide that a number of her former colleagues were incompetent, inebriated, or worse. In the spring of 1996, after the success of the anti-Clinton inside-the-White-House book by former FBI agent Gary Aldrich, Tripp told Tony Snow, a columnist and talk show host who had been a Bush speechwriter, that she too was thinking of writing a sexy "tell-all" book about the Clinton White House. Snow introduced her to a conservative New York writer and agent named Lucianne Goldberg, who arranged for her to work with a ghostwriter.

In the spring of 1996, Tripp met Lewinsky, who had just been transferred to the Pentagon, and they quickly became friends. Soon Lewinsky was confiding about her affair with the president. In September 1997, Tripp told Goldberg about Lewinsky, and the following month, at Goldberg's suggestion, Tripp began to tape her telephone conversations with Lewinsky.

Lucianne Goldberg was a literary agent, writer of salacious novels, and conservative political junkie who had once worked as a researcher at Kennedy's White House and ended up as a Nixon spy on George McGovern's campaign plane. She was a natural wheeler-dealer with a flair for public relations and she conspired with the press, the prosecutors, and the Jones lawyers—all in a non-stop effort to destroy Bill Clinton.

Within a matter of a few months, the words, tapes, and actions of these three women would touch off a spiral of reactions that led ultimately to the impeachment of the president. It would turn out to be a far more challenging story for the press than the Gennifer Flowers revelation. It would test the judgment and balance of the Washington press corps as they moved from the familiar terrain of the Whitewater financial scandal to the unknown landscape of an X-rated presidential sex scandal.

CHAPTER 2

A PLAYER IN THE
SCANDAL CIRCUS
January 13–15, 1998

THE PROFESSIONAL TERRAIN IN REPORTING ON SUCH MAT-
TERS WAS TREACHEROUS; THE RULES WERE BLURRY AND EVER-
CHANGING. . . . NOW, HERE I WAS, A PLAYER—ONE OF THE
ACTS IN THE SCANDAL CIRCUS.

—Michael Isikoff, *Uncovering Clinton*

No other Washington reporter devoted more grit, time, and energy to Bill Clinton's sexual misadventures than Michael Isikoff. In fact, he has been credited with helping to invent a new genre of contemporary journalism called "sexual investigative reporting." When he was in college, Isikoff had been inspired by *The Washington Post*'s Bob Woodward and Carl Bernstein, who doggedly pursued Nixon and ultimately drove him from the presidency. After a number of warm-up assignments, Isikoff landed a job at the *Post* in 1981. He covered the Justice Department, drug busts, and finally the 1992 presidential campaign.

If Hollywood executives were casting someone in the role of an investigative reporter, they would have to look no further than this rumpled, bespectacled sleuth. Blessed with a chronic look of skepticism, Isikoff didn't "cover" the Clinton/Lewinsky story so much as he prowled through its underbrush, a Dostoevskian figure undisturbed by the need, which frequently arose in his research, to cozy up to felons and other disreputable sources to get another quote, another fact, another insight. He didn't mind dirtying his hands. Colleagues said his commitment to investigative journalism bordered on the obsessive. Occasionally, as he dipped deeper into the scandal, he would cross a "blurry" line between journalistic objectivity and subjective engagement, and his role would suddenly become suspect, even to himself. "I was part of the story," he wrote in his account of the scandal. "I didn't like it." When he went after a story, he went for the jugular. He was relentless, fierce, almost as suspicious of an editor as of a source.

Like his colleague Schmidt, Isikoff was assigned to the Clinton watch, which he pursued with characteristic doggedness in Little Rock and Washington. He developed a fascination for Arkansas politics—"the bizarre characters, the southern folklore, the strange mix of rumor, fact and tabloid fantasy." During the '92 campaign he got a tip about a private investigator hired by the Clinton campaign to keep tabs on the so-called bimbo eruptions—a phrase that Clinton aide Betsey Wright coined to describe the numerous women coming forward to sell stories to the tabloids claiming they had had affairs with the governor. Isikoff then discovered that the Clinton campaign had not reported any payments to the investigator in its reports to the Federal Election Commission (FEC); the initial payments of $28,000 had been listed as "legal fees." Isikoff later explained, "That was something I fixated on. If you look at FEC reports, as some of us do, you can find . . . every last nickel reported under expenditures. But here was a rather substantial portion of funds going to a private investigator for the Clinton campaign, and it was nowhere reported." The following year, Isikoff continued combing through the voluminous records of the FEC and found that the campaign had paid the investigator more than $100,000—most of it after the election. He wondered why the campaign staff had not conformed with FEC regulations. What were they trying to hide?

Isikoff spent a lot of time in Little Rock in 1993. Each of his stories about Clinton, Whitewater, or Troopergate contributed to his Rolodex of colorful sources, and with each story he kept returning to one question: Was Clinton just reckless with women, or was he pathologically incapable of controlling his sexual urges? His instinct told him that Clinton was both a liar and a philanderer and that the two were related.

Among the Clinton-haters, Isikoff became a valuable prospect, a reporter on the "liberal" *Washington Post* who seemed to share their acid assessment of the president. They cultivated and used Isikoff, and he cultivated and used them. Each met the other's needs, a perfectly normal arrangement between a source and a reporter. Over the next couple of years, however, Isikoff allowed routine cooperation to evolve on more than one occasion into unhealthy collaboration.

Isikoff's journey from cooperation to collaboration started on February 11, 1994. That morning, right-wing GOP political consultant Craig Shirley telephoned Isikoff with a "heads-up" on an appearance later that day by Paula Jones, a twenty-seven-year-old former state employee in Arkansas, before the Conservative Political Action Conference at the Omni Shoreham Hotel. This was to be Jones's debut in Washington, and Shirley wanted to generate coverage of her charge of "sexual harassment" against the president. Shirley wanted bombshell coverage—Jones "live" on CNN, excerpts on the evening news, front-page stories in the *Post* and the *Times,* radio reports on the hour. Shirley had high hopes. Here at last was a woman who would openly discuss her charges against the president. It was no longer a question of whispers or rumors about Clinton's womanizing, so easily dismissed by the White House. Here was a real, live woman with a story the Washington press corps could not ignore.

At the news conference, covered by some fifty reporters and a half dozen television crews, Jones lifted the lid on her story. For some unexplained reason, though, she chose not to tell all of it. One frustrated reporter asked: "Will you tell us in your own words something about what really happened in that room?" Jones and her lawyers conferred but refused to provide any fresh information. "I will not speak on that," Jones said flatly. Reporters left feeling they had wasted their time. Later, Isikoff cornered one of his favorite Little Rock sources, lawyer Cliff Jackson. What's up? Isikoff asked. If she has anything to say, why didn't she say it? Jackson was delighted to tell Isikoff "the whole story"—that in 1991 Clinton had summoned Jones to his hotel room, dropped his trousers, and asked for oral sex. Jones had refused, he said. Isikoff demanded proof, and Jackson produced two sworn affidavits from friends Jones had confided in after her encounter with Clinton. Isikoff said he needed more proof, and Jackson then proposed that he interview Jones. A deal. The next morning, in her hotel suite. But it had to be an exclusive. No problem.

Isikoff raced back to the *Post* newsroom. It was 3 p.m. He had a story to write. Almost immediately, he ran into a problem in the person of Robert Kaiser, then the *Post*'s managing editor, a former foreign corespondent who, as Isikoff put it, "didn't have much use for me." Kaiser, after listening to Isikoff's summary, waved it off as inconsequential, but Isikoff, undeterred, took his story to Len Downie, who thought enough of it to convene a meeting of his top editors. Several of them, like Kaiser, were skeptical of

Isikoff and his reporting. How trustworthy were the affidavits, they wanted to know. How credible was Jones? Isikoff, who had had a running quarrel with his editors for years, argued that the affidavits were signed and, besides, months earlier, these same editors had raised similar questions about the Troopergate story. Where were the women? they had asked then. Well, Isikoff replied, here was one of them, and he would probably be able to interview her in the morning. Downie decided that Isikoff had a point. "Let's go ahead," he said; but first he wanted more reporting on the story. What, for example, did the White House have to say?

Isikoff turned first to George Stephanopoulos, at the time one of the president's top aides, whose responsibilities included burnishing the president's image with the Washington press corps. Stephanopoulos, helpful to Isikoff in the past, sounded "irritated." He tried to dissuade Isikoff from writing the story, citing Jackson's instigation of the whole event. If this was Jackson's idea, he asked, how reliable could it be? Moreover, Stephanopoulos added with a degree of confidence that exceeded his knowledge, Clinton did not even know Jones. Stephanopoulos was spinning his tale on "background," and Isikoff needed an "on-the-record" quote. They shadowboxed for a while longer, until finally Stephanopoulos yielded. The charges, he said for publication, were "not true. It's just a cheap political fundraising trick."

Next on Isikoff's list was Danny Ferguson, the trooper who had allegedly brought a woman named Paula to Clinton's hotel room. Isikoff found Ferguson at his home in Arkansas, but it proved to be a fruitless conversation. Ferguson was totally uncommunicative: "I'm not going to have anything to say."

Next was David Brock, who had first broken the Troopergate story in the *American Spectator.* He sounded defensive when Isikoff pressed him about his original story and said only that Jones "corroborates the essence" of what he had written.

Pressed by a fast-approaching deadline, Isikoff started writing his 800-word story about the Jones news conference at just about the same time that Downie sent another *Post* reporter, Lloyd Grove, to the Omni Shoreham to try to interview Jones. Downie knew that Isikoff was going to interview her the next day, but he was thinking about that day's story, and to him it still seemed thin and insubstantial. Aside from the White House denial, which was utterly predictable, Isikoff had been unable to break any new ground. He had nothing beyond what Jones had said and Jackson, "on background," had alleged. Grove found Jones in her suite, and while she was friendly, she refused to provide any more information. After an hour, Grove returned to the *Post*, unable to tell Downie whether Jones, in his view, was lying or telling the truth.

For Downie, it was "a dicey call"—he said, she said, Jones against the president, an unlikely pairing that was to lose its exotic quality over the next few years. It was 6:30 p.m., and Downie again summoned his top editors to his office. This time White House correspondent Ann Devroy joined the discussion. "How can we run this story?" she asked. "We have no idea if any of this is true." Others added that Jackson's involvement itself undercut the legitimacy of the Jones charges. Were it not for Clinton's known enemies, there would have been no news conference and no Paula Jones. The editors seemed disposed not to run the story. Isikoff, as he later remembered, was getting hot under the collar. He suspected Devroy was simply protecting her White House turf, blocking another reporter from writing about Clinton. "How could we not print anything?" Isikoff asked in defense of his story. "How can we just ignore this?" He assumed at the time that other news organizations were going to give extensive coverage to the Jones news conference.

The argument in Downie's office lasted for another half-hour. The clock was now the editor's enemy, a decision had to be made, and Downie decided against running the story—not, he stressed, because the *Post* wasn't interested in it, but because it needed more exhaustive reporting. Jones and her supporters should be interviewed, and Isikoff should do the reporting.

The following morning, Isikoff returned to the Omni Shoreham and found Jones, her husband, and her Little Rock attorney in her suite. They were depressed. The ballyhooed news conference had barely made news. CNN not only had not carried it live; the cable network had made only scant reference to the Jones charges in its regular news broadcasts. Two of the three major broadcast networks had not said a word; the third, ABC, mentioned the charges briefly but then quoted the White House as dismissing it all as "pathetic." *The Washington Post* carried nothing; *The New York Times* ran only a four-paragraph story deep inside the paper. From a public relations perspective, it was a dismal flop, a fact Isikoff quickly noted and exploited to his own advantage. The salesman in him argued that if Jones told him everything, holding back nothing, then the *Post* might publish the whole story—assuming of course that her story checked out. Everyone else in the world of journalism would then pick up the *Post* exclusive; that was the way journalism worked. Jones conferred with her lawyer and quickly bought Isikoff's argument. Her relieved attorney turned to Isikoff and, extending his hand, proclaimed: "Izzy! Pleased to meet you, Izzy." Then, for the next three hours, chain-smoking all the way, Jones, propped up on pillows on her large bed, told Isikoff the whole sordid tale, skipping no detail, no matter how gross.

Isikoff had his story, but Downie was not ready to publish it. The editors had begun to lose patience with what they considered Isikoff's crusading, self-centered, muckraking style of journalism, and they were reluctant to proceed until they had much more convincing evidence. They sent Isikoff back to Little Rock to do some more reporting. By mid-March, Jones and her lawyer, who had made an exclusive deal with Isikoff and *The Washington Post*, were starting to get impatient. So was Isikoff. At one point he lost his cool and clashed with deputy national editor Fred Barbash. "You fucking asshole," he shouted. Barbash complained to Downie, and Downie felt he had no option but to suspend Isikoff for two weeks without pay. The conservative *Washington Times* got wind of the incident and turned it into an ideological attack on the *Post* for spiking Isikoff's story and trying to bury the charges against Clinton. Isikoff's popularity with Jerry Falwell and other right-wing activists soared; but his popularity at the *Post* hit a new low.

In fact, *The Washington Post* did not publish a story about Paula Jones until May 4, 1994, when they had a solid news peg: the president had hired Bill Bennett to represent him in the case. After the story appeared, Isikoff resigned and quickly joined Evan Thomas at *Newsweek*, his reputation as a tough-minded reporter easing his way in an increasingly competitive journalistic market. "He was helpful to the *Post*," Downie recalled, "but he's really a very difficult person to deal with."

As one of *Newsweek*'s two investigative reporters, Isikoff covered a wide variety of political issues, including Whitewater, but for a time the Clinton sex scandals were placed on the back burner. In 1994, according to a Lexis-Nexis search, he wrote fifteen bylined stories for the news magazine, only one of which touched on Clinton's sex life. In 1995, he wrote thirty-three stories, none of which touched on this subject. In fact, the White House chose to leak Whitewater and other documents from Vincent Foster's office exclusively to Isikoff, hoping to convince this skeptic that there had been no cover-up. The story appeared in *Newsweek* on July 9, 1995, and White House officials were pleased with it.

In 1996, Isikoff wrote forty-four bylined stories, six of which mentioned Clinton's problems with Paula Jones. *Newsweek*'s interest in the Jones story was piqued in the fall of 1996 by Stuart Taylor, legal correspondent for the *National Journal*, who met with Isikoff while writing a long piece for the *American Lawyer* reexamining the validity of Jones's claims. The Supreme Court was about to hear arguments about the president's immunity from civil suits while in office, and *Newsweek* decided to do a cover story about it.

From that time until the Lewinsky story finally broke on January 21, 1998, Isikoff was hooked on the journalistic narcotic of Clinton's sex life. He pursued one clue after another, one woman after another, all the while persuading himself that it was not the sex that propelled him to investigate the president's private life; rather, it was Clinton's lying about it. Of one thing there can be no doubt: it was Isikoff's story. He was a key player (at times, *the* key player) in the unfolding of this historic scandal. His reporting forced the actions, strategy, and timetable of other lead actors in the drama. He was, for a journalist, in very heady terrain. "What do you do when you find yourself sucked into the story?" Isikoff asked rhetorically toward the end of his book. "What happens when you become beholden to sources with an agenda? There are no easy answers here." Driven by curiosity and ambition, encouraged by his editors, he kept plunging more deeply into the story. A few other reporters had similar opportunities, but none possessed his determination to "get" the story, which in this case was the same as getting the president.

Isikoff's road to the president's women led through the Jones lawyers, who were trying to establish a pattern of sexual behavior that would bolster their client's case against Clinton. As the case developed, the stable of "Jones lawyers" came to include many who would provide tips and leaks to Isikoff and other journalists.

First, there were the "lawyers of record," who argued the case publicly. Jones's original Little Rock lawyer, Danny Traylor, was replaced by a pair of more experienced Washington lawyers, Joseph Cammarata and Gil Davis, before she filed suit against the president in May 1994. They represented her for three years but quit in September 1997, after Jones turned down a $700,000 settlement. At that point their bills were over $800,000 and they saw little chance of recovering any of their money. They were replaced by a team of born-again Christians recommended by the right-wing Rutherford Institute—Donovan Campbell, Jr., Wesley Holmes, and Jim Fisher—who would handle the crucial period involving Monica Lewinsky.

Then there was the secret legal team—young, high-powered, smart, very conservative, former prosecutors and government lawyers, members of prestigious law firms in Chicago, New York, and Philadelphia—who provided behind-the-scenes advice to the official Jones attorneys from the beginning. In fact, they helped recommend lawyers for Jones, and later, at the height of the crisis, would provide Linda Tripp with a lawyer as well. Their existence was not known to the public until October 1998, but Isikoff stumbled upon two of them in August 1997: Ann Coulter, a right-wing lawyer and columnist for *Human Events;* and George Conway, a partner at a New York firm where, ironically, he worked closely with former Clinton White House counsel Bernard Nussbaum. Conway did not want his anti-Clinton legal activities made public. The others were Richard Porter, a former aide to Vice President Dan Quayle; Jerome Marcus, a former prosecutor in the U.S. Attorney's office in Philadelphia; and Nelson Lund, who had clerked for Justice Sandra Day O'Connor. All three were graduates of the University of Chicago Law School. Linked by their shared antipathy to Clinton, they kept in close touch, passing along suggestions about strategy and writing briefs for the Jones legal team. Coulter referred to them as "elves"—as she told Isikoff, "There are lots of us busy elves working away in Santa's workshop"—and the name stuck. It suggested a playfulness at odds with their role as members of a legal cabal.

Finally, there was Starr. When named independent counsel on August 5, 1994, he was already a controversial figure. For one thing, he had considered filing a friend-of-the-court brief in support of Jones's sexual harassment suit against Clinton. He had also consulted "about six times" with Gil Davis, one of Jones's lawyers. "He was a constitutional scholar," said Davis, "and I wanted his counsel. No payment was involved." And Starr had carried his argument into the public arena, objecting during a televised debate on PBS to the White House position that, while president, Clinton was immune from prosecution. Starr believed no president was immune from prosecution. Clinton backers strongly opposed Starr's appointment, but after a few days, having no other option, they reluctantly supported the White House's public position that Starr was a fair and honorable prosecutor.

On January 13, 1997, the Supreme Court heard oral arguments in the Jones case. The historic Jones brief was written by two of the secret Jones lawyers, Conway and Marcus. A few days later, when Isikoff called Jones's official lawyer for his reaction to the Supreme Court hearings, Cammarata gave him a tip about a woman who had called and claimed that she had had a sexual encounter with the president in the Oval Office on November 29, 1993. "He pulled me to him," she had told Cammarata. "He kissed me," and then she had volunteered other details. Cammarata at the time was collecting names of "other women," but the caller refused to give her name. Still, she left enough clues with Cammarata for Isikoff to track her down. She turned out to be Kathleen Willey, a Democratic Party activist and White House volunteer from Virginia. Isikoff then pursued her until at last she confided to him on an "off-the-record" basis but in "gripping and microscopic detail" that the president had "groped" her during an Oval Office visit when she had gone to ask him for a paying job. "His hands were everywhere," she said. "He put his hands up my skirt."

Willey had then steered Isikoff to two other sources, who could, she claimed, confirm her tale. One was her close friend Julie Hiatt Steele and the other was Linda Tripp, who worked at that time in the White House counsel's office. Steele informed Isikoff that Willey "told me everything" about the presidential grope. She also said that Willey, after learning the following morning that her husband had committed suicide for unrelated reasons, found her situation more desperate than ever. She begged the White House for a job and got one—briefly—in the White House counsel's office. Later, she was sent on trips with diplomatic delegations to Copenhagen and Jakarta. Steele, knowing her friend had no diplomatic qualifications, remarked: "This is just trying to keep you quiet." And it did for a while.

Although Willey had expected Tripp to confirm her account as well (why else give Isikoff her name?), Tripp put her own spin on the story. As she related it to Isikoff and later to the grand jury, she saw Willey shortly after she left the Oval Office, but far from seeing a woman whose pride had been wounded, she saw someone joyful if somewhat "disheveled—her face was red and her lipstick was off." Tripp continued: "I can tell you that she was very excited, very flustered. She smiled from ear to ear the entire time. . . . She seemed almost shocked, but happy shocked."

To Isikoff, this was a major story: it was the first time a woman had charged Clinton with sexual misconduct in the White House. But he knew it would not be enough for his editors. He kept on digging.

Monica Lewinsky had told the story of her relationship with the president to her mother, her aunt, and seven or eight close friends. No one had breathed a word of it. But her new confidante, a fellow exile from the White House whom she met at the Pentagon in the spring of 1996, was a different matter. Tripp was a volatile, ambitious woman with a grudge against the Clinton White House. Lewinsky's revelations were made to order for her. On March 24, 1997, when Isikoff asked her about Willey, Tripp hinted at a bigger story: "You're barking up the wrong tree," she said.

Intrigued, Isikoff kept calling her. In April, she agreed to see him again. They talked for hours at her home, late into the night. She told him an astonishing story about a president consumed by sex, about a White House preoccupied with cover-ups, and finally about a twenty-three-year-old intern who was having an affair with the president at that very time. Isikoff kept writing, filling up his notebook, and Tripp kept talking. She and the intern, whose name she withheld, had become close friends, she said, close enough for the intern to share intimate secrets with her: specifically, that the president and the intern had hidden in a small passageway near the Oval Office where she would "service him with oral sex"; that on many occasions, after midnight, the two had engaged in "phone sex," with the intern sexually stimulating the president with evocative descriptions; that the president had confessed to the intern that he had had hundreds of affairs—so many that he was able to circle on a calendar the days he'd been faithful to his wife; and, finally, that the president had confided that he expected to be alone after his presidency, suggesting to the intern that he would be divorced and she might then be his choice for a mate.

On May 28, after the Supreme Court's surprising 9–0 decision permitting the Paula Jones trial to proceed, Isikoff told his bureau chief Ann McDaniel for the first time about the information he had gathered about three women claiming connections to Clinton: Willey, Tripp, and the unnamed intern. He didn't reveal the names he knew even to McDaniel. He didn't want reporters in Washington or editors in New York gossiping about what he had learned. He insisted the information be kept strictly confidential, and McDaniel accepted his terms, believing *Newsweek* might be on the edge of a huge story.

The following day, McDaniel flew to New York, as she did every week, and briefed *Newsweek*'s editor, Maynard Parker, and her other senior colleagues. She stressed the importance of confidentiality and requested that he make only one decision: that Isikoff be allowed to focus on this story. No other decision was necessary at that time. Parker agreed, emphasizing that Isikoff's pursuit itself had to be kept absolutely secret. "If word were to leak out that *Newsweek* was reporting on this, he warned, it was almost the same as publishing it."

The top editors in Washington and New York then circled the *Newsweek* wagons around Isikoff's pursuit of the Clinton story. In Washington, McDaniel and Thomas were his closest allies and supporters. The level-headed McDaniel had been with the magazine since 1984, covering, among other things, the Supreme Court and the Justice Department. Then, "kicking and screaming," as she put it, she had been assigned to cover the hurly-burly world of politics. She did so well that she quickly became chief of correspondents, and then, in 1996, Washington bureau chief, succeeding Evan Thomas, who had had the job for ten years. After a while, Isikoff's tight circle expanded to include his colleague Daniel Klaidman, who then covered the Justice Department.

On July 25, Cammarata, hoping to pressure the president into a settlement, issued a subpoena for Kathleen Willey to testify in the Jones case. Isikoff believed that this gave *Newsweek* enough of a news peg to run a story about Willey, but Evan Thomas objected. "All we've really got here is one source—Linda Tripp," he argued. No, Isikoff responded, "We have a subpoena." Eventually, Isikoff got his way: the story was published in the August 11, 1997, issue of *Newsweek*.

To some degree, *Newsweek*'s decision to publish was forced by Matt Drudge, the dot.com epitome of the "new news," who would later play a major role in the Lewinsky coverage. Drudge placed no journalistic restrictions on the material he published on his Internet Web page. If the story was juicy, sexy, and eye-catching, he would run it. Conway, one of the elves, had become impatient with *Newsweek*'s delays and had leaked the essence of the Willey story to Drudge, who ran it on July 29 and 31 as an illustration of the "establishment press" suppressing the real news.

On October 6, Isikoff met for the first time with a source who was at the center of the web of intrigue surrounding the Jones case: Lucianne Goldberg. For months Tripp had been passing along Lewinsky's secrets to Goldberg, hoping to work out a lucrative book deal. Goldberg had persuaded Tripp to tape her frequent phone conversations with Lewinsky, and they planned to provide Isikoff with selected tidbits of information to whet the public's appetite.

Goldberg later described Isikoff as one of her "heroes." Back in 1994, he had pressed his editors at *The Washington Post* to publish the Jones story and in the process had won brownie points with every Clinton-hating conservative. "When I heard that he had gone to *Newsweek,* I was saddened, for to me that meant the end of the 'bimbo beat' for Isikoff," Goldberg later wrote. But she need not have worried, for Isikoff carried his expertise to the news magazine.

Tripp told Isikoff that she had begun to tape her conversations with the intern and showed him the tapes. No bombshells in them, she cautioned, but would he like to hear them? Isikoff squirmed. "Wait a minute," he said. "I'm not sure I should be doing this. It probably isn't a good idea for me to listen to this." Occasionally, Isikoff anguished about whether he was becoming too much of a player in the story. Now Isikoff demanded to know the intern's name. As he recounted the story, "Tripp hesitated. She looked at Goldberg, who seemed to nod. 'Okay,' said Tripp. 'Her name is Monica Lewinsky.'"

From then on, the pace of events quickened. Tripp and Goldberg kept providing Isikoff with intriguing information to document the affair. From them, he obtained receipts for the courier service that Lewinsky used to send letters and packages from her Pentagon office directly to Clinton at the White House via his personal secretary, Betty Currie. They told him of a hurriedly arranged meeting between Lewinsky and Clinton in his private study at the White House while Mexican president Ernesto Zedillo waited outside. And they told him about a navy blue dress in Monica's closet that had the president's semen on it. Tripp claimed she had actually seen the dress. She offered to steal it and give it to Isikoff so he could have it tested. He told her that was a crazy idea.

Isikoff was uneasy about his role in this situation. "I realized I was in the middle of a plot to get the president," he later wrote. He was covering the story as a journalist, but he was covering it "from the inside, while it was unfolding, talking nearly every week with the conspirators as they schemed to make it happen." At the same time, he was convinced that his earlier assessment of Clinton as a lying philanderer was accurate and should be reported.

But there were questions. Was it relevant to Clinton's work as president? How? And was there a "zone of privacy" to which he (or any American citizen) was entitled? Isikoff frequently engaged in semi-academic debates with his two top editors in Washington, McDaniel and Thomas. They kept returning to the question of "relevance." Specifically, why was *Newsweek* investigating the president's sex life?

Thomas was disturbed by the "unseemly spectacle," by a "sinking feeling in the pit of my stomach that the public would be turned off government even more than they were." He worried that this kind of journalism would only increase "public cynicism" and "distrust." But Thomas appreciated the story's potential, and, like Isikoff, he decided to continue to play the game.

While Tripp and Goldberg were feeding nuggets about Lewinsky and Clinton to Isikoff, they were also feeding similar information to the Jones legal team. Tripp volunteered to testify, but she wanted it to look as if she were being forced to do so, in order to conceal her treachery from Lewinsky. Goldberg worked it out through the elves, and Tripp received her subpoena on November 24. Goldberg also informed the pro-Jones lawyers of the existence of Monica Lewinsky. Thus, when Isikoff interviewed Donovan Campbell, one of the new Jones lawyers, on December 17, he seemed well aware of the former intern.

On December 19, Lewinsky was served with a subpoena demanding that she appear for a deposition in the Jones case on January 23, 1998, and turn over all correspondence with the president as well as all gifts she had received from him. Three days later, the president's good friend Vernon Jordan, a Washington superlawyer who had been trying to help Lewinsky find a job in New York, took her to see a lawyer with a sterling ethical reputation, Francis D. Carter. Lewinsky told him there had been no sexual relationship between her and the president. Carter said he would draw up an affidavit for her to sign that might make it unnecessary for her to testify.

On December 22, in a taped conversation, Tripp tried to draw a distraught Lewinsky into damaging admissions about herself, the president, and Jordan. The tape of December 22, which was to become a prime piece of evidence, was ambiguous, but it could be interpreted to mean that

Lewinsky was planning to lie about her relationship with the president and that Jordan was encouraging her to do so; moreover, she seemed to be asking Tripp to lie as well. Goldberg sent this information to the secret Jones lawyers, ignoring the ambiguities, and they immediately raised questions about perjury, subornation of perjury, and obstruction of justice.

Meanwhile, Tripp could not resist the temptation of boasting about her high-level intrigues, no matter how risky it might be. She kept her weekly bridge partners up to date about the details of the Lewinsky-Clinton affair. According to later testimony by Maryland state prosecutor Stephen Montanarelli, she told them that she was "tape-recording a woman named Monica who was having a sexual relationship with the president." She even invited Lewinsky to her home for a Christmas party so her neighbors could meet "the woman who was unwittingly being taped." Tripp's friends—like the friends in whom Lewinsky had confided—were remarkably discreet. The news never leaked.

For Goldberg and Tripp, the only missing step now was to get the information to Starr's prosecutors. Once again, Goldberg worked through the elves, who told her startling story to Paul Rosenzweig of the OIC staff. The following day, Rosenzweig took the story to Starr's deputy, Jackie Bennett, and on January 12 Starr approved an interview with the person who had all the damaging information, Linda Tripp. OIC lawyers arrived at Tripp's home that evening and spent hours listening to her version of the story. Tripp was concerned that the tapes she had made from her home in Maryland might be illegal. Bennett reassured her that she was doing the right thing, and then, without checking further with Starr, ordered a body wire for Tripp to use in her meeting with Lewinsky the following day.

The trap was ready to spring. The plot was on the verge of success. The two parallel investigations into the Clinton scandals—Starr's Whitewater inquiry and the Jones sex inquiry—were about to converge.

Early Tuesday afternoon, January 13, 1998, Isikoff was sitting in his *Newsweek* office, a windowless, cluttered cubicle on the eleventh floor of 1750 Pennsylvania Avenue, a half block from the Executive Office Building and the White House. He was thinking about how he would report the president's deposition in the Paula Jones case, which was scheduled for

Saturday, January 17, only four days away. Saturday was usually deadline day for weekly magazines and he wondered if he would have enough time on Saturday to check with his sources and get the essence of the president's position on the Jones charges.

Isikoff's reverie was interrupted by a phone call from a man he has refused to identify. Isikoff maintains that the caller insisted on anonymity, and that he as a reporter is "bound by the ethics of my craft" not to disclose his name. "I don't exist," the caller said. "You know that woman you quoted last summer in the Kathleen Willey piece?" "Tripp" flashed through Isikoff's mind. The caller stated that "a little event" was about to start at the Ritz-Carlton Hotel in Arlington, Virginia. What little event? "FBI agents working for Ken Starr have wired her for a lunch with a former White House staffer named Monica Lewinsky," the caller continued. A sting. How did this all happen? The caller claimed he had no idea.

This story about the sting astounded Isikoff. Starr was trying to nail Clinton by way of Lewinsky. A bombshell, Isikoff thought. He quickly called Goldberg, one of his favorite sources. "Do you know anything about this?" he asked. "You heard?" she replied, obviously surprised. She knew. Goldberg later told me that she had spoken with Isikoff, whom she called "Spikey"—a reference to his spiked stories—almost "every single day" during this period, giving him one nugget after another, and she did talk to him that day. "I definitely did tell him about the sting," she said, "but did I tell him before the sting, or after he already knew about it?" As she later mused, "That week was an absolute blur. Very cops-and-robbers-like atmosphere. We were like a bunch of kids playing in the dark."

Isikoff recalled this time in similar terms. "Everything that had happened up until this moment—my conversations with Tripp and Goldberg, the courier slips, the dress, all of it—always had a playacting quality," he wrote. "I had felt at times as if I had wandered into one of those murder mystery weekends in which I was acting out the role of a reporter in a written-for-modern-day-Washington Agatha Christie play. Having the chance to peer into Linda Tripp's world was seductive, there was no question about that. It offered an eerie and fascinating, if tinted and very blurry view of what purported to be seedy conduct inside the White House. But it had been hard to connect it with any objective reality, no way to be sure the whole thing wasn't some gigantic, psychotically induced mirage." But once Starr entered the play, "objective reality" entered with him—and did

Isikoff a huge favor. He no longer had to prove to his editors that Tripp's story about the Clinton-Lewinsky affair was true; no longer had to prove that the affair had enough relevance to justify a news story. Starr's sudden intrusion in the story was proving it for him. "This was [no longer] about sex, or even about the Paula Jones case," Isikoff wrote. "This was about a special prosecutor launching a secret criminal investigation of the president—and targeting his supposed girlfriend in an effort to nail him. It was breathtaking news."

So breathtaking, in fact, that he felt "a little dizzy and weak." He fought the fleeting temptation to burst in on the Tripp-Lewinsky lunch at the Ritz-Carlton, imagining a headline in the next day's paper: REPORTER DISRUPTS CRIMINAL PROBE OF PRESIDENT. He decided to go the traditional route—work his sources and then check and double-check his facts. Isikoff informed his incredulous colleague Klaidman, and then his bureau chief, McDaniel, about the Starr/FBI sting.

McDaniel, who was in New York, immediately instructed Isikoff to start "crashing"—meaning that he should drop everything else and work nonstop, even without sleep, to finish the story. They were both thinking it would be a cover story. McDaniel informed her senior editors. Everyone understood that the political world in Washington was about to turn upside down, and so was theirs. Up to that moment, Isikoff's romancing of Jones, Tripp, and Goldberg, while absorbing and titillating, was not reportable, at least not in *Newsweek*. Now, with Starr launching a secret taped investigation of the president's relationship with Lewinsky, a once-in-a-lifetime story loomed on the near horizon. McDaniel told me, it "completely changed the way *Newsweek* dealt with the story."

For Isikoff, "crashing" on Wednesday, January 14, meant, first, learning a lot more about Monica Lewinsky, the woman in the scandal; and second, getting the Tripp tapes—the very tapes he had declined even to listen to a few months earlier.

Isikoff called Willie Blacklow, a source who had recently retired as deputy director of the Pentagon's public affairs office. Did Blacklow know Lewinsky? Sure, he answered. She was "a sweet young kid," who had done "a fine job" in the office. But he was puzzled about a couple of things. One was that she seemed a bit young and naive to hold such a high clearance and sensitive position; and the second was that she often implied she had important friends at the White House—she seemed to be a name-dropper.

In December 1996, Lewinsky proved to him that she had at least one important friend there. Blacklow accompanied her to the White House Christmas party. She was "dressed to the hilt, with a semi-low-cut red dress." When they got to the Clintons on the reception line, the president greeted her with a "Hi, Monica" and "hugged" her. Mrs. Clinton shook her hand. "I was kind of stunned," Blacklow recalled. "There was no question that she was something more than just another gofer."

Isikoff then called Goldberg and learned that Tripp had decided that day to change lawyers. She no longer had confidence in her lawyer, Kirby Behre. Instead, she was hiring James Moody—aggressive, ideological, recommended by Goldberg's anti-Clinton lawyer friends. Tripp had instructed Moody to go directly to Behre, who was keeping her invaluable tapes, and deliver them to Starr's prosecutors. "Wait a second," Isikoff shouted. "I need to hear those tapes." Goldberg promised that, to be helpful, she would call Moody, but recommended that in the meantime Isikoff should try to call him, too. Isikoff called and left a message.

Next on Isikoff's list was Jackie Bennett, the pugnacious prosecutor who had led the OIC interrogation of Tripp two days before. After hearing Tripp's saga of illicit sex in the White House, Bennett was strongly of the view that Starr should now broaden his investigation of the president and that he needed no additional authorization to pursue leads that went directly into the president's sexual misbehavior in the Oval Office. A number of Bennett's OIC colleagues took immediate exception to this course, which they considered unwise and unnecessarily provocative. They distrusted Tripp, questioned her veracity, and actively discouraged Starr from expanding his investigation of the president to include the Lewinsky connection.

On numerous occasions in Little Rock and Washington, Bennett had grudgingly helped Isikoff and other reporters, often with a wink and a nod, sometimes with a suggestion, a lead, a fact. But on this Wednesday morning, Bennett chose not to take his call. A few hours later, Isikoff called again, his voice conveying a deeper sense of urgency. Bennett got the message and, according to Isikoff, told one of his colleagues: "I think he may already know." Bennett assumed that Isikoff had learned about the Tripp tale and that he was calling for confirmation.

Bennett was afraid the story would become public—that *Newsweek* would publish Tripp's account of a White House affair and thus deny

Starr's OIC the element of surprise and the opportunity to ensnare the president in an embarrassing scandal. McDaniel was afraid that *Newsweek* would lose the exclusive that it had had for months, that all of Isikoff's efforts would be blown. "We were running on separate courses that at some point were going to collide," McDaniel said. The collision was now only days away.

Bennett argued with his colleagues, this time persuasively, that the OIC no longer had the luxury of time and that it had to expand its investigation. Isikoff was on their trail. Bennett got Starr's permission to inform the Justice Department. By the time he placed a call to Eric Holder, the deputy attorney general, it was 9:30 p.m., and Holder was at the MCI Center watching the end of a basketball game between the Washington Wizards and the San Antonio Spurs. Holder, usually conscientious, ignored his beeper. Bennett called again at 10:18 p.m. This time, Holder returned the call. "We are sort of into a sensitive matter," Bennett began. According to his notes, which were to become part of the OIC record, Bennett remained artfully vague yet suggestive. "Breaking. Paying close attention to jurisdictional limits—confident sufficient jurisdictional nexus. Involves people at and associated with the White House." Holder, who was calling from a pay phone, had no option but to be equally vague. "We need to meet with you in person," Bennett said. They agreed to meet the following day.

On Thursday, January 15, 1998, journalism, at least as practiced at *Newsweek,* entered treacherous terrain.

Over the years, American journalism has developed standards of professional conduct. They can be simply defined: be objective and fair; tell the truth, meaning don't lie or dissemble even in pursuit of the truth; build a high wall between the editorial and financial sides of the industry; keep a respectful distance between you and the government; resist the urge, no matter the competitive pressures, to impose yourself on or in the story—you are the storyteller, not the story. Unfortunately, these standards have been steadily eroding.

Newsweek at this time was experiencing a leadership crisis. Maynard Parker, its legendary editor, was in the hospital with leukemia, and a committee led by Richard Smith and Mark Whitaker was making the big decisions. Smith, the editor in chief, was a former foreign correspondent who had covered Vietnam with courage; Whitaker was a bright young reporter/executive and Parker's heir apparent. Committee decisions were characteristically cautious, rarely bold. When the senior editors gathered in Whitaker's office to hear McDaniel's latest report on Isikoff's sensational findings, they were both intrigued and worried: intrigued by the prospect of a bombshell exclusive; worried about the responsibility (both editorial and financial) of having to base their decision on one reporter's controversial sources and style. "The credibility of the magazine was at stake," said Whitaker.

What if Monica Lewinsky proved to be a totally unreliable source? What if Linda Tripp was psychotic? What if Goldberg proved to be little more than a Clinton-hating zealot? What if, by next Monday, when the magazine hit the newsstands, the charges against the president and Vernon Jordan were found to be baseless?

Would it be possible, they asked McDaniel, for Isikoff to get the tapes? Maybe they would then be better able to judge the reliability of Lewinsky's allegations. Smith and Whitaker felt that McDaniel herself had to hear the tapes; in their minds, it was not enough to leave the full responsibility to Isikoff.

In the end, they reached two decisions: first, prepare two cover stories for the next issue—one with and one without the Lewinsky scandal; and second, tell Isikoff to get the tapes. They knew that on this story no other reporter had the sources, the contacts, the inside knowledge. What he knew had the potential to destroy a president.

For months, Isikoff had worried about his role in covering the scandal, about crossing the line between aggressive reporting and personal participation in the story. On this day, he crossed the line and became a player, an actor, a negotiator.

His first call was to Kirby Behre, the Washington lawyer whom Tripp had just fired. Isikoff's technique was to share what he knew with a source: to open his cupboard, display his wares, and then judge the source's response. If the source confirmed the information, and if Isikoff believed the source, then he was halfway there. All he then needed was a second source to confirm the validity of the information, although on rare occasions one perfectly placed source could be sufficient. On the other hand, if the source openly disputed the information, then Isikoff had a serious problem. Was the source lying or telling the truth? If Isikoff (or any reporter, for that matter) believed the source was probably telling the truth in disputing the accuracy of the information, then he had to readjust his approach to the story and perhaps even drop it. But if a source chose the middle ground, refusing to either confirm or deny the information, then the journalist had to go with his own judgment: he could assume that the source could not speak to the issue because of lawyer-client privilege or doctor-patient confidentiality, that the source knew nothing, or that the source did not want to get involved. In this case, Behre refused to answer any of Isikoff's questions, citing lawyer-client privilege, and Isikoff took his response to be a form of silent confirmation.

Next, Isikoff called Betty Currie, the president's personal secretary. When Isikoff identified himself, she later told the grand jury, she felt a "thud" go off in her head. Isikoff reviewed what he knew from courier slips he had obtained from Tripp and Goldberg detailing the delivery of packages and letters from Lewinsky to Currie that were intended for the president. Did Currie know anything about these deliveries? She answered in a voice remarkably calm for the occasion: "I'm not quite sure. But I'd be happy to look into it and get back to you." What Isikoff did not know at the time was that Currie promptly called Lewinsky to discuss strategy and then called Jordan and left a message: "Betty/POTUS [President of the United States]. Kind of important."

But his most important call that day was to Jackie Bennett. This time, he refused to take no for an answer, and Bennett accepted the call. "I know what you guys have been doing," Isikoff stated. "I know everything. We need to talk. Right away." Bennett, "anxious and extremely upset," agreed. He told Isikoff to come immediately to Suite 410 of the Office of the Independent Counsel.

The Isikoff-Bennett encounter, witnessed by two OIC prosecutors, Michael Emmick and Stephen Bates, proved to be an exceptional exchange between a reporter and a source. A reporter could work energetically at his or her craft for a lifetime and never experience anything remotely like it. Isikoff went beyond generally accepted rules governing a reporter's conduct with a source. He not only dug for information—he cajoled, threatened, blackmailed, and taunted Bennett. He played every card in his hand. "We'd have been thrilled if Isikoff was not hounding us and we could operate on our own timetable," Bates told me, "but we couldn't—we were operating on a timetable dictated by journalism's needs."

"Let's face it," Bennett began with undisguised anger. "You've got us over the barrel." He proposed a bargain: If Isikoff agreed to delay publishing his story, giving the OIC more time, he would be rewarded with "hard evidence" of a conspiracy.

Isikoff was tempted, but he stood his ground. What "hard evidence"? Isikoff wanted to know. A document of some kind?

Bennett refused to be specific. He wanted—and needed—information to prosecute his case against the president. "We need to know everything you know," he said. Everything Isikoff had done, everyone he had called, everywhere he had gone. Basically, Bennett wanted to know whether the OIC investigation had already been compromised.

Isikoff wrote that he took Bennett's questions to be "implicit confirmation" of his information. "I played along." But instead of just listening to the OIC prosecutor in an effort to pick up new insights or new tidbits of information, Isikoff decided to disclose most of what he had been accumulating for months. What McDaniel, as Isikoff's editor, had learned after many months of confidential consultation, Bennett, as Isikoff's source, now learned in a matter of minutes: what Isikoff knew about the Tripp tapes, her treacherous relationship with Lewinsky, her confessional talks with Bennett and the OIC, the sting attempt at the Ritz-Carlton. Bennett, sensing soft turf, pushed Isikoff: Tell me more. What else do you know? Was the OIC investigation still whole?

Isikoff asserted in his book: "I couldn't tell him sources." But he did tell him about his calls to Behre and Currie, and they were among his sources. Then Isikoff took the offensive, apparently on the assumption that he had demonstrated his goodwill and now it was Bennett's turn to talk.

"Look, you guys are the ones that need to cooperate with me," Isikoff said. "You need to lay out your evidence, or at least your basis for starting this investigation." He reminded Bennett and his colleagues that Starr was under critical attack for prolonging the investigation and that straying into the Jones case "without adequate justification would give his critics even more ammunition." Isikoff then threatened Bennett—which, as a reporter, he should not have done. "Unless you show me what you've got and establish the predicate for this, you're going to get roasted." Isikoff later reflected: "It was, in a way, a form of blackmail. I was threatening to make him look really bad if he didn't give me information."

Bennett replied: "We can take the heat. I'm 100 percent comfortable that we have adequate justification for getting involved in this."

Bruce Udolf, another prosecutor, entered the sparsely furnished conference room at this point. "What have I missed?" he asked. Isikoff took the initiative and explained that he knew all about the Clinton/Lewinsky affair and "planned to move ahead with a story on it." Udolf was stunned. "You can't do that," he said. The OIC needed time.

Isikoff relentlessly pursued his quarry. He told Udolf that he knew everything. He wanted to know if the sting had produced evidence of a federal crime. Udolf paused, nonplussed. "I can't believe I'm having this conversation. I've never had a conversation with a reporter like this in my life." Udolf appealed to Isikoff's sense of justice. If he published the story, the OIC's case would be finished.

"We bargained," Isikoff recalled later. The OIC needed time. Isikoff argued that *Newsweek* would not be publishing until Sunday, so the OIC had time. Udolf and Bennett said that there were things Isikoff didn't understand—that, in any case, the OIC could not strike a deal with Isikoff until Friday. Bennett asked who else Isikoff would have to call before writing his story. Jordan and Lewinsky, Isikoff said. They would have to be called, and soon, he stressed. He had no choice.

Bennett asked how long Isikoff could delay making those calls. "Not long," Isikoff replied. Then, arbitrarily, Isikoff set a deadline of 4 p.m. Friday. Without so much as checking with his editor, Isikoff had accepted Bennett's request for a temporary hold on his pursuit of the story, meaning that *Newsweek*—a news organization—had just struck a deal with the OIC—an arm of the government. The terms were imprecise, but the effect was that the OIC had another day to continue its investigation of the president without fear that a journalist would sabotage its effort.

Isikoff rationalized his unorthodox approach by acknowledging that it was "tricky" but insisting that he had made only a "relatively modest concession." He wouldn't call Jordan or Lewinsky until 4 p.m. Friday while the OIC pursued its undercover probe of the president's sex life. "It wasn't my job to help Starr sting the President. . . . But by the same token, it wasn't my job to get in the middle of their investigation." He left his momentous meeting with the OIC feeling that he was about to expose "a pretty damn good story."

Isikoff's bargain with the OIC's Bennett was highly unusual. Ever since the Vietnam War and the Watergate scandal, relations between

reporters and government officials have been prickly. Reporters are skeptical, even cynical, about the government; officials are distrustful and dis-
dainful of the press. In this case, both sides cooperated, in part because
both sides, for different reasons, were intent on "getting" the president.
They needed each other.

After his encounter with Bennett, Isikoff returned to his office and
briefed McDaniel. If she as bureau chief objected to Isikoff's deal with the
OIC, or to his journalistic improvisation, she didn't let on during my interview with her—nor did Isikoff disclose any editorial concerns of this
nature in his book. "The entire situation was surreal," Isikoff wrote. "The
prosecutors were pleading with us for time so they could nail the president
on sex and perjury." McDaniel sensed an additional reason. "I suspect,
although they didn't say so specifically, that they would have preferred that
we veer off and back down," she told me. "I don't think they saw a good
solution for themselves in this." Though *Newsweek* and the OIC cooperated, she said, they were "not working toward the same end." She had her
eye trained on a single objective. "Our goal was to tell the story of a federal
investigation of the president of the United States for an affair with a
younger woman who happened to be on the federal payroll."

Once his negotiation with the OIC was over, Isikoff returned to his
effort to get the Tripp-Lewinsky tapes. He begged for the tapes, whenever
there was anyone at the other end of the phone to listen. He was, Goldberg later recalled, "occasionally hysterical." Isikoff was certain that by this
time, James Moody, Tripp's new lawyer, had the tapes. In fact, late that
afternoon, Moody had obtained them from Behre, Tripp's old lawyer, and
brought them to his office; but Moody didn't want to talk to Isikoff and
refused to answer his repeated calls. Isikoff was now functioning on high
octane. Unable to reach Moody, he called Tripp, but she had changed her
number. Then he called Goldberg and read her the riot act. Didn't she
realize, he screamed, that if he couldn't listen to the tapes, he couldn't write
a story supporting Tripp's charges against the president; and that if he
couldn't write such a story, their whole effort would collapse. Starr would
look stupid. Tripp would look like a liar.

Isikoff later wrote: "That at any rate was what I was telling them. It is the
way reporters operate. We threaten, we cajole, we feign sympathy. But the
truth for me was slightly different: whatever was on those tapes, listening to
them, and quoting them, would make this a much more compelling and dra-

matic story for *Newsweek*." Once again, as he had on a number of other occasions, Isikoff argued that his frenetic, theatrical, at times deceitful and free-wheeling style was typical of the craft—it's what most other journalists did. Not so. Most journalists operate according to different standards of engagement. For his part, Isikoff was so deeply enmeshed in his story, so determined to get the tapes, that he was prepared to say and do just about anything.

At the end of the day, Jackie Bennett and three of his colleagues went to the Justice Department for a meeting with Eric Holder and one of his deputies. Bennett overstated his case, claiming that there was "explicit" evidence of perjury involving Lewinsky, Clinton, and Jordan. Holder was stunned. Bennett went on to assure Holder that the OIC had had no contacts with the Jones attorneys, which was not true. Here was an example of one arm of the government misleading another.

Then, to bolster his plea for speedy action, Bennett explained: "A seriously complicating factor came to our attention this evening. Mike Isikoff is on to this. He has been receiving information from a friend of Tripp's. We met with him and he is disturbingly far along. So we have a very short window of opportunity to try to move this along." Holder asked: "His article will come out next week?" Bennett nodded. "I'm sorry to leave you with this." Thus Bennett used Isikoff as leverage on the Justice Department. He kept stressing that *Newsweek* was working on the story and would publish it on Sunday. "This was meant as a way of explaining why we had to act fast," said one Justice Department participant. "But the way he said it and kept saying it, it also was clear to us that if we turned down the request, *Newsweek* would know about that, too. We had no choice."

Holder promised to contact the U.S. Attorney General.

Isikoff at this point was a threat to Starr's best-laid plans. To expand his investigation to include the president's sexual escapades, Starr needed the permission of the Justice Department and the authorization of the three-judge panel that had appointed him as independent counsel. If Isikoff lived up to his promise to Bennett not to call Lewinsky and Jordan until Friday at 4 p.m., Starr might still have the time to clear these bureaucratic hurdles.

CHAPTER 3

"SOMETHING ABOUT PERJURY"

January 16, 1998

"THIS IS WHAT IMPEACHMENT IS MADE OF. YOUR POLITICAL
ENEMIES WILL EAT YOU ALIVE IF THERE IS ANYTHING IN THAT
DEPOSITION THAT IS NOT TRUTHFUL."
—Quoted in Bob Woodward, *Shadow*

"THESE WOMANIZING STORIES ARE OLD HAT AND STILL
HAVEN'T GONE ANYWHERE."
—Lanny Davis, *Truth to Tell*

On Friday, January 16, 1998, Viveca Novak, an investigative reporter for *Time*, began hearing rumbles about a *Newsweek* exclusive. "Something about perjury," she recalled, "something about the president." At the time, she didn't know much more, but she began to get a bit concerned. A word like "perjury" linked to the president was enough to alert a reporter to make a few calls—especially one who had spent time in Little Rock covering the Paula Jones sexual harassment suit for *The Wall Street Journal*. Novak first telephoned a source at the White House on the assumption that *Newsweek* would have had to call there for confirmation of its story. Her source was not helpful, or was simply uninformed. She then called David Kendall, the president's personal attorney. He too was not helpful, claiming absolute ignorance of any exclusive, but he did give her his cell phone number. He was taking his family to New York for the weekend, but if she really needed him, he said, she was to feel free to call.

As fierce competitors, *Time* and *Newsweek* had ways of checking on each other. "We would often get the drift of what *Newsweek* was going to go with, just as I'm sure they'd get the drift of what we were going to go with," Novak later told me. She checked with a few colleagues but in this case hit a dry well. Not even an echo. "I wasn't frantic," she said, "but I was concerned."

Early that Friday morning, Attorney General Reno met with two of her principal deputies, Holder and Lee Radek, and one of their leading investigators, Josh Hochberg, who had just returned to the Justice Department from a visit to the Office of the Independent Counsel. There Hochberg had read the transcript of the "sting" arranged by Starr and the FBI the previous Tuesday at the Ritz-Carlton. The taped conversation between Tripp and Lewinsky raised serious questions, Hochberg said, and further investigation was clearly required. Starr had specifically requested authority to expand his existing mandate to look into the Clinton-Lewinsky entanglement. If Reno rejected Starr's request, the Justice Department could be accused of trying to protect Clinton. She had little choice.

Starr's staff, anticipating her decision, had drafted a formal request for an expanded investigation to the three-judge panel headed by Judge Sentelle that was responsible for overseeing all OIC activities—the same panel that had named Starr in the first place. Starr justified his request by arguing that there was a connection between his original investigation and the new charges. "We are already investigating Vernon Jordan for having helped arrange employment for Webster Hubbell," Starr wrote, referring to the former associate attorney general and Hillary Clinton law partner who had gone to prison and then reneged on his promise to cooperate with the Whitewater prosecutors. Now, Starr continued, there were indications that Jordan was involved in finding a job for another person whose testimony might be damaging to the president.

The panel formally reviewed the request and, within hours, authorized Starr to investigate Lewinsky, Jordan, "and others" for "crimes" relating to the Jones case. Radek objected to the inclusion of Jordan's name. Judge Sentelle discussed the objection with his two colleagues and then called Bennett with final approval of a sealed and secret two-page order giving Starr the power to investigate "whether Monica Lewinsky or others suborned perjury, obstructed justice, intimidated witnesses or otherwise violated federal law." Neither Jordan nor the president was mentioned. Only the name "Monica Lewinsky" was in the judge's order. Up to this point in her life, she had been an unknown. In the next few days, her name was to become known to a wider but still very small circle of lawyers, reporters, and government officials. Then, on Wednesday of the following week, she was suddenly to be rocketed to international fame.

At *Newsweek* that morning, the talk was all about the tapes. From the moment Isikoff arrived and started briefing McDaniel and Thomas, he realized that if he didn't get the tapes and if his editors didn't have a chance to listen to them, he might not get his story in the magazine at all. Visions of past struggles with his editors at the *Post* rose in his mind. Isikoff assured McDaniel that he still hoped to be able to hear the tapes, perhaps before day's end, but he could not assure her that he could bring the tapes, or copies of them, to the office so that she and Thomas could hear them. McDaniel understood the concerns the editors in New York had expressed the previous day. Smith and Whitaker wanted her and Thomas to hear the tapes, too. They did not want to publish the story only on the basis of Isikoff's sourcing and reporting.

McDaniel proposed as a backup that it would be a good idea—"just in case"—for Isikoff to prepare a story about Clinton's upcoming deposition on Saturday in the Jones case. Did she mean New York was getting cold feet, Isikoff asked. No, McDaniel replied, but "just in case." Isikoff actually had fresh information for a good story—that Willey had testified the previous Saturday about the infamous presidential grope. But he knew that the Willey story, while interesting, paled in comparison with his latest discoveries.

In the office at the OIC, Jackie Bennett was negotiating an immunity agreement with James Moody, Tripp's new lawyer. Bennett was following up on his assurance to Tripp at their January 12 meeting that he would deal with her concern about possible prosecution in Maryland, where taping of another person without consent was illegal. The terms were simple: Tripp would get immunity as soon as Moody delivered the potentially incriminating December 22 tape to the OIC. The tape was of the conversation Tripp recorded shortly after Lewinsky received a subpoena to testify in the Jones case. On it, Lewinsky referred to a meeting she had had that day with Vernon Jordan. Tripp, trying to entrap both Lewinsky and Jordan, asked whether Jordan had asked her to lie in her affidavit. Lewinsky's answer was artfully vague; it could be read as either confirmation or evasion, depending on one's legal needs and political views. While negotiating with Bennett, Moody hyped the prospective value of the December 22 tape, claiming that it proved Jordan's involvement in a possible obstruction of justice and would therefore "especially interest the OIC."

Bennett wanted the tape—indeed, he wanted all the Tripp tapes. He proposed that Moody bring the December 22 tape to the OIC that morning and all the other tapes later in the afternoon and in exchange Tripp would obtain her immunity. Moody accepted the proposal with only one caveat—that he obtain copies of all the tapes he was to bring to the OIC. After all, Moody's agenda was not only to get immunity for his client but also to get publicity for their anti-Clinton campaign. That was where Isikoff entered his calculation: Moody realized he would have to cooperate with him, however unwelcome the prospect. Both Moody and Goldberg considered the *Newsweek* reporter to be a key component of their "conspiracy" to dismantle the Clinton presidency, and Goldberg had been badgering him to help Isikoff. Bennett promised to get copies of the tapes back to Moody as quickly as possible.

Later that morning, Moody hand-delivered the first tape to the OIC, activating Tripp's immunity.

Isikoff was anxiously awaiting Moody's call. When it came, Isikoff recalled, "I nearly jumped out of my chair. Where the hell have you been? I shouted. Don't you realize how important it is that I hear those tapes? Don't you realize that Linda is going to get clobbered if I can't prove how serious all this is?" Isikoff's language was deliberately designed to suggest that he and Moody shared common aspirations and purposes. Moody responded, with disingenuous surprise, "Oh, you're calling me about that," as if the tapes were tangential to his professional concerns. "Cut it out, I snapped. I'm not bullshitting here." Moody finally focused on Isikoff's request. He agreed that it would be "in the public interest" if Isikoff heard the tapes, but said first there were "some things he had to work out." Moody said he would call back later. "When?" Isikoff demanded. "My deadline is tonight. I've got to hear those tapes tonight." Moody assured the frustrated reporter that he would be back in touch.

Lanny Davis was a White House lawyer, hired primarily to deal with legal questions the press might raise on Clinton's various scandals. He was a short-timer, preparing to return to private practice after a period of intense service. On this wildly busy day, Davis had a farewell lunch with Isikoff— on reflection, Davis later wrote, a rather "strange" lunch. Usually, Isikoff was the sort of impatient reporter who would begin pushing for information about sensitive legal matters at the White House even before a drink could be ordered, but on this occasion he seemed preoccupied and troubled, and his questions focused less on the latest White House embarrassment than on what Davis had heard about the activities and interests of other reporters. When reporters called the White House these days, he wanted to know, what were they asking about? Any interesting questions? Any particular story line? Any gossip? Then Isikoff asked what seemed like an odd set of questions about a conversation he and Davis had had months before. Why, Isikoff asked, had Davis called last July 4 to inquire about whether he was working on a story about the president and another woman? Davis recalled the exchange, which took place a week or so before Isikoff first broke the Willey story. "Who asked you to call? [Isikoff] prodded. Why? What had you heard at that point? From whom?"

Davis ducked Isikoff's questions. "These womanizing stories are old hat and still haven't gone anywhere," he responded with studied casualness. Isikoff, he remembered, turned coy. "They're more real than you think," he said.

At 12:30 p.m., Monica Lewinsky was sitting at the Food Court of the Pentagon City Mall waiting for Linda Tripp to join her for lunch. Fifteen minutes later, she saw Tripp descending on the escalator. As Lewinsky rose to meet her, two FBI agents stepped forward, flashed their badges, and informed Lewinsky that she was the subject of a criminal investigation and that attorneys for the OIC wanted to talk to her. Naturally she was shocked, frightened, and utterly bewildered. The two agents escorted Lewinsky and Tripp to room 1012 of the Ritz-Carlton Hotel, where one of Starr's prosecutors, Mike Emmick, an experienced white-collar prosecutor from Los Angeles, was waiting. He informed Lewinsky at the start of a highly emotional twelve-hour interrogation that the Attorney General had authorized Starr to investigate criminal activity related to the Jones case. He showed her photographs of her Tuesday lunch with Tripp and told her of tapes from the same lunch revealing that she had lied under oath and signed a false and misleading affidavit. Emmick capped his summary by telling Lewinsky that she could be charged with a number of federal crimes, such as perjury, obstruction of justice, and witness tampering. If found guilty of these crimes, Emmick warned, she could go to prison for twenty-seven years.

"I just felt an intense stinging pain, an overriding terror," Lewinsky recalled. "It was surreal. I couldn't understand how this was all happening." Emmick later described Lewinsky as "nearly hysterical with tears. She would sob, then cry out, then stare into space, then cry for long periods."

Emmick took advantage of a relatively quiet period to describe a possible way out for Lewinsky. If she would cooperate with the prosecutors, then maybe they would not indict her. Lewinsky wanted to know what "cooperate" would entail. Emmick explained that, like Tripp, she would have to agree to be wired, or be fitted with a microphone, and then call or meet a number of people under investigation for the purpose of trapping them into providing incriminating testimony. As Lewinsky recalled the conversation, Emmick mentioned Betty Currie or Vernon Jordan or possibly the president. Starr denied that specific names had been mentioned.

Lewinsky asked if she could call her lawyer. Yes, Emmick replied, she had a legal right to do so, but if she chose to exercise it and inform her lawyer of her situation, the news about the OIC investigation might leak and her value as an undercover informant would decrease. Over the next few hours, Lewinsky froze into an uncommunicative silence.

Emmick, after a while, tried another approach. If Lewinsky cooperated, the OIC would give her full immunity, and the immunity would extend to her mother too, suggesting that the OIC was also considering criminal charges against her mother. If she didn't cooperate, the offer would be withdrawn that day. Lewinsky was again jolted into a bout of uncontrollable tears. She wanted to call her mother. Jackie Bennett, periodically calling in from his office to check on the Emmick-Lewinsky exchange, decided to come to the Ritz-Carlton and talk to Lewinsky. The negotiation needed some "gray hair," he later said. When he arrived, Bennett sat opposite the obviously distraught young woman and adopted a tough, unbudging stance known to any lawyer who had ever faced him in court. As Lewinsky later recalled, he said, "You're twenty-four years old, you're smart, you're old enough, you don't need to call your mommy." Displaying the resilience she was later to show the world, Lewinsky responded coldly, "Well, I'm letting you know I'm leaning toward not cooperating." Later, she recalled: "Emotionally I was shut down now. Like a rape victim who screams for the first five minutes and then just stops, I had just closed down."

At 3 p.m., as agreed earlier with Bennett, Moody arrived in the conference room of the OIC and handed over sixteen audiotapes (with explanatory notes from Linda Tripp) to Stephen Bates, one of Starr's prosecutors.

Moody repeated to Bates what he had already told Bennett—that he had not retained copies of the tapes and would appreciate copies "once the OIC prepared them, if possible." He informed Bates that "he had received many messages from Michael Isikoff of *Newsweek*," who urged Moody to call him because he was preparing an article "highly damaging" to Tripp. Bates kept the tapes with him until Friday evening, when he delivered them to an FBI agent, Steve Irons, working with the OIC prosecutors at the Ritz-Carlton Hotel.

While Monica Lewinsky was facing Starr's prosecutors, led by Jackie Bennett, President Clinton was facing his own lawyer, Bob Bennett, who was trying to prepare him for his unprecedented deposition in the Jones case, scheduled for the next day. Clinton was likely to be asked about his questionable relationships with nine different women, including Gennifer Flowers, Kathleen Willey, and a relative newcomer, Monica Lewinsky. According to Bob Woodward, Bennett told him, "Mr. President, I find your explanation about one of the women frankly unbelievable." He went on to warn the president, "'This is what impeachment is made of. Your political enemies will eat you alive if there's anything in that deposition that isn't truthful.' . . . 'I hear you,' the president said."

Bennett was referring to a woman in Arkansas, not to Lewinsky. Woodward says that Bennett found it "totally improbable that the president had taken up with a young woman, age 23 or 24, who apparently brought pizza and mail to the Oval Office." Besides, Clinton had assured him a few days earlier that there was no reason for the Jones lawyers to be asking about Lewinsky. When Bennett asked if Lewinsky had made any other visits to the Oval Office, Clinton said that "Betty Currie had invited her church group to look at the Christmas decorations . . . and Monica tagged along and maybe she poked her head in." Moreover, Bennett had received a copy of Lewinsky's affidavit stating, "I have never had a sexual relationship with the president."

Isikoff was still worrying about the competition. "The first sign of trouble came mid-Friday afternoon," he later wrote. He got a call from Deborah Orin, Washington bureau chief of the *New York Post*, a tabloid that prides itself on giving credit for every story it appropriates from a competitor. Orin, a friend, told Isikoff that she had heard he was writing a "blockbuster." Could she get an advance copy late Saturday for her Sunday paper? "With full credit, of course," she added. Isikoff told her nothing at all. "Then, I slammed down the phone, quite agitated," Isikoff wrote. "What the hell was going on?"

Isikoff believed that Orin had gotten her tip indirectly from Lucianne Goldberg, who had probably alerted her buddy, Marc Kalech, the managing editor of the *Post*, that *Newsweek* "had a hot one coming." Goldberg was on retainer with the *New York Post* and often passed along gossip and information.

Orin had a different recollection of her Friday call to Isikoff. She told me that she had picked up "something linking Ken Starr to Paula Jones." What could it be? "It sounded totally outlandish," Orin recalled. She tried to connect the dots linking Starr, Jones, and Whitewater. "I remember saying to Mike, 'I hear you got a big story.' Mike would normally be very helpful, so long as we gave him credit. And we always did. He'd normally say something like, 'I can't help you now, not this week, but call me or call somebody else on Saturday or Sunday.' But this time all he did was say nothing and hang up. Something was up, but I didn't know what it was. I didn't know anything about an intern. I only knew that it had something to do with Starr and Jones."

No sooner had Isikoff finished one disturbing call than he got another. On Thursday, Isikoff had struck a deal with Bennett in which he agreed not to call Jordan or Lewinsky for a comment about Starr's investigation until 4 p.m. on Friday; now, with that deadline approaching, Bruce Udolf of the OIC was asking him to wait until Saturday. Udolf didn't tell Isikoff—and Isikoff didn't know at the time—that the OIC had picked up Lewinsky and so far had failed to persuade her to cooperate with its investigation. The OIC needed more time.

"Under normal circumstances," Isikoff wrote, "I would have told him to take a hike." But these were not normal circumstances. Having crossed the line with Thursday's highly controversial arrangement with the OIC, Isikoff felt that he had no choice but to agree to the OIC's latest request. He could do nothing without the tapes. "My hands were tied," he wrote in his book. "I had been told to sit tight. I would get to hear the tapes that evening." Isikoff has never spelled out the precise role of the OIC in providing the tapes, but his account suggests that the arrangement he reached with Bennett on Thursday may have involved a promise that they would be made available to him.

Isikoff reported the news to McDaniel. "This was making me crazy," he told Steven Brill. "How was I gonna reach Jordan on a Saturday?" McDaniel seemed amazingly untroubled. "Don't worry," she said. "We'll be able to track Jordan down on Saturday if we need to. . . . There are ways to retrieve Jordan's phone numbers from the right Rolodexes."

"Extremely reluctantly," Isikoff told Udolf that *Newsweek* would wait until Saturday morning—but no longer.

Actually, no matter what brave front Isikoff showed Udolf, there were doubts among *Newsweek*'s top editors in New York about whether they should proceed with this story, even if Isikoff did get to listen to the Tripp tapes. "New York was sounding like they thought this wasn't enough," Isikoff said. "Friday night, Spikey called and told me there were some problems," Goldberg recalled. "But he said it looked like they would go with it."

Orin was not the only reporter outside *Newsweek* who was beginning to pick up the whiff of a story. "It was in the ether," Orin said. "There was something out there—hard to describe." Journalists can often sense an approaching story.

Late in the afternoon, Michael Weisskopf, a respected political reporter for *Time*, called Lanny Davis at the White House. "Hear anything about the president coaching a witness who has been called before a grand jury?" he asked. "Something relating to notes or tapes regarding the Jones case?" Weisskopf then referred cryptically to the possible involvement of a young woman. With Weisskopf, as with Isikoff earlier in the day, Davis could not be helpful, because he knew nothing about the story. "How strong is your source of information?" Davis inquired. "Pretty good—but won't go on the record. This is worth your checking it out," Weisskopf replied.

Davis had the highest regard for Weisskopf: he was too good a journalist, Davis believed, to be calling a White House counsel on the eve of the president's deposition by Jones's lawyers unless his information and instincts told him that there was a good story out there. Davis pressed, "Can you tell me anything more? Otherwise, you know, I'll have difficulty getting people to help me." Weisskopf was under deadline pressure. "Can't tell you much more right now. Get back to me."

Davis pondered the possibilities. The only grand jury activity involved Whitewater. Davis at the time knew nothing about Starr's expanded authority, and, besides, he wrote, "I had the strong impression that Starr's efforts to implicate the President and the first lady in these matters had come to a virtual dead end." Davis at the time was echoing the common Washington assumption that Starr was spinning his wheels, unable to score a big hit against Clinton.

Still, Weisskopf was Weisskopf, and Davis wanted to be helpful. He called a few colleagues in the counsel's office as well as political and press people, prefacing his questions with urgent requests for confidentiality. His calls produced nothing. He then took his questions to a higher level in the counsel's office. "Any chance you could check this out with the president or Bob Bennett?" he asked. "You know we don't go to the president with press questions on something like this," his colleague replied. Davis called Kendall, a classmate from Yale Law School. Kendall was unreachable. Davis tried Bennett. Unreachable, also. Finally, he called Weisskopf and asked whether there was anything else the reporter could share with him. "No," was Weisskopf's answer. Davis said that in that case he could neither confirm nor deny Weisskopf's queries.

Like many other network correspondents and producers, Jackie Judd and Chris Vlasto worked as a team, responsible to the Washington bureau of ABC News and to the executive producer and anchor of *World News Tonight,* the marquee evening news broadcast of the network. Judd was the solid on-air presence, a reporter of reliable, tested judgment with enough ambition to push a story but not over the edge. Vlasto was her perfect companion, younger, far more committed to causes, often hanging on the edge. Veterans of the Arkansas Whitewater press corps, they generally divided up their responsibilities—Judd keeping in close touch with Jackie Bennett and other sources at the OIC, and Vlasto working his sources among the Jones lawyers. On Friday evening, they came up with a solid story: Kathleen Willey had testified about the president's sexual advances. It was the same story Isikoff had, except that Judd, working for a network, had a huge advantage—she was ready to break the story on *World News Tonight.*

Anchor Peter Jennings opened his broadcast with what he regarded as the more important story—the president's deposition scheduled for the following morning. "Paula Jones is on her way to Washington tonight," he began. "She will be present tomorrow when President Clinton gives a deposition in her sexual harassment suit against him. The President met today with his attorney [Robert Bennett] to prepare for his testimony. Our legal analyst Jeffrey Toobin joins us this evening." Jennings then turned to the studio monitor. "Jeffrey, this has all had something of a circus-like atmosphere. What will really go on over the weekend, and how much of his personal life will they get into?" Toobin responded, "Well, Judge Susan Webber Wright . . . will do her best to make sure it's not a circus. She is going to limit the questioning to what went on in that Little Rock hotel room, potentially to whether state troopers were ever used to arrange trysts, perhaps also relations between the then-governor and his employees. But she will not allow a generalized inquiry into his personal life by any means."

As it turned out, Judge Wright allowed not only a "generalized inquiry" into the president's personal life but a very specific inquiry involving controversial ground rules for defining "sexual relations" between the president and a number of Jane Does, including Lewinsky. Jennings then said: "ABC's Jackie Judd reports today that Kathleen Willey swore under oath in a deposition that, against her will, the President made sexual advances towards her when she was working at the White House. What's the significance of this today?" Judd had offered not this "tell item," as it's called, but a complete story with pictures, a quote, and her own analysis. It was rejected primarily because the executive producer and the anchor considered other news to be more important.

Toobin offered his analysis. "Well, it's potentially very significant, because the plaintiff's lawyers want this to be more than just a 'he said, she said' case. They want to show that there is a pattern of behavior on the President's part, and this could be part of it. But the term 'unwanted sexual advances' is so vague, and it could mean so many different things, that the judge is going to want to make sure it really is similar to what Paula Jones [is] claiming before she lets the jury hear it."

Having highlighted and analyzed the lead story and the Willey exclusive, Jennings then turned to the other "news of the day," including events in Iraq and Bosnia, the pope's upcoming visit to Cuba, John Glenn's return to space, and the abortion issue. A pattern was set for television news: over the next year, with few exceptions, the president's sex life was to be the opening story, and news about the rest of the nation and the world would follow at a respectful distance.

At 10 p.m., Lewinsky's mother, Marcia Lewis, finally arrived at the Ritz-Carlton. Bennett might not have believed that she was necessary, but her daughter would not make any decisions without her. Once contacted and informed of Monica's desperate plight, she boarded a train from New York to Washington. Emmick still hoped that he could persuade Lewinsky to cooperate in a sting of Currie and Jordan. He had very little time: Clinton was to be deposed the following morning and, so far as he knew, *Newsweek* was to publish its blockbuster story on Sunday.

Lewis listened to Emmick's case, conferred with her daughter, and decided to call her ex-husband, Bernard Lewinsky, an oncological radiologist in Los Angeles. Mother and daughter spoke with Dr. Lewinsky and then Emmick spoke with him, conveying a sense of urgency. Lewinsky wondered if his daughter shouldn't speak with a lawyer before deciding on her next step. "I said that was fine," Emmick remarked, "but we needed a decision quite soon, and I wasn't sure if an attorney could be contacted that soon." Lewinsky promised Emmick that a lawyer representing his daughter would call him soon.

Lewinsky immediately called a close friend, a medical malpractice lawyer named William Ginsburg, who was soon to have his fifteen minutes of fame. "Monica's in some kind of trouble," he said. Ginsburg let his imagination run wild and promptly assumed she was involved in espionage; after all, he figured, she had worked at the Pentagon. No, not exactly, her father disclosed. "She may be involved with the president." She had been picked up by FBI agents and questioned about a false affidavit in the Jones case. Don't worry, Ginsburg said. A few minutes later, he called Emmick and said he would be boarding a "red eye" and arriving in Washington early Saturday morning. In the meantime, Monica Lewinsky was to say and do nothing.

Emmick was unhappy about this delay. He couldn't explain the urgent need for Lewinsky to cooperate in a sting of Jordan, Currie, and possibly the president. *Newsweek* was waiting in the wings. Instead, he told Ginsburg that he could arrange a possible immunity agreement for Lewinsky but he needed it now. Ginsburg suggested that Emmick fax a copy of the agreement to him. Emmick refused, saying he could not run the risk of a leak and he was running out of time. Ginsburg said he couldn't allow his client to accept an agreement he hadn't seen or negotiated and that he would see Emmick on his arrival in Washington. At 12:45 a.m., Lewinsky and her mother were allowed to leave the hotel and return to their Watergate apartment. In ten hours, Clinton was going to be deposed by the Jones lawyers—he was walking into a trap, and Lewinsky couldn't help him.

At 12:30 a.m., Isikoff's long night of anxious waiting came to a successful close. James Moody, Tripp's lawyer, delivered the key December 22, 1997, tape to the *Newsweek* office. For the next four hours, in McDaniel's large office, Isikoff, Thomas, and Klaidman joined their bureau chief to listen to the tape. McDaniel had assured Smith and Whitaker, the editors in New York, that she would listen to the tape and judge its authenticity. "We loaded up the recorder, and the four of us listened intently—scribbling notes as fast as we could," Isikoff recalled. There on the tape were the voices of two of the principals: Lewinsky and Tripp. "I heard Monica's voice, that whiney, awful voice," said Thomas. "Within five or ten minutes, it was clear to everybody that this was compelling stuff." "Astonishing," Klaidman said. "All of a sudden, it was real, it was authentic. You could tell that while Monica Lewinsky was immature, this was genuine."

McDaniel and Thomas had approached the story with an understandable degree of skepticism, but after a brief time they concluded that the conversation between Lewinsky and Tripp sounded very real indeed. What Tripp had told Isikoff was transparently true—it was right there on the tape; but . . . Lewinsky? Was she telling the truth? Had she invented the story of her sexual relationship with the president? Had she exaggerated? Embroidered? They were not sure.

McDaniel wondered aloud whether Lewinsky had concocted "an elaborate fictional world" in which she and the president were lovers. There was, in fact, no explicit reference by Lewinsky to having sex with the president; it was implied but never stated. McDaniel raised another question: was there on the tape any evidence of a crime, such as an obstruction of justice? Tripp was clearly trying to get Lewinsky to confirm that the president was urging her to lie, but Lewinsky wouldn't bite.

Tripp: "He knows you're going to lie. You've told him, haven't you?"
Lewinsky: "No."
Tripp: "I thought that night when he called you established that much."
Lewinsky: "Well, I mean, I don't know."
Tripp: "Jesus. Well, does he think you're going to tell the truth?"
Lewinsky: "No . . . Oh, Jesus."
Tripp: "So he's at least feeling somewhat safe that this is not going to go any further right now, right?"
Lewinsky: "Yeah."

There was no confirmation of an obstruction of justice, and, in any case, even if there were, it would just be her word against the president's. McDaniel and Thomas left after a few hours, having reached no decisions, and Isikoff and Klaidman began the tedious job of transcribing long passages of the tape made all the more difficult by repeated computer breakdowns. By 4 a.m. Saturday, both were exhausted but buoyed by the hope that their story was going to run. New York wanted the tape; they got it. "We felt the tape was authentic," Klaidman told me, "and that the conversations authenticated the idea that Monica Lewinsky was not making this up. She might have been a little bit flaky, but not a total flake." McDaniel said they would reconvene in several hours. The two bleary-eyed journalists left their office and went home for a few hours' rest.

Isikoff's account of the scandal, *Uncovering Clinton*, is remarkably detailed, filled with an insider's insights into the intimate interrelationships between a reporter and his sources. But it skims over one crucial question: How did Isikoff obtain the December 22 tape for *Newsweek*? It seems likely that it was part of an arrangement Isikoff reached with Bennett. Isikoff would not pursue his story for twenty-four hours, and Bennett would get twenty-four hours to pursue his case. In exchange, Bennett would give Isikoff access to inside information, perhaps including the tapes—but Isikoff could not reveal his source, either in *Newsweek* or in his book. The reason, he later explained in a footnote to the paperback edition of his book, was that he had pledged "confidentiality" to a source "that evening" and could not break his word. He added that at the time *Newsweek* was "mercifully kept in the dark" about how the tape actually reached his office.

According to Justice Department guidelines, a prosecutor such as Bennett is barred from disclosing investigative information like the December 22 tape to the press.

Throughout this period, Bennett was protected not only by Isikoff but by other reporters who benefited from the prosecutor's leaks in the days before the scandal broke and immediately thereafter. The press was clearly in collusion with the prosecutor, receiving extremely damaging information while refusing to divulge its sources. In a period of unprecedented scandal, the public often had no idea where the information was coming from or the motivation of those who leaked it.

Of course, on the evening of January 16, Isikoff had no way of knowing for sure that he was going to get the tape. If Bennett wanted to be sure he did, Bennett needed the equivalent of a CIA cutout—someone who could provide him with cover so that he himself could not be accused of providing forbidden material to a reporter. Moody, Tripp's lawyer, was the obvious candidate. But Moody, who distrusted all reporters, was reluctant to give the December 22 tape to Isikoff. Still, he had made a deal with Bennett and he was under continuing pressure from Goldberg and George Conway—the most active of the elves—to see the wisdom of working with Isikoff to undermine Clinton. "I had to fight with Moody until the last minute to let *Newsweek* hear those tapes," Goldberg said. "He just didn't get it."

In the end, Moody and Bennett met shortly after midnight at the Howard Johnson hotel opposite the Watergate complex (an eerie echo of the Watergate scandal a quarter of a century earlier). Bennett brought Bruce Udolf, and Moody brought George Conway, almost as if each needed a witness. If Bennett gave Moody the December 22 tape with the understanding that Moody would then deliver it to the *Newsweek* office on Pennsylvania Avenue, Bennett had to have known that he was violating the spirit, if not the letter, of Justice Department guidelines. His rationalization could only have been that he didn't deliver the tape to a news organization; it was Moody who delivered it.

CHAPTER 4

AN INCREDIBLE SEVEN-HOUR
DIALOGUE
January 17, 1998

SCOOPS ARE WHAT IT'S ALL ABOUT. IT'S WHAT WE STRIVE FOR
EVERY WEEK.
—Michael Isikoff, *Uncovering Clinton*

"EIGHTY PERCENT JUST WASN'T GOOD ENOUGH."
—Ann McDaniel, *Newsweek* editor

Isikoff had been "crashing" since Wednesday, and by early Saturday morning, when he returned to the *Newsweek* bureau from his Chevy Chase home, he was exhausted and testy. He was increasingly concerned that his editors in New York were developing serious doubts about publishing his Monica scoop even though he had produced the tape they wanted. He had won rows of ribbons battling his editors, not only at the *Post* but at *Newsweek* too, and he was ready for the upcoming fight, convinced that publication in this case was not only justified but necessary.

Bypassing the narrow corridor that led to his own office, Isikoff walked directly into McDaniel's. For much of this momentous day, Isikoff was to be in and out of this large, well-appointed office with its breathtaking view of Washington. McDaniel was one of Isikoff's staunchest supporters.

I've got to have a decision, Isikoff told her—"like in the next few hours." His reasoning was unassailable. If *Newsweek* was to publish the Clinton-Lewinsky story, he had to have enough time to contact the principals: Vernon Jordan, Betty Currie, and Monica Lewinsky. He needed their responses. On the other hand, if *Newsweek* was not going to publish the story, then he should not be calling the principals in a criminal investigation. He didn't want to be accused of interfering with Starr's newest probe. McDaniel was sympathetic to Isikoff's position, but she was also concerned about her New York editors, who continued to agonize about their pending decision. After listening to the December 22 tape, she had concluded that Tripp was probably telling the truth. But she was uncertain about Lewinsky. In fact, she wondered whether the young intern was "nuts." At a minimum, McDaniel felt that she needed more information. She promised Isikoff a timely answer—"soon," she assured him.

Normally, it is the reporter who calls the source. This time it was the source who called the reporter. When an anxious Isikoff returned to his office, uncertain about whether he was going to write about Lewinsky or about the president's deposition in the Jones case, he found a puzzling message on his desk from John Podesta, the deputy chief of staff at the White House. The two men were on friendly terms. During the previous summer, in fact, Podesta had taught a course at Georgetown University's law school about, of all things, media coverage of White House scandals, and he had invited Isikoff to be a guest lecturer. The message asked Isikoff to call Podesta at the White House.

"So I hear you got quite a story coming," Podesta pushed.

"Oh, really," Isikoff said, trying to sound innocent.

"Something about tapes and obstruction of justice and Ken Starr," Podesta went on. He then explained that *Time* reporters had been calling officials all over the White House asking about a *Newsweek* bombshell. "So," Podesta asked, "what's going on?"

In his book, Isikoff writes that he was "in a bind." He couldn't very well tell Podesta what he knew. For one thing, New York had not yet made a call. For another, *Time* was sniffing around the White House. "I dodged, mumbling something about not working on anything relating to White-water. He took my response as a no."

It was time to turn the tables on Podesta; time for the journalist to ask questions, not answer them. Isikoff remembered that Podesta was supposed to have been the "senior official" who arranged Lewinsky's job interview in October 1997, with UN Ambassador Bill Richardson. Though Isikoff could hardly be described as casual, certainly not on this special Saturday, he tried to sound casual as he asked Podesta, "Do you know somebody named Monica Lewinsky?" Podesta replied that he thought she had been an intern. "What's the deal with Bill Richardson, getting her an interview with him?" Isikoff asked. Podesta answered matter-of-factly that, yes, she had been looking for a job and, yes, he had helped her. Podesta added that he had even met her once at a funeral. So what? Isikoff pushed a little harder. "I told him I understood her name had come up in the Paula Jones case, and I had some questions about her." Podesta said that only Bob Bennett, the president's lawyer, could answer questions about Lewinsky, and he was "tied up in Clinton's deposition." Podesta promised Isikoff that he would check with Bennett and call back as soon as possible. It was, Isikoff later told me, "a very weird phone call."

What Podesta actually did was to head to the White House counsel's office to see Cheryl Mills, one of the president's lawyers. "I talked to Isikoff," Podesta told her. "He said he wasn't working on a matter having to do with the grand jury and Ken Starr. . . . He was working on a Paula Jones matter that involved Monica Lewinsky." In other words, Podesta had indeed concluded that Isikoff was digging into the Lewinsky story and that *Newsweek* might publish it. Isikoff had wrongly concluded from the same awkward conversation that Podesta had not yet drawn a link between Lewinsky and his scoop.

On Saturday morning, President Clinton arrived at the Washington law firm of Skadden Arps Slate Meagher & Flom for his deposition in the Paula Jones case. Presiding over the proceedings was U.S. District Court Judge Susan Webber Wright—a former law student of Clinton's appointed to the bench by President George H. W. Bush. She had agreed to fly in from Arkansas at the request of the president's lawyer, Bob Bennett, in an effort to protect the dignity of the presidency. She imposed a "gag order" on all discussion of the deposition, meaning that no one in the conference room was permitted to talk about the case with anybody.

The gag order worked at first. If you looked at the front-page stories about the president's deposition the following morning expecting juicy details about Clinton and Jones, you would have been disappointed. Only *The New York Times* ran a slightly textured story, quoting one source who gave a bit of the flavor of the deposition, but even the *Times* failed to provide any facts about Clinton's exchange with the Jones lawyers. *The Washington Post* and the *Los Angeles Times* published the bare story—very few details, very little color. After a day or two, though, the gag order began to collapse, as it often does in major cases. In the current celebrity climate, enticing to lawyers as well as politicians, lawyers talk, especially to journalists, when they consider such talk to be helpful to their clients or their careers.

Before the president entered the room, Bennett told Judge Wright that he was concerned about leaks that might embarrass the presidency and hold it up as "the laughingstock of the world." The judge shared his concern, but added a sense of perspective. "What was initially very shocking and embarrassing to the Court," she said, "is not quite as shocking and embarrassing anymore."

Clinton took an oath to tell the truth, the whole truth, and nothing but the truth. James Fisher, one of Jones's lawyers, opened his interrogation with a surprise. Since so much of the case revolved around the question of "sexual relations," he had developed a definition drawn from the federal criminal law on sexual abuse and the Violence Against Women Act of 1994, which the president had signed into law with considerable fanfare. Bennett objected vigorously. He argued that the definition, consisting of three parts, was too sweeping and complicated. Judge Wright, agreeing with Bennett, struck parts two and three from Fisher's definition, but she left part one, which covered "intentional sexual contact."

Fisher began his examination by raising questions about the president's relationship with Kathleen Willey. Clinton "emphatically" denied any improper behavior. This exchange broke no new ground. After an hour or so, Fisher reached into his bag of Tripp-triggered questions. "Now," Fisher asked, "do you know a woman named Monica Lewinsky?" The president replied, "I do." Fisher delicately began digging into sensitive areas—how often had he seen her? Where? Any talk about her affidavit? Was he aware that she had met with Vernon Jordan to discuss this case? The president said yes, he knew that they had met. Jordan, he said, was giving her advice about moving to New York. (Bennett was astonished; he had never heard of such a meeting.)

Fisher asked whether the president and Lewinsky had exchanged any gifts. Now Clinton's answers began to sound revealingly noncommittal—"I don't recall," "I don't remember," he kept repeating. Fisher then took aim at the president's heart.

"Did you have an extramarital sexual affair with Monica Lewinsky?"

"No."

Fisher sharpened his question. "Have you ever had sexual relations with Monica Lewinsky as that term is defined in Deposition Exhibit 1, as modified by the Court?" Judge Wright suggested that Clinton study the definition. The president responded: "I have never had sexual relations with Monica Lewinsky. I have never had an affair with her." Fisher did not probe more deeply into what the president meant by "sexual relations" and "an affair." It was left to Kenneth Starr and his prosecutors to probe more deeply and then to charge in their impeachment drive that the president had lied under oath when he denied having "sexual relations" with Lewinsky. However those two words were ultimately to be defined, there was little doubt that Clinton had been not only "unhelpful," as he was later to concede, but dishonest.

When it was Bennett's turn to ask questions, he read from Lewinsky's affidavit. "I have never had a sexual relationship with the president," he quoted her as saying. "He did not propose that we have a sexual relationship." Bennett asked: "Is that a true and accurate statement as far as you know it?" The president replied: "That is absolutely true."

The only admission made by Clinton that contradicted his previous denials concerned Gennifer Flowers. Clinton acknowledged that on one occasion, in 1977, he had had sexual relations with her.

At 4 p.m., the deposition ended, and the president left the conference room with Bennett and Charles Ruff, who was then the White House counsel. Ruff told Clinton he thought the deposition had gone "great." Bennett agreed. They were almost ready to crack open bottles of champagne and celebrate. Why? Because so few of Fisher's questions had to do with Jones, whose legal argument had worried the president's lawyers. And because foolishly they believed that the president had put Lewinsky behind him.

The "gang of four," as they would later be called, reconvened in McDaniel's office at 10:30 a.m. for the start of a seven-hour dialogue between Washington and New York that ended with one of *Newsweek*'s most controversial decisions. Dialogues between Washington and New York are not new to American journalism. New York is generally where editors in chief, anchors, publishers, and producers live—it has been the editorial and financial capital of the nation for more than a century. Washington is where power is concentrated—it has been the political capital of the world since the outbreak of the Cold War. It is where news happens. These journalistic dialogues have often been tense, with Washington arguing for more space and time and New York resisting the pressure while pooh-poohing the importance of Washington's "inside-the-Beltway" stories. It is not only populist politicians who decry Washington's inflated sense of self and distorted sense of values. The journalistic chieftains of New York also resent Washington's centrality and power. Though connected, Washington and New York are polar opposites in journalistic warfare.

So it was perhaps appropriate that the Saturday struggle about whether *Newsweek* should publish its Monica scoop took place on a telephone line between Washington and New York. In Washington, Ann McDaniel was joined by her deputy, Evan Thomas; her chief investigative reporter, Michael Isikoff; and Daniel Klaidman, whose legal expertise and contacts at the Justice Department would soon prove helpful. In New York, editor in chief Richard Smith and managing editor Mark Whitaker were joined by Jon Meacham, the national affairs editor. Smith and Whitaker made the big decisions about covers and lead stories; Meacham dealt with smaller decisions about placement and length.

Isikoff had sensed there might be trouble. He had even alerted Lucianne Goldberg on Friday evening to the possibility that New York might delay running the story, but he had also told her that he thought that by day's end the decision would likely be made to proceed. He still thought, as the crucial debate began on Saturday morning, that the story was simply too big, too explosive to be put on hold. Besides, if *Newsweek* decided not to run it, Isikoff was certain that other news organizations, already on the scent of the Monica bombshell, would come up with the information and go with it.

To begin, Smith asked two key questions: What do we know? And how do we know it? Unspoken at the time was the feeling, later acknowledged by a few participants, that if the forceful, dynamic Parker were well, he would have "scrambled the jets"—his favorite command for all-out war. Every reporter would have been ordered into battle, every source contacted, and no one would have had to wonder about whether *Newsweek* was going to publish a story of this magnitude. That would have been assumed. But now it was not Parker who was in charge of the troops; it was the ad hoc troika of Smith, Whitaker, and Meacham, and they didn't want to blow the first big call on their watch. They wanted to be certain about the accuracy and fairness of the story.

McDaniel responded: We know that we have three elements of a very big story.

- Starr has launched a criminal investigation of the president: Did Clinton in fact have an illicit romance with Lewinsky, and did Clinton recruit Vernon Jordan's help to get her a job in New York?
- Starr conducted a "sting" of Lewinsky while she was having lunch with Tripp on Tuesday.
- Tripp has been taping telephone conversations with her young friend for months. We heard one of them, dated December 22, 1997, late last night. The tape seemed to confirm what Tripp has been telling Isikoff for months—that Lewinsky had in fact been having an affair with the president.

Smith listened to McDaniel's report and raised a number of questions. How much did they really know about Jordan's involvement? His name had come up repeatedly on the tapes, Isikoff told his New York editors, over-stating the degree of his knowledge, and Starr was targeting him. Yes, Smith and Whitaker said, but there was the matter of fairness. Was Isikoff being fair to Jordan? Isikoff couldn't help wondering about his editor's motivation. After all, Jordan cut a very large figure in Washington. He was often a dinner guest at the home of Katharine Graham, the legendary boss of the Washington Post Corporation. Smith knew him—they had even played golf together. Perhaps Smith was allowing Jordan's social position to influence his editorial judgment. McDaniel acknowledged that she had heard nothing on the tape to indicate that Jordan had asked Lewinsky to lie about her affair with the president. Smith reminded everyone that when McDaniel had first pitched the story, a few days before, she had assured him there was "evidence" that Jordan and the president had asked Lewinsky to commit perjury. Now there was no such evidence. Might there not be another "fact" that was later discovered to have no supporting data? McDaniel moved quickly to protect Isikoff, on whose shoulders so much of the credibility of the story rested. Mike never said there was such evidence, she told Smith. She said that she herself might have oversold the story.

"Can we really accuse Jordan of suborning perjury without something harder?" Smith returned to one of his principal concerns. "Can we really accuse Clinton of committing an impeachable offense?"

Smith was the first to raise the question of impeachment. Isikoff, stunned, glanced at Klaidman, as if to say who's thinking about impeachment. Within a week, many journalists would be openly discussing the possibility of impeachment and resignation.

Then Smith switched to Lewinsky. According to Isikoff's account, he raised a series of questions. "What do we really know about her? We've never even talked to her, we've never laid eyes on her. She's a private person—and we are about to thrust her into a media maelstrom."

Isikoff argued, "This is as much a Ken Starr story as it is a Clinton story. What Starr is doing here is extraordinary. It is news by any definition. It is potentially a bombshell. Washington will go nuts over the fact that Starr has done this. We can't ignore it."

The telephone line between Washington and New York was getting hot. Smith was unimpressed. "You can talk all you want about Starr and obstruction of justice," the editor said. "But at the end of the day, people are going to look at this as a sex story. That's what they are going to think this is—a story about Clinton having sex with a young woman." In fact, if Starr, in his investigation, had not been able to raise doubts about the president's credibility during the Jones deposition, the story might well have gone down in history as simply "a sex story."

Whitaker was equally unimpressed. If we can't publish exactly what happened between Clinton and Lewinsky, "then it just becomes another 'Ken Starr is investigating' story." Isikoff was, as he later understated his emotional response, "quite agitated." This is the "ultimate 'Ken Starr is investigating' story," he thought.

As the noon hour approached, New York, as represented by Smith and Whitaker, seemed to be tilting against publication. Meacham had said nothing. He was lost in practical problems. How would such a story read? he was thinking. What would it look like? News magazines have a dual responsibility: to present the news but also to illuminate personalities with photos. No reader had ever heard or seen Monica Lewinsky. Who was she? What was she like? According to Isikoff's account, Meacham said much later, "I kept thinking what will the second paragraph look like?"

It was a freewheeling exchange. "It was so free," Klaidman later remembered, "that a guy like me who had not been at the magazine all that long—I'd met Mark and Rick, but I didn't know them all that well—I felt utterly free to express my opinions about the story and to do so without reservation."

In Washington, McDaniel was a kind of noncommittal middleman, fielding and answering questions but offering no opinions of her own. Klaidman and Isikoff passionately favored publication. Isikoff described Thomas as favoring publication, "the only [editor] who did."

Viveca Novak of *Time* kept calling David Kendall over that weekend on the assumption that as one of the president's lawyers he would have been informed of any brewing story or scandal. Kendall was in New York City with his family hopscotching from one museum and play to another. He had given her his cell phone number, so he wasn't surprised that she called—it was just the frequency and intensity of her calls that surprised him. Novak told me that she must have called Kendall three times or more. "I was persistent," she explained. "I was not frantic." She was in fact calling other sources, too, but with no success. Unfortunately for Novak, and *Time*, Kendall knew nothing about a *Newsweek* story. After taking Novak's third call, Kendall finally said in humorous exasperation, "Viveca, get a life. It's Saturday afternoon." Kendall, though so close to the president, was to remain in the dark about the Lewinsky problem until the following Tuesday evening. So too was Novak. So too were most Washington reporters.

It was close to noon. In McDaniel's office, the dialogue continued, though it had lost energy, in part because Smith and Whitaker seemed disposed to delay publication and McDaniel and Thomas were not aggressive advocates of publication. Isikoff felt trapped. Deep in his gut, he was positive that the story should run and that if Parker were making the decision, it would run. But, even if the Lewinsky exclusive was temporarily spiked, Isikoff would still need to produce a story on the president's deposition. And if they did decide to proceed with the Lewinsky story—which seemed unlikely at this point—Isikoff had to get busy on the phones and try to get through to Jordan, Currie, and Lewinsky. He didn't have much time. "I couldn't believe we were still debating this," Isikoff told editor Steven Brill, "when I've got to try to reach Vernon Jordan."

Smith tried to convey his concerns to the journalists in Washington. Suppose we publish the Lewinsky story, he told them, and after we publish it, we find out that Lewinsky invented the whole thing, or most of it. And there we are, sitting on every newsstand in the country, in the world, with a presidential scandal that might not have happened, with a president who might not have lied, with a *Newsweek* exclusive that's a bummer. What do we do then? Say we're sorry, Mr. President? We are not a daily newspaper. If we were and we were wrong, he continued, we could explain it all within twenty-four hours, or less. With a weekly, we'd have to wait a week.

"Mike and I were pretty adamant about the story running," Klaidman recalled. A year or so later he could see the logic of Smith's concerns, but at the time he was frustrated. He decided to return to his office and do some reporting. Would Starr have launched this new phase of his investigation without first having checked with the Justice Department? And would the Justice Department have given its approval without first having checked with the three-judge panel? Unlikely. Klaidman called a number of sources at the Justice Department. He reached only one of them, but in this case one source was enough. The source told Klaidman that yes, Attorney General Reno had referred the matter to the three-judge panel, and yes, the panel had given its approval. Starr, in other words, had gone to the proper authorities and had official permission to proceed with the Lewinsky/Clinton investigation.

To Klaidman, this was big news, and he "dashed back, breathlessly," to McDaniel's office. "From the expression on their faces," he concluded that his editors had decided to postpone publication. Perhaps Smith and Whitaker had reached such a decision, but Thomas was suddenly infused with new excitement. "If we were *The Washington Post* or *The New York Times*," Thomas later said, "we would print."

McDaniel had yet another concern—the ethical problem of a news magazine interfering with an ongoing law enforcement operation. Someone suggested that they call Starr and let him make his case for postponement. Isikoff thought, quite sensibly, that his editors were beginning to crack under the pressure. Obviously Starr, if contacted, would itemize a thousand reasons why postponement made sense. It was in his interest. But rather than have McDaniel call Starr directly, Isikoff was asked to call

Jackie Bennett and arrange for Starr to call McDaniel. Starr flatly refused. A prosecutor, he angrily told Bennett, does not beg a news organization.

When the seven-hour dialogue resumed, Isikoff and Klaidman were at wits' end. "You know this is not the Bay of Pigs," Isikoff said. "Human lives are not at stake here. The national security isn't hanging in the balance. Why the hell shouldn't we publish this?" Thomas agreed that the Lewinsky story was no Bay of Pigs; indeed, there was no comparison. "This is a pretty dipshit investigation," he snapped. For years, Starr has been trying to nail Clinton—and failed. Now, Thomas added, he's trying to nail him on sex. "So what if we blew this investigation," Isikoff quoted him as saying. "It wasn't as if they were about to catch a terrorist or something." Klaidman echoed roughly the same theme. "We are already players in this story no matter what," he said. "If we run the story, yes, there's a potential that it will blow Starr's investigation. If we don't run it, we're giving this already controversial prosecutor a green light to run what might be the most controversial investigation in the history of law enforcement. This wasn't a case of life or death. There was no national security imperative at work. We should report the story. Check it for accuracy. Give everyone involved an opportunity to explain why it shouldn't be run and then just run it." He later returned to this theme. "Look, we're players in this drama. That being the case, we should just do journalism, as opposed to trying to decide whether or not our publishing the story will impact Ken Starr's investigation."

Still McDaniel was unpersuaded. She kept wondering whether they had all the information, or even enough information to go with the story. "There are times when it's just not worth being first," she said. "Sometimes it's just not the right thing to do." She told me later that she was 80 percent sure that Lewinsky was telling the truth. But, she added, "eighty percent just wasn't good enough."

By late afternoon, Isikoff and Klaidman had just about given up hope. Each, in exhaustion and disappointment, had retreated to his office. At 5:30 p.m., McDaniel asked Isikoff to return to her office. Smith was on the line. He told Isikoff that he had decided to hold the story. This was not to be interpreted as a reflection on Isikoff's reporting. Smith said, "We think you've done a great job, and we appreciate it." It was a question of time, Smith stressed. If *Newsweek* were a newspaper, it could have done more reporting and waited a day to publish. Smith later cited three basic reasons for the magazine's' decision: their "uneasiness about what they had heard and not heard about Jordan on the tapes; their inability to question Lewinsky directly; and an inclination to take Starr up on his offer of waiting and not impeding the investigation while getting a better story." He added: "We talked about just doing an item on the expanded investigation [without naming Lewinsky], but we thought we knew too much for that. It wouldn't have been leveling with our readers."

Isikoff was drained of anger and energy. He said quietly that it must have been a "tough call" for Smith and the other editors. He left McDaniel's office "utterly defeated." And in this state he should perhaps have gone home and gone to bed. Instead, Isikoff made three calls, which proved to be major blunders.

His first call went to Jim Moody. Isikoff informed him that, "after a lot of debate," the editors had decided that the evidence linking Jordan to suborning perjury and obstructing justice was simply too flimsy. The second call went to Lucianne Goldberg, who had been an enormous help to Isikoff. He told her what he had just told Moody—that the evidence was not strong enough to persuade his editors to publish the story. Finally, Isikoff called John Podesta at the White House. He told this senior official that the story they had discussed earlier in the day was not going to be published after all.

Isikoff then went home, "barely conscious, and ate dinner. My in-laws were visiting," he recalled, "and I had no energy left to speak. I apologized and went upstairs to bed."

Neither Michael Weisskopf nor Viveca Novak, despite all their efforts, could help *Time* catch up with *Newsweek*'s Lewinsky exclusive. By early Saturday evening, the two major news magazines went to press without Monica Lewinsky. Instead, they both focused on what *Time* called "The Big Face-Off," Clinton finally facing Jones, each combatant flanked by a small army of lawyers. Because of the gag order, no news organization had much news about the deposition, but *Time* did manage to find out about the president's mood—at least, about his lawyers' spin on his mood.

Time reported: "At the end of six hours of questioning by Jones's attorneys, Clinton departed in what sources close to him say was an ecstatic mood. The President felt the deposition had gone smashingly well for him. Describing the mood Saturday night at the White House, one person close to the President said: 'Everyone is going to sleep well tonight.'" In fact, the president canceled the dinner plans he had with his wife, met almost immediately with his close aide, Bruce Lindsey, called Vernon Jordan, and then arranged a get-together with Betty Currie for the next day.

At 6:30 p.m., network news time, the *CBS Evening News*, like its competitors at ABC and NBC, led with a report on the president's deposition. Reporter Scott Pelley had an exclusive: "CBS News has learned," he said, "that part of the questioning was based on the depositions of four women who also claim Mr. Clinton made sexual advances. Three of them are from Arkansas. One of the women is a former White House employee." He added, interestingly, that Clinton arrived in a car that did not sport the usual presidential seal on the back door.

On ABC's *World News Tonight*, the reporter was Jackie Judd, who, as usual, worked closely with her off-camera producer, Chris Vlasto. She also described the president's arrival, his limousine disappearing into an underground garage to avoid the camera crush on the sidewalk. Paula Jones, though caught in the crush and jostled from side to side, enjoyed "wading through the mob, posing for pictures." Judd used two sound bites—one from Susan Carpenter McMillan, Jones's public relations person, who said that Jones wanted to "look him [Clinton] right in the eye" and one from Jonathan Turley, a George Washington University professor, who said the Jones lawyers had a "right" to hurl "every alleged infidelity" at the president. Judd, in her on-camera close, raised the possibility that under certain circumstances the president's deposition could be seen at some later time. "The president's videotaped deposition will remain under seal," she said, "but portions of it could be used at a trial if Mr. Clinton chooses not to testify. If there is a settlement in this case, the deposition may become a piece of history, never to see the light of day."

After Clinton's deposition, Paula Jones's lawyers, like the president's lawyers, were feeling giddy, but they had more reason. Clinton, by admitting to a single instance of marital infidelity with Gennifer Flowers, had proven himself to be a liar. Jones, on the other hand, was feeling awful. "That chickenshit," she sobbed, sitting alone on a bench in a corner of the conference room. "He wouldn't even look me in the eye. He lied. He just lied." McMillan had promised the press that Jones would make a comment after the president's departure, but her client looked puffy-eyed and miserable, clearly unable to convey the vindicated, stylish, and self-confident image McMillan had in mind for her. So they hustled Jones through the waiting cameras and reporters and drove her back to her hotel, leaving McMillan behind to administer the requisite spin and inform one reporter, in particular, that Jones and her advisers would indeed agree to dine with him that evening at the Old Ebbitt Grill, a fashionable Washington restaurant.

The reporter was Chris Vlasto, the young ABC producer who had been following Clinton's indiscretions for many years. Like Isikoff, Vlasto had spent months in Little Rock cultivating Arkansan sources, especially Jim McDougal, and, like Isikoff, he had developed an acute distaste for Clinton and his "semantical games." McDougal was a very special source for Vlasto. In Arkansas, they had spent a great deal of time together, and they had become close buddies. "Though Chris had the lean and hungry look of a young journalist," wrote McDougal in his book with Curtis Wilkie, *Arkansas Mischief,* "his manner was that of a scholar. I discovered that the man belonging to the gentle voice on the phone had the cunning of a con artist but the soul of a true friend. I soon trusted Chris more than my own lawyer." When McDougal fell into a deep depression because of his Whitewater involvement and faced another jail sentence, Vlasto flew to Arkadelphia to bolster his spirits. "Not only was I despondent," McDougal wrote, "I felt weak and feeble. 'I'm not going to last a year,' I said. 'I'm going to die in jail.'" Transforming himself from journalist into political adviser, Vlasto responded, "You don't have to go out this way. If you walk in to see Ken Starr, he'll greet you with open arms." The next day, McDougal "sent word to Starr that [he] would be interested in talking to him." McDougal died in prison in March 1998, in the middle of the Lewinsky scandal. The following year at the Radio and Television Correspondents Association dinner, Vlasto and Judd received a prize for their reporting of the story. Vlasto took advantage of the occasion to praise his friend McDougal for his role in uncovering the Whitewater scandal—an "in your face" gesture as Bill and Hillary Clinton sat grimly on the dais not five feet away and three thousand journalists and politicians applauded the ABC news team's accomplishment.

Vlasto was a journalist with attitude. He apparently felt that it was his responsibility to "get" the president. A number of his ABC colleagues tried to persuade Vlasto to limit his ambitions to just covering the news. Vlasto rejected such advice, believing that his power as a journalist must be used to cleanse society of political wrongdoing. "It was a most infuriating thing—the president's parsing of words," Vlasto told me. "We all knew it. We'd been parsing him for years. From the very beginning, his problem was just telling the truth, but it was so hard." Vlasto said illustratively that David Gergen had once advised the president to release all of the White-water documents. "There would be one bad week of publicity," Gergen supposedly said, "and that would be the end of it." Vlasto said that the president in a weak moment seemed to agree with Gergen, but nothing happened. Why? "Because Hillary killed the idea."

Vlasto was the only reporter close and trusted enough to accompany Paula Jones, her husband Steve, her hairdresser (who had come all the way from California), her team of lawyers, and her public relations adviser McMillan to a large window table at the Old Ebbitt Grill for a dinnertime celebration. The very public nature of the dinner was McMillan's idea. "I don't care whether you want to or not," she told a reluctant Jones, "but you are going to dinner." And just as she anticipated, this scene of "family" joy was captured in photos and included in the next day's coverage. Every-thing was included, that is, except for the fact that the unfamiliar face at the table belonged to a reporter, whose news organization, ABC, ended up paying the huge bill. But in the process he acquired a bundle of editorial goodies, which were to appear over the next week in a succession of Judd stories about the unfolding scandal. When questioned about the dinner, Vlasto sounded like a "senior official" who had been found with his hand in the cookie jar. "Yes, I took Paula Jones's lawyers to dinner. That's public, and that's all I'm going to say."

At around 11 p.m. on Saturday night, Matt Drudge called Isikoff. He wanted to check on a story. Isikoff, dead tired and deeply disappointed, had fallen asleep. His wife, Lisa Stein, told Drudge that her husband was asleep and she wasn't going to wake him.

At 1:11 a.m. Washington time, the *Drudge Report* scooped Isikoff on his own story, just as it had done in July 1997 on the Kathleen Willey story. Not once, but twice, the experienced Isikoff has been outfoxed by a Holly-wood gossipmonger. Drudge put out a "**World Exclusive**" on his Inter-net Web site to the effect that *Newsweek* had "killed" a story about a "sex relationship" between President Clinton and a "23-year-old former White House intern."It was, as Drudge correctly stated, a "blockbuster report." The Isikoff exclusive was no longer exclusive. *Newsweek* had had its chance, and for very good journalistic reasons, it had forfeited it. Now the story was sprung onto the Internet, into a new world of instant communications.

How did it get to Drudge? Once again, it was the anti-Clinton legal cabal. After Isikoff called Moody, the disgruntled lawyer called Conway, who decided to e-mail the essence of what he knew about the *Newsweek* decision to Drudge. If the elves couldn't get their story out by way of the mainstream press, through Isikoff, they didn't mind getting it out by way of Drudge.

In this way, Isikoff and *Newsweek* lost control of their story, the *Drudge Report* achieved new prominence, many members of the Washington press corps awakened to the prospect of a hot presidential scandal—and American journalism was forever changed.

CHAPTER 5

ENTER MR. DRUDGE

January 18, 1998

"IF KRISTOL WANTS TO GO WITH SOMETHING BASED ON
DRUDGE, THAT'S HIS PROBLEM."
—Michael Isikoff, *Newsweek*

"IF THAT'S THE KIND OF STORY ISIKOFF IS WRITING, THEN
HE'S WELCOME TO IT."
—Doyle McManus, *Los Angeles Times*

The two-tiered, bold-faced headline on the *Drudge Report*'s "**World Exclusive**" read:

**NEWSWEEK KILLS STORY ON WHITE HOUSE INTERN
BLOCKBUSTER REPORT: 23-YEAR-OLD,
FORMER WHITE HOUSE INTERN
SEX RELATIONSHIP WITH PRESIDENT**

As with other Drudge exclusives that might trigger lawsuits, the young "scandalmonger," to borrow William Safire's word, framed his story as a report on the media. Drudge began: "At the last minute, at 6 p.m. on Saturday evening, *Newsweek* magazine killed a story that was destined to shake official Washington to its foundation: A White House intern carried on a sexual affair with the President of the United States!" He continued, "The Drudge Report has learned that reporter Michael Isikoff developed the story of his career, only to have it spiked by top *Newsweek* suits hours before publication."

Drudge's rendition had all the elements of a racy television soap opera:

a two-year-long romance, an intern's visits to the White House "after mid-night," "a small study just off the Oval Office where she claims to have indulged the president's sexual preference," "a secretary named Betty Curry [sic]," "love letters," and "tapes of intimate phone conversations."

Of the hundreds of "**World Exclusives**" Drudge had written and released since he started the *Drudge Report* in 1995, none had the impact of this hastily composed bombshell.

When Isikoff awoke on Sunday morning, his wife told him that Matt Drudge had called. Suddenly Isikoff understood that his exclusive might no longer be exclusive. The phone rang.

It was his friend David Tell, an editorial writer for the conservative *Weekly Standard,* who was, he explained, only doing his boss's bidding. Editor Bill Kristol, who was at the time a regular panelist on the ABC show *This Week,* had asked him to check with Isikoff on a middle-of-the-night item on the *Drudge Report* claiming that *Newsweek* had spiked his story about a sexual relationship between the president and an intern. Was that true? And what if anything could he tell Kristol, who seemed intent on mentioning it on the broadcast? Isikoff's finely tuned sense of conspiracy led him to the quick and, for the most part, accurate conclusion that either Moody or Goldberg, frustrated by *Newsweek*'s decision to delay publication of the Lewinsky scandal, had told Conway, the most active member of the lawyers' cabal, and Conway had then leaked it to Drudge, just as he had leaked the Willey story to Drudge the previous summer. "This is going to be ugly," Isikoff thought. "I never imagined they were going to do this. Then again, how could I have thought they would do anything different?"

Isikoff asked Tell to read the entire Drudge item to him. It was clear that Drudge had not been given Lewinsky's name, or he would have used it. Nor apparently had he been told about the most significant part of the story: Starr's expanded investigation of the president. At least, Isikoff thought, Drudge didn't have the whole story. "Maybe it could [still] be contained," he thought. Isikoff reacted by playing a game of Washington poker with Tell. "Look," he told his friend disingenuously, "if Kristol wants to go with something based on Drudge, that's his problem." Then Isikoff added with a rhetorical flourish, "How could he rely on anything that guy writes?"

Kristol had indeed gotten the tip from Conway as well as from

Richard Porter, his former colleague in Vice President Quayle's office. They were attempting to use Kristol's new position as a television commentator on ABC to amplify and legitimize their leak to Drudge. Kristol did not mind being used, as long as the leak made news and he and his relatively new magazine were quoted.

The phone shattered McDaniel's Sunday morning slumber. She too had been exhausted from the Saturday negotiation and frustrating result. The caller was a reporter asking about the Drudge item that spoke of a spiked Isikoff exclusive. Did she have any comment? The usually unflappable McDaniel, on any other occasion only too eager to help another reporter, on this occasion declined the opportunity. "No comment," she said. "It's what we had feared all along," she later told me. After months of secret legwork and deliberation, McDaniel knew in her gut that it was now only a matter of days, if not hours, before other news organizations would join the chase. Isikoff and Klaidman had warned—correctly—that the story would not hold for another week; it was simply too explosive. But their editors made the right decision in delaying publication without further investigation. They had not counted on the fluid borders now separating the old and the new journalism. From out of nowhere, Drudge had struck again: not *Time,* nor *The New York Times,* nor any other traditional news operation, but a gossip columnist on the Internet. On this particular story, *Newsweek* had been light-years ahead of everyone. But now, by way of Drudge and the Internet, they would all become competitors. *Newsweek* would lose both its scoop and its edge.

Just who was this Matt Drudge?

The young man with the Walter Winchell fedora, the cocked eyebrow and the unshaven chin was born in a Washington suburb in the Nixon years. His parents were liberal Democrats, but Drudge was always a conservative; he loved Reagan. From an early age, he was intrigued by the news. His favorite program was CNN's *Crossfire.* He was curious, but did not do well at school, and he never went to college. For a time Drudge worked at a neighborhood 7-Eleven food store, but soon decided that he wanted to move to Hollywood. With help from his parents, he rented a small $600-a-month apartment in a seedy part of town. He got a job in the CBS gift shop, which was as close as he could get to the stars and celebrities, and he took advantage of his location. His interest was Hollywood folklore. He accumulated gossip, sometimes by picking through trash bins for discarded trivia. In 1994, his father bought him a computer. Within a few months, Drudge began posting gossipy news items on the World Wide Web, and he began to acquire a modest following. Entrepreneurial and supremely self-confident, Drudge expanded his after-hours hobby into a passionate one-man operation. He established an e-mail distribution service for his hottest Hollywood items, and then he linked his Web site to news organizations, wire services, and columnists, so that if you logged onto his Web site, you also could conveniently log onto a range of columnists, from David Broder of the *Post* to Maureen Dowd of the *Times*—and all for free. He was "fun" for those who didn't take their journalism too seriously, and he attracted hundreds and then thousands of "visitors." He was irreverent and irascible, totally untutored in journalism, and he blossomed on the Internet.

At the beginning, this didn't add up to much money, but it did add up to a "virtual" business in the totally new world of cyberspace. Drudge kept using whatever money he had accumulated to buy new equipment. *Brill's Content* described his apartment as crammed with "a cheap Sanyo television monitor tuned to CNBC, another to CNN, another to C-Span, a Sony radio purring phone talk, an RCA satellite dish bringing in European news, show tunes, and extra TV channels, a police scanner looking for local action, and, most important, two computer screens linked to chat rooms, e-mail, news wire services and the Internet."

Soon, all this gadgetry produced a few genuine scoops: in 1996, Drudge was first to report that GOP presidential candidate Bob Dole had chosen supply-sider Jack Kemp as his vice-presidential running mate. His scoops ranged from the substantive to the silly. And, of course, each generated more publicity for Drudge and more subscribers for his Web site—ninety thousand by the time he broke the Lewinsky story.

In April 1997, two years after launching the *Drudge Report* on the Internet, Drudge was already enough of a celebrity to be invited to the White House Correspondents Dinner in Washington, where Clinton consultant Mandy Grunwald greeted him with a hug and others were drawn to him like moths to a flame. Fans asked for his autograph; journalists interviewed him. Political heavyweights such as Mary Matalin, the GOP operative-turned-pundit, and Susan Estrich, the Democratic Party operative-turned-professor/pundit, claimed to start each morning by going to their computers and reading the *Drudge Report*. The *Independent* in London ran a long profile on Drudge. So did the *Atlanta Constitution and Journal, The Washington Post,* and the *Los Angeles Times.* Drudge had become hot news, especially among Washington conservatives who had tired of Rush Limbaugh and were hungering for another media hero.

In June 1997, Drudge returned to Washington, by now one of the acknowledged darlings of the right. Ann Coulter, the conservative attorney who coined the term "the elves," and David Brock, author of the "Troopergate" article in the *American Spectator,* hosted a kind of debutante weekend for Drudge. He was guest of honor at a bustling party of young conservatives. Like a visiting head of state, he addressed the National Press Club and then toured *Newsweek,* creating quite a fuss there. Among many other journalists, he met Isikoff, who inadvertently gave him an innocuous bit of information about a Starr story soon to be released to the public. Drudge converted Isikoff's "tip" into a hyped bulletin on the *Drudge Report.* Isikoff later acknowledged that he had made a mistake in even talking to Drudge. A week later, Drudge, always on the prowl for tips, called Isikoff, and the Hollywood gossip got the Washington pro to confirm rumors that he was working on the Willey story. Was Isikoff trying to impress Drudge? Was Drudge simply stroking Isikoff's ego? Either way, within a week, Drudge had the Willey sex story on the Internet and Isikoff had egg on his face.

In the course of researching the Willey story, Drudge exchanged e-mail messages with a young White House staffer, or so he wrote. He had such "chats" with many officials who labored in the anonymity of government cubicles but enjoyed the private rush of sharing a secret, of seeming to be in the know. Drudge asked his White House contact about Kathleen Willey. What did the staffer know about her and the president? The staffer, puzzled at first, promised to check; he returned in a panic. "OK, I'll give you this," responded the staffer. "I just asked Podesta about it and he knows what it is and asked me to check to see if Isikoff was writing it for tomorrow's magazine. He's not, but you knew that. You and I did not have this conversation. I just got a lot of people very riled up around here about this Willey thing. We'll talk later. Do not mention this conversation."

Drudge not only "mentioned" the conversation; he published it verbatim on his Web site, proving to his growing audience that although he was not one to play by traditional background rules, he still had real-time access and knowledge of what was happening in newsrooms and government offices. The Internet was innocent, inviting, and insidious—it took Drudge everywhere, even into private cubicles in the White House, and some officials responded, often anonymously. They couldn't give their names, and Drudge had no way of knowing how reliable their information was—but he used it. After his Willey scoop in July 1997, Drudge claimed that White House officials logged onto his Web site 2,600 times to read his coverage of the scandal. He had made it. Drudge understood that most people loved gossip. And he was there to provide it.

A month later, Drudge hit a big bump on the road. He published a malicious and totally inaccurate story about Sidney Blumenthal, who was just moving from *The New Yorker* to the White House as a presidential adviser. Drudge, relying quite often on unchecked tips from anti-Clinton sources, reported that Blumenthal abused his wife. When Blumenthal responded with an angry $30 million lawsuit, Drudge admitted on his Web page the next day that he had made a mistake. Not good enough, Blumenthal replied, the suit stands. According to Lewinsky, Clinton, who supported Blumenthal, began to refer to Drudge as "Sludge." Drudge became persona non grata in the power corridors of the White House, but he remained a popular addiction in the cubicles.

In Washington and elsewhere, a generational and technological divide opened between those who "drudged" and those who didn't "drudge." The younger reporters, raised on the Internet, made it a practice to check Drudge's Web site three to five times a day. Some liked and trusted Drudge; many others did not. The older reporters knew little to nothing about Drudge. For example, ABC's Jackie Judd, who was later to play an important role in reporting the Lewinsky scandal, told me that up until that Sunday, "I don't think I had ever heard of him. I didn't even have the proper computer programs." At *The New York Times*, several key reporters, even those familiar with the Internet, had no knowledge of Drudge's story. White House correspondent John Broder said that he never saw or even heard about the original story. Investigative reporter Don Van Natta, Jr., said, "I didn't know very much about Drudge." CNN's Wolf Blitzer confessed, "I was basically in the dark until Wednesday morning. I just didn't know anything about Drudge or his report." NPR's Daniel Schorr was typical of many Washington reporters who remembered January 18, 1998, as the first time they had ever heard of Matt Drudge or imagined the Internet as a possible source of news.

Both David Shuster of Fox News and Jim Warren of the *Chicago Tribune* saw the Drudge item but "didn't believe it" and "certainly didn't pursue it." Doyle McManus of the *Los Angeles Times* recalled spotting the Drudge item on Sunday and thinking, "If that's the kind of story Isikoff is writing, then he's welcome to it."

Among the many younger, more Web-savvy journalists was Mark Stencel, editor of OnPolitics, washingtonpost.com's Politics and Election 2000 site, a new and expanding branch of *The Washington Post*'s media empire. Stencel said that his staff of young reporters were attuned to the Drudge culture—they were very much part of it. They might be called e-journalists. They didn't cover the news so much as collect and collate it from many sources and then disseminate it on the *Post*'s Web site. Bright and eager, fresh from the best colleges, poorly paid, inexperienced, but ready for adventure, they were part of the ever-mutating world of journalism/media/information/entertainment.

They represented for the *Post* (and for most other major news organizations) an investment in the future. The Post had been pouring money into washingtonpost.com on the assumption that the Internet was a vast marketplace with unlimited potential for profit and power. No matter their reservations, of which there were many, few editors and producers dared stand in the way of that potential. In 1999 alone, for example, the Post invested $85 million in its Web site while earning only $20 million from it. The Post has been prepared to take this loss (and presumably others) for the opportunity to establish itself as an on-line player. "So many people already are accessing information that way; you have to be a part of it," said Kevin Lavalla, managing director of Veronis Suhler & Associates, a New York–based consulting firm for the communications industry. "If you aren't a part of it, you'll lose out." That was the prevailing view anyway until early 2001, when the stock market dropped sharply and economic calculations changed.

On Sunday mornings, when affairs of state were not pressing, President and Mrs. Clinton usually went to church. On this particular Sunday morning, with *The Washington Post* sporting a front-page photo of Paula

Jones and her attorneys raising champagne toasts at a very visible dinner intended to convey a sense of celebratory vindication, they were definitely in need of spiritual comfort—they didn't want to suggest in word or action that the Jones case was affecting their lives in any way. After services, the president smiled but refused to respond to shouted questions about his deposition from a gaggle of reporters kept behind police barricades. None of the questions concerned the Drudge item. With one hand, he clutched his Bible; with the other, he held his wife's hand—the picture most appropriate for the television news that evening and the newspapers the next morning.

Later, Hillary Clinton, who rarely gave interviews, chose that day to tell NBC–Mutual Radio that she and her husband had learned to shield themselves from cruel and unpleasant intrusions. "We do box it off," she explained. "You have to box it off, because there is no way you can let people with their own agendas, whatever they might be, interfere with your life, your private life or your public duties. And that's what my husband does every single day." Mrs. Clinton also said that the sermon "just built us up again. And we . . . came home and actually cleaned closets and did things that we'd been meaning to do. . . . Just a way in which we try to keep our lives as normal as possible, despite what's going on around us."

Although Isikoff for his part was upset by the news of the Drudge scoop, he was not totally devastated. After all, he had been able to get his Willey exclusive into the magazine. When *Newsweek* highlighted the Willey story in its advance publicity kit on Sunday, it proved to be perfectly timed for maximum exposure. The gag order had limited the Jones lawyers to hints about the president's deposition, but there were no details and reporters were hunting for a fresh lead. Isikoff provided one that had the effect of steering reporters away from the essence of the Drudge account and back to the basics in the Jones case.

Washington is a capital of many little wars. One of them is waged every Sunday morning, when *Fox News Sunday,* NBC's *Meet the Press,* CBS's *Face the Nation,* ABC's *This Week,* and CNN's *Late Edition* clash on the field of ratings, bookings, and newsmaking. The winner is determined not only by the number of people who watch each program but by the front-page headlines each generates in Monday morning's newspapers. Win the ratings war but lose the battle of the headlines, and if you are a network executive or producer, you still haven't carried the day. Indeed, you are probably in trouble.

On this particular Sunday, the newspapers featured a photo of the champagne dinner attended by Paula Jones and her husband, and the morning talk shows each had a Jones lawyer making essentially two points: first, that he was under a court order not to talk about the president's deposition; but second, that he was going to do his very best to nibble at the edges of the court order, leaving hints here and there, while pushing his client's bitter charge of sexual harassment against the president. Clinton's lawyer, Bob Bennett, could have joined the video slugfest. Instead, he chose to occupy the high ground by affirming his commitment to the court order but telling a few reporters that the torrent of press speculation about the president's sex life was "absolute nonsense—absolute reckless, irresponsible nonsense."

All of the shows focused on the president's deposition in the Jones case. Only one—*This Week*—mentioned the Drudge story. News from the Internet was still being treated by mainstream journalists as news from an electronic netherworld—mysterious, essentially uncheckable, and there-fore unreliable. And yet this attitude was on the edge of dramatic dissolu-tion. Within a week, not only would the *Drudge Report* become the source for an endless rush of unsourced stories about Lewinsky's affair with the president, but the gossip columnist himself would be invited by host Tim Russert of *Meet the Press* to join Broder and Safire for a discussion of the scandal's impact on the Clinton presidency. The new and the old news would meet on the changing terrain being shaped by presidential scandal.

On Sunday, January 18, 1998, it was still the president's problem with Jones, not the intern, that captured the attention of most of the journalists and political pros who gathered around their television sets for the politi-cal news of the day. On CBS's *Face the Nation,* lawyer James Fisher out-lined the Jones strategy. "We think it would be highly relevant," he told host Bob Schieffer, "if we were to prove at trial that there were other instances of similar conduct, not only on the part of Mr. Clinton, but the state troopers that guarded him while he was governor." Could he prove such conduct? he was asked. Fisher, who already knew about Lewinsky,

Willey, and others, replied: "I think there is a substantial basis for our contention, yes." Another Jones lawyer, David Pike, appearing on NBC's *Meet the Press*, demonstrated that he and his colleagues were all singing from the same sheet of music. "What we're attempting to prove in this case," he told Tim Russert, "is that he [Clinton] engaged in a pattern of sexual harassment, and that's what we intend to prove." James Carville, the idiosyncratic Cajun defender of the Clintons, lacerated Jones. "It's all about money, plain and simple," he seethed, "and a healthy dose of right-wing politics."

Russert knew about the *Drudge Report*. His executive producer had informed him of it before the show began. On this Sunday, though, still operating on pre-Lewinsky standards, he opted to ignore Drudge and use the *Newsweek* story about Willey. "There's not enough there," he told his producer. On the show, he asked Carville about the Willey charge of presidential "groping." "Is there in fact a pattern of behavior that those who support President Clinton are worried about . . . ?" Carville snapped: "The president denies it, and . . . frankly, I know the president's telling the truth." (Even later in the day, when Russert was again discussing the Drudge story with the executive producer of *Today*, he again recommended against using it. "We hadn't confirmed anything yet," he explained.)

At the ABC studios, located in the shadow of the historic Mayflower Hotel, the stars of *This Week* were preparing to go on the air—Sam Donaldson and Cokie Roberts as co-hosts, and George Will, George Stephanopoulos, and Bill Kristol as co-pundits. Kristol was a bright conservative who had worked for Dan Quayle, and Stephanopoulos was a bright liberal who had worked for Bill Clinton. ABC in this way attempted to balance the political ticket, but if you added conservative columnist Will to the mix, it gave the conservatives a distinct two-to-one advantage in pundits.

When Kristol told Stephanopoulos about the Drudge story, the former Clinton aide had decided to check with the White House. He called Podesta, who had spoken with Isikoff on Saturday but still lacked details about the spiked *Newsweek* exclusive. An inside-the-Beltway course named "Spin Strategy 101" would suggest that if you can't confirm or deny an allegation, attack the credibility of the source, which is exactly what Podesta advised his old friend. "The only way you can respond to it is to say, 'This is Drudge, he's a rumormonger . . . and you can't believe what you read in the *Drudge Report.*'"

This Week, like the other Sunday morning talk shows, is divided into two parts: first, one to three interviews with prominent figures; then a segment devoted to commentary, in which all five of the show's stars exchange ideas, the more controversial the better. Stephanopoulos, raising a question that seems painfully amusing in hindsight, asked whether the Jones suit could possibly have any additional harmful effect on the Clinton presidency. "What worse can come out than already has been out?" the aide-turned-pundit asked. "He has been accused of murder, my goodness, from Jerry Falwell. What else can come out?" Kristol attempted to answer the rhetorical question. He said: "The story in Washington this morning is that *Newsweek* magazine was going to go with a big story based on tape-recorded conversations, which a woman who was a summer intern at the White House, an intern of Leon Panetta's . . ." at which point, unceremoniously, Kristol was interrupted by Stephanopoulos, who scoffed, "And Bill, where did [the story] come from? The *Drudge Report.* You know we've all seen how discredited that is . . ." Kristol shot back: "No, no, no. They had screaming arguments in *Newsweek* yesterday. They finally didn't go with the story. It's going to be a question of whether the media is now going to report what are pretty well-validated charges of presidential behavior in the White House."

Donaldson broke into the exchange. "I'm not an apologist for *Newsweek*," he said. "But if their editors decided they didn't have it cold enough to go with, I don't think that we can sit here without—unless you've seen what they were basing their decision on—how can we say *Newsweek* was wrong to kill it?"

When the televised Kristol-Stephanopoulos debate ended, the speculation in Washington (and elsewhere) began. What in fact did *Newsweek* spike? Susan Estrich e-mailed Drudge: "Drudge, this better not be true." Karen Wheeler, the head of *Newsweek*'s publicity department, called Isikoff at home and complained that her "phone was ringing off the hook." Isikoff and Wheeler were old friends, who had shared many confidences about their bosses. "Michael," she asked, "what can you tell me about all this? I need to know." Isikoff responded coldly, "Nothing. I can't say anything. You'll have to call McDaniel." There was an angry pause, followed by Wheeler's sarcastic response, "Okay, fine," and she slammed down her phone.

Late that Sunday afternoon, President Clinton conducted an extraordinary "memory session" with his secretary, Betty Currie. He had called her after his Saturday deposition and suggested a Sunday meeting. As Currie later testified, they sat at her desk outside the Oval Office, and Clinton explained that he had had to answer a few questions about Monica Lewinsky. He thought that Currie ought to know about them. Then he popped a string of now memorable statements—"in a very quick manner, one right after the other," she later testified. "You were always there when Monica was there." "I was never alone with Monica, right?" "Monica came on to me and I never touched her, right?" "Monica wanted to have sex with me and I cannot do that." Currie followed each statement or question with a one-word answer. "Right," she said. The president insisted that his conversation with Currie was simply to "refresh" his memory—not to coax or coach her into remembering these events in the same way that he did. Possibly, but it precipitated a frantic attempt by Currie to contact Lewinsky, which proved to be difficult. She paged Lewinsky at 5:12 p.m., then again at 6:22 p.m., and again at 7:06 p.m. and 8:28 p.m. Finally, at 10:15 p.m., Lewinsky called and made a fleeting reference to "Hoover," hoping Currie would get the hint that the FBI was on her tail.

A few weeks later, when *The New York Times* broke this story, it went to great lengths to avoid using the verb "coach," deliberately staying away from a verb that might be interpreted legally as the president engaging in the act of obstructing justice. The *Times* was trying to be super-careful, yet report an important element of the emerging Lewinsky scandal. But within an hour, the *Associated Press* and *Nightline* rewrote the *Times* account, using the verb "coach," dropping any pretense of subtlety, and suggesting that indeed the president had been trying to influence Currie's testimony and thereby obstruct justice. At the moment of their reports, both the AP and *Nightline* had no way of knowing the president's true intention; they simply *presumed* that he was trying to coach Currie, even though later in her grand jury testimony she said she didn't think he was trying to coach her at all.

The evening news on Sunday has always been the stepchild of the networks. If it isn't preempted by a golf match or a football game, it is often shortchanged on personnel, attention, and news. The anchor is either a comer or a goner, but is seldom a weekday star, unless a huge story is breaking, in which case Dan Rather is likely to reoccupy the anchor's chair on CBS, Tom Brokaw on NBC, or Peter Jennings on ABC. Most of the time, the U.S. government is closed, foreign embassies are shut, and news bureaus operate with limited staff. If news is ever made on a Sunday, it is an accident of nature or an unanticipated eruption of war, a coup d'état, a plane crash. And yet, according to the television schedule, there is an evening newscast on CBS, another on NBC, a third on CNN, and a fourth on ABC, and they all must be filled with "news," the definition of which is extremely flexible on Sundays. At least one story, often the lead story, is a reworked rendering of the morning newspaper and the morning talk shows, a headline providing the theme and a talk show a relevant sound bite or two.

On this Sunday evening, the story was still the president's Saturday deposition in the Jones case, a story now twenty-four hours old but still compelling enough for a Sunday. There was the *Drudge Report* on the Internet, but no broadcast or wire service made any mention of his "**World Exclusive**" about the president's romance with a young intern. Why were most Washington journalists ignoring the Drudge story on this Sunday? Was it because Drudge broke his story on a long weekend (the United States was to celebrate Martin Luther King, Jr., Day on Monday) and few reporters were working? Was it because Drudge was not considered a reliable source of information? Was it because even if a mainstream reporter had fastened on to the Drudge exclusive, he or she could not have gotten any confirmation, or enough confirmation, for a major newspaper or network to go with it? Not on a Sunday, when nothing was expected to happen, when no one in a position of authority was reachable anyway. The explanation probably lay in a combination of these factors.

In any case, when it came time early Sunday evening for CBS, ABC, and

CNN (NBC was preempted for a sports event) to air their newscasts, the focus was unmistakably on the Paula Jones case. It was legitimate and safe.

CBS's evening news program on Sunday began at 6 p.m. The anchor was Sharyl Attkisson, a recent, still unproven CNN transplant, who began her broadcast with two brief items about the president: the first that *Newsweek* was running an "exclusive" about how President Clinton "kissed" and "fondled" a "former White House aide" in a "hideaway off the Oval Office" (no confirmation or independent reporting by CBS, no mention of Kathleen Willey's name); and the second that Paula Jones was leaving Washington after listening to Clinton's six hours of testimony on Saturday. Attkisson then ran a sound bite from CBS's Sunday talk show, *Face the Nation,* showing Jones lawyer Jim Fisher asking for presidential accountability in his client's sexual harassment suit.

Having thus briskly disposed of the lead story in 246 words, Attkisson leaped to bigger things—"Still to come on tonight's CBS Evening News," she pronounced, "Dan Rather shows us how Cuba feels about the Pope's visit. Also, why some utility companies kept customers in the dark during the ice storm. And the struggle to keep the Olympic flame alive in Japan." Pope John Paul II was not scheduled to arrive in Havana until Wednesday, but Rather went there in advance to do a few pieces on what was expected to be a historic journey, the pope's first to Castro's Cuba.

At 6:30 p.m. on ABC, veteran newscaster Carole Simpson began *World News Tonight Sunday* with a 448-word story that Paula Jones was leaving town—again news that was hardly riveting, but it still topped Simpson's agenda. It featured the president in an unprecedented story about sexual harassment, and no anchor could escape its lure.

Sam Donaldson, who covered the White House and also anchored *This Week* on Sundays, was the correspondent for this story, a classic example of Sunday news. It contained four sound bites and ended with a Donaldson close, filled with sourced and unsourced information. "Behind the scenes, the spinning of the story continued," he boomed. "Paula Jones and her group dined Saturday night with champagne, professing to be pleased with the way things had gone. Friends of the president one-upped that by telling *Time* magazine the Clinton camp is ecstatic about the way the deposition went. And what did the president say yesterday? That's concealed because of the gag rule. But already leaks have it that he continued to maintain that he doesn't remember Ms. Jones. And questioned about other women allegedly obtained for him by state troopers, he is said to have denied in various ways that he's ever sexually harassed anyone. A messy business, but it's likely to get worse before it's over."

At 7 p.m. on CNN, anchor Laurie Dhue introduced a 622-word lead story by White House correspondent John King. Easily the longest of the three network stories, it contained four sound bites from the morning talk shows—two by Jones's lawyers, one by her spokesperson, and one by Clinton supporter James Carville—and it ended with a question-and-answer exchange between the anchor and the correspondent, speculating about whether a financial settlement between Jones and Clinton was likely before the projected May trial. At one point, King concluded that a settlement was still a "possibility." But he added, "for now, all signs point toward a trial that could prove a political and personal embarrassment for the president whatever the verdict."

William Ginsburg, a legal meteor across Washington's media sky, had arrived from Los Angeles on Saturday and spent most of the day reacquainting himself with the twenty-three-year-old woman he had known as a child. He was shocked at Lewinsky's fragile condition. She was, he thought, in a state of near hysteria, possibly suicidal. She needed medical attention, urgently. In fact, she asked to be checked into a psychiatric hospital, but Ginsburg persuaded her to rest, with her mother, in their small apartment at the Watergate. He also found that he was repelled, truly angered, by Clinton's seduction of Lewinsky, as he imagined the relationship. He wanted Clinton to be exposed as a "misogynist," even as a "molester."

But first he had to meet with Starr's prosecutors. On Saturday evening, he had gone to the independent counsel's office, where he had met with Jackie Bennett, Bob Bittman, and Mike Emmick. They still wanted Lewinsky to serve as their agent—to make "controlled calls" to Clinton, Currie, and Jordan. And they seemed ready to indict her for perjury if she didn't cooperate. Ginsburg was appalled. Who ever heard of prosecuting a twenty-three-year-old for lying about an affair? Later, Ginsburg called one of his Washington friends, a criminal lawyer named Nathaniel Speights, and asked for his help.

On Sunday, while the rest of political Washington, including the White House, obsessed publicly and privately about the Jones case, Ginsburg drove Lewinsky to Speights's home in Chevy Chase, so his new comrade-in-arms could get a raw glimpse of their desperate client. Speights ruled out a plea bargain with Starr's deputies—he thought they were bluffing. With Ginsburg's approval, he called Emmick and warned him that if Starr was intending to prosecute Lewinsky, he could forget about winning her cooperation in any form. Speights demanded immunity, or there would be no negotiation. Soon Emmick called back—immunity was a possibility, he said, but Starr and his deputies would first have to hear Lewinsky's whole story. Toward this end, he invited Ginsburg, Speights, and Lewinsky to come to the OIC office on Monday morning.

A small number of Washington reporters were busily pursuing the intern angle.

At *Newsweek,* Isikoff and Klaidman—who knew the most about Lewinsky, including her name—were trying to learn more. Who were her friends? Who would talk?

At *Time,* Michael Weisskopf called sources at the White House, the Pentagon, and on Capitol Hill: did anyone know about the president coaching a witness? About tapes? About an intern?

At ABC, Chris Vlasto and Jackie Judd were piecing together a complicated puzzle, pieces of which Vlasto had assembled from his Saturday dinner with Jones and her lawyers. They didn't yet know about Lewinsky, Reno, the three judges, and Starr's new pursuit of Clinton.

At NBC, Russert had alerted political reporter Lisa Myers to the Drudge story about an intern. What could she find out? Myers had excellent sources at the OIC.

At *The Washington Post,* Susan Schmidt had heard whispers on Friday about a presidential scandal having nothing to do with Paula Jones, and she had been calling sources everywhere. She too had particularly good sources at the OIC.

Once again, despite their efforts, it was not these traditional, experienced journalists who advanced the story. It was Drudge, who was in close contact with Goldberg and the behind-the-scenes Jones lawyers. On Saturday night, Conway had been Drudge's principal source. Now, late Sunday night, after calls to Conway, Goldberg, and others, Drudge had another exclusive, in which, for the first time, Monica Lewinsky's name appeared in print.

At midnight, Washington time, Drudge ran the following story:

FORMER WHITE HOUSE INTERN CALLED; NEW BACKGROUND DETAILS EMERGE

> *The "Drudge Report" has learned that former White House intern, Monica Lewinsky, twenty three, has been subpoenaed to give a deposition in the Paula Jones case.*
>
> *About the young woman, this is known . . .*

Drudge then disclosed that Lewinsky had worked as a summer intern and staff assistant at the White House and then as an assistant to the Pentagon's spokesman, Kenneth Bacon. He also disclosed that Lewinsky, a 1995 graduate of Lewis and Clark College with a major in psychology, was proficient in the use of a word processor and had "access to top secret and sensitive information."

Because of their timing and their subject matter, Drudge's reports contributed to the media's preoccupation with sex and sensationalism. They encouraged the publishing and broadcasting of poorly sourced information. And, as much as anything, they highlighted the problems of Internet journalism—an "Open Sesame" to a world of speeding and colliding fragments of unchecked data fired into cyberspace without any assurance of accuracy or reliability.

CHAPTER 6

THE GATHERING STORM
January 19, 1998

" . . . WHAT IS WHISPERED IN THE CLOSET SHALL BE PRO-
CLAIMED FROM THE HOUSE-TOPS."
—Louis Brandeis and Samuel Warren, *Harvard Law Review* (1890)

On Monday, January 19, 1998, a holiday commemorating the birth of Martin Luther King, Jr., readers of *The Washington Post* found two front-page stories dealing with Clinton's sexual indiscretions. In one, White House correspondent Peter Baker raised an important question: As the Paula Jones case proceeded, could Clinton "prevent a more unsavory portrayal of his private life from being etched into the public consciousness?" Baker suggested that it might be too late, citing three news reports:

- Scott Pelley's exclusive on Saturday's *CBS Evening News* about four women alleging "unsolicited sexual advances" by Clinton;
- the *Newsweek* story about "a former White House aide" who made similar charges;
- the ABC Sunday *This Week* discussion of a "long-running tryst" while Clinton was in the White House. (This was the initial Drudge intern story, raised on the program by Kristol.)

By referring to these three reports in a front-page story, the *Post* gave them added credibility and legitimacy.

In the second front-page story, reporter John Harris raised another question that puzzled Clinton-watchers: How could one account for his 65 percent approval rating amid rising discussion of his private peccadilloes? Harris explained, "Some of the president's intimates note his remarkable ability to compartmentalize his life: the policy wonk who genuinely admires his wife resides in one space; the rogue who risks political standing through personal indiscretion occupies another."

Monday provided an excellent example of the president's ability to compartmentalize his life. In one compartment was the threat of exposed infidelity—not in Arkansas, but in the White House. Clinton had spent much of the night on the phone, anguishing not about Jones, who was old news, but about Lewinsky, who was about to be new news. As late as 11:02 p.m., he had called Currie, waking her, to inquire whether she had been able to reach Lewinsky. The sleepy secretary had responded, no. "I was almost too tired to talk to him," Currie recalled in grand jury testimony. The next morning, at 8:42 a.m., she called the president to tell him that, despite six efforts to reach Lewinsky on Monday morning from 7:02 a.m. to 8:37 a.m., leaving messages with appeals that the former intern return her calls, she still hadn't heard from her. Try her again, the president said. At 8:44 a.m., Currie called Lewinsky a seventh time. At 8:50 a.m., Clinton called Currie, only to learn that she still had not reached Lewinsky. At 8:55 a.m., Clinton called Jordan, believing that if anyone could reach the suddenly and uncharacteristically reclusive Lewinsky, it would be Jordan. He tried twice—at 10:33 a.m. and again at 11:16 a.m.—and still no luck. Jordan then lunched with his friend, attorney Francis Carter, who had handled Lewinsky's affidavit at Jordan's suggestion, and showed him a copy of the *Drudge Report*. "You need to talk to your client about that," Jordan cautioned. Carter told Jordan that Lewinsky was no longer his client.

And yet, in another compartment, there was the Clinton who had to get on with his job. Like Superman changing in a phone booth from one costume to another, Clinton emerged from his secret and frantic White House deliberations looking for all the world like an ordinary citizen out to do good work for his community. He wore a Stanford T-shirt, blue jeans, and cowboy boots and went to Cardozo High School in D.C. to help paint a classroom, telling reporters along the way that he had "no comment" on the Jones deposition. There was a gag order, after all. When a reporter asked Clinton about his upcoming Middle East negotiations, which were to start Tuesday morning, he responded with a diplomatically upbeat assessment. There was a subject he could discuss. "I'm committed to making it a success," he said with proper determination. "I'm going to do my part, and I just want us to have constructive relations where we can move this forward."

Not only the president and his closest aides and friends but just about every reporter in town had read the *Post* accounts of Clinton's troubles. Most simply assumed that it was more of the same—more women, more Arkansas foolishness—and they did little or nothing to pursue the leads. But a small handful of reporters, "three or four of us," had been "working this story very energetically, competing against each other," recalled the *Post*'s Susan Schmidt. They sensed "something special" looming on the near horizon, and each was determined to get it first. In addition to Schmidt, this group included Judd and Vlasto of ABC, Weisskopf and Novak of *Time,* and Isikoff, who knew more about the story than all of them combined, and whose sources, while unsavory, were superb.

In *Newsweek*'s office on Monday, an increasingly frustrated Isikoff, feeling his story slipping through his fingers, was frantically working the phones in an attempt to reach Currie, Jordan, or Lewinsky, or perhaps some of her close friends in whom she might have confided about her strange affair with the president of the United States. Klaidman was helping his colleague. They had no luck reaching Lewinsky. Currie and Jordan kept their distance. But they did reach a number of informed lawyers in and out of government, a few of Lewinsky's friends, and, of course, Goldberg, who had just spoken with Linda Tripp. By day's end, Isikoff and Klaidman felt that they were prepared to answer the questions posed on Saturday by their New York editors and to write a solid story. Sadly for them, they worked for a weekly, which meant their story would not hit the newsstands until the following Monday. They had a special respect for the hardworking Schmidt, and they were certain that Schmidt and the *Post* would beat them to their exclusive, just as Drudge already had on the Internet.

At the *Post*, Schmidt, who had barely left the office since Friday, was calling people "far and wide" but was still at that awkward stage in the reporting process when a journalist has a number of facts but not yet a coherent story. Not until very late Sunday night did Schmidt hear the name Lewinsky—and her source was Drudge. "Someone in the office came upon it on the Internet and told me about it, that she was the intern in question. I checked around and found that she worked at the Pentagon, and then things began to come together. Then I heard about Linda Tripp. I knew that she had testified at the Whitewater hearings—I knew because I covered them. She worked at the Pentagon, and now I had to find out where Linda Tripp lived, and when I did, I drove right out there to talk to her."

At ABC, Judd was working on a totally different story for Tuesday's *World News Tonight*—a special "Your Money" piece on what she called a "Wisconsin porkbuster." It was Vlasto, her New York producer, who was busily working on the Lewinsky story. He later told me that he had heard a "rumor" about an unnamed intern and the president in December but had done nothing about it. At the celebratory Jones dinner on Saturday evening, he learned, among other things, that Tripp was a key source in the deepening drama about the president's sexual adventures. Vlasto remembered her from the Whitewater hearings. "A very strange witness," he said. "Very strange. A woman who engaged in gossip, who exchanged endless e-mails with girlfriends, who took notes on everyone who entered and who left the [White House] counsel's office." Vlasto called Tripp at her home in Maryland, and he called Ashley Raines, one of Lewinsky's friends, who was soon to testify before the grand jury. Raines never returned his call, but one of the White House spokesmen, Barry Toiv, called, apparently at her request. "What do you want?" he asked somewhat belligerently. Vlasto punted—it was Raines he wanted, someone who knew Lewinsky well, who might be able to tell him about her relationship with Clinton. Vlasto didn't want a spokesman who represented a suddenly anxious White House, waiting for a mainstream journalist to confirm what an Internet gossip had alleged over the weekend—that a more damaging scandal was lurking just beyond the Jones embarrassment. Vlasto had very little respect for Drudge. "Read what he wrote that weekend," Vlasto told me. "Not much really. But I have to say it did have a big effect. It got a lot of people involved in this story who wouldn't have been. It created a frenzied atmosphere." Vlasto thought at the time that he was working on two separate stories, one focusing on Jones, the other on Lewinsky.

At *Time*, Weisskopf was on the phone, asking Lanny Davis whether he had seen the *Drudge Report* over the weekend. "No," Davis replied. "I don't read the *Drudge Report*." Weisskopf, the reporter, began briefing Davis, the source—an unnatural exchange that was to repeat itself frequently in the next few days. "Drudge says that a young intern, Monica Lewinsky, may have had an affair with the President." He added that Isikoff and *Newsweek* had been working on the story. Suddenly, Davis recalled Isikoff's odd demeanor at lunch on Friday. He told Weisskopf that he had never before heard the name "Monica Lewinsky" and wondered why anyone would take Drudge seriously. Weisskopf would not be deflected. "Something's popping," he said briskly. "Can't tell you any more right now."

Vlasto, Weisskopf, and Schmidt did not write a word on Monday. They were building a story, piece by piece, widening their circle of sources, accumulating information and impressions, absolutely determined to beat their competitors.

At noon Washington time, Rush Limbaugh, whose affection for Bill and Hillary Clinton would not fill a thimble, rapturously reported to his many millions of die-hard "dittoheads" on radio that another sex scandal was about to envelop the White House. How did he know? Because just as "someone in the office" had told Schmidt about the *Drudge Report,* someone in Limbaugh's office had told him about it, too. Schmidt kept reporting, while Limbaugh went straight to his microphone. Although many Americans assumed that Limbaugh lived in the same media tent as *New York Times* and *Washington Post* reporters, he was not a journalist; in fact, he had contempt for most journalists, whom he defined as "liberals." Limbaugh felt no obligation to check Drudge's report: all Limbaugh had to do was tell his listeners what Drudge had reported, just as Kristol, another non-journalist in the universe of journalism, had done on Sunday on ABC's *This Week.* Limbaugh loved the Lewinsky story. Day after day, for more than a year, Limbaugh chewed on the red meat of the scandal.

The evening news programs touched lightly on the president's deposition in the Jones case. None of them mentioned the various *Drudge Reports,* and the name "Lewinsky" never crossed an anchor's lips. The story had not yet ripened for network use.

At 8 p.m., CNBC, one of the cable operations that depended on a constant stream of chatter, provided a contrast with the networks' coverage. *Equal Time,* which blurred the line between journalism and politics, had no hesitation about devoting an hour to presidential scandals. It featured two women anchors, one a liberal, the other a conservative, and, as on many of the other cable talk programs, every topic was reduced to a shouting match between two opposing parties or positions. On Monday, the anchors were Stephanie Miller, a liberal lawyer from Los Angeles, and Bay Buchanan, Pat's conservative sister and campaign manager of his quadrennial run for the presidency. Also politically balanced were their guests: Jennifer Laszlo, a Democratic loyalist; Ann Coulter, the Republican activist; and Stuart Taylor, the controversial journalist who had criticized his colleagues for adopting a less than respectful attitude toward Paula Jones. Buchanan quickly steered the conversation toward the Willey charges, which Laszlo promptly discounted, and the new, whispered White House scandal involving an intern, which Laszlo dismissed as a Hollywood fantasy. She suggested that Isikoff had "confused reality with the movie *Wag the Dog.*"

Buchanan summoned Taylor to her rescue. "Not one jot or tittle of Michael Isikoff's detailed reporting on this case and other Clinton problems has been proven wrong yet," Taylor insisted. Later in the program, Buchanan returned to the story about the "23-year-old intern," who had had a "two-year affair" with the president. Already the "affair" was being discussed as a fact, though no one on the program, including Taylor, had done any reporting on the story or knew anything beyond what Drudge had written about *Newsweek*'s "spiking" of Isikoff's story. Coulter, who knew a lot more about Lewinsky than she was prepared to acknowledge on the program, chose to restrict her comments to published or broadcast reports. "I know what I read on the Drudge Report," she noted carefully, "and it's certainly broken there and on Rush [Limbaugh]. And apparently there is a 23-year-old intern who's supposed to have had a lengthy affair, and tapes recounting this, with the President."

Unlike the Limbaugh program, which attracted a weekly audience of 18 million, *Equal Time* attracted a very modest audience—200,000 to 400,000 homes on a very good evening. Its impact was limited.

Lewinsky, Ginsburg, and Speights spent most of Monday at the OIC, Ginsburg and Speights negotiating in one conference room, Lewinsky crying in another. The prosecutors had one major demand: they wanted to speak directly to Lewinsky. Her cooperation and her testimony were essential to their plans to prosecute the president. Ginsburg also had one major demand: he wanted the OIC to grant full immunity to his client.

Otherwise, he stressed, he would not allow his client to meet with the prosecutors. All communication between Lewinsky and the OIC would have to go through him. Tempers rose, Ginsburg cursed, Lewinsky wailed.

At one point in the afternoon, negotiations were interrupted when the prosecutors received a copy of the latest *Drudge Report*, which revealed Lewinsky's name. Suddenly the situation had changed. The prosecutors could no longer hope to use her to entrap Jordan, Currie, or Clinton. She had become, in Jackie Bennett's word, "radioactive."

In the course of the day, Drudge continued to release updates on the Lewinsky story, not all of them accurate. At 5:31 p.m., he reported briefly that Lewinsky had denied "in a sworn affidavit" that she had ever had a "sexual relationship with President Clinton." Drudge added that NBC had obtained a copy of Lewinsky's affidavit in the Jones case for a story planned for Tuesday. (In fact, NBC had no such affidavit.) At 6:52 p.m., Drudge released a report that was essentially an elaboration of the previous report, adding only that NBC's copy had been "leaked" (he didn't say by whom) and that *The Star* tabloid was also preparing a story on the Lewinsky affair.

Who was Drudge's source? How did he know so much, so fast?

For most of Monday (and Tuesday and Wednesday, too), it was none other than an impatient and manipulative Lucianne Goldberg, who kept funneling sensational and unsourced tips to her new "client," Drudge, who was, understandably, ecstatic. "This thing just fell into my lap," he told Howard Kurtz of *The Washington Post*. Goldberg's old "client," Isikoff, had turned out to be a bitter disappointment, since he was unable to persuade his editors to publish the story. Drudge, on the other hand, being essentially indifferent to the normal constraints of journalism, barely paused to catch his breath. He was his own editor. He ran a one-man operation with a reach as wide as the Internet. He rewrote Goldberg's stream of scintillating tips and fired them into cyberspace. They fell to earth in many computers, including the busy OIC office in the nation's capital, where they affected the negotiations between Bennett and Ginsburg.

Bennett had always been reluctant to offer immunity to Lewinsky. He believed that the OIC should insist on Lewinsky's cooperation in this criminal investigation—or else. In fact, one of his colleagues, Solomon Wisenberg, believed that the OIC decision to let Lewinsky leave the hotel with her mother on Friday night rather than frighten her into cooperation was a tactical blunder.

"She wasn't strong, like Susan McDougal," he told me. "We could have got her to break within a day. It was our biggest mistake." He dismissed later accounts of the OIC's treatment of Lewinsky, "stories about Starr using Gestapo tactics—they weren't true," he insisted.

By 10:30 p.m., after both sides had restated their positions, it was obvious that there would be no agreement. Bennett handed Ginsburg a subpoena for Lewinsky's mother, Marcia Lewis, whose name had come up repeatedly in the Tripp-Lewinsky tapes, and he warned that in the absence of Lewinsky's cooperation, he might be obliged to subpoena her father as well. Ginsburg responded with an angry eruption of profanity. He stormed out of the conference room, violating the norms of legal etiquette, grabbed Monica, and said, "Come on, we're leaving." "I fell to the floor in a delirium of despair," Lewinsky later told her biographer. "It was this feeling of never-ending torture. What were they doing to my family? I couldn't handle it anymore."

Up to this point, Lewinsky's privacy had been invaded by only a small circle of lawyers. Soon her private life would become known to the entire world.

Journalists did not concern themselves with the question of whether Lewinsky was entitled to what Hillary Clinton had always called "a zone of privacy," some space where she could feel safe from public scrutiny. But journalists had to concern themselves with the question of whether a president was entitled to "a zone of privacy." Should a president's private life be open to their coverage if his public performance was beyond reproach, or if it was at least acceptable to the American people? In other words, should journalists make a distinction between a president's private life and his public performance?

Though much has been written in recent years about these recurrent questions, no one has done a better job of identifying the underlying problems than Supreme Court Justice Louis D. Brandeis and lawyer Samuel D. Warren, who penned their analysis on "The Right to Privacy" in the *Harvard Law Review* a century before the Clintons arrived at the White House. Brandeis and Warren worried especially about the technological advances then pressuring the news business into undermining what they took to be a sacred right of the American people—"the right to be let alone." "Instantaneous photographs and newspaper enterprise have invaded the sacred precinct of private and domestic life," they wrote, "and numerous mechanical devices threaten to make good the prediction that 'what is whispered in the closet shall be proclaimed from the house-tops.'"

The journey between the closet and the housetop could be defined as gossip, both then and now—unsubstantiated, unchecked, but titillating information that appealed to many people while at the same time lowering moral standards, driving more substantive issues out of newspapers, and destroying "robustness of thought and delicacy of feeling" throughout society. These two legal scholars regarded gossip as the principal culprit.

They wrote:

The press is overstepping in every direction the obvious bounds of propriety and of decency. Gossip is no longer the resource of the idle and vicious, but has become a trade, which is pursued with industry as well as effrontery.

To satisfy a prurient taste the details of sexual relations are spread . . . in the columns of the daily papers. To occupy the indolent, column upon column is filled with idle gossip, which can only be procured by intrusion upon the domestic circle.

The intensity and complexity of life, attendant upon advancing civilization, have rendered necessary some retreat from the world, and man, under the refining influence of culture, has become more sensitive to publicity, so that solitude and privacy have become more essential to the individual; but modern enterprise and invention have, through invasions upon his privacy, subjected him to mental pain and distress, far greater than could be inflicted by mere bodily injury. Nor is the harm wrought by such invasions confined to the suffering of those who may be the subjects of journalistic and other enterprise. In this, as in other branches of commerce, the supply creates the demand.

Each crop of unseemly gossip, thus harvested, becomes the seed of more, and, in direct proportion to its circulation, results in a lowering of social standards and of morality. Even gossip apparently harmless, when idly and persistently circulated, is potent for evil. It both belittles and perverts. It belittles by inverting the relative importance of things, thus dwarfing the thoughts and aspirations of people.

When personal gossip attains the dignity of print, and crowds the space available for matters of real interest to the community, what wonder that the ignorant and thoughtless mistake its relative importance. Easy of comprehension, appealing to that weak side of human nature which is never wholly cast down by the misfortunes and frailties of our neighbors, no one can be surprised that it usurps the place of interest in brains capable of thought and delicacy of feeling.

No enthusiasm can flourish, no generous impulse can survive under its blighting influence.

Brandeis and Warren were prescient. Remember, this was written in 1890.

They did not know about cable television, talk radio, and the Internet, or about fifteen-second ads and eight-second sound bites. Yet they were already preoccupied by the threat that "instantaneous photographs" posed to private life. Privacy, to these jurists, was an essential right, without which a democratic people could not flourish. If Brandeis and Warren were on the Supreme Court today, would they place the right to privacy ahead of the right to know? Would they sanction restrictions on freedom of the press to protect the privacy of the public official? Would they, in the final analysis, blame the press or the president for the great meltdown of morality and standards in January 1998?

On Monday night, Washington was only a day away from the most intrusive press invasion of presidential privacy in the history of the nation. If fragile boundaries did once exist around a president's "right to be let alone," they were about to be shattered.

CHAPTER 7

THE GINSBURG QUOTE

January 20, 1998

"GINSBURG SAID . . . THAT EITHER THE PRESIDENT WAS A
MISOGYNIST OR STARR WAS A MONSTER. THAT OPENED THE
FLOODGATES."

—Susan Schmidt, *The Washington Post*

"HIS WAS A REALLY FLAMBOYANT QUOTE."

—Chris Vlasto of ABC News

"WE'VE GOT A PROBLEM. WE ARE IN UNCHARTED WATERS."
—David Willman of the *Los Angeles Times*

On Tuesday, things began to come together.

By midday, reporters and cameramen were already unruly, as they muscled their way into the White House briefing room for another performance by a harassed spokesman whose leash seemed to be getting shorter by the day. Spokesman Mike McCurry's exchanges with the White House press corps, usually spicy, were becoming sullen and tiring. Tuesday was no exception. The president's public calendar was filled with diplomacy and domestic politics: meetings with PLO chairman Yassir Arafat and Israeli prime minister Benjamin Netanyahu and a fund-raising pep talk at the Democratic National Committee. But ABC's Sam Donaldson for one did not seem interested in the interminable Mideast negotiations or another presidential speech. He was interested in Drudge's tantalizing exclusives, and he needed an official comment.

Donaldson: "Someone said that you or someone here has put out the
word that staffers at the White House should not be
allowed to log onto the *Drudge Report*. Is that true?"
McCurry: "I—I don't discuss that subject."

Donaldson: "What? Whether you have put out the word that you
             can't log on?"

McCurry: "I've heard calling it a report is too generous."

Donaldson: "Well, whatever you want to call it is fine with me, but
             have you forbidden people to actually . . ."

McCurry: "No. People—it's a free country, and people can do what
             they want to on the Internet."

McCurry was expressing the prevailing White House view that Drudge was a gossipmonger unworthy of a serious response. Yet Donaldson was a serious reporter digging into sensitive turf, and McCurry quickly understood that he was going to have to get an official comment on the Internet scoops. Drudge represented a new and unavoidable challenge of a sort no White House spokesman had ever confronted before.

An hour after the briefing, McCurry distributed a press release, in which the president was quoted as saying that the American people should celebrate the upcoming Chinese New Year as a time "to embrace the challenges of the year ahead." Little did he know how challenging the year ahead would be.

At *Newsweek,* which had suffered the humiliating sting of Drudge's hijacking of Isikoff's story Saturday night, Ann McDaniel was now sensing a more traditional challenge. She had come to share Isikoff's concern that Schmidt of *The Washington Post* would soon pick up the threads of the Lewinsky story and that the *Post,* because it was a daily newspaper, would then become the first mainstream news organization to publish the extraordinary details of this presidential affair with an intern. Someone outside journalism, who knew that *Newsweek* and the *Post* were both owned by the same corporation, might logically ask: what difference would it have made which outfit published first? The answer is that news organizations remain fiercely competitive, no matter who owns them. Moreover, as more and more news organizations gobble up one another and then merge with Internet giants to become unprecedentedly huge media conglomerates, there is an increasing likelihood that competing news organizations will end up belonging to the same national or global enterprise without losing their individual identities. At least, that is what optimistic observers of the media scene believe. Pessimists see the drive toward the creation of more conglomerates as foreshadowing not just a dumbing down of news standards but also a homogenization of news identities.

In this case, when I later asked Schmidt if she had benefited from Isikoff's spadework, she bristled with indignation. "We share nothing with *Newsweek*," she fumed. "I don't even know where their office is." McDaniel echoed her disdain for intracorporate collaboration. "We don't cooperate," she insisted. "We didn't share any information on this story." Actually, editor Len Downie of the *Post* decided on Tuesday to inform Donald Graham, chairman of the board of the Washington Post Corporation, that Schmidt was close to breaking the Lewinsky story. "I wanted to give him a heads-up," Downie explained. He learned that Graham already knew about the story, because the editor of *Newsweek* had briefed him earlier. Still, Graham told Downie nothing of substance. "I'm in a very tough situation," Downie quoted Graham as saying, "because *Newsweek* has already kept me informed on the story. Just keep going."

At ABC News, Vlasto was furiously working the phones. He knew he was close to pay dirt, but what was he missing? Lewinsky, of course, held one of the keys, but she wasn't answering the phone. Vlasto kept calling—persistence being one of his singular qualities. Finally, much to his surprise and delight, she answered around 3 p.m. Vlasto, oozing charm, asked Lewinsky a number of questions about her relationship with the president. Lewinsky, maintaining her cool, referred Vlasto to her lawyer, since, for the time being, she couldn't talk to reporters. And who is your lawyer? Vlasto asked. Bill Ginsburg, she answered, in a refreshing glimmer of candor. And how do I reach him? Vlasto wondered. She gave him Ginsburg's cell phone number, adding that the lawyer was on his way back to Los Angeles. Vlasto was excited; he had actually talked to Lewinsky, he had her lawyer's name, and he also had his cell phone number.

Vlasto went into high gear. He had an associate call Ginsburg. She reached him at Dulles Airport outside Washington just minutes before Giusburg was to board a transcontinental jet to Los Angeles after his inconclusive and bitter exchanges with Starr's deputies. The associate asked the obvious questions, and Ginsburg, while refusing to answer most of them, unrolled one response that he seemed to have rehearsed for journalists—he was to use it a few more times on Tuesday. "If the allegations are true that there was a sexual relationship with the president," Ginsburg said, "then he was a misogynist and I have to question his ability to lead. If they are not true, then why is the independent counsel ravaging the life of a twenty-three-year-old girl?" Vlasto knew immediately that Ginsburg had just made "news." He alerted his assignment desk to send a television crew to the Los Angeles airport to meet Ginsburg on his arrival there and get him to repeat this extraordinary comment on camera. ABC thus became the only network agile enough to get Ginsburg on camera that day. Then, impetuously, without checking with senior editors, Vlasto put the quote on the ABC News Web site. In other words, by late afternoon Tuesday, the Ginsburg quote was in play, available to anyone who logged onto ABC's foothold in cyberspace. Finally, Vlasto called Starr's office for a reaction. He read the quote to an OIC spokesperson, "who took it down verbatim," he remembered. "That's when the OIC panicked."

This was to be the pattern: a journalist called the OIC for information or a reaction; the OIC asked the journalist what he or she knew; the journalist usually shared his or her information with the OIC, hoping with this display of goodwill to generate additional information from the OIC—which proved to be an invaluable service, since it made clear to the OIC what elements of the story were in play and which sources might have been leaking. This then allowed the OIC to feed the journalist its slant on the evolving story.

"That was one of the key moments of the day," Vlasto later recalled. "His was a really flamboyant quote—linking Monica to Starr and the president." Up to this point in his reporting, Vlasto, like most other journalists, had no idea of the relationship between the Lewinsky affair and the independent counsel. Now, thanks to Ginsburg, Vlasto understood for the first time that Lewinsky, Jones, and Clinton were all characters in a single unfolding story about presidential dalliances connected somehow to the Office of the Independent Counsel. But how? Vlasto's partner, Jackie Judd, was on Capitol Hill, where she had gone to do an on-camera close for her "Your Money" piece. Her plan at the time was to fly to Hawaii on Wednesday to do another "Your Money" piece. She was not thinking about Lewinsky or Starr when Vlasto called with the latest news about Ginsburg. In other words, as late as Tuesday afternoon, ABC's lead correspondent on the story was not even aware of how close she was to breaking it. She and Vlasto alerted the producers of *World News Tonight* that they were working on a "big, big story." Vlasto thought that the Ginsburg quote "unified" the piece, pulling together formerly disparate elements into a coherent whole, but they still felt that they didn't have enough reliable information—or time—to do the story for the 6:30 p.m. news program. At the time they were thinking about proposing a piece for *Nightline,* which aired at 11:35 p.m.

Judd wasted no time returning to the office, where she joined Vlasto in an effort to learn more about Starr's role in the scandal. What did he have to do with Lewinsky? At about 5 p.m., Vlasto called David Kendall, one of the president's attorneys, and asked about the brewing scandal. Kendall, who was reached on his cell phone, said that he did not know about it and in any case did not want to comment; he promised Vlasto he would check and call back later in the evening. For her part, Judd started calling "people who would know," she said, "a variety of sources." Soon "the outline of a story" formed in her mind. One source told her, "This is big, this could be historic," a phrase that further fueled her curiosity.

At NBC and CBS, there were rumors that ABC was about to broadcast "a big one." But ABC's *World News Tonight* time came and went without a bang. NBC's Tim Russert later claimed, "We had access to the same information," but it just wasn't "hard enough." Others in his Washington bureau disputed this claim, saying that NBC knew nothing about the story until Wednesday. Judd left ABC and drove home to Chevy Chase. She figured that there would be plenty of time later in the evening to make other calls.

At *The Washington Post,* Susan Schmidt was also approaching decision time.

What did she know? And was it solid? She knew she had a big story, an explosive story about a presidential affair with a young White House intern named Monica Lewinsky—she was certain that much was true. She had covered Whitewater and knew Starr and his prosecutors, especially Jackie Bennett, who was proving to be exceptionally helpful to her and her newspaper on this day when all of the pieces were coming together into a huge story. Was she being spun? Of course, she assumed, but she was a pro and could adjust to the spin. Did she have enough for publication? And another obvious question: Had the affair interfered with the president's capacity to do his job? She suspected Downie would ask a variation of that question. Did she know for a fact that the affair interfered with government business? Could she prove it? Not really— how could she? And short of such proof, could she justifiably push for publication? In her judgment, the answer was yes. She had been told that Starr had authority from the three-judge panel to investigate allegations of perjury involving Lewinsky and the president, but she wanted confirmation if possible from the Department of Justice. She told Downie that she was close to finishing the Lewinsky story. Downie told her to call Starr's prosecutors and then Tripp, and he told Peter Baker to call the White House and then Jordan. "When we get close to publication on a story of this sort, we like to check with the principals," Downie said. His final decision to publish was still hours away.

Late in the afternoon, a "key piece of information" crossed Schmidt's desk, an example of chance intermingled with diligent legwork. It was a quote from Ginsburg, who enjoyed speaking to reporters "on the record," in contrast to other lawyers in this case, who enjoyed dropping their tidbits "on background," that is, anonymously. Schmidt got the Ginsburg quote from Baker, who had been working on the Jones story and helping Schmidt when possible. He got Ginsburg's cell phone number from his secretary in Los Angeles. "At first, it all seemed so fanciful," Baker said, "but Ginsburg pulled the pieces together."

First, Ginsburg stated that he had been in negotiation with Starr's deputies. Second, he described his client as a vulnerable victim caught between two powerful men. Third, he refused to comment on whether his client had had a sexual relationship with the president. But then he added the quote soon heard around the world: "If the president of the United States did this—and I'm not saying that he did—with this young lady, I think he's a misogynist. If he didn't, then I think Ken Starr and his crew have ravaged the life of a youngster." Ginsburg said that someone like Lewinsky could be devastated, "if you're not terribly sophisticated and you're misled by the people at the center of the political system, and that includes the president and his staff and the special prosecutor."

What Ginsburg was now saying to Baker and Schmidt was that Starr was an integral part of the Lewinsky/Clinton story—else why would Ginsburg, who represented Lewinsky, place his client in the middle of a still unexplained war between Starr and Clinton? "That quote," Schmidt told me, "opened the floodgates." Suddenly, Schmidt understood that she had been focusing on only part of the story; now she had to uncover the rest of it, and quickly. What was Starr's role in this drama? And would his office now confirm it?

In the Washington bureau of the *Los Angeles Times*, tucked away in a modern complex on I Street, investigative reporter David Willman was working on an exclusive story about the serious side effects of Rezulin, a relatively new drug for diabetes. Late in the afternoon, Willman got a call from a source who was knowledgeable about the president's serious legal problems and who was, according to bureau chief Doyle McManus, "behaving strangely." Reporter and source had been engaged in "an erratic ongoing dialogue" for days. Now, for the first time, Willman sensed "vague intimations of genuine, building excitement." What's going on? he asked. Willman, who had covered Whitewater, with a special emphasis on the Webster Hubbell angle, believed that the White House was getting into deep trouble.

An hour later, as Willman was preparing to call it a day—with nothing yet clear enough for a story on either Rezulin or Lewinsky—the source called him once again. This time the source was no longer vague, indeed, he was dramatically specific and informative. For whatever reason, he told Willman the whole story: the president's affair with a young intern, the tapes, Starr, the three-judge panel approving an expanded OIC investigation of Clinton, the charge of "obstruction of justice," everything. The story simply dropped into Willman's lap, just as it had dropped into Drudge's lap. Was it a source at the OIC, who knew the *Post* and ABC were close to breaking the story? Was it one of the lawyers? Was it someone at the White House engaged in the practice of "inoculation"? Willman wouldn't say.

Willman, still wearing his coat, strode into McManus's large office. "Boss," he said glumly, "we've got a problem. We are in uncharted waters." He then told McManus the story conveyed by his source. "The problem now is threefold," he said. "First, it'll take months for this story to unwind and it'll be a huge distraction for everyone. Second, it's really salacious stuff, and the paper is not going to be happy publishing it. And third, I really want to work on the Rezulin story." Still, Willman knew that he was the paper's star investigative reporter, an "expert" on presidential problems.

If he didn't research and write the story that night, he would have to do it the next day. He solicited help from his colleague, Ron Ostrow, who was "well wired" at the Department of Justice and the OIC. Together, they started looking for confirmation. For the mainstream journalist—unlike Drudge—the story, even when dropped in his lap, was still not enough; confirmation was essential.

For his part, McManus had known "something" was "cooking" ever since late Saturday night, when he learned from Drudge that *Newsweek* had killed Isikoff's story. However, Drudge was describing a sex scandal, and, McManus thought, "If that's the kind of story Isikoff is writing, then he's welcome to it." Only when he learned that the sex scandal had morphed into a criminal investigation of a sitting president did he change his mind; then it became a legitimate story for him and the *Los Angeles Times*. Willman, on the other hand, knew nothing about Drudge; indeed, until late Tuesday afternoon, he had no idea who Matt Drudge was or what he was reporting. Everything then started moving very fast. "Firewalls were smashing," McManus observed.

The Washington Post and the *Los Angeles Times* share a syndication wire; stories and columns scheduled for the next day's edition of both newspapers appear on the wire at 6:30 p.m. If a *Post* editor likes an *L.A. Times* story, he or she can decide to run it—with proper credit, of course. Normally, editors read the wire simply to learn what the competition is planning to publish. A routine practice, a check, a courtesy. On Tuesday, January 20, 1998, neither the *Post* nor the *L.A. Times* released publication plans for the next day. The explanation for this unusual omission was twofold: first, editors did not want to disclose that a bombshell exclusive was about to explode—why tip off the competition? and second, at both newspapers, editors were not yet certain that the Lewinsky story would be ready for publication.

Just as Vlasto and Schmidt sought clarification and confirmation from the OIC, their collaborating colleagues sought clarification and confirmation from the White House. Late Tuesday afternoon, as calls went from ABC and *The Washington Post* to the OIC, other calls went to McCurry at the White House. He was the spokesman, the official on the front line of journalistic inquiry. Questions big and small usually ended up on his desk.

Ever since late Saturday evening, when Drudge ran his first piece about a presidential scandal, McCurry sensed that a real problem might be brewing, although he hoped it would all prove to be "the same old-fashioned poppycock" he'd been hearing for years. But there had been very few actual queries from reporters—that is, until Vlasto and Baker began calling with the Ginsburg quote. McCurry, of course, ducked; he provided neither denial nor confirmation, promising only that he would check and call back. First on his list was Podesta, who said he knew nothing. Then McCurry called the president's lawyers; they too knew nothing, or feigned ignorance. Finally, he thought about asking the president, but there was no opportunity. At that time, Clinton was rushing from one meeting to another about the Middle East and preparing for the Democratic Party fund-raiser. (Besides, who would have had the courage to buttonhole him and ask, "Mr. President, have you been having an affair with one of your White House interns?") Ask Mrs. Clinton? No way. Then whom? Bruce Lindsey? But even if he knew, he would never have breathed a word about it. Lindsey was that discreet, that loyal. On a story of this sort, McCurry had few genuine options. Moreover, he wasn't sure how hard to push the White House bureaucracy, because he still didn't know for sure that the *Post* was going to publish its story the next morning.

Ever since Vlasto had called in midafternoon and dictated the Ginsburg quote to a press person, the OIC was in a frantic state. Vlasto wanted confirmation; soon Schmidt wanted confirmation, too. And then Willman and other reporters called. Was it true, they wanted to know, that the OIC was negotiating an immunity arrangement with Lewinsky's attorney, as Ginsburg told Vlasto and then Baker? And to what end? Was the OIC investigating Clinton for allegedly having encouraged Lewinsky to lie in her Jones deposition? What was the OIC's response to Ginsburg's charge that Starr and his deputies were "ravaging" his client?

The pressure on the OIC for answers became "enormous, unimaginable," according to Solomon Wisenberg, one of Starr's deputies, largely because the rules governing OIC dealings with the press were crumbling. Up to this point, only two people were authorized to talk to the press—Starr and Jackie Bennett—and only Bennett did so regularly. Now, as the

Ginsburg quote prompted a rush of press queries, Bennett found himself in the eye of a growing storm.

Bennett felt the OIC had no option but to confirm the core of the Ginsburg quote and then, with carefully timed leaks to key reporters, to disclose information helpful to Starr's case and harmful to the president's. In the early evening, with Starr's permission, Bennett began to return calls, and soon ABC, *The Washington Post,* and the *Los Angeles Times* got the confirmation they needed to proceed with their stories.

Soon thereafter, McCurry got a fresh round of calls: Could he respond to the OIC confirmation? It was the latest example of the Washington merry-go-round, and once started, it wouldn't stop until the story was published or broadcast. Then a new cycle would start all over again.

On Tuesday evening, the Democratic National Committee fund-raiser at the Corcoran Gallery of Art showcased Clintonian "compartmentaliza-tion" at its most brilliant. Watching Clinton deliver a practiced yet inspir-ing 3,932-word speech, filled with historical allusions and political challenges, no one could have imagined that he was hours away from the worst crisis of his presidency. He proudly proclaimed an era of peace and prosperity and spoke of the United States as "the greatest . . . democracy in human history," leading the information revolution, nearing a balanced budget, cutting unemployment and expanding job opportunities, stand-ing up to ethnic hatred in Bosnia, Ireland, and the Middle East. "I didn't come here tonight for a pat on the back," he said. ". . . We've got lots of time left, lots of work to do, and I want you to leave here with your energy renewed for the fights, the struggles and the issues of 1998 and beyond." For almost an hour of soaring rhetoric, it was as if the Lewinsky threat did not exist.

Behind the scene was an unfolding mystery. Hillary Clinton and Tip-per and Al Gore, who had intended to be with the president, did not attend the fund-raiser—a fact that did not seem to disturb the party faith-ful, who interrupted Clinton with bursts of sustained applause as they cel-ebrated the fifth anniversary of the Clinton-Gore administration. And yet the small pool of print reporters and cameramen noticed their absence. The other journalists were corralled into a dim basement room, where they had time to read and study the White House press release, which announced that the Clintons and the Gores would attend the fund-raiser. When reporters observed that of the four only the president was present, White House aides tried to get an explanation.

Mrs. Clinton, they finally told reporters, was suffering from back pain, and she couldn't attend. (The following day, looking radiant, she traveled to Baltimore to deliver a speech at Goucher College.) Later, more flustered by the minute, these aides returned to the basement press room to tell reporters that Tipper Gore was "not feeling well" and that the vice president had decided to accompany her to their residence on Massachusetts Avenue.

White House reporters, accustomed to White House spin, were skeptical of the official explanations. They sensed an unusually high level of anxiety among presidential advisers. Photographers, who were among the best sleuths and gossips in the White House press ensemble, were whispering among themselves, and Carl Cannon of the *National Journal* overheard one photographer telling another, "Monica's in town." Cannon, whose father, Lou, had covered the Reagan White House, had no idea who Monica was or why she was being discussed by his colleagues. Puzzled, Cannon called his bureau chief. Know anything about a Monica? he asked. His chief told him about the Ginsburg quote. Cannon knew enough to sense something big was breaking. He tried to get a reaction from White House officials, but they all stonewalled with a response that, while true, seemed evasive—that the president was returning to the Executive Mansion after the speech for a late night meeting with Israeli prime minister Netanyahu.

Of the dozens of government bureaucracies in Washington, only the White House, the Justice Department, and the OIC were working at a feverish pace on this Tuesday evening. The others had already slowed to a nighttime crawl. Of the hundreds of news bureaus, only four—*Newsweek,* ABC, the *Post,* and the *Los Angeles Times*—were producing copy about the Lewinsky scandal. The others had settled for more routine stories. Of the thousands of lawyers who occupy K Street, only a handful were busy advising the president, the intern, Tripp, and Starr. The others had retreated to family dinners in the suburbs or to business dinners in the city. Most of the nation's capital was absorbed with normal business; only a small corner of it was absorbed with final preparations for a crisis none had ever confronted before.

Judd, from her home in Chevy Chase, kept calling her key sources. At 8 p.m., she "nailed it from an impeccable source." My guess, from the evidence, is that her source was the OIC's Bennett. She denied vehemently that her source was Lucianne Goldberg. "I have never checked with Lucianne Goldberg about anything," she insisted. "Not a single story." Vlasto, from the ABC bureau, successfully reached four lawyers: David Kendall and Bob Bennett, working for the president; Francis D. Carter, who briefly helped Lewinsky; and William Hundley, who represented Jordan. With each lawyer, Vlasto unloaded his merchandise—all the elements of his story—and waited for reactions, which tended to be revealing. Kendall, for example, told him that he'd never heard of a Monica Lewinsky and doubted the story, but wanted to check further. Bennett dismissed the story, but in an unpersuasive way. Sometimes the strength of a dismissal unintentionally conveys the impression of a weak confirmation.

In any case, "everything came together on Tuesday evening," Vlasto told me. "It was a compilation of many little things. The Ginsburg quote was the major moment. He was on the record. But we also had three real good sources. What sent the story over the edge was that Ken Starr and Paula Jones became one story. Up to that point, I had covered both of them separately. Suddenly they came together." Vlasto and Judd then conferred on their next step. *Nightline*, they agreed; they would try to get their story on *Nightline*.

By 8:30 p.m., at the *Los Angeles Times*, Willman and Ostrow had the confirmations they needed to write the story—one from the OIC, presumably from Bennett; another from the Justice Department; and a third from an informed lawyer. But, according to McManus, his reporters still treated the information cautiously. For example, they did not put Lewinsky's name in the first draft until they learned that Ginsburg, soon after arriving in Los Angeles, had named her at a news conference. Then they added her name so deep into their story that it didn't appear on the front page at all. At the time, Willman and Ostrow didn't know that Lewinsky was a native of Beverly Hills.

At the *Post*, editor Bill Hamilton was looking at the clock. In another half-hour—at 9 p.m.—Len Downie and Bob Kaiser would have to make an important decision: whether to let the first edition of the paper (with a limited run of 70,000 copies) go to bed without the Lewinsky exclusive and hold it for the second edition (with a far more substantial run of 800,000 copies) later in the evening, when presumably all of the elements of the story would be confirmed to their satisfaction. In a newsroom, these are usually the most difficult decisions. Schmidt and Baker had most of the story—the sex scandal, the Ginsburg quote— but they were still seeking greater clarification of Starr's role. Hamilton had asked *Post* reporter Toni Locy, who then covered the U.S. District Court, whether she could find out from her sources at the Justice Department whether Starr's pursuit of the president was in fact based on solid legal grounds.

Locy, who was at home, knew that Schmidt had been agonizing about the story since at least Friday evening, when she had called in a sweat to say she had learned that "Isikoff's got something"—did Locy know what? No, she didn't then, but after checking with an informed source at the Justice Department, she knew now. "I lucked out," she recalled. From her source, she learned that indeed Starr had received proper authorization from the three-judge panel after his deputies had presented their evidence to Janet Reno's "shocked" officials. Locy quickly conveyed this new information to Hamilton, who brought it to Schmidt, Baker, Downie, and Kaiser. They now had the story in all its dimensions. Schmidt and Baker began to redraft it for the second edition. Downie decided to add Locy's name to this historic byline—she had produced a key element of the story. Finally, Downie asked Baker to give the White House another chance to explain the president's position.

Kendall had just sat down for dinner with his wife when the phone rang. It was Mike McCurry. "Can you take a conference call in twenty minutes?" McCurry asked. "*The Washington Post* is going with its Monica Lewinsky story." Kendall, who had been told about Lewinsky by Vlasto a few hours earlier, responded, "Who is Monica Lewinsky?" Kendall obviously wanted to appear poorly informed on the story. McCurry told him that the *Post* was probably going to report in Wednesday's paper that Starr had been authorized to investigate whether Clinton and Jordan had encouraged Lewinsky to lie about her relationship with the president. Kendall called a colleague at the Justice Department to find out whether there might be an inaccuracy in the *Post* account, some reason for asking the *Post* to delay publication. His colleague, in an attempt to be helpful, suggested that Kendall would be wise not to deny the story.

At 9 p.m., Judd called Robin Sproul, ABC's Washington bureau chief, told her the whole Lewinsky saga, and urgently suggested they organize a conference call with ABC's top brass, all of whom had congregated in Havana to oversee coverage of the pope's arrival on Wednesday. If Judd was to do the story for *Nightline*, she didn't have much time. Joining ABC chairman Roone Arledge on the phone were ABC News president David Westin, *Nightline* anchor Ted Koppel, executive producer Tom Bettag, and a number of other vice presidents and producers. Judd and Vlasto briefed the brass for forty-five minutes. They were good reporters, and they had the story—no doubt about it. Still, Bettag asked for their sources. "No way," they replied. "Take our word for it." Bettag conferred with Koppel. It was, they recognized, "a challenge—to see if we could mount a story from Cuba." They concluded, finally, that "this one demanded more, we had only part of the story, we didn't have it yet." They decided "to pass on the story. Everyone made the decision, and it was the right decision," Bettag added. Judd was furious, and she expressed her disappointment in no uncertain terms. "I was very frustrated," she said. "I wanted the story to be on the air. Our handicap was that everyone was in Cuba—a miserable way to operate."

At 9:00 p.m., Lanny Davis was at home when his pager buzzed. It was Podesta's office. Call Peter Baker, an assistant said. Odd, thought Davis. Normally, Baker would have called him directly. Davis called Baker. "Are you seated or standing?" Baker asked. "Seated," Davis replied. (Later, Davis told *Brill's Content:* "I told him he was interrupting a good scotch. He said, 'You're going to need that scotch.'") "We have a pretty important story and we need White House comment right away," Baker said. Davis asked, "What's your deadline?" Baker answered, "About ten-thirty, but we might be able to extend that if you can get us a reaction." Then Baker told Davis what the *Post* knew about the Lewinsky story. Davis promised a White House comment. Then, for a moment, he sat in shock. "This could be the worst story of the Clinton presidency," he told his incredulous wife. "It could threaten the Clinton presidency itself."

Davis called Podesta immediately. Much to his surprise, the usually overburdened Podesta picked up the phone himself. "John," Davis began, "the *Post* is running a story with three key facts confirmed, and they want our comment." Podesta asked, "What are they?" Davis answered, "First, they've confirmed that a White House intern named Monica Lewinsky claims to have had an affair with the president, and this is corroborated by tape recordings between Ms. Lewinsky and a friend. Second, they've confirmed that Ken Starr got the tapes, went to the attorney general, and has received authority from the three-judge panel to investigate the president's role, which includes possible perjury, subornation of perjury, and obstruction of justice. Finally, they've confirmed that as a result of suspicions about this affair someone at the White House caused Ms. Lewinsky to be transferred to a job in the Pentagon." Podesta sighed. "You better come down here right away," he said. Davis stressed that Baker only had an hour and a half before his final deadline. He suggested they talk to the president. Podesta replied, "I doubt it—he's with Prime Minister Netanyahu in the Oval." Diplomacy trumped scandal, but only for a while.

While driving to the White House, Davis felt his pager vibrating. "Call David Willman, *Los Angeles Times.* Urgent," it said. He expected other reporters to call, too, and a few did. Most still knew nothing about the story and had never heard of Lewinsky. Davis called Willman, who had the same story as the *Post* but with a few more details. No sooner had Davis reached his White House desk than Frank Murray of the *Washington Times* called—he implied that he had spoken with Lewinsky's lawyer, who had bad-mouthed the president. He wanted a White House response. Wolf Blitzer of CNN called—he had heard that the president had had an affair with an intern and the FBI had interviewed her. Davis pleaded for time and promised an official response; he just didn't know when.

Davis joined Podesta, McCurry, and a few others in the spacious office of White House counsel Charles Ruff. McCurry was hoping they could agree on a response. Ruff asked for more time. He called Kendall—what did he know? Kendall said he'd call back soon. And he did, with the unhappy news that the *Post* and the *Los Angeles Times* were correct. They had "the basic facts right." That still left the open question about whether Podesta, or anyone, would ask the president for guidance on a response to the press. Davis argued that it would be wiser for the White House to get its response into the *Post* now, while it still had the chance, rather than respond post facto tomorrow. No one disagreed, but no one could summon up the courage to confront the president.

At 9:52 p.m., Drudge struck again.

CONTROVERSY SWIRLS AROUND TAPES OF FORMER WHITE HOUSE INTERN, AS STARR MOVES IN! **WORLD EXCLUSIVE**

> *Federal investigators are now in possession of intimate taped conversations of a former White House intern, age 23, discussing details of her alleged sexual relationship with President Clinton, the DRUDGE REPORT has learned. The development has completely consumed high-level Washington, with Starr's investigators working past midnight in recent days.*

Now, for the first time, Drudge was reporting a *federal* investigation of the president. The big secret was out—but not yet all the way out. It was out only on the Internet—not yet in the mainstream press. But widespread dissemination could be only hours away.

At 10 p.m., Vlasto called Isikoff. "We're about to scoop you on your story," Vlasto said. The ABC producer still thought there was a chance that *Nightline* would broadcast the Lewinsky exclusive on Tuesday evening; but the decision had already been made to pass.

At 10:30 p.m., Baker called Lanny Davis. Did the White House have an official response? Baker asked. The *Post* could not wait any longer. On his own, without authority, Davis informed Baker "on deep background" that the White House had indeed confirmed that Starr had been given formal authority to investigate the president in the Lewinsky scandal. But, Davis added, he could not go any further. Perhaps Davis went this far only because he knew he was leaving his position within a week.

Davis then sent his deputy, Adam Goldberg, to the *Post*'s loading dock on 15th Street to pick up a copy of the early edition. By the time Goldberg returned empty-handed, Davis had learned that the *Post* was holding the story for the second edition and that it would not be available for distribution until after midnight.

At 11:30 p.m., Vernon Jordan shouted into his hotel phone in New

York. "Jesus! Jesus! Jesus! I never told her to lie." Jordan was talking to his lawyer, William Hundley, who had called to tell him about the *Post* story. They quickly agreed that neither would say anything to the press except that Jordan would cooperate fully with the Starr investigation.

At midnight, Clinton learned what was in the *Post* story. He called his lawyer Bob Bennett at 12:08 a.m. and spoke with him for a half-hour, after which Bennett told the *Post,* "This story seems ridiculous, and frankly I smell a rat." Then the president called and spoke with Bruce Lindsey for a half-hour. At 1:16 a.m., he called Betty Currie and spoke with her for twenty minutes. "Have you heard the latest thing that's happened?" Currie recalled him asking. He told her that she would be mentioned in the *Post* story about the Lewinsky relationship. He kept talking and talking. "I got the impression that I think he just wanted to vent or whatever. He just talked." Then, Clinton spoke once again with Lindsey and, at 2:30 a.m., left word that he was to be awakened at 7 a.m.

At 12:34 a.m., the second edition of Wednesday's *Washington Post* began to circulate through the capital. The *Post* was the first mainstream news organization to put the Lewinsky scandal on the front page. The editors then posted the whole story on their Web site.

At 12:38 a.m., Judd's account was broadcast on ABC Radio. Frustrated by *Nightline's* decision to delay her exclusive, she had written a few radio scripts and sent one to the ABC Web site. She had also written a one-page, single-spaced memo and faxed it to all the people at ABC she thought needed to know about the story. She was positive that Wednesday was going to be a very busy day.

At 1:40 a.m., Willman finally left the *Los Angeles Times* bureau in Washington. It had been a frustrating night's work. With Ostrow's approval, he had filed their story at 9:30 p.m., both reporters believing that they had three excellent sources and a full account of Starr's role in the criminal investigation of the president. They assumed that their Los Angeles editors would give quick approval to their story. They were wrong. Their editors kept stalling, communicating not with Willman but with an editor in Washington. Willman grew increasingly impatient with this three-quarter-time minuet of editorial inaction. Finally, editor in chief Michael Parks approved publication. He had delayed for two reasons: first, because Lewinsky was a local woman and the *L.A. Times* felt that it had to be absolutely certain about the facts; and second, because the paper was always uncomfortable with stories about sex. This was a story about a president having sex with a local girl. When Willman read his story in the paper, he learned that his editors had taken anonymous quotes from the *Post* story and inserted them into his own story without so much as telling him. Apparently the editors wanted to protect the *L.A. Times* from a possible lawsuit by putting a bit of editorial distance between their reporter and some of the details about the presidential affair.

CHAPTER 8

ONE SEXY SCOOP

January 21, 1998

"A TOTALLY NEW PHENOMENON. IT FELT LIKE THE WHOLE
WORLD HAD CHANGED."

—Joseph Lelyveld, *New York Times* editor

"WE WANTED TO BE FIRST, BUT WE WERE ALSO AFRAID TO BE
FIRST."

—Lisa Myers of NBC News

"NO REPORTER WANTS TO BURN HIS BRIDGES TO SOURCES."

—Evan Thomas, *Newsweek* editor

It was 7 a.m. in New York, and Lucianne Goldberg was ecstatic. "It's breaking! It's breaking!" she shouted on the phone to her son, Jonah, in Washington. "We've done it."

Goldberg, Tripp, Jones, and their lawyers, both official and unofficial, felt a sense of deep satisfaction. They had got what they wanted. They had shepherded the Lewinsky scandal through Tripp's tape recordings into Isikoff's notebooks and through their legal cabal of elves onto Starr's agenda. Then, by way of a Drudge detour on the Internet, they had planted leaks with key journalists until the story exploded on the front page of *The Washington Post* on January 21, 1998. Suddenly, all of journalism resembled an unchecked and uncheckable maelstrom of facts and hearsay, rumor and buzz that ricocheted from Drudge's Internet into the newsrooms of the *Los Angeles Times* and ABC News, from Limbaugh to Koppel. It was, *New York Times* editor Joseph Lelyveld later observed, "A totally new phenomenon . . . like the whole world had changed."

Jonah Goldberg, while denying the existence of "some grand conspiracy," basked in the reflected glow of his mother's "triumph" even two years later, echoing almost word for word what he had told Steven Brill in the summer of 1998. "Here was everything we'd done . . . breaking right there on *Good Morning America,* with Sam Donaldson standing in front of the White House and George Stephanopoulos talking . . . impeachment," he told me. His mother added perspective. "For five years," she told Brill, "I had had all kinds of Clinton stories that I had tried to peddle. Stories from state troopers, from other women, you name it. And for five years I couldn't get myself arrested. Now I was watching this [and] I was loving it. Spikey [her nickname for Isikoff] and Linda and us had really done it." And she was determined to keep the story rolling. "I wanted to keep this beast alive," she said. "I gave the *New York Post,* which I love and work for, a story a day for eight straight days."

"My mom was the only one who was absolutely truthful," declared Jonah. "She never made any secret of the fact that she really disliked Clinton."

It was not a six-column banner headline stretching across the top of *The Washington Post*—the kind that announces the election of a new president or the outbreak of war—but it was big enough: a four-column headline reading CLINTON ACCUSED OF URGING AIDE TO LIE. Beneath it was a smaller subhead: "Starr Probes Whether President Told Woman to Deny Alleged Affair to Jones's Lawyers." The story featured an unusual triple byline—"By Susan Schmidt, Peter Baker and Toni Locy"—and an extraordinarily heavy reliance on unnamed sources. It left the capital in a state of shock and every reporter in a sudden rush for information. For months, the Washington press corps had felt "irrelevant." According to Michael Oreskes, bureau chief of *The New York Times,* "They felt themselves adrift, their editors putting Washington news alongside foreign news as ignorable stuff." Now, he told me, "Monica gave them a new lease on life." And they seized it.

The *Post* story began: "Independent counsel Kenneth W. Starr has expanded his investigation of President Clinton to examine whether Clinton and his close friend Vernon E. Jordan Jr. encouraged a 24-year-old former White House intern to lie to lawyers for Paula Jones about whether the intern had an affair with the president, sources close to the investigation said yesterday."

The three reporters based much of their story on what "sources" had told them about the information on the tapes Tripp provided to Starr, which prompted him to ask the Justice Department and the three-judge panel for expanded authority. "Sources said Tripp provided Starr with audiotapes of more than 10 conversations she had with Lewinsky over recent months in which Lewinsky graphically recounted details of a year-and-a half-long affair she said she had with Clinton," they wrote. "In some of the conversations—including one in recent days—Lewinsky described Clinton and Jordan directing her to testify falsely in the Paula Jones sexual harassment case against the president, according to sources."

"It took us four or five days to get our bearings," acknowledged Joseph Lelyveld, who represented *The New York Times,* arguably the best newspaper in the country. In other newsrooms around the capital and the country, journalistic standards dipped noticeably, as reporters wrote or broadcast stories based on questionable or even nonexistent sources.

Nothing more dramatically illustrated the challenge of covering this scandal than the use or misuse of "sources." The initial *Washington Post* story ran 1,608 words. It contained four "on the record" quotes—the crucial one from Lewinsky's lawyer Ginsburg, who confirmed that Starr was "investigating his client's involvement with Clinton"; one from presidential lawyer Bob Bennett, who said the president denied any such relationship; and two brief and inconsequential quotes from lawyers Hundley and Moody. It also quoted twenty-four anonymous sources, who were loosely identified in any number of different ways. For example, there was one "sources close to the investigation," used in the lead of the story; six references to "a source" or "the source"; four "according to a source or sources"; five "source or sources familiar with" (sworn statement, job history, testimony, document, her account); one "White House officials"; one "associate"; five "a Justice Department official or officials"; and one "a colleague." The "background/on the record" ratio was an unhealthy twenty-four to four, a pattern that improved only slightly in *Post* coverage over the next few weeks.

Following a burst of criticism by scholars and media critics, the *Post* felt the need to run a special column by managing editor Kaiser explaining its reliance on anonymous sources. "Trust us," he seemed to be saying—we are no less unhappy than you about the use of anonymous sources, but in this case they are necessary if we are to tell you the whole story.

One explanation, rarely acknowledged or denied, was that *Post* reporters, especially Susan Schmidt, leaned heavily on Jackie Bennett and other sources in Starr's office, and their cooperation was based on the assumption that they would not be quoted or traced. Such background rules were not uncommon in Washington. If Schmidt (and many other reporters) had not played by these ground rules, said Toni Locy, "we would all have been dead in the water." But once playing by these ground rules, reporters found themselves excessively beholden in the early days of the scandal to the OIC version of events.

Until the breaking of this story, *The Washington Post* had rigorously abided by its two-source rule, imposed by Ben Bradlee during the Watergate scandal. If a reporter did not have two sources for each fact, then he or she could not use the fact. During the first few days of the Lewinsky scandal, though, the *Post* often disregarded its own rule, especially on the use of anonymous sources. For example, according to one reliable study, only 16 percent of its reporting depended on named sources. Thirty-eight percent was based on two anonymous sources, and 26 percent on one anonymous source—meaning at least 64 percent of its early reporting was based on anonymous sourcing, more than triple the *Post*'s average.

But in these early hours of the Lewinsky scandal, as Lucianne Goldberg danced a jig of joy in her New York apartment, dozens of reporters and cameramen raced to battle positions at the White House and the OIC, and pundits had their noses powdered in television green rooms, no one was counting sources. For the second time in the last quarter of the century, the *Post* had mounted a journalistic assault against a sitting president, and everyone—*everyone!*—wanted to get a piece of the action.

NBC's *Today* dominated—and still dominates—the morning television ratings, but on January 21, 1998, ABC's *Good Morning America* was the place for breaking news. At 7 a.m., anchor Lisa McRee breathlessly reported "explosive new allegations" that "strike at the very heart of the presidency." With Jackie Judd and Bill Kristol in Washington, Sam Donaldson at the White House, George Stephanopoulos in Birmingham, Alabama, Jeffrey Toobin in New York, and Cokie Roberts and Peter Jennings in Havana, ABC fielded an all-star team to cover and comment on the breaking Lewinsky scandal.

Although *Newsweek, The Washington Post,* and the *Los Angeles Times* also had a rather large hand in breaking this story, *Good Morning America* proclaimed (for the purposes of pride and publicity) that Judd "broke this story overnight," as though she were flying solo. She opened the first segment of the two-hour program with a comprehensive report based on both her reporting and Vlasto's. Like the Schmidt-Baker-Locy "exclusive" in the *Post,* Judd also used the Ginsburg and Bennett quotes and then eight anonymous sources. Twice she exploited the promotional gimmick— "ABC News has learned . . . ," meaning the reporter offers information without any personal, political, or geographic indication of origin. Five times she resorted to variations of "sources" ("a source," "the source," "another source," and "according to sources"), and once, when discussing the attitude of the "Starr investigation," she spoke of "investigators" as the source of her observation, suggesting she was using the plural to conceal the identity of a single person in the OIC, who was probably Jackie Bennett or someone speaking on his behalf.

After Judd's hard news report, the rest of the program was devoted to a combination of gossip, analysis, and speculation—punditry at its least responsible—which became the hallmark of television news coverage of the scandal. On *Good Morning America,* in those early days, 72 percent of all of its statements were based on anonymous sources or characterized as analysis or punditry, as distinct from hard reporting—that is, the conveying of clearly sourced fact; 46 percent of all statements on *Today;* 72 percent on *Larry King Live;* 64 percent on ABC's *World News Tonight;* 72 percent on the *CBS Evening News;* 70 percent on NBC's *Nightly News;* 81 percent on CNN; and 48 percent on *Nightline.* What that meant was that most of what the public heard and saw was unsourced, speculative, or derivative.

Shortly after 7 a.m., before Sam Donaldson could even have made his usual round of checks, he was already on network television saying: "The danger here . . . is very, very great. If Kenneth Starr can mount sufficient evidence that the president of the United States told this young lady to lie, that's a federal crime, that's suborning perjury. And, clearly, a serious impeachment investigation would begin on Capitol Hill." Donaldson, while urging caution, referred to the *Post* and Judd reports as "shocking evidence," and argued that "from the standpoint of the president," Lewinsky had "to be destroyed." He explained, "I mean by that . . . any suggestion of these tapes that he put the arm on her to lie must somehow be destroyed." Impeachment, he said, adding historical perspective to his analysis, was a "political judgment" that depended on "the court of public opinion." Donaldson's analysis was prophetic. Clinton would be impeached by the House of Representatives, but a year later, public opinion, among other things, saved him from conviction in the Senate. But at the time Donaldson was engaging in nothing more than speculation.

By 8 a.m., Donaldson had spoken briefly with Mike McCurry and Vernon Jordan. McCurry was quoted as saying, "I don't know anything one way or the other," and Jordan went no further than "No comment." But ABC's veteran White House correspondent chose to up the ante anyway. "An impeachment investigation will begin on Capitol Hill of a very serious nature," he said, if it could be proven that Clinton urged Lewinsky to lie. Stephanopoulos, now a Donaldson colleague, jumped on the impeachment bandwagon. He said he had talked to "some people in the White House," and they all agreed that the scandal stories were "probably the most serious allegations yet leveled against the president. There's no question that . . . if they're true, they're not only politically damaging, but it could lead to impeachment proceedings." Yes, Donaldson agreed, but since impeachment was "a political question," public opinion was crucial, and the president's "popularity rating" was 64 percent—too high, he suggested, for a successful impeachment drive.

President Clinton was awakened at 7 a.m. He called one of his top lawyers, Kendall, at 7:30 a.m. and spoke to him for a half-hour. He called his other principal lawyer, Bob Bennett, at 8 a.m., and spoke to him for fifteen minutes. To both, Clinton denied the *Post* story. He lied to his own lawyers.

At 7:45 a.m., the president's chief of staff, Erskine Bowles, a successful southern businessman, convened a meeting of his shaken senior staff, many of whom had not slept all night. They were anxious, disappointed, and angry. Bowles delivered an odd kind of pep talk. Looking for shafts of light in the dark clouds, he reminded his grim staff that Clinton had faced similar crises in the past—and survived and even flourished. He urged everyone to concentrate on their jobs; there was work to do. Then, in a determined effort to convey the impression that normal White House business would continue despite the scandal reports, he asked Gene Sperling, one of Clinton's chief domestic advisers, to discuss tax policy proposals the president intended to reveal during his State of the Union Address.

Sperling lectured to his distracted colleagues. "There's an air of unreality here," one senior aide later told a reporter.

Lewinsky was stunned when she saw the morning paper. Quickly, she turned on the television set. She was on every channel, everywhere, her life suddenly and radically altered. She spoke with Ginsburg, furious about his sharply negative characterization of the president. "Once the story broke," she told her official biographer, "we stayed inside and this whirlwind roared around our heads. Everyone was talking about him having to resign. I couldn't believe that. I was still very much in love with the president, very protective of him and I did not appreciate Bill Ginsburg saying that he was a misogynist. At the same time, there was a sense of frustration because these charges were simply not true. He never told me to lie."

At 8 a.m., Evelyn Lieberman, who as White House deputy chief of staff had exiled Lewinsky to the Pentagon in the spring of 1996, walked briskly into her morning editorial meeting as the recently appointed head of the Voice of America (VOA). Lieberman had already read the *Post*. Her Washington-based staff of editors, reporters, and broadcasters was linked, by way of a special audio hookup, to all foreign bureaus of the VOA. Everyone was waiting anxiously for Lieberman's first big decision: How would the VOA handle the delicate matter of a White House sex scandal?

Lieberman turned to her deputy and asked for his ten top stories. The deputy complied, putting Lewinsky in the eighth slot. "What? Are you mad?" she exclaimed. "She's the lead story everywhere. Move it up. Move it up." It was the right journalistic decision. The VOA treated the Lewinsky story as if it were any other news organization, not as a government agency under orders to protect the president. In the past, the VOA had often got into trouble for wrapping the truth in propaganda handouts. Not on this occasion.

McCurry joined a small group of White House lawyers meeting at 8 a.m. in the spacious office of White House counsel Charles Ruff to review a press statement that Ruff had drafted and that McCurry had just cleared with the president. The draft said that Clinton was "outraged by these allegations" and that "he never had a sexual relationship with this woman."

When he was in the Oval Office, McCurry wondered, did Clinton have *any* relationship with Lewinsky? McCurry, sensing the extraordinary sensitivity of the moment, chose not to raise this question with the president. He had told Clinton, who seemed very subdued, "I'm going to make it clear that I'm saying this on your behalf." Clinton agreed.

Normally, when the White House confronted a major problem, the legal and political advisers to the president clashed and produced radically different recommendations. The lawyers were cautious—they weighed every word, worrying more about the legal implications of a statement than about politics or public opinion. The political pros were bolder—they, too, worried about every word, but they were ready to take risks to protect the president's image and popularity, his policy program and legacy. On this very special morning, Lanny Davis recalled, one lawyer suggested they change "sexual" to "improper," and McCurry agreed. No one argued about it, even though they recognized that the press would jump on the difference between "improper" and "sexual." "The usual atmosphere and routine in our damage-control sessions seemed to be virtually inoperative," Davis wrote. "It was a different, almost surreal atmosphere. All our usual instincts were frozen. . . . We just sat in silence. There was no real debate."

Before Lewinsky loomed as a threat to the Clinton administration, McCurry had scheduled three interviews for the afternoon of January 21, 1998, with Jim Lehrer of PBS's *NewsHour*, Mort Kondracke of *Roll Call*, and Mara Liasson and Robert Siegel of NPR's *All Things Considered*. Someone asked whether it was a good idea for the president to do these interviews. Instead of focusing on his State of the Union speech, they would obviously be focusing on Lewinsky and Starr. Should the interviews be canceled, perhaps postponed? Everyone understood that a decision to cancel the interviews would be widely interpreted as proof that the president was in serious trouble. On the other hand, proceeding with the interviews opened him to phenomenal embarrassment and political danger. Yet no one argued one way or the other. "The atmosphere of intellectual and political paralysis was palpable," recalled Davis.

Early Wednesday morning, Jill Abramson, Washington enterprise editor for *The New York Times*, picked up her copy of *The Washington Post* and knew instantly that the *Times* had been scooped; but she later admitted, "I still didn't grasp how big a story this would turn out to be." A tough, curious reporter who had done her share of investigative reporting for *The Wall Street Journal* before joining the *Times*, Abramson enjoyed gossiping with "colleagues from other news organizations, picking up leads, threads, knowing what others were going to publish or broadcast. But in this case," she said, "I was not plugged in." Ordinarily, she would have known about the gathering storm—a sense of an imminent story, a hint about *Newsweek*'s decision on Saturday to postpone publication, a whisper about Drudge filling the Internet with sensational stories, or about the *Post, Time,* and ABC digging into Starr's expanded mandate. "I simply didn't know," she admitted, "and that's not like me."

She didn't rush to the office. At 8 a.m., as if it were just another day, she went to the "Y" for her daily workout, and at 9 a.m. she joined the other *Times* editors and reporters at the Corcoran Gallery for a special exhibition of an artist's version of *Times* front pages from 1996. Everyone was there, including bureau chief Mike Oreskes. By 10 a.m., they all started to leave for the office.

At 10:30 a.m., Oreskes opened a memorable meeting of shaken reporters and editors. They had been embarrassed and humiliated. Not a single one of them had written a word about the story. From New York, Lelyveld, his back against the journalistic wall, e-mailed a message of encouragement to Oreskes and his troops—let's rally and cover the story. He was, he later said, "very unhappy," but he had no option but to encourage his reporters to go out and produce their own scoops.

Oreskes, who had been bureau chief for less than a year, explained his thinking at the time. "From the moment Ken Starr was given jurisdiction over the Lewinsky matter, the issue for us changed entirely," he told a group of editors in October 1998. "Now we had a duly constituted prosecutor conducting a criminal investigation of the President of the United States. There were lots of questions for the society—and thus for us—about how this investigation came to be. But there was no longer any question that it was a story, a message I had to deliver very clearly that first difficult morning, the morning that our competitors had broken the story. I had a group of reporters that needed to know. Some of them wondered even at that point whether we wanted to be in this one. . . . I explained that we were in this now, and if we were going to do it, we were going to do it to our standards."

His message delivered, Oreskes deployed his reporters. Jeff Gerth, one of the *Times*'s many investigative reporters, was quickly able to confirm the major elements of the *Post* account of the new White House scandal, and Abramson began to look for new angles that had not yet been explored.

The *Times* was not alone in Washington in its belated awakening to the Lewinsky scandal. With few exceptions, every newsroom was surprised and stunned by the story.

Frank Sesno, bureau chief of CNN, sensed "something in the air," but he knew nothing about the scandal until he read the *Post* account. Once he read it, he thought Clinton was "toast." His successor as White House correspondent, Wolf Blitzer, had heard about an intern (even checked inconclusively with one official on Tuesday evening), but, like Sesno, he really knew nothing until he read the *Post* on Wednesday morning. Once he read it, "there was no question where most of the story was coming from," he said—the OIC.

David Mazzarella, then editor of *USA Today,* later recalled that he was "totally in the dark" until Wednesday morning, when he picked up the *Post.* His first of three daily editorial meetings was originally scheduled for 10:30 a.m. On this morning, it was held at 9:45 a.m. "Like the *Times,* we were playing catch-up journalism from day one. . . . My directions were simple: we were to be extra careful with this story. There had already been too much sensationalism. I wanted our coverage to be clear, unbiased and not sensational."

Les Crystal, executive producer of PBS's *NewsHour,* had been planning Lehrer's interview with the president for weeks. "When I opened my door and saw the headlines in the *Post* and realized it was the same day as our interview, 'Oh my God,' I thought, 'Oh, my God!' The White House will surely cancel it."

Lisa Myers, NBC's chief political reporter, was covering the travels of House Speaker Newt Gingrich. Every morning during the trip, she would call the executive producer of *Nightly News* to see if he thought she had enough for an offering. On this morning, the producer wasn't even listening to her pitch. "We just got creamed by ABC," he screamed. "Creamed!" He gave her the headlines of the *Post* and ABC stories about Lewinsky. Myers remembered, "We didn't have much of anything."

Jim Warren, bureau chief of the *Chicago Tribune,* shared the same sense of shock when he picked up his copy of *The Washington Post* that morning. He knew nothing about the expanded Starr investigation of the president and the intern, but he made one immediate and important decision. Nothing would be reported in the *Tribune* unless his reporters could independently confirm the information, even if that meant the *Tribune* would miss the story.

At 12:19 p.m., Drudge ran an alert on his Web site, no longer easily dismissible on this story.

LEWINSKY NIGHTMARE CONTINUES

UN Ambassador Richardson offered me a job during breakfast meeting at Watergate Hotel, she said; Investigators probe possibility of Clinton DNA....

DNA? What was he talking about? The only journalist who knew was Isikoff, and he was not about to report it.

McCurry was late for the daily press briefing at the White House, but this time he had a good reason. He knew it was going to be hell. For more than a year, the White House press corps had felt that the president was "slip-sliding his way through the scandalous muck," to quote *Washington Post* media reporter Howard Kurtz. But not any longer. Not after the *Post* and ABC had set off their bombshells that morning.

At last, McCurry, looking somber, entered the briefing room. It was a standing-room-only crowd. Cameras squeezed into the tight space behind the wooden seats. Photographers crouched in front of the podium. CNN, Fox, and MSNBC were carrying the briefing live. McCurry read the Ruff draft, cleared by Clinton, denying "any improper relationship" with Lewinsky. The room erupted with questions, and this tumultuous scene was transmitted live throughout the nation and the world. What did he mean by "improper"?

"I'm not going to parse the statement," McCurry answered.

NBC's Claire Shipman: "Does that mean no sexual relationship?"
McCurry: "Claire, I'm just not going to parse the statement for you;
   it speaks for itself."

NBC's David Bloom: "Mike, would it be improper for the President
of the United States to have had a sexual relationship with
this woman?"

McCurry: "You can stand here and ask a lot of questions over and
over again and will elicit the exact same answer."

Bloom: "So, Mike, you're willing to . . ."

McCurry: "I'm not leaving any impression, David, and don't twist my
words."

The Washington Post's John Harris: "Would you be up here today if
you were not absolutely confident these are not true?"

McCurry: "Look, my personal views don't count. I'm here to represent the thinking, the actions, the decisions of the president.
That's what I get paid to do."

The *New York Post*'s Deborah Orin: "What is puzzling to many of us
is that we've invited you probably two dozen times today to
say there was no sexual relationship with this woman and
you have not done so."

McCurry: "But the President has said he never had any improper
relationship with this woman. I think that speaks for itself."

ABC's Donaldson: "Why not put the word 'sexual' in?"

McCurry: "I didn't write the statement."

A reporter asked McCurry whether he knew anything about UN
Ambassador Richardson offering a job to Lewinsky. The spokesman
ducked—he knew nothing about the subject, raised fleetingly by Drudge
on his Web site.

The briefing lasted thirty-six minutes—agonizing for McCurry and
electrifying for reporters. At the end, a reporter shouted: "Mike, what's
your next move, or counsel's next move, or the President's next move?"
McCurry tried humor for an exit line. "My next move," he shot back, "is to
get off this podium."

He retreated hastily to his office, while the reporters rushed to their
cubicles. For the next year, what Susan Schmidt and Michael Weisskopf
called "the political story of a generation" would dominate their personal
and professional lives.

The press briefing offers a picture window on what preoccupies
Washington reporters. Had Lewinsky not popped out of the White

House cake on January 21, 1998, two major stories would have dominated the agenda: the president's upcoming State of the Union Address and the U.S. military buildup against Iraq. Ordinarily, reporters would have focused their questions on these stories—but not on this day, nor on others over the next year leading to the House impeachment of President Clinton.

The pattern was set on January 21. McCurry was asked 128 questions in his 36-minute briefing, 113 of which (88 percent) related to the Lewinsky story. Fifteen questions concerned other matters, such as Iraq. On January 22, he was asked 97 questions, 81 of which (83 percent) concerned Lewinsky. Sixteen questions addressed other matters, mostly Iraq. On January 23, he was asked 79 questions, 52 of which (66 percent) concerned Lewinsky and 27 of which focused on domestic and foreign issues to be raised in Clinton's speech. On January 26, the following Monday, the day before the speech, McCurry was asked 117 questions, 84 of which (72 percent) concerned Lewinsky and 33 of which concerned other issues. On the day of the president's speech, when often there is no formal briefing, McCurry convened a short one. Not to his surprise, 85 percent of the questions touched on the scandal.

All told, in the week beginning with January 21, 1998, 75 percent of all questions directed at McCurry during his midday briefings concerned the breaking scandal. These exchanges rained down on all newsrooms and radio and television talk shows, sparking a round of sensational stories on Capitol Hill and encouraging a flow of leaks from Starr's OIC headquarters.

At 1:42 p.m., Drudge amplified his earlier alert. On his Web site was the usual "**WORLD EXCLUSIVE**" but this time added to his eye-catching logo was the alluring phrase: CONTAINS GRAPHIC DESCRIPTIONS. The story did, unmistakably.

The *Drudge* item contained two pieces of new information: first, that Lewinsky had told Tripp in December 1997 that Richardson had offered her a job at the United Nations; and second, that she had kept "a garment with Clinton's dried semen on it—a garment she allegedly said she would never wash." Drudge continued, "investigators have become convinced that there may be a DNA trail that could confirm President Clinton's sexual involvement with Lewinsky, a relationship that was captured in Lewinsky's own voice on audio tape." Goldberg had struck again. It would not now be long before the dress/DNA/semen story leaped onto the front pages of the mainstream press.

For PBS's Jim Lehrer, January 21, 1998 was to be a special day. On his calendar, confirmed by McCurry only the day before, was an interview with the president. Actually, the interview originally had been scheduled for mid-December, but a *New York Times* interview at that time had produced so much news that McCurry was under fire from White House reporters to shoehorn a press conference into the president's busy schedule. Clinton wouldn't tolerate both a press conference and a *NewsHour* interview in the same week, so Lehrer was asked to wait until the third week of January. That morning, as he looked in astonishment at the front page of the *Post*, he wondered whether he would have to wait a bit longer.

His executive producer, Les Crystal, a former president of NBC News, shared that same sense of uncertainty. Crystal rushed to his office. Everyone there expected the interview to be canceled. The *NewsHour* crew arrived at the White House at 9:30 a.m., as scheduled, and, Crystal recalled, everything seemed fine. An hour later, the crew called and said that the interview was being delayed until 3:30 p.m. Crystal had planned to tape and possibly edit the interview, but now he decided to feed it live to the studio, still in plenty of time for the 6 p.m. broadcast. Another complication intervened, though. "Everyone was calling us for a live feed," Crystal remembered. After much deliberation, he agreed to give a short live feed to ABC and CNN, but then realized that he couldn't pick and choose among the radio and television networks. Give to one, give to all.

After lunch, when Crystal joined Lehrer for the ride to the White House, the cool, unflappable anchor "was absorbed with the question of how far he could go with Monica." They decided that Lehrer would begin and end the interview with the Lewinsky scandal. The White House, Crystal noted, was "filled with tension. Everyone there was thinking about the scandal, but not talking about it." Shortly after 3:30 p.m., the president, looking puffy and slightly dazed, entered the room with his dog, Buddy, "which produced a few laughs and that helped ease the tension somewhat."

In his opening question, Lehrer paraphrased the *Post* lead, asking the president whether he had asked Lewinsky to lie about their relationship. "Is that true?" Lehrer wanted to know.

"That is not true," the president responded. "That is not true. I did not ask anyone to tell anything other than the truth. There is no improper relationship."

Lehrer pressed a bit harder. He asked the president to define "no improper relationship."

The president answered: "Well, I think you know what it means. It means that there is not a sexual relationship, an improper sexual relationship or any other kind of improper relationship."

Lehrer: "You had no sexual relationship with this young woman?"
Clinton: "There is not a sexual relationship. That is accurate."

The president's apparently deliberate use of the present tense exploded like a thousand firecrackers at the White House. Reporters used to parsing Clinton's rubbery language instantly latched on to "is." NPR's Mara Liasson, watching the PBS feed from the newsroom, later remembered: "We went wild. It was, like, Aaaaagghh!" NBC's Claire Shipman called Lanny Davis. "Did you notice he used the present tense?" she remarked. "Come on, Claire, give me a break," Davis answered. "That wasn't intentional. He's denying there was a sexual relationship. Period." Dozens of other reporters called with the same question. *Newsweek*'s McDaniel watched Clinton's denials and wondered: "How can he stand there and lie?" McCurry, also watching, was not sure the president was denying a sexual relationship. He thought the president was transparently evasive. "Well, that was a disaster," he told his staff. "We've got to do something." Crystal, who was with Lehrer and Clinton, was one of the few journalists who missed the "is" explosion. "I didn't sense that he was parsing his words so carefully," he said. "My sense at the time was that the president was flatly denying the story."

After the PBS interview, McCurry flew to Clinton's side. "Look, you used the present tense," he said. "Were you meaning to communicate anything?"

"Oh, no, no, no, no," Clinton answered.

Mort Kondracke then called for his telephone interview, as planned. He too thought the president's use of "is" was a lawyerly way of ducking the question of whether there "was" a sexual relationship. This time, Clinton's answer was even more puzzling to reporters, because he used both "is" and "was" in his responses. "It is not an improper relationship," Clinton said, "and I know what you mean, and the answer is no."

"*Was* it in any way sexual?" Kondracke put special emphasis on "was."

"The relationship *was* not sexual," the president replied firmly.

At 4:40 p.m., it was NPR's turn. Robert Siegel of *All Things Considered* joined his colleague, Mara Liasson, and they both went into the Oval Office, where the president awaited them. The questions were the same, but the answer was a presidential attempt to squelch the budding "is/was" controversy. "I think it's more important for me to tell the American people that there wasn't improper relations." Clinton created what was to become a self-justifying mantra—that he had been elected to do a difficult job, that "some people" resented his political triumph, that he had to "box out" the scandal hullabaloo. He would cooperate with Starr, he would tell the truth.

The White House press corps was not buying this line—they had heard it all before. By the time Lehrer and Crystal returned to their office, there were dozens of calls and questions about "is" and "was." "I'll never forget it," Crystal said. "Never."

Whether Hillary Rodham Clinton knew of her husband's relationship with Monica Lewinsky before it erupted into a national scandal may have to await her memoirs—or his. Although she had complained of a backache on Tuesday evening severe enough to keep her from accompanying her husband to the fund-raiser at the Corcoran Gallery, she kept to her schedule on Wednesday, including a speech at Goucher College in Baltimore. She might have intended to discuss matters of public policy, but her suddenly ballooning press corps had Monica in mind. "Can you say," one reporter shouted, "that you flatly believe these latest accusations are false?" The first lady replied: "Certainly I believe they're false. Absolutely." She was then asked if the publicity pained her personally. Mrs. Clinton acknowledged the obvious. "You know," she said, "I wouldn't say that it is not hard. It is difficult and painful anytime someone you care about, you love, you admire is attacked and subjected to such relentless accusations as my husband has been. But I also have now lived with this for more than six years. And I have seen how these charges evaporate and disappear as they're given the light of day."

One of the journalistic ironies of the day was that the president's televised denials appeared on ABC, CBS, CNN, Fox, and NBC (and its cable outlets) before they could be seen on PBS, which conducted the interview. The reason was that PBS would not allow its schedule of programs to be interrupted by news. Still, the *NewsHour* had the whole interview and ran it, thereby providing the public with a very special service.

The live network inserts began at 3:32 p.m., when ABC anchor Peter Jennings broke into the network from Havana, where he was awaiting the arrival of Pope John Paul II, to report the president's first official response to the breaking Lewinsky scandal. (Ted Koppel had already left Cuba to return to Washington so he could more effectively anchor *Nightline* from the scene of the scandal.) Two minutes later, NBC's Tom Brokaw, also in Havana, opened his coverage of the scandal. More than twenty minutes later, at 3:58 p.m., Dan Rather cut into CBS's regularly scheduled soap operas.

The ABC insert featured excerpts from the PBS interview, in which the president denied that he had asked anyone to lie or had an "improper, sexual" relationship with Lewinsky, and then commentary from Cokie Roberts in Havana and Jackie Judd, Bill Kristol, and George Stephanopoulos in Washington. "The next three years of the Clinton presidency," opined Stephanopoulos, "rest on the shoulders of Monica Lewinsky." The former White House aide had called many of his old colleagues. "They were up all night," he said. "There were also conference calls through the night and into the morning, right up until noon today with lawyers, political aides in the White House. This has, for better, for worse, consumed the White House this morning. And people are a little bit shellshocked, a little bit depressed." Cokie Roberts noted that the president had been "quite unequivocal" about denying a sexual relationship with Lewinsky, "but unfortunately," she added, "this president is not always believed." Bill Kristol said that the president had been "dodging bullets" for five years but that this crisis, he felt, was "different."

The NBC insert also showed excerpts of presidential denials, but Tim Russert's commentary later drew critical fire as an example of an unnecessarily hasty judgment call. The Washington bureau chief seemed to be predicting a Clinton resignation within days. "The next 48 to 72 hours are critical," he said. At one point, quoting "one of President Clinton's best and dearest friends," Russert said the friend told him that if Starr "sets us up, we will get him and destroy him." But if the president "lied . . . and obstructed justice, he's going to have to leave town in disgrace." Russert added, "One of these men, Bill Clinton or Ken Starr, has a terrible week ahead of them."Russert explained a year and a half later that he had spoken with "key close aides" to the president, who told him they believed Clinton's denials but were also prepared to be bitterly disappointed in him. Russert said he was merely reflecting and reporting their feelings. "Given Clinton's past record," Russert went on, "a number of aides kept wondering" if he wasn't in fact lying to them to keep his job and to protect his family.

The evening newscasts opened with the day's events, each running at least three stories about the Lewinsky scandal but adding nothing new to the mix. ABC, CBS, and NBC each ran a story about allegations of a Clinton-Lewinsky affair, another story about the relationship between Tripp and Lewinsky, and a third about how Starr became involved in the investigation. For the many millions of Americans who caught only snatches of gossip at the office during the day and wanted a clear review of the day's dramatic events when they got home, the three network news programs provided the perfect cocktail of information, rumor, analysis, and speculation. In recent years, the evening newscasts have rarely been watched for breaking news so much as for a review and analysis of news read in the morning paper or heard on the drive home.

That evening, none of the three flagship news programs ran a separate story on a major development that came across their fax machines at exactly 6:43 p.m. It was a press release from Revlon. "Monica Lewinsky," it read, "was referred to MacAndrews & Forbes by Vernon Jordan, a member of the board of directors of Revlon, a MacAndrews affiliate, for a possible entry-level public relations position." The Revlon press release then went on to say that MacAndrews & Forbes had offered her a job but was now rescinding it—obviously because Lewinsky had become, to quote Jackie Bennett, "radioactive."

Isikoff, who had been angry for days, as the *Post,* ABC, and the *Los Angeles Times* moved into position to break *his* story, smiled for the first time on Wednesday. "What do you know? I thought. It's true. It really is all true." Though he knew more than any other reporter about the Lewinsky story, he still hungered for more information and confirmation. And here was Revlon admitting that a member of its own board of directors was using his influence to get a job for Lewinsky out of Washington, out of government, out of the president's hair; in other words, one of the president's best friends was doing Lewinsky a favor, perhaps to purchase her cooperation. Legally, this proved little, but it was highly suggestive of suborning perjury and obstructing justice. It played to Starr's needs—and to Isikoff's.

There were times that Wednesday when neither Isikoff nor McDaniel thought life was fair. This was, after all, their story—*Newsweek's* story— and yet their competitors were capturing much of the glory. For McDaniel, the day had started very early. At 1:30 a.m., a journalist friend, who had been an editor at the *Post* but now worked for *U.S. News & World Report,* woke her with a depressing report. "Now I know what was wrong with you," he said. They had been at a party Monday evening, and McDaniel had struck him as especially withdrawn and preoccupied. When he asked what was wrong, she had replied, "I just can't tell you." Now he understood her problem. "Sorry to upset you, but I think you are going to want to see *The Washington Post.*"

What McDaniel had feared for days had apparently happened. By deciding not to publish on Saturday, *Newsweek's* editors knew they would be running the risk of seeing their scoop reported by others. McDaniel couldn't go back to sleep. What could she do? She wanted to make sure that Isikoff got the credit he deserved. McDaniel began to consider a totally different, unorthodox option—the possibility of breaking the story on *Newsweek's* Web site. For a journalist of the old school, this was a revolutionary idea. "We had never broken a major story on the Web before," she said. Newsweek.com was "an important part of our operation," but it was untested in the big leagues of competitive journalism. The Web was still considered somewhat flaky, a place for Matt Drudge perhaps, but not for *Newsweek.* "To make the first big offering on your Web site be perhaps the most controversial story you've ever had. . . ." McDaniel shrugged her shoulders.

Now, with dawn still hours away, she outlined the story, highlighting key points of continuing exclusivity, and strengthened her argument for publication on the Web. At the crack of dawn, she called Richard Smith, her editor in New York, informed him of the *Post* publication, and made her pitch. Smith asked, "Can we write it slightly differently on the Web than we would in print?" Yes, she replied—how about doing it as a diary? Go for it, he said.

On Wednesday morning, McDaniel turned to Isikoff and Thomas—Isikoff the reporter, the ultimate expert on this story; Thomas the better writer, the fastest edit man in the business. Write it, she said—crash for our Web site. All day, Isikoff and Thomas wrote, edited, and added to "Diary of a Scandal," their long rendition of Isikoff's controversial and pivotal sleuthing. It was a day-by-day account, starting on January 12 and ending on January 19. They were trying to be fast and accurate. They had more information on this story than any other reporters in Washington, but combing through dozens of Isikoff's notebooks took time. In the end, they produced a 10,000-word essay that included most of the journalistic gems Isikoff had accumulated: Lewinsky's history, Starr's strategy, Tripp's maneuvers, and above all, the tapes. Since the *Newsweek* group had actually heard one or more of the tapes, they were able to provide a far more nuanced account of the charges against Jordan and Clinton than the journalists who had to rely on secondhand reports from the OIC.

In the course of the day they came up with a major new piece of what the Starr team regarded as damaging evidence: "talking points" that Lewinsky had given to Tripp on January 14 with suggestions for her affidavit to the Jones lawyers regarding her former friend Kathleen Willey. According to Isikoff and Thomas, the "talking points" urged Tripp "to modify comments she had made to *Newsweek* back in July—that she had seen Willey coming out of the Oval Office with her make-up smeared." Lewinsky suggested instead that Tripp "tell Jones's lawyers that 'you do not believe that what she claimed happened really happened. You now find it completely plausible that she herself smeared her lipstick, untucked her blouse, etc.'" Starr assumed that Lewinsky did not write these talking points herself, and he was "investigating whether the instructions came from Jordan or other friends of the president."

Finally, Isikoff and Thomas added the Revlon nugget and submitted the "Diary" to McDaniel. She cleared it with her senior editors in New

York. Isikoff was delighted. "We had a ton of exclusive material," he later wrote. "We were in the middle of this story. The public was starving for details. We should tell them what we know." At around 7 p.m., *Newsweek* made journalistic history by putting a story of this magnitude on its Web site. "Clinton Accused," the headline read, as Isikoff's reporting, denied its debut on Saturday, burst into cyberspace on *Newsweek Interactive*. The Associated Press immediately plucked the "Diary" clean for the wires. The evening talk shows feasted on it. *Newsweek* reporters and editors appeared on many interview programs. Their reporting later won a number of journalistic awards, including a National Magazine Award.

On Wednesday evening, CBS, NBC, and ABC each ran a "Special Report." CNN ran four "Breaking News" bulletins. Talk shows went absolutely wild. Ginsburg appeared on *Rivera Live!* on CNBC, the first of dozens of interviews he was to give over the next few days. Against this frenetic backdrop, the president donned a black tie and Mrs. Clinton a formal evergreen suit as they hosted a gala fund-raiser at the White House, yet another stunning example of "compartmentalization." They ignored the press and smiled for their guests as they turned their attention to celebrating the preservation of the "historic glory" of the White House, for which they had helped raise an estimated $25 million. One guest, a longtime admirer of Clinton, later told me that he stood in dumbfounded astonishment at Clinton's performance. "He was backslapping his way through the crowd," this businessman recalled, "shaking hands, laughing, as though nothing else was going on. I thought he was going to cancel the whole thing."

"You poor son of a bitch." Not exactly a proper way of addressing the president of the United States. Yet, in this circumstance, if anyone could employ profanity, it was Dick Morris, the Clinton consultant who was bounced from the 1996 presidential campaign for his own sexual indiscretion. Clinton had called him in the morning for advice, and Morris had recommended a private poll. Clinton tried to explain himself: "I didn't do what they said I did. I've tried to shut myself down, sexually, I mean. But sometimes I slipped up, and with this girl I just slipped up." Late that night, Morris telephoned with the results. The American people, he said,

One Sexy Scoop -147-

would forgive Clinton for adultery, but if he were guilty of lying and obstructing justice, 56 percent thought he should be removed from office. "Well," Clinton said, "we'll just have to win then."

Having passed on the Lewinsky story the night before, anchor Ted Koppel and producer Tom Bettag, back at their *Nightline* desks at 1717 DeSales Street, were certain that Clinton would try to spin his way out of this mess too, just as he had so many others over the years. But this time, like other Washington reporters repeatedly outmaneuvered by a White House battalion of master spin merchants, they were determined that he would not succeed. Bettag later said: "We have had a complicated relationship with the White House. They've used us, and we've used them."

The story, as Bettag saw it, was a titanic struggle between a president and a prosecutor, and it was not a new one. "We devoted lots of time to the Whitewater scandal, well before Monica," Bettag explained, "and the White House was furious with us then too." Ann Lewis, a Clinton adviser, counted the number of times *Nightline* had directed its critical fire at the Whitewater scandal. "Forty-seven times," she said. Lewis wanted to be clear that she respected Koppel, but really couldn't figure out why he appeared to be so determined to "attack us relentlessly, to get us." Bettag believed that "the American people needed a cool place to reflect on this scandal—we could provide that space; few others could."

On Wednesday night, *Nightline* opened an extraordinary series of fifteen broadcasts, night after night, devoted exclusively to different aspects of the Lewinsky scandal. In its unrelenting preoccupation with the scandal, the best of late night television news was no different from the cable talk shows that couldn't get enough of Monica. "Crisis in the White House" was the most commonly used title, but some broadcasts were called "The First Family in Full Battle Regalia," "White House Intern," "Who is Ken Starr?" and "The Clintons versus the Media and the Right Wing."

Bettag later proudly reflected on the series. "We helped people sort out a complicated story every day," he told me. "It was a real story, with a real voice. We were not alarmist, we were analytical. I feel very good about what we did. I don't feel that I have betrayed any of my principles."

Koppel, opening his broadcast, felt the need to explain why he had decided not to devote his Tuesday program to the Clinton/Lewinsky scandal even though his colleague Jackie Judd had the story. "It was clearly an important story," Koppel told his viewers, "but to rush something that explosive on the air, to shoehorn it in at the last minute into a photograph that was primarily about the Pope's visit and its impact on Cuban and Cuban-American families would have seemed awkward at the very least." He stressed that though "it has not yet been established that any of the charges are true . . . over the last 24 hours, the story has already metastasized."

Koppel introduced Judd, who, he said, "broke the story." Judd certainly "broke the story" for ABC, but other reporters "broke the story" for *The Washington Post* and the *Los Angeles Times*. Technically, by only a matter of minutes, the *Post* in fact was first on the Internet and the newsstands with the story.

Judd, as usual, presented a clear chronology of the scandal. She used network lingo to describe one element of her story as a hot exclusive: "ABC News has obtained what is potentially one of the most damaging pieces of evidence indicating a cover-up." She had hit upon the "talking points," which, she said "seems to have been drafted by a lawyer" and "allegedly handed to Tripp." Much of the same information had been published hours earlier in Isikoff's "Diary" on *Newsweek*'s Web site.

Judd concluded her report by suggesting that she (or her unnamed source) did not believe Lewinsky wrote the talking points. "It is hardly the kind of language that a 24-year-old secretary would draft," she said, implying that only a lawyer could have written them. At the time, many other reporters took the same line. But it turned out that not even Starr in his final report alleged that anyone other than Lewinsky had drafted the "talking points" and given them to Tripp.

Reporter John Donvan's report for Koppel was also framed as a chronology filled with superb illustrative quotes: McCurry saying the president was "outraged by these allegations"; Stephanopoulos saying the White House was "in full crisis mode . . . really as shocked as I've ever seen"; Bennett again "smelling a rat"; Clinton telling Lehrer that "there *is* not a sexual relationship." Donvan concluded: "A fair question seems to be whether the worst days for this White House are yet to come."

Koppel interviewed the loquacious Ginsburg, fresh from *Rivera Live!*, who stressed that Lewinsky was being "victimized" and that she deserved blanket immunity from prosecution.

Chris Bury then reported to Koppel that Starr would have "a rare news conference" the following day. Starr, who seldom talked to reporters, clearly wanted to put his own spin on the evolving story.

Michel McQueen's piece highlighted GOP congressman Lindsey Graham of South Carolina, who was soon to catapult himself into the national spotlight as a Clinton critic. "If he is indicted," Graham said, latching onto yet another far out possibility at the time, "it is time for us to have an inquiry into an impeachment."

Toward the end of his broadcast, Koppel faced David Gergen and George Stephanopoulos, a duo on whom Koppel was to rely repeatedly over the next year. In the understatement of the day, Gergen stated: "We are either facing the worst act of self-destruction or the worst smear of any president in the twentieth century." Finally, Koppel turned to Sam Donaldson, who had been on the air many times during this exceptional day. The veteran correspondent, reflecting the widespread opinion of the press corps, concluded wearily that if the president "is not telling the truth, he's cooked." Cooked, in the sense that his resignation or his impeachment was now a distinct possibility.

And with this bold prediction, an amazing if not glorious day in the history of American journalism came to an exhausted end.

CHAPTER 9

STAMPEDE

January 22, 1998

"CBS NEWS HAS LEARNED . . ."
                              —Scott Pelley, CBS Evening News

"ABC NEWS HAS OBTAINED . . ."
                              —Jackie Judd, ABC News

"I GO WHERE THE STINK IS."
                              —Matt Drudge, on NBC's *Today*

"IT MAY . . . ULTIMATELY COME DOWN TO THE QUESTION OF
WHETHER ORAL SEX DOES OR DOES NOT CONSTITUTE ADUL-
TERY."

                              —Ted Koppel, *Nightline*

Thursday, January 22, 1998, provided an example of catch-up journalism unparalleled in the history of the craft. *Newsweek,* ABC
News, *The Washington Post,* and the *Los Angeles Times* had parts of the
story, but every other news organization was in a state of panic. With the
competitive pressure so intense, journalists committed many professional
sins. One was to publish or broadcast information that had not been properly checked or confirmed. Another was to rush to judgment. Pundits
operated on a presumption of presidential guilt. Many reporters followed
their lead, basing their stories on "sources," often unnamed and sometimes
unknown. Still another sin was the strong urge to report news simply
because it was "out there," swirling around the rumor mill, not because an
editor or producer knew it to be true. It was journalism run amok.

This was the morning that Matt Drudge broke into mainstream journalism. He was a guest on NBC's *Today.* Co-host Matt Lauer described the
Drudge Report as "a media gossip page known for below-the-Beltway
reporting" and Drudge as some kind of right-wing kook, who "targeted the

White House" and engaged in "partisan politics." Drudge described himself as "a reporter, not overly educated, not underly educated." He said, "I go where the stink is." Lauer pressed him: "Is it journalism, or is it gossip? Are the facts checked and doublechecked? Do you take what you hear and just put it out there?" Drudge, like a coiled snake, bit back. "Oh, you mean like Richard Jewell?" he asked, a snide reference to the innocent man NBC had inaccurately identified as the bomber at the Atlanta World's Fair. Clearly Drudge could hold his own in this form of journalistic combat.

Lauer then probed for Drudge's sources—"Where did you first hear about this story?" he asked, as if a journalist, even one of Drudge's questionable reputation, would reveal his sources. Drudge replied in the abstract— the Lewinsky story had been given to him by "sources, citizens who were concerned . . . sources who are familiar with the situation, in and out of the White House." To prove his sources were truly informed, Drudge repeated the bombshell story he had first broken on his Web site the day before. "There's a potential DNA trail," he said, "that would tie Clinton to this young woman." Lauer leaped at this assertion, choosing words for his next question that suggested he had been briefed on Drudge's earlier report but didn't want to raise the DNA issue himself: "You say Monica Lewinsky has a piece of clothing that might have the president's semen on it? What evidence do you have of that?" That was not what Drudge had said but he replied: "She has bragged about this to Mrs. Tripp, who has told this to investigators, it's my understanding." Lauer couldn't resist. "But you don't have any *confirmation* of that?" "Not outside of what I've just heard," Drudge answered, with surprising candor, "but I don't think anybody does at this point."

Lauer thanked Drudge and turned to Mike Isikoff, making his second appearance of the morning on the program. All told, *Newsweek* reporters and editors appeared on forty different radio and television programs Thursday to talk about the scandal. Adopting a more respectful tone, Lauer asked *Newsweek*'s investigative ace if he could confirm Drudge's report about a DNA trail from Clinton to Lewinsky. Isikoff's answer defined the difference between Drudge and a weekly news magazine in terms of their approach to reporting. "Look, Matt," he answered, "there's lots of things I've heard about this and other things."

Lauer: "Have you heard that, though?"

Isikoff: "I have not reported that, and I'm not going to report that
until I have evidence that it is, in fact, true."

Lauer: "You're not telling me whether you've ever heard it?"

Isikoff: "I've heard lots of wild things, as I'm sure you have. But you
don't go on the air and blab them and talk about them unless
you know you have some confidence that it's true."

It was by that time 7:41 a.m., but already every viewer of the popular *Today* program, even if he or she were still sleepily making their way through the morning paper, had heard something about a "dress," about "DNA evidence," about Clinton's "semen," all linked somehow to an intern named Lewinsky. The "dress" story was aired on NBC. It was not "reported" on NBC—that is, an NBC journalist did not do a special report on the "dress/DNA" story; in fact, not a single NBC reporter had any hard information to substantiate it. But the dress story was now "out there," a sensational piece of information that was unconfirmed and, in a technical sense, unreported.

The New York Times, "the newspaper of record," was also playing catch-up. For editors and reporters there, it was an uncomfortable feeling.

Everyone in the 43rd Street office of the *Times* in New York was anxiously awaiting "Joe's reaction" to the nine stories in the paper that related to the scandal. "Joe" was Joseph Lelyveld, the soft-spoken, cerebral editor, who rarely showed emotion, even on this sort of story.

Two of the nine stories appeared on the front page. The lead story, placed as usual in the top right-hand corner, sported a three-line headline spread over three columns:

SUBPOENAS SENT AS CLINTON
DENIES REPORTS OF AN AFFAIR
WITH AIDE AT WHITE HOUSE

Written by Jeff Gerth and Francis X. Clines, who had the reputation of being one of the paper's best writers, the story ran 2,002 words: a well-crafted reworking of Wednesday's widely reported news. It jumped from the front page to page 24, where the *Times* ran excerpts of relevant White House and presidential statements alongside an unbylined feature story about television anchors fleeing Havana, where the pope was starting a historic visit, to Washington, where Lewinsky was hiding from the journalistic hordes now descending on her Watergate apartment. The other front-page story, featuring photographs of the new and notorious trio of Lewinsky, Tripp, and Clinton, focused on the "fateful friendship" of the two women. It was written by Jill Abramson and Don Van Natta, Jr., who based their story on "government investigators and people who have worked with the two women." On page 25, reporter Stephen Labaton reviewed Starr's strategy, reporter Richard Berke profiled Vernon Jordan, one of the central characters in the drama, and reporter James Bennet wrote specifically about the president's denials. On page 28, the *Times* published an editorial of no special distinction. On page 29, the op-ed page, columnist William Safire, hardly a Clinton apologist, chose to "presume innocence," noting that the president could not possibly have engaged in such "senseless risk"—"I just can't believe that"—because, among other reasons, "the world's crises will not take a holiday." It is of course possible that Safire "presumed" Clinton's "innocence" only so that he could clobber the president in his next column, assuming more damning information would have surfaced by that time.

Of all nine stories, none revealed more about the shortcomings of scandal coverage in those opening days than the *Times* lead. That story was based on forty-four different sources, meaning not necessarily forty-four different people but rather that there were forty-four references to sources of one sort or another. Of the forty-four, fourteen were named, "on the record" sources, including Clinton, Bennett, Ginsburg, and Starr. Nineteen were "background" sources, loosely defined in this case as "lawyers close to the investigation," "individuals," "lawyers familiar with the case," or simply "lawyers." There was no way of knowing the name or judging the reliability of these sources. The reader was left to fly blind. The remaining eleven were "deep background" sources, ranging, for example, from "the subpoenas were said to be seeking" to "amid reports that . . .". Here information was conveyed to the reader but hooked to totally unreported origins and sources, who probably refused to provide any information unless guaranteed in advance by *Times* reporters that their identities would be fully protected.

This pattern persisted through the early days of the scandal, when *The New York Times* ran an unusually large number of stories. For example, from January 22, 1998, to January 27, 1998, a six-day span, the *Times* ran ninety-six stories on the scandal, an average of sixteen per day. Legitimate questions could be raised about whether there was really that much news to publish, or whether competitive pressures were forcing editors to publish more than they knew for sure.

One editor who read every story in this brief period was Martin Baron, then associate managing editor of the *Times*, who was to become editor of the *Miami Herald.* Lelyveld asked Baron, who had been on vacation, uncontaminated by any editorial responsibility for what had already been published in the paper, to critique *Times* coverage of the scandal during the "initial firestorm"—the week from January 22, 1998, to January 30, 1998. It was, even for a confidential, "closely held" document, a remarkably candid "consciousness-raising exercise," as Lelyveld described it in his covering memorandum. It ran only six pages, but it took a self-confident, courageous editor to order it.

Baron's criticism centered on "two major lapses": bad sourcing and sloppy editing. With respect to the January 22 lead story, he wrote, "major portions . . . were largely unsourced—omissions that were thinly disguised, often through use of the passive tense, with phrases like 'said to be' and 'reportedly were to be.'" Baron then quoted at length from questionable parts of the story, which I have highlighted in bold type:

- *Late tonight, F.B.I. agents sought interviews with people in whom the intern might have confided in the White House and at the Pentagon, where she later worked. The subpoenas **were said to be seeking** White House logs showing when visitors were admitted to the executive mansion. These **reportedly were to be crosschecked** with detailed records kept by the Secret Service that show the President's minute-to-minute whereabouts.*

- *The President made his denial in a television interview **amid reports that** the former White House intern had admitted to the affair and to the alleged advice to deny it under oath in secret tape recordings made by her confidante, Linda R. Tripp, and then by F.B.I. agents working with Ms. Tripp.*

- ***There were reports** that Mr. Starr already possessed hours of secret tape recordings of the intern as possible evidence of alleged perjury and obstruction of justice by the President and his close friend and troubleshooter, Vernon Jordan.*

- *Mr. Starr . . . **was reported investigating** possible evidence that the President himself left in the alleged affair, including telephone messages subsequently re-recorded secretly for prosecutors. . . .*

• ... *In another **reported disclosure**, Ms. Lewinsky told her friend that Mr. Jordan, the President's confidante, took her for a ride in his car and advised her that if she kept quiet, nobody would go to jail.*

Baron was especially disturbed about "problems of attribution." The *Times* offered the Tripp tapes as "a source of our information." Which would have been fine, in fact excellent, except that, at the time, the *Times* did not have the tapes:

• *Mr. Jordan is reported to have counseled that she deny the affair, said individuals close to the investigation and **some of the passages of Ms. Lewinsky on tape**.*

Baron then listed a number of editorial blunders that went undetected or ignored:

• Quotes we never heard but felt free to recount without attribution.
   "I worked at the White House," Ms. Tripp explained to Mr. Starr's investigators. "I saw what happens when you go against them. They smear you. They crush their dissidents."
• Repeating sensational reports of others without confirming them ourselves.
   And ABC News reported tonight that she received a package for the President from Ms. Lewinsky believed to contain love letters. Baron asked: "Believed to contain"? Who believed?
• Questionable exercises in mind-reading.
   "She was in love with the guy," said the person after listening to the tapes. "She felt she was his soul mate."
• Passive voice as a substitute for sourcing.
   *Two members of the Cabinet ... **were described as** particularly distressed by the accusations.*
• Speculation.
   But confidantes of Mr. Clinton have said privately that Mr. Clinton and his personal secretary, Betty Currie, may have befriended Ms. Lewinsky because the President recognized that she had had a troubled childhood, and may have simply needed a friend.
   "He's drawn to troubled types," one friend said tonight. "So is Betty

Currie." Baron then asked: "Is this anything more than self-serving speculation? Does someone whose parents divorce necessarily experience a troubled childhood?"

- Overstatement based on evidence seen or heard.
  Lewinsky's sworn affidavit in the Paula Jones case, flatly denying a sexual affair with the President, conflicts with twenty hours of taped conversations in which she reportedly discussed a sexual liaison in detail. Baron: "Have we heard all twenty hours of taped conversations?" It was a rhetorical question. The *Times*, at the time, had not heard even one hour of the tapes.

Only an insider like Baron could have produced such a critique, and only a proud newspaper like the *Times* could have tolerated its stinging candor.

And how did *The Washington Post* resume its conquest of the story on January 22, 1998? It ran fourteen stories about the scandal, five more than the *Times*—three on the front page, one on page 2, two on page 12, two on page 13, one on page 14, plus one editorial. There were also four additional stories in the Style section: one on press coverage; another on Jay Leno jokes ("After five years of investigating and $35 million, Kenneth Starr has found the smoking gun, and it's apparently in President Clinton's pants"); a third on a "webguide for scandalmongers"; and finally a "news you can use" story about "breaking the news to children." This was saturation coverage—every angle, every personality, every joke was covered, often in excruciating detail.

From January 22 to January 27, *The Washington Post* published 120 stories about the Clinton-Lewinsky entanglement, 24 more than *The New York Times* over the same period, averaging 20 stories a day on the subject.

The three front-page stories, clustered in the top right-hand corner, dominated the page. A single large headline—FBI TAPED AIDE'S ALLEGATIONS—topped a photograph of the president. Below him to the right and left were the same photographs of Lewinsky and Tripp that appeared in the *Times*. At this point, few people had heard or seen the two women; within a matter of days, they were to become familiar images of immorality and betrayal. White House reporter John F. Harris wrote that Clinton "spent his afternoon [Wednesday] with a revolving door of reporters in a campaign to keep his presidency from buckling under the force of allegations about his relationship with a former White House intern." His story had the advantage of depending upon named sources, particularly the president.

Another front-page story, by Dana Priest and Rene Sanchez, described two "exiles"—Tripp and Lewinsky—who had "shared lively chat, confidences." Phrases such as "according to sources" studded this report. The third story, written by Susan Schmidt and Peter Baker, highlighted Starr's so far unsuccessful efforts to win Lewinsky's cooperation in nailing Clinton and Jordan. It focused on Starr's strategy, and though it too was resplendent with "sources," it was obviously dependent on the cooperation of the OIC, not exactly an objective actor in this drama.

Like the Clines-Gerth lead in the *Times*, the Schmidt-Baker lead in the *Post* was also based on unnamed, unaffiliated, and unknowable "sources." Of the thirty-nine sources used in this story, seven were named and "on the record," among them Clinton, *Newsweek,* and Davis, who was quoted as refusing to comment. Twenty-eight of the sources were used "on background"—"sources familiar with the investigation," "a source familiar with her legal strategy," and just plain "sources," among others. Four were on "deep background"—"including reports that" and "other information emerged yesterday that." Decidedly different from the *Times* story, though, was the *Post*'s unusually heavy reliance on no sources at all. Time and again, Schmidt and Baker conveyed information that had no cited antecedent. For example, "hidden nearby were numerous FBI agents monitoring every word." How did the reporters know this? They knew this because they were told, and they were told with the understanding that they would not reveal their sources, even on "deep background."

While researching this story, Peter Baker roamed far and wide on his hunt for sources, going well beyond his familiar White House terrain. According to Jonah Goldberg, Baker called him "three times in an hour," desperately trying to match *Newsweek*'s Isikoff and get his hands on Tripp's tapes, copies of which mother Goldberg and perhaps Jonah had in their possession. To avoid having Jonah hand the tapes directly to him, Baker suggested a number of far-fetched schemes. One was for Jonah to give the tapes to a "friend," who would then give them to Baker. Another was for Jonah to leave the tapes on his stereo and then deliberately leave his apartment door ajar so Baker could slip into the apartment and pick up the tapes. Neither scheme was implemented.

Schmidt also roamed among many sources, but she returned to the OIC for a substantial portion of her material: she needed them, and they needed her and the *Post*. In fact, so excellent were her contacts at the OIC that when she and Michael Weisskopf of *Time* decided to write *Truth At Any Cost*, published in April 2000, they were given extraordinary access to Kenneth Starr and his top deputies. Schmidt and Weisskopf—who also interviewed fourteen presidential aides and lawyers—enjoyed the benefits of ten lengthy interviews with Starr and many long talks with twenty-five of his normally reticent assistants, all with Starr's advance approval. The upshot was a sympathetic, well-written portrait of Starr, containing dozens of unsourced insights into Starr's state of mind similar in style to unsourced news accounts in the *Post* outlining Starr's investigation as well as his step-by-step strategy.

Lars Erik Nelson, a columnist for the *New York Daily News* who distrusted Starr as much as he disapproved of his pursuit of Clinton, described Schmidt in his book review as "a central figure in this sordid story." Nelson explained that Schmidt got information from the OIC that was then often sourcelessly featured on the front page of the capital's most influential newspaper and in this way tilted the legal and political struggle between Starr and Clinton in favor of the prosecutor. As a reporter, Schmidt felt she was doing her job as well as she could, given the journalistic turmoil of the time. Editor Robert Kaiser acknowledged that *The Washington Post* ran stories with "only the vaguest sourcing" during those early days, strongly implying that was the only way his reporters could protect their contacts in Starr's office. Nelson then quoted critic Steven Brill of *Brill's Content* saying: "She absolutely knows that he [Starr] leaked to her. You can't write about that [in the book] as if it's a mystery. This whole thing has an air of unreality." Schmidt had—and presumably still has—utter contempt for Brill, telling me on more than one occasion that he "misquoted me—I'd disregard everything that Brill wrote or said." While expansively critical of anyone who questioned her approach to covering the story, Schmidt shed no light on why she, as an experienced reporter, resorted to the use of so many sourceless quotes.

If journalism is, in fact, "the first draft of history," then Schmidt and Baker, in those early days, wrote a good first draft. But like many other first drafts, this one contained errors and misjudgments—understandable perhaps in the reporters' frantic rush to deadline. For example, in their January 21 and 22 stories, they leaned heavily on the OIC-spread presumption that Clinton and Jordan had urged Lewinsky to lie. And if they had urged her to lie, then they were both guilty of perjury, suborning perjury, and possibly even obstruction of justice. This was the OIC line and the basis of its legal strategy. Clinton repeatedly denied that he'd urged Lewinsky to lie—and his denials were reported—but his credibility with the press was at such a low ebb that his denials quickly lost their authority and readers and viewers were left with the clear impression that he had indeed urged Lewinsky to lie; an allegation that appeared in just about every *Post* account of the scandal. This then had the snowballing effect of encouraging other newspapers and networks with poor access to the OIC to publish or broadcast the *Post* version of the truth.

But the *Post* version of the truth was questionable. Even Starr admitted in his report to Congress that he had no evidence to support the allegation. Editor Len Downie provided the official explanation of the *Post* error, saying that Tripp must have assumed from the tapes that Clinton and Jordan had urged Lewinsky to lie, and she had conveyed her assumption to her sources and they had conveyed it to Schmidt. "Yes, it's true, the story didn't hold up completely," admitted Downie, "but it's what Sue's source told her."

The Wall Street Journal was in a world of its own.

It could easily be argued that it was where all of the rest of journalism should have been, but its January 22, 1998 edition was distinctive in its cautious approach to the scandal. It seemed as if it deliberately wanted to be slow on the pickup. Political scandal was not its thing unless it affected the market, and the market was booming.

Published since 1889 by the Dow Jones Company, the *Journal* focused on financial and business news, though in recent decades it also has done a highly professional job of covering domestic and foreign news. Also in recent decades a deep chasm of political and philosophical differences has opened between the editorial page and the rest of the paper. Its front page is designed not for the eye but for the mind—it is divided into six even columns of print, like soldiers lined up for a routine inspection. Nothing is supposed to be visually dramatic. Photographs are off-limits, though an ink drawing of a notable personality is a common feature.

On January 22, 1998, the only reference to the scandal on the front page of *The Wall Street Journal* was a short item, which topped the "Worldwide" column. It read:

> Clinton was hit with allegations of an affair with a young White House intern. Responding to reports that the Whitewater prosecutor has expanded his investigation to include the new accusations, Clinton denied having a sexual relationship with Monica Lewinsky, 24, and said he never told her to lie to lawyers in the Paula Jones sexual harassment suit. Lewinsky denied an affair in an affidavit taken in the case, but a former White House aide reportedly secretly taped her discussing the affair and efforts by Clinton and confidant Vernon Jordan encouraging her to lie. *Lewinsky's age and the talk of extramarital relations in the White House threaten to turn the public against the president in a way other cases haven't.*

What is clear from this brief account is that the *Journal* simply rewrote *The Washington Post* story, or an AP version of the *Post* story, twice referring to "reports" and "reportedly" to indicate the information came from others, as if it wanted to put distance between itself and the salacious details of the scandal. The *Journal*, like the *Times*, was not even in the hunt for this story—it came as a complete surprise. In the Washington bureau at 1025 Connecticut Avenue, reporters quickly split into two camps. One camp, according to bureau chief Alan Murray, felt that the *Journal* was right not to have been in the hunt and that it should not now be rushing to claim proprietary rights to this scandal. "We didn't do O.J.," one of them said, "and we don't have to do shit like this—we are *The Wall Street Journal*." The other camp believed that Starr, who had been near oblivion because of his inability to get Clinton, suddenly had been resurrected by the Lewinsky scandal and that the president's impeachment was now his goal. Murray was in the "impeachment" camp. "On Wednesday," he explained, "we all read the *Post* and we were able very quickly to confirm that Starr was knee-deep in this new investigation. Once we knew that, we also knew that Starr was going for impeachment. No doubt about it. He was building a perjury case."

On page A20, reporters Brian Duffy and Michael Frisby wrote the only news story touching on the scandal to appear in the *Journal* on January 22, 1998. They outlined the basic facts, as reported by the *Post,* and embellished their story with the results of the latest WSJ/NBC poll, conducted by Peter Hart and Bob Teeter, which showed that the president's approval rating for the preceding week had climbed to 62 percent—his highest mark ever. Their implied question was whether a president so popular could be impeached.

All other comment about the scandal was reserved for the editorial page, run as an autonomous fiefdom by the brilliant, conservative, and controversial Robert L. Bartley. His view of journalism was that *The Wall Street Journal* should report not only what it knows but also what it believes. So long as the news conformed to Bartley's vision of truth and reality, it should be published, and, on his turf, it was published on the morning of January 22, 1998. First, of course, was his own editorial, headlined "The Outrage Arrives." Bartley started by quoting Stephanopoulos's prediction that this scandal could lead to Clinton's impeachment. The president had survived other scandals, but this time he had wandered into unacceptable terrain—sex with an intern in the Oval Office. "Now comes the outrage," Bartley wrote, "pouring out of the mouths of every Beltway pundit with access to a TV talk show. The ceiling is suddenly caving in on Mr. Clinton's presidency on the testimony of two or three courageous women."

A small box in the middle of the editorial featured an extraordinary advertisement in bold type: "**Clinton Scandals Collected. 'A Journal Briefing: Whitewater—Vol. III' is available for $16.95 plus shipping. All three volumes for $39.95. Call 1-800-635-8349.**" The collection could well have appealed to readers who relish anti-Clinton "documentation." Its provenance was known to Bartley, but he chose not to share it with his readers.

Bartley also ran an op-ed offering from Congressman Bob Barr, a Georgia Republican. Although it was headlined THIS IS WHY WE HAVE IMPEACHMENT and featured a photograph of Lewinsky, the piece itself had very little to do with Lewinsky or the scandal. It was, ironically, an argument against renewing the independent counsel statute. Bartley obviously wanted to exploit the scandal by displaying the photograph of Lewinsky and the headline about "impeachment."

Finally, Albert Hunt, in his weekly column headlined A MOMENT OF PRESIDENTIAL PERIL, wrote that if anyone in Washington heard an odd noise on Wednesday, it was "the sound of Teflon cracking." Hunt reflected his own personal uneasiness about the whole subject, writing that this sex scandal could be different from earlier ones. If Starr could prove that the president was guilty of witness tampering and obstruction of justice, Hunt concluded, then this scandal could develop into a genuine threat to the Clinton administration.

USA Today, founded in 1982, has a remarkable national daily circulation of 3.2 million copies, far more than any other newspaper in the country. Its founder, Allen H. Neuharth, has always considered it "a family newspaper." On January 22, 1998, it could not avoid the Lewinsky scandal, though it was clear that its journalistic heart was in Cuba with Pope John Paul II. A large picture of the pope and his host, Fidel Castro, filled the center of the front page. A bold headline—CUBA, CASTRO EMBRACE POPE—topped the picture. But, above it, a much bolder, sensational headline—CLINTON DENIES AFFAIR; RECORDS SUBPOENAED—caught the reader's eye. The lead story, written by Tom Squitieri, was a mirror image of the one that had appeared the day before in *The Washington Post*. On a number of occasions, Squitieri cited no sources and, like many other reporters, hid behind phrases such as "people familiar with the investigation" and "persons familiar with Starr's probe" (presumably the OIC). To the left of the headline and story was a 2 × 2-inch photograph of the same smiling young woman, Monica Lewinsky, who was quickly giving a bad name to the battalions of college students who invade Washington every summer to work as interns. The cover story, a daily front-page feature, showed a picture of Clinton under the headline PRESIDENT'S RESILIENCE FACES BIGGEST TEST. Susan Page, an experienced White House correspondent, quoted "scandal-tested Clinton aides" as acknowledging privately that "they were shaken and demoralized." The scandal, she wrote, "ricocheted around the capital like some supercharged billiard ball."

It was sufficiently supercharged to compel editor David Mazzarella to run seven other stories in the paper that morning—nine in all, plus an editorial. "Like the *Times*," he told me, "we were playing catch-up journalism from day one." A former foreign correspondent with extensive experience in Italy and the Middle East, Mazzarella said that "amid the flood of accusations, rumors and spin," he believed that his reporters had to be "extra careful." The paper's "primary mission," in his view, was "to help readers get their bearings. We had to be sure. . . . We had to be cautious. I wanted our coverage to be clear, unbiased and not sensational." His directions were that "there were to be no unnamed sources." But in fact "unnamed sources" populated *USA Today* in the early days of the scandal, just as they did every other newspaper.

On page 2, *USA Today* ran a revealing but questionable poll of 676 people contacted between 6 and 9 p.m. on Wednesday evening. The poll, conducted with CNN and Gallup, was rushed, unreliable, and yet interesting. It showed that 62 percent of the American people still approved of Clinton's job performance, the same as the week before; 82 percent had heard the news of the sex scandal; but that if Clinton had urged Lewinsky to lie and thus obstructed justice, slightly less than half of the American people (46 percent) favored his impeachment. The poll seemed to be saying that infidelity was acceptable, but getting caught lying about it was not. Also on page 2 was a story about the meaning of an "improper relationship."

Deeper into the fourteen-page paper were five other stories, all on page 9. They appeared under a banner headline: WHITE HOUSE TRIES TO RIDE OUT THE STORM. With each story was a photo: a large one showing Clinton hugging his dog Buddy, while a smiling Jim Lehrer waited to begin his *NewsHour* interview; another of a pained Mike McCurry attempting to answer unanswerable questions; a third of Clinton with Vernon Jordan palling around on a golf course; a stock photo of Starr; and the same photo of the increasingly ubiquitous Lewinsky that was on page 1. The stories were similar to those that appeared that day in the *Times* and the *Post*.

The editorial on page 12A was entitled "Another Sex Scandal Clouds Clinton Character." It featured photos of Lewinsky and Tripp. It was the third time that this photo of the smiling "former intern" appeared that day in *USA Today*—clearly the editors wanted to exploit her notoriety and just as clearly they had no other photo. The editorial was balanced, expressing astonishment that Clinton would risk a sexual relationship with a twenty-three-year-old intern in the White House but warning too that if Starr was found to be on a "witch hunt," he should be fired. The larger point concerned the president: if the "multiple, anonymously sourced media reports" were accurate, and Clinton did urge Lewinsky to lie, said *USA Today,* then "his presidency will be in ruins, either because his credibility is destroyed or—if crimes are proved—he is impeached." Even balanced, careful *USA Today* was discussing impeachment.

Mazzarella was pained by the sourceless sourcing of the stories, not just in *USA Today* but in other papers as well. He assigned a number of reporters and researchers to a most unusual and unorthodox news story for the next day. "How the Clinton News Story Evolved Over the Past Week" was the headlined result. Journalists, as a rule, never disclose or even discuss their sources. Yet, on page 6A of the January 23, 1998 edition of *USA Today,* a newspaper was discussing where journalists got their information. (In addition, there were thirteen other stories in the paper that day about the scandal, plus another editorial.) Mazzarella explained that he wanted "to tell people who was reporting what and where it might have come from." It was a worthwhile attempt to help readers figure out the reliability and origin of a story—which news organization broke it, who were the sources, who might have leaked it. The paper had the right idea.

The *New York Post* is a proud, conservative, struggling tabloid, locked in daily combat with the *New York Daily News.* It too was stunned by Wednesday's *Washington Post* story, even though its Washington bureau chief, Deborah Orin, had sniffed a scandalous something in the air since Friday, when a conversation she had had with Isikoff ended on an odd but intriguing note. Still, despite a number of calls, she ended up knowing nothing specific about the Lewinsky scandal until, like so many of her Washington colleagues, she awoke on Wednesday and read *The Washington Post.* But, unlike many of her Washington colleagues, Orin had an ace in the hole, and its name was Lucianne Goldberg, a regular reader, fan and friend of the *New York Post.* For eight straight days, Goldberg fed a juicy exclusive tidbit or two—or three—to the *New York Post,* and all it had to do was cite "sources," not Goldberg, and run with it after a perfunctory check. She was a valued leaker, not just to the *New York Post* in those early days but to other favored publications and reporters too, including Drudge.

How does a leaker leak? In this case, every day, Goldberg called Marc Kalech, a managing editor with special responsibility for the Sunday section of the paper. They were friends who had a business relationship. Kalech had used Goldberg as his literary agent for a time and as an adviser on which books to excerpt for the Sunday paper. Goldberg had a personal and financial interest in helping Kalech and the *New York Post*. Their daily conversations were filled with irresistibly sexy gossip. Goldberg briefed Kalech on everything Lewinsky had told Tripp, and Tripp had told Goldberg. "I gave him a story every day, a good story," she boasted. "I love Marc." Each Goldberg call was like a playfully tossed dagger at the Clinton administration.

Joyous that the story had finally broken in the mainstream press, Goldberg was now determined to spread it. And the journalistic craving for any and every whisper of gossip, rumor, and fact was so powerful that she had no problem. She was called by everyone, even reporters repelled by her political agenda. For his part, Kalech distributed the Goldberg nuggets to key *New York Post* colleagues with the understanding that the information would be considered safe and sound and its source would be protected. How best to protect a source? Refer to her as "sources," shielding her with the plural. Were Goldberg's nuggets then checked and confirmed by *New York Post* reporters and columnists? Kalech first insisted that the "journalistic rule about two sources" was honored, but he later acknowledged that the "deadline pressures" were "enormous" and "maybe the rule was broken." The pressures on every newspaper, but especially on a New York tabloid, were in fact so unrelentingly brutal that confirmation was considered a hindrance and rarely pursued. The goal was to transform a nugget into a headline, with maximum speed. Confirmation could await a calmer time; besides, who'd remember a mistake, an exaggeration, a fumble?

On January 22, 1998, the *New York Post* ran ten news stories, four pieces of commentary, and one editorial. The headlines in a tabloid are often revealing and sometimes more deftly crafted than the stories themselves:

WHITE HOUSE BUSY CIRCLING THE WAGONS

BILL "FESSES UP" TO FLOWERS FLING

JORDAN IS A MASTER BEHIND THE SCENES

INTERN-AL "AFFAIR" HAS BILL IN DENIAL

SOCCER MOM HAS GIVEN CLINTON A SWIFT KICK

"SOAPHEAD" MONICA BECOMES SPICE GIRL

THIS WILL DESTROY HER, FLOWERS SAYS

SIZZLING TALE OF THE TAPES HEATS UP
IMPEACHMENT TALK

EX-INTERN MIGHT BE STARR WITNESS

Every *New York Post* reporter worked hard on these stories, but none worked harder or benefited more from the Goldberg leaks than Orin. Her stories that day contained dead giveaway phrases betraying their provenance. Orin referred to "sources" to disguise the *New York Post's* reliance on Goldberg as she wrote about one revelation after another: that Lewinsky had called Clinton "the Big Creep"; that Clinton had told Lewinsky to lie about their affair and then she had told Tripp to lie; that Tripp had secretly taped Lewinsky at a nearby Ritz-Carlton Hotel; that Lewinsky had visited the president at the White House but pretended she was visiting his secretary, Betty Currie; that Lewinsky had told Tripp that she and the president had oral and phone sex but not intercourse; and so on.

The four commentaries, illustrating the relentless anti-Clinton bias of the *New York Post*, were headlined:

HIS PRESIDENCY IS NOW WORTH, UH, ZIP

NETWORKS SCRAMBLE AS ALL HELL BREAKS LOOSE

GRAVEGATE WIDOW "AFFAIR" ON DECK IN CLINTON
SCANDALS

NEW DOG, SAME OLD TRICKS

The "Zip" piece by Andrea Peyser began "ZZZZZZZZIP," and it ended with "This woman hears a presidency sinking under the weight of an uncontrollable zipper. ZZZZZZZZIP." The *New York Post* editorial, called SMELLING A RAT, a phrase repeatedly used by presidential lawyer Bob Bennett, showed uncharacteristic caution for a conservative tabloid in judging the president's guilt. "Much remains to be learned," it said, ending with an allusion to a clock ticking toward impeachment.

The 9:00 a.m. gaggle of impatient reporters around McCurry's desk had only one story in mind—what was the president going to say about

Lewinsky? And when? The spokesman, as so often happened in crises, tried to deflect their attention to another story. Big news from Bosnia, he announced. An infamous war criminal had just been captured. McCurry had more details. A question or two about Bosnia followed, but reporters quickly returned to Lewinsky. McCurry riffled through a stack of announcements. There would be a 10 a.m. photo-op, he said—Clinton and Arafat. The president planned to spend the rest of Thursday on his State of the Union speech. Reporters rapidly retreated from McCurry's office, knowing that they would get a crack at the president in an hour.

In the Oval Office, the president was meeting Lanny Davis, who had resigned for personal reasons. Clinton's eyes were red and puffy, and he looked exhausted. Davis wondered whether the reason was an allergy or lack of sleep. Davis wanted to give some advice to the president. In your interview with Jim Lehrer yesterday, he said, you looked "evasive, untruthful, unsure of yourself." Do what you do best, Davis suggested, "better perhaps than any president in modern history: take your case to the American people, tell them everything, everything there is to tell. Let them judge." Let your lawyers do the lawyering, Davis continued. "You do politics—what you were born to do." Clinton nodded, and then asked Davis for his reading of the press. Davis thought the press believed that Clinton "has had an affair and that he was guilty" of lying. The president said that "there was nothing new there."

Later Davis wrote: "He was very uncomfortable about something, something causing him a deep, deep internal conflict, something tearing at him from different directions, something very elemental. I saw the pain, the fatigue, in his eyes."

All morning a battle had been raging between the president's political advisers (Rahm Emanuel, Paul Begala, and Douglas Sosnik) and his legal advisers (Charles Ruff, Robert Bennett, and David Kendall). The issue was how much information to release to the public. The lawyers wanted to impose a tight clamp on all information about the scandal. They warned that public comments must be terse and uninformative. The politicians, fearful of plummeting public support for the president's program, pleaded for maximum transparency. According to *The Washington Post*, the battles were "robust" but not "acrimonious."

A few days later, Davis met one of the president's lawyers in the corridor and repeated his pitch about releasing the relevant documents. "The pressure is immense from the press," he said, "and every day we delay will look like we're trying to hide something. It's going to get out at some point anyway."

"No," replied the lawyer.

"Why? We've always put out . . . records preemptively—so we could be sure to get our context and interpretation as part of the story. Starr is going to get them anyway. They speak for themselves—whatever they say, they say."

"No information is going to be put out to the press by the White House about this matter—period."

Davis was "stunned." He "couldn't believe" what he had just heard—the White House was going to impose a strict policy of delay and deny. In his view, the effect would be to intensify journalists' skepticism and speculation, leading to "the old classroom whisper game," which is exactly what happened.

"I would get a call from a reporter," he wrote,

> asking me whether I had heard about a particular rumor. I would call several White House people to ask them whether they had any knowledge of this. Often those whom I called had already heard about the rumor from the same reporter, but wouldn't tell me that, only that they had heard the same rumor. Or sometimes the same reporter would call the individual whom I had just called, and get some type of confirmation that the individual had heard the same rumor. Every so often, a new piece of information would be leaked, its origins and reliability uncertain, further stoking the flames. And around and around, within virtually a closed loop of the same people talking to each other, we would go again and again. Often, to my astonishment, at least initially, the next morning I would actually find these rumors printed in certain newspapers, attributed only to anonymous "sources."

Yassir Arafat must have thought that the United States had gone crazy. On previous visits to Washington, he had been able to generate news, even sympathy, for his cause; now he had been relegated to the back pages by an alleged affair between the president and a young woman. Just as twenty years earlier, during the Watergate crisis, diplomats could not believe that a great country would destroy a president over a "third-rate burglary," so now Arafat and his diplomatic entourage began to search for hidden meanings to this madness. In Washington, up and down diplomatic row, the word was that the Palestinian delegation was scratching its head, wondering whether Lewinsky was an Israeli agent, planted in the White House to seduce and destroy the president because he had been too sympathetic to the Palestinian cause. A number of Arab diplomats were utterly bewildered by the sight of the world's surviving superpower going into journalistic and political convulsions over a presidential affair. In their countries, when caught in an embarrassing "private matter," every politician lied, every journalist lied, and nothing would ever appear in a newspaper.

But this was the United States, and at 10:11 a.m., a small pool of reporters and cameramen from both the American and Palestinian sides were allowed into the Oval Office for a photo-op with Clinton and Arafat, both seated decorously in front of the fireplace. Photo-ops generally lasted five minutes or so, enough time for a half-dozen questions.

The president opened with a brief summation of his recent meetings with the Israeli and Palestinian leaders. An American wire service reporter asked the first question and a quick follow-up. Arab reporters, speaking in Arabic, asked one question of Clinton and one of Arafat. Both leaders stressed the "urgency" of breaking the Middle East diplomatic deadlock. Then the inevitable happened: the question about Lewinsky. "Could you clarify for us, sir," a pool reporter asked, "exactly what your relationship was with Ms. Lewinsky, and whether the two of you talked by phone, including any messages you may have left?"

The atmosphere was surreal: the Middle East was on the edge of unraveling once again, the president of the United States had a chance to spark a resumption of peace talks, and yet a member of the White House press corps could not resist the urge to ask about Clinton's "zzzzzzzzzip" problem.

Clinton, no novice at photo-ops, was highly adept at the spin game. His answer, so carefully phrased, suggested that he had anticipated the question and that he was ready with his reply. "Let me say, first of all, I want to reiterate what I said yesterday. The allegations are false and I would never ask anybody to do anything other than tell the truth. Let's get to the big issues there, about the nature of the relationship and whether I suggested anybody not to tell [*sic*] the truth. That is false. Now, there are a lot of other questions that are, I think, very legitimate. You have a right to ask them; you and the American people have a right to get answers. We are working very hard to comply and get all the requests for information up here, and we will give you as many answers as we can, as soon as we can, at the appropriate time, consistent with our obligation to also cooperate with the investigations. And that's not a dodge, that's really why I've—I've talked with our people. I want to do that. I'd like for you to have more rather than less, sooner rather than later. So we'll work through it as quickly as we can and get all those questions out there to you."

With this one answer, the president provided every journalist in Washington with his or her lead for the day.

Anchors Away!

The network anchors had cleared out of the Havana Libre Hotel in Cuba on Wednesday evening, immediately after their newscasts. By late morning Thursday, their expensive operations were already being dismantled. They had been accompanied by more than a hundred technicians at a cost of hundreds of thousands of dollars. Now the news focus changed, and they were gone. *"Escandalo sexual, eh?"* joked the cab driver, as he chauffeured ABC executives, reporters, and technicians back and forth from the hotel to the airport. Pope John Paul II was, like Arafat, reduced to a sidebar story. "First we heard that Brokaw was going back," Dan Rather remembered with embarrassment. "Then we heard Jennings was . . . clearing out. . . . I truly wanted to stay there and report on the Pope, but I got the distinct impression [from executives in New York] that if I stayed another minute, I would have been there all alone and without a job." Brokaw and Rather flew directly to Washington, Jennings to New York.

ABC cameramen from Moscow, Mexico City, and Paris "marveled" at the ABC command decision to dump the pope for "a presidential dalliance," which was how they saw the Lewinsky story. Bill Blakemore, an ABC correspondent who'd covered the pope since the early 1980s, shared their sense of bewilderment. He had arrived in Havana breathless with the excitement of the papal visit. John Paul II was going to blast the U.S.

embargo on Cuba. "I've got it here, it's written, I've got it in my notebook," Blakemore shouted, only to learn moments later about Lewinsky. "Bill," Jennings informed him, "we're leaving." Blakemore, obviously deflated, replied with a trace of sarcasm: "I suppose the only story you'll want tomorrow is reaction from the Vatican, or the Cuban government, to the President and the intern."

If Clinton had spoken, could Starr be far behind? In the OIC, the argument revolved around whether Starr should engage in a sound-bite–for–sound-bite war with Clinton. No, decided Starr. "The emphasis of style over substance was anathema to Starr," wrote Schmidt and Weiss-kopf. But there was an immediate problem. Outside the building an army of rebellious journalists and cameramen had besieged the OIC, blocking traffic and frustrating pedestrians, and Starr was encouraged to agree to a limited compromise: he would make a brief statement to the cameras, while his prosecutors dropped a blizzard of subpoenas on Betty Currie, Vernon Jordan, Lucianne Goldberg, and anyone else even remotely connected to the scandal.

The moment Starr emerged from his office, he was mobbed by reporters desperate for a taped on-camera comment. Starr was clearly startled. Slowly, with the help of security guards and even a few sympathetic reporters, he made his way to a top-heavy stand of microphones. The questions erupted in an incomprehensible chorus, so loud no one could hear anything. Finally, someone in the jostling crowd shouted: "Shud-dddupp," and, at 11:08 a.m., Starr began to speak.

In a quiet, controlled voice that many later described as prissy and condescending, Starr told the reporters that he could not discuss the details in the case but promised to move "as promptly as we possibly can" and cautioned reporters not to jump to conclusions. "Let's bear in mind," he said, stressing what was not only obvious but proper, "that each individual in our country enjoys a presumption of innocence. I think that's very important in terms of fairness." When he paused, questions came from every corner of the crowd. There was one he wanted to answer—the one about whether his prosecutors had been, as reported, harshly threatening to Lewinsky. The judge who had never been a prosecutor asserted: "We use appropriate investigative techniques that are traditional law enforcement techniques. We conduct this investigation the way any other investigation would be conducted. . . . Any officer carrying out the activities of the federal government must be properly within his or her jurisdiction." The questions continued, but Starr retreated to his office and reporters raced to their phones and cameras.

McCurry's briefing was live, one episode in a political soap opera that started with *Today* and ended with *Nightline*. The briefing, which began at 1:35 p.m., was carried by all the networks, and the cable channels such as MSNBC and CNN beamed it to the world. ABC's Sam Donaldson stood in front of the bursting-at-the-seams White House press room, killing time in conversation with Peter Jennings while waiting for McCurry and his harried entourage to enter the battle zone.

"The president said this morning he thought the country deserved answers," Donaldson was saying, "that he would like to give answers, but he said he was going to cooperate with the investigators and therefore he was not going to answer until the investigation was finished. However, Peter," Donaldson continued, "we will do our best to make certain Mike McCurry answers."

As if on cue, McCurry entered and walked past Donaldson, who sensed his moment, smiled, bowed slightly, and beckoning toward the spokesman's podium said: "Mr. McCurry, if you will, sir." According to Tim Kiska, a reporter for the *Detroit News*, Donaldson looked like a game show host introducing a contestant. The White House press corps, "struck by the strangeness of the situation, collapsed in laughter." Viewers might have wondered whether the Donaldson and McCurry act really warranted laughter, but the reporters understood that their act had become an integral part of American governance, even in a moment of crisis.

That day, McCurry had an impossible task. He sympathized with the president's *political* advisers, but his mandate was defined by the president's *legal* advisers. It was thin and grudging. Moreover, he had deliberately absented himself from a number of White House meetings he would normally have attended, because he did not want to attract a Starr subpoena and incur legal costs beyond his means. Nevertheless, although he was a short-timer, he remained loyal to the president and, to the best of his ability, defended him.

Q: "Would it be normal for the president to leave messages on her [Lewinsky's] home phone answering machine?"

A: "I'm not going to speculate on that. I'm not going to speculate on anything related to the specifics."

Reporters wanted to know whether the scandal was interfering with the president's work.

A: "Obviously he's got to deal with this matter as it comes up and arises. But he's still got an enormous amount of work to do on things like the Middle East peace process."

Q: "The effect on the staff at the White House—are people shocked, disheartened, disspirited? It must be some distraction on the staff at any rate."

A: "Of course it is and I think, you know, people just have to keep going forward."

One subtext of these exchanges was the matter of Clinton's credibility, which had dropped to a new low following *The Washington Post*'s disclosure that morning that the president had admitted during his Jones deposition to having had a sexual relationship with Gennifer Flowers. Was the *Post* right or wrong? If the paper was right, then Clinton had lied in 1992 (when he denied an affair) and was probably lying now. If it was wrong, then the press corps felt that the spokesman should say so. McCurry's answer was misleading. "The president knows," he said, "that he told the truth in 1992 when he was asked about that relationship, and he knows that he testified truthfully on Saturday, and he knows his answers are not at odds."

Well, reporters continued, what kind of relationship did Clinton have with Lewinsky? McCurry repeated the president's denial. Was it sexual? McCurry ducked. Had he made passes at an intern? No, McCurry replied. "That's common sense and common decency, and of course that applies to everyone." Except, obviously, in this case, many reporters felt that it did not apply to the president.

After McCurry's briefing, "Clinton aides," as they were described in Friday's newspapers, explained on background that the president had only been denying the description of the affair offered by Flowers—not that he had not had sex with her. No longer a "Clinton aide" speaking on background, Stephanopoulos later told ABC's Chris Bury: "He was trying to be open about the fact that he had not had a perfect marriage, that there had been affairs, but not necessarily give credence to every ounce of her story because many of the details in that story were probably wrong."

Journalists felt they now had to check and double-check everything Clinton said. Could his denials any longer be believed?

From the very beginning, Starr had more than Clinton in his legalistic cross-hairs. He also targeted Vernon Jordan, the president's friend and confidant, a tall, impeccably tailored, sixty-two-year-old lawyer, an avid golfer on Martha's Vineyard during the summer, a skilled, self-confident Washington insider at all other times. At 3:30 p.m., in a ballroom at the Park Hyatt Hotel jammed with reporters and cameras, Jordan walked to the microphones. "May I have your attention?" he asked, as if he really had to ask for it. "My name is Vernon Jordan," he continued, as if they didn't already know. He spoke for five minutes in a slow, deep voice, hitting each word for special emphasis and drama, and he allowed no questions. Only Jordan on this day could have appeared before cameras, stated his position, and walked off without answering a question.

"I want to say absolutely and unequivocally that Ms. Lewinsky told me in no uncertain terms that she did not have a sexual relationship with the President. At no time did I ever say, suggest or intimate to her that she should lie," he said. Jordan promised to testify "directly, completely and truthfully" before the grand jury. His personal photo-op was choreographed to help the president, and for a brief time it did.

Yes, he told reporters, he had tried to find Lewinsky a job. Yes, he had also found a lawyer for her. And yes, it was odd, he agreed, that someone so powerful should spend so much time trying to help a young intern, but the former civil rights leader who now served on eleven corporate boards and earned more than $1 million a year invoked a biblical admonition to explain his actions—"To whom much is given, much is required," he said. "I was pleased to be helpful to Ms. Lewinsky, whose drive, ambition and personality were impressive."

Like Starr, reporters couldn't lay a glove on Jordan, even if they had wanted to, and none did. Jordan seemed to rise above the squalor, his reputation as clean after the impeachment of the president as it was before.

Naturally, Peter Jennings's lead story on *World News Tonight* was about "the intern." "So much depends," he said, "on what Monica Lewinsky does or says, more specifically, next. No one knows that better than ABC's Jackie Judd." By this time, only one day into the biggest political story of the decade, Judd had already become the network's number one reporter on the scandal. (By year's end, she was the most visible female correspondent in television news, and the thirteenth most visible in the business, having appeared ninety-nine times.) She had helped break the story for ABC on Tuesday night, and she took the lead in Wednesday's extensive coverage. She had colleagues, of course. Every morning at 9:15, she met with other reporters and producers in the Washington bureau to share information and discuss what was likely to develop in the course of the day. They were connected by telephone to reporters and producers in New York, who were also working on the story. As Jackie Judd recollected more than two years later, "it was impossible for one person to do the whole story, to check every fact—it was just physically impossible. There was the White House angle, Justice, the OIC, everyone speaking for Monica."

Judd was not alone. Donaldson was at the White House—he had his sources. Chris Vlasto, her energetic producer, had a fat Rolodex of Jones lawyers and other Little Rock sources. Dorrance Smith, executive producer of *This Week with David Brinkley,* knew Linda Tripp from their days at the Bush White House, where Smith had worked as a communications adviser. Indeed, for a time, Tripp had been his secretary, and they remained friends. Smith also knew Gary Aldrich, a former FBI agent who had also worked at the White House and written a book that was sharply critical of the president. Shelley Ross, who was Diane Sawyer's producer, exploited a connection she had with Lucianne Goldberg—they spoke frequently in the days immediately after the story broke. "Juicy tidbits" was the way Goldberg described what she gave to Ross. From all of them apparently came information or insights that enriched Judd's reporting. On a story of this magnitude, ABC benefited from a spirit of collegial collaboration, uncommon in network coverage.

Thursday's piece was a typical example of television scandal coverage.

It was divided into three parts. Judd opened with a timely taped interview with Lewinsky's lawyer, William Ginsburg, who had just returned to Washington from Los Angeles. His client was supposed to be deposed by Jones's lawyers on Friday. Ginsburg disclosed that U.S. District Court Judge Susan Webber Wright would determine later that evening whether the deposition would proceed as scheduled or be postponed. Ginsburg implied that he favored postponement—he needed the time to arrange an immunity deal for Lewinsky.

Then Judd introduced the second part of her piece. Leading with the breathless "ABC News has learned . . . ," she reported that Lewinsky had been "offered leniency if she agreed to wear a wire and secretly tape conversations of others—presumably, Vernon Jordan, Mr. Clinton's secretary and possibly the President himself." "Leniency" was intended to be a softer, looser word than "immunity." Judd was referring to Lewinsky's seizure the previous Friday by FBI agents working with Starr's prosecutors, who then interrogated and even threatened her. Quoting "a source," Judd went on to say that the "talks fell apart." A brief sound bite from Starr followed. He defended his prosecutors, saying that they had behaved "properly" within their "jurisdiction."

The third part of Judd's story concerned "this document," as she displayed it, "obtained by ABC News." Again, she patted herself on the back. She did not tell her viewers how or from whom ABC News had obtained it. The "document," she said, "contain[ed] talking points—instructions for how to answer" questions posed to Tripp by Jones's lawyers. One instruction, according to "sources," was that Tripp say Lewinsky left her White House job "because she was stalking the 'P,' the president, not because she was having an affair with him."

Finally, Judd concluded by pointing not to vague "sources" but rather to "prosecutors" (presumably from the OIC), who believed that the talking points came "from a lawyer obviously concerned about limiting damage to President Clinton." In this way, Judd reflected the prevailing OIC view at the time that Bruce Lindsey or another of the president's lawyers was the likely author of the talking points. Judd was not the only good reporter spreading questionable information at that time. *The New York Times, The Washington Post, Newsweek,* and other newspapers and networks also did their share.

CBS, once described as "the Tiffany network" but now languishing in third place in network ratings, was—like so many other news organizations—playing catch-up journalism, which, on a story of this force, imposed unbelievable pressures on reporters, anchors, and producers. The competitive Dan Rather, the White House serving as his brilliantly illuminated backdrop, opened his broadcast with loaded phrases designed to inject immediacy and drama into his broadcast: "possible pivotal night here at the White House," "it's stand and deliver time for the president and for special prosecutor Kenneth Starr," "frenzied photo-op," and "details that became clear just before broadcast time." Scott Pelley, who was then the CBS White House correspondent, just as Rather had been during the Watergate scandal, used sound bites from Clinton, Jordan, and McCurry to highlight a stream of self-proclaimed "exclusives" to convey the impression that his information was so hot-off-the-press precious, timely, and important that he couldn't possibly source any of it.

Pelley got caught up in the breathlessness of the moment. "Dan," he began, "we understand . . . ," and then Pelley unloaded his "exclusives."

First, "lawyers for Monica Lewinsky" planned to tell a "federal judge" that the now famous intern was going to plead the Fifth Amendment in Friday's deposition.

Second, "CBS News has just learned" that Starr had subpoenaed Betty Currie. (Here Pelley inserted the Clinton clip denying an improper relationship.)

Third, without citing a single source, Pelley reviewed what *Newsweek*, ABC, and *The Washington Post* had already reported—that Tripp had taped Lewinsky, that Lewinsky had been subpoenaed to testify in the Jones case, that she had sworn (in an affidavit) that she'd never had an affair with Clinton, but in the Tripp tapes she had claimed there was such an affair but Clinton and Jordan had "encouraged her to lie under oath." (Here Pelley inserted the Jordan clip saying he would answer grand jury questions "directly, completely and truthfully.")

Fourth, "CBS News has learned" that Lewinsky complained to Tripp on the secretly recorded tapes that Clinton had other affairs and she named four women, three of whom supposedly worked at the White House, and she was very upset that "Mr. Clinton [was] cheating on her."

Fifth, Clinton denied in his Saturday deposition that he had had a "sexual relationship" with Lewinsky, but, "CBS News has learned," he admitted to an affair with Gennifer Flowers, an affair he had denied in January 1992. (Here Pelley inserted the relevant clip from the *60 Minutes* interview.) The Clinton admission about the Flowers affair had appeared that morning in the *Post*. Pelley followed with a clip of McCurry's denial.

Pelley's on-camera conclusion contained his fourth "CBS News has learned" reference. With each use, the phrase lost currency. Pelley reviewed what had happened to Lewinsky after she was seized by the FBI the previous Friday. Finally, Pelley said: "According to Secret Service documents, Lewinsky was cleared to enter the White House as recently as last month, Dan." Pelley did not tell his viewers whether he had actually seen such "documents" or whether he had simply been told about them.

Pelley's coverage of the Lewinsky scandal rocketed him into second place among the most visible television reporters in 1998, behind only anchor Peter Jennings. In all, Pelley would do 214 stories, 5 fewer than Jennings.

Impeachment was in the air. Pundits had been playing with the possibility from early Wednesday morning, when the story first broke. In fact, according to the Committee of Concerned Journalists, 68 percent of such speculation originated with the press, while only 32 percent was attributed to "congressional" or "administration" or "official" sources. If the president was actually to be impeached, then the vice president, according to the U.S. Constitution, would assume his full responsibilities. Al Gore was suddenly thrust into a controversial spotlight, where he clearly did not want to be. How would he respond? One way would have been to cancel all public appearances and avoid the press. Instead, Gore decided to maintain his normal schedule.

Five newspaper columnists had been invited to Gore's office to discuss a range of issues, including the president's upcoming State of the Union speech. Not surprisingly, the Lewinsky story intruded into the vice president's carefully calibrated plans. The columnists arrived in his office more absorbed with scandal than with policy projections. David M. Shribman of the *Boston Globe* observed that Gore appeared to be saying, by both word and body language, that he intended to remain solidly behind Clinton, even as he prepared to launch his own presidential campaign. "The president has denied the charges," the vice president said in a serenely detached manner, "and I believe him. He has said that he will cooperate fully with the independent counsel, and you will see that is exactly what he does." In his first on the record comments, Gore stressed that the president had fundamental responsibilities at home and abroad that the vice president expected him to fulfill. "For six years I have watched him pursue the agenda he has set for the American people . . . in spite of attacks of various kinds. He is maintaining his focus now." Gore made certain that the press saw no daylight between him and Clinton. "He is not only president of the country," Gore said, "he is my friend." Pundits could discuss impeachment—and they did, more and more in the days that followed. But Gore's public comments and actions were perfectly tuned to the personal and political sensitivity of the occasion.

As William Ginsburg had anticipated, Judge Wright arranged an early evening conference call with lawyers representing Lewinsky and Jones. She informed them that she had decided to postpone indefinitely Lewinsky's scheduled deposition by Jones's lawyers on Friday. The judge, who was in Little Rock, never explained her reasons in public, but the effect of her decision was to clear the path for Ginsburg to try again to arrange an immunity agreement with Starr. Since Monday's unsuccessful negotiation with OIC prosecutors, Ginsburg had had no contact with them, nor they with him. "I wish [Starr] would call me," Ginsburg told reporters plaintively. "I haven't heard from him. I haven't heard from his staff either. Obviously, if there's jeopardy [to Lewinsky], I'd like a deal."

With no one from the OIC with whom to negotiate, Ginsburg had extra time on his hands that he decided to exploit in print and on the airwaves. He started to escort Lewinsky to upscale restaurants, answer all journalistic inquiries, and accept every invitation to appear on a talk show. He didn't want Lewinsky to speak to reporters, and she complied. CBS correspondent Wyatt Andrews managed to get through to Lewinsky on the phone. He found her to be "polite, tired and beleaguered." She told him: "I really can't comment. Could you please talk to the family's attorney?" Andrews pressed for a response to his questions. She stuck to her ground. "I'm very sorry but I shouldn't have said this much. I don't want to have to hang up on you."

Oral sex, as an issue in the scandal, had been raised before, even "reported" before, a quote here or there from the Tripp tapes. But when Ted Koppel of *Nightline* opened his Thursday broadcast with an unembarrassed reference to "oral sex," it was obvious that the Lewinsky scandal had moved even the best of mainstream journalism onto new terrain: a murky place where talk of sexual activity, formerly reserved for off-color comedians or racy late night Web sites, was deemed to be acceptable—indeed, even central—to understanding the news of the day.

"It may ... ultimately come down to the question," said Koppel, "of whether oral sex does or does not constitute adultery." Sensing the need to explain this assertion, he added: "If the question seems both inappropriate and frivolous, it is neither. It may bear directly on the precise language of the president's denials. What sounds, in other words, like a categorical denial may prove to be something altogether different. It is by its very nature an offensive issue, but be forewarned, we will be dealing with it later on."

On air, Koppel then made the obvious point—that he could have selected, as his subject for the evening, the pope's journey to Cuba, or Ted Kaczynski's admission that he was the Unabomber, or Arafat's checkerboard journey to a Middle East accommodation. But he had selected the Lewinsky scandal. As a journalist, he felt that he had no option. He divided the program into four parts: John Donvan reporting on the feeding frenzy engulfing the White House; Chris Bury on Flowers, oral sex, and Clinton's slippery language; Michel McQueen on the criminal investigation centered on the talking points; and finally a Koppel interview with one of Lewinsky's former classmates. It was the second of fifteen straight *Nightline* programs on the scandal.

Donvan began with pictures of a half-empty press room—half-empty because the speaker was Secretary of State Madeleine Albright and the subject was the Clinton-Arafat negotiations. Donvan then cut later in the day to a SRO briefing room. The speaker was McCurry and the subject was sex in the Oval Office. Not much real news, Donvan observed, but it was still a feeding frenzy. Not much real news either when Starr appeared at his news briefing, but it didn't seem to matter to the press corps. The story, Donvan said, had become an "obsession" in less than forty-eight hours, explained in part by the subject matter, but also by the live, instantaneous, and continuous coverage, marked by nonstop talk.

Reporter April Ryan told Donvan: "I mean I can't get it out fast enough. Literally while we are up in the briefings, I'm getting paged to make sure I have that quote, make sure I have this, make sure I have that. So I mean it's something that they're like, you know, chomping at the bit for." Columnist Walter Shapiro said: "In a normal week, the idea of Yassir Arafat going to the Holocaust Museum would be on the cover of news magazines. [Actually, he never did get there.] We'd be talking about it for weeks. Here, you can barely notice it."

Donvan closed by noting that the White House had originally planned on highlighting the president's negotiating skills on the Middle East and his visionary agenda on the economy. "Now, obviously not," he said.

The second piece reviewed "several scandalous allegations against Bill Clinton during his long political career," especially the one involving Gennifer Flowers. "What she said then and how he responded bear re-examination," Koppel said.

Chris Bury used a surgeon's scalpel on Clinton's prose. He returned first to the *60 Minutes* interview. CBS reporter Steve Kroft asked about Flowers's allegation of a "twelve-year affair with you." To which Clinton snapped: "It, that allegation is false." Maybe, Bury observed, "that precise allegation, a twelve-year affair, may indeed have been false. But," he continued, "Bill Clinton also carefully avoided answering or denying the fundamental question, did he have an affair with Gennifer Flowers?" Clinton then said: "You know, I have acknowledged wrongdoing. I have acknowledged causing pain in my marriage." Stephanopoulos, the former Clintonite, had the task of dissecting the president's message. "What the president was trying to do," he said, "was acknowledge that he wasn't perfect, that he had had affairs at some level, but not to give more credibility to Gennifer Flowers than she deserved."

Bury then played audiotapes of telephone conversations between Flowers and Clinton dating back to the late 1980s. The tapes strongly suggested that the two had had a close relationship. Flowers asked at one point if Clinton was "going to run." He answered: "I want to. I wonder if I'm just going to be blown out of the water with this." The "this" was unclear, but it appeared to refer to stories about their relationship. In one of the taped conversations, Flowers was heard talking about having oral sex with Clinton. Bury said, "Several Arkansas state troopers assigned to the Governor's detail have said on the record that Clinton would tell them oral sex is not adultery." Clinton was also heard advising Flowers how to answer journalists who ask about their relationship. "If they ever hit you with it, just say no and go on. There's nothing they can do."

In fact, Bury then showed that Clinton had a long history of "splitting semantical hairs."

- On smoking marijuana: "I've never broken the state law and that when I was in England, I experimented with marijuana a time or two and I didn't like it and didn't inhale and never tried it again."
- On avoiding the Vietnam draft: "I was against the Vietnam War, but I gave up a deferment and put myself back in the draft. I got a high lottery number."
- On Whitewater: "It turned out to be a bad investment, and we lost what was for us a lot of money."
- On campaign finance irregularities: "I'm not trying to disclaim responsibility, but I am trying to point out that there is a, there's a difference between what the party does and what the campaign does."

Bury then discussed this Clintonian quality of semantical evasion with NPR's Mara Liasson, who had interviewed the president on Wednesday. "What set off alarm bells," she recounted, "is when the president said to Jim Lehrer, 'There is no improper relationship,' and of course everybody thought, Uh, oh, he's pulling a Clinton. He's saying there was one but there isn't now." Liasson widened the lens of her analysis: "He has such a high burden of proof now, everything he says is parsed, you know, put under a microscope because, you know, because that's what he, that's his modus operandi."

Even with Bury, in the course of an otherwise first-rate report, "ABC News has learned" reared its boastful head. "ABC News has learned," Bury concluded, that Lewinsky was heard on the Tripp tapes saying "the president draws a distinction between oral sex and adultery. According to a source, who has listened to the tapes, Lewinsky is heard saying there was only oral sex, we never had intercourse. Such distinctions may prove important in the context of what constitutes an improper relationship. And now, when President Clinton tries to answer these new explosive charges, all of Washington will weigh his every word, comma and clause, just as carefully as he does." Bury did not identify his one source by name or organization, so his viewers had no way of judging the reliability of the information.

Michel McQueen's piece zeroed in on "a second broad category of allegations against Mr. Clinton," Koppel said in his introduction, "which legally speaking may be far more threatening." He had in mind the talking points—the idea that one of Clinton's lawyers wrote them on the president's orders or with his knowledge in order to "suborn perjury" or "obstruct justice." If that could be proven, then he would be guilty of a crime and would almost certainly be impeached. McQueen's piece included sound bites from former prosecutors who operated on the assumption that Lewinsky could not possibly have written the talking points herself.

Joseph diGenova, a Washington lawyer and former independent counsel, said that he would first like to have the document. "I would then want to have Ms. Lewinsky explain to me where she got it, who gave it to her, when it was given to her, what she was asked to do with it, was she threatened, was she cajoled, was she paid in some way to do this?" diGenova, too, clearly could not imagine that Lewinsky had the brains or experience to write it herself.

McQueen read key sections of the document, including specific recommendations to Tripp on what she should say during her deposition. Then came McQueen's blunt conclusion: "It is not the language one would expect an inexperiencd young secretary to use in advising a friend."

Barbara Nicastro, another former prosecutor, went even further: "It's not 21-year-old language," she proclaimed. "It's semi-legal. It's got legal-speak in it, if you will."

The issue was whether Tripp was being coached. Since no one seemed to believe that Lewinsky could be the one doing the coaching, it followed that someone had to be coaching Lewinsky. That someone, according to this scenario, had to be either Clinton or Jordan. A third former prosecutor, Alexia Morrison, outlined her problem with the talking points. "Probably the most troubling thing," she said, "is that the documents suggest that there was an effort to persuade the recipient, who we believe was Ms. Tripp, to change her recollection from what she may have believed was the case to something closer to something the president was already on record as saying."

Equally troubling was that no journalist seriously entertained the possibility that Lewinsky could have written the talking points. As a result, all stories were based on the faulty premise that she did not. Even *Nightline* got caught.

Finally, Koppel interviewed Stephen Enghouse, a former classmate of

Lewinsky's at Lewis and Clark University in Portland, Oregon. Koppel asked about Lewinsky's credibility: On a scale of one to ten, "where would you put her?" Enghouse answered, "Somewhere around a five or a six." Koppel seemed puzzled. Why so low? he wondered. "Well," the former classmate answered, "just because I know her and I know that she's kind of young and seeks attention and I believe would be prone to sensationalize or overdramatize or exaggerate specific areas or instances in her life that would lead her to gain more attention."

Koppel:	"You believe she is not only capable of but likely to have made up that kind of a story?"
Enghouse:	"Yes. You know, I don't like to say that. Monica's my friend. But I would not be at all surprised and I think it's probably likely that yes, she's making that up."
Koppel:	"Why do you say that?
Enghouse:	"I don't think she had any idea that it would get any further than this woman she was talking to. I'm very confident she had no idea it would go to this proportion, you know, and had she known that I don't think she ever would have said anything."

Koppel concluded his broadcast by saying, "The White House will very likely seize on Stephen Enghouse's assessment of Monica Lewinsky as evidence that she is not to be believed." And yet, Koppel said, she was probably granted "late evening" access to the White House, she was probably helped by Vernon Jordan, she was probably implicating the president in embarrassing and possibly illegal situations on the Tripp tapes. Koppel was not drawing specific conclusions, but he was surely suggesting a few; and they all led inexorably to the view, unspoken by the anchor, that the president had been lying under oath and that the constitutional ground beneath him was shaking.

CHAPTER 10

GREENROOM CHATTERBOXES

January 23, 1998

"SHE IS STRATEGIC, SHE IS SAVVY, SHE IS A CRISIS MANAGER,
AND SHE IS IN BATTLE MODE."
                                        —A friend about Hillary Rodham Clinton

"THERE IS A KOOKY QUALITY TO ALL OF THIS. YOU JUST HAVE
THE FEELING THERE'S ONE BIG PIECE MISSING."
                                        —Robert Bennett

"BOY, JACKIE, THAT'S PRETTY STRONG STUFF, ESPECIALLY
WITH THE SEMEN. THAT COULD BE FORENSIC EVIDENCE."
                                        —ABC's Barbara Walters to Jackie Judd

I t had happened at least once before.

Six years earlier to the day, on January 23, 1992, Ted Koppel did a pio-
neering story on *Nightline* about an alleged affair between presidential candidate Bill Clinton and an Arkansas woman named Gennifer Flowers, an
affair first "reported" that morning by *The Star*, the supermarket tabloid,
which faxed the story to major news organizations. It was tempting bait, but
in those days most news organizations kept a respectable distance from stories about the private lives of public officials. Clinton had spent much of that
snowy day in New Hampshire denying the report, and ABC, for one, had no
independent confirmation. Neither did any of the other large news organizations. Short wire service stories fed local radio and television news, which
ate it up. The story hovered around the far edges of the mainstream press
until late in the evening, when *Nightline* produced and broadcast a highly
original approach to the telling of the Flowers "scoop," an approach copied
by other news programs a thousand times since then. It focused on how
the media covered the tabloid report—*The Star* faxing the story to news
organizations, reporters gossiping about it while trying unsuccessfully to confirm it, the governor denying it at one campaign stop after another, and

then of course the pundits and political operatives wondering what if any impact it would have on the presidential campaign.

This new approach allowed a news program to slip around direct coverage of a scandal by reporting on how the press covered it—in this oblique and sophisticated way, covering the scandal by focusing on the coverage of the scandal. The *Nightline* broadcast had one other important effect: it legitimized coverage of the scandal by other news organizations. If Koppel could cover it, albeit indirectly, then so could they.

Now, half a dozen years later, Koppel's role was not to cover the coverage but to explore the importance of oral sex in the president's definition of a "sexual relationship." This proved to be, as Koppel said on Thursday night, a crucial element in the story. By raising and discussing this sensitive issue on network television, Koppel eased the way for Matt Lauer to pursue the same subject on NBC's *Today* program the following morning. Lauer had no fresh information, but oral sex as an issue was now "out there." If anyone had complained to Lauer, he could have explained his willingness to discuss the president's novel definition of a "sexual relationship" by saying, "Hey, Koppel talked about it; why can't I?"

"New information coming out last night says" that "the president makes a distinction, draws a line, between having oral sex with a woman and that being considered an adulterous affair," Lauer began, turning to Isikoff, his expert on Clinton's sex life.

Isikoff answered primly, "Well, you asked the question, so I'll answer." Isikoff reminded viewers of the Tripp tapes. "Yes, on the tapes, there is—there are discussions along those lines." Isikoff was at the time one of the few Washington reporters who had actually heard any of the tapes. He reached back several years and disclosed that "during Troopergate some of the troopers were quoted as saying the president made that distinction. . . . We do know that Monica Lewinsky, in her discussions with Linda Tripp, says that President Clinton made that distinction."

Isikoff expressed the impatience of many journalists that Friday morning who wondered how much longer Clinton could avoid a substantive response to the questions about the Lewinsky scandal. "The president clearly has to make some sort of public statement that's going to convince the public that—that his position on this is tenable and that he's telling the truth," he said.

Isikoff then referred to the WAVES, the records kept by the Secret

Service on White House visits. If Lewinsky had actually visited the president "at unorthodox hours, either on weekends or late in the evenings," that would be in the record. "What explanation is going to be given for why Monica Lewinsky made those visits?" Isikoff asked.

Lauer reminded Isikoff: "Although keeping in mind there's nothing illegal about visiting the White House."

"No," Isikoff agreed, as the studio clock moved toward 7:15 a.m., "but the president's problem right now, I think, is less legal, although he certainly faces that, than political. He's got to lead the country. He's got to maintain his credibility as a leader, and if most of the public doesn't believe him on this . . . it's going to be very difficult, if not impossible, for him to do that."

Every television studio in the nation's capital has a "greenroom," the inappropriately named (it's almost never green in color) and inexpensively outfitted room where the reporters and their guests—pollsters, politicians, prime ministers, arms control experts, economists, and government officials—gather to exchange rumors, check their hair and makeup, and wait for their turn to be brilliant under the lights.

At ABC headquarters in Washington, the star on that Friday morning was William Ginsburg, Lewinsky's attorney, who was appearing on *Good Morning America* as part of an extraordinary run of interviews designed, first, to coax Starr's prosecutors into negotiating an immunity deal for his client, and second, to launch a sharp attack against their professionalism—two goals that on the surface seemed totally irreconcilable. For Ginsburg, there was an additional dividend: he enjoyed the spotlight, the publicity, the limos, the nonstop cell phone courtships by the network divas, the round of interviews and restaurants, the oohs and aahs. Bill Ginsburg, by God, had arrived in the big time! He had a kind of power—he had access to Monica, the one woman everyone wanted to interview, the one woman who could tell her half of the story and possibly bring down a president.

Once their on-air interview began, anchor Lisa McRee asked Ginsburg about Lewinsky. How was she?

"Devastated, concerned, upset and fearful, does not know what the future holds," Ginsburg replied.

What was her relationship with the president?

"She worked with the president in the White House, and other than that she has no relationship that I'm aware of."

Ginsburg repeated what was to become his mantra: "I can't talk about the details of the case," he said. "Anything that would invade the attorney-client privilege would be unethical for me to broach."

McRee asked if Ginsburg thought Starr's investigation was "legitimate." The question was like a fastball over the plate. Ginsburg, angry that *The Washington Post* and *The New York Times* had both run anti-Lewinsky stories that day that, he thought, could only have come from Starr's office, blasted it out of the ballpark. "I don't like the way the investigation has been conducted," Ginsburg said. "Right off the bat, you talk about stings, and wires and traps. I'm not happy with that at all, and especially when you are dealing with a 24-year-old girl. It's not nice."

McRee, quoting from the newspaper accounts, led Ginsburg into a discussion of Starr's wiring of Tripp for her meeting with Lewinsky the week before. "Goes a step further," Ginsburg jumped in. "He lured Miss Lewinsky to the Ritz Carlton Hotel . . . and with the help of four or five FBI agents and three or four U.S. attorneys, managed to detain her, although she was technically free to go, for eight or nine hours without an attorney. That should frighten anyone who is involved in the process here in America."

McRee: "Were they telling her that they had evidence against her
          and threatening her in any way, legally?"
Ginsburg: "I don't know. I wasn't there. . . . I can say that repeatedly
          during the course of discussions with the office of the
          prosecutor, we have been squeezed. How's that for a
          direct statement? And they've even made threats to
          involve her parents."

Ginsburg then raised the issue of the Lewinsky-Tripp tapes. He found it "very disturbing" that the press seemed to have copies while he did not. "Would you believe it?" he exclaimed. "I haven't heard those tapes. I don't have the information that the press has. I've been fortunate to be invited onto shows like yours. I have heard quotes from the tapes. And I have had to ask the press if they would send me transcripts of the tapes. I wonder why the Office of the Independent Counsel won't let me listen to the tapes and comment on them."

McRee asked about the talking points, quoting "sources within the prosecutor's office," who suggested the information might have come from "someone associated with Vernon Jordan." Ginsburg acknowledged that he had "seen" this "piece of paper" but did not know who wrote it.

Lewinsky's lawyer used the forum of a network program to build sympathy for his client. "She finds herself caught between the president of the United States, Vernon Jordan and Kenneth Starr," he said, "probably three of the most powerful people in the world if not this nation."

Having featured ABC's Ginsburg "exclusive"—easily the most overused and undervalued word in journalism that week—McRee then turned to Jackie Judd, "the woman who broke this story." Judd opened her morning report by crediting Ginsburg with success in persuading Judge Wright to "indefinitely postpone Lewinsky's deposition in the Paula Jones case." The Jones lawyers wanted Lewinsky to help them "establish a pattern of alleged sexual misconduct" by Clinton, said Judd, and Starr wanted Lewinsky to help him "establish a pattern of alleged obstruction of justice by the administration." Judd also reported that Lewinsky had "sworn under oath she did not have an affair with the president." But, Judd added, "If she lied, she could be subject to perjury; and if she lied at the behest of Jordan and the president, then she could also be subject to conspiracy charges."

McRee introduced Sam Donaldson, who was already at the ABC battle station on a White House lawn crammed with cameras, satellite gear, cables, and technicians. "What do you think the White House will say this morning?" McRee wanted to know. "It's a terrible dilemma down here," Donaldson responded, explaining that Clinton's lawyers wanted silence while his political advisers favored a degree of transparency. Donaldson, who remembered Watergate, recalled for his viewers that Nixon had often said that it wasn't the crime that hurt, "it's the cover-up." McRee asked a cream puff question, mostly to trumpet ABC's "exclusive" with Ginsburg, about whether the White House agreed with Ginsburg—how could it not?—that Starr had been acting improperly. Actually, the White House had a split-level response, Donaldson responded: on the record, being very proper and correct, but on background, excoriating Starr and his deputies for conducting "a political witch hunt."

At 8 a.m., McRee returned for the second hour of *Good Morning America*, running a long clip from her Ginsburg interview. Her supporting cast, as usual, consisted of Judd and Donaldson. "I've been told by a source," Judd began, that Starr had subpoenaed Lewinsky to appear before a grand jury, thus putting pressure on Ginsburg to strike a deal with Starr or watch his client face "potential criminal charges, possibly perjury, possibly conspiracy." Was Ginsburg her source that morning? And why depend on only one? More than two years later, Judd explained why she occasionally used only one source, when two would have been safer. Quoting *Washington Post* columnist David Broder, she said that it depended on the "quality" of the source, the "trust" she had in him. Broder had said that one excellent source was better than two acceptable sources. There were times, Judd added, when she might have been "too honest," acknowledging in a story that her information came from "a source" when she could just as easily have said "sources" and no one would have known the difference. Judd closed her piece by citing "sources," who told her there might be "several messages from the president" on Lewinsky's voice mail at home. "And you can bet that Ken Starr would love to get his hands on that," she concluded.

Donaldson reported that the president was going to hold a cabinet meeting later in the day. Usually, such meetings were used as photo-ops, a way to push an administration policy. Not this time, Donaldson said. The meeting would be closed to the press. Donaldson also reported that former President Jimmy Carter, "a very straitlaced Baptist," would be paying a call on Clinton later in the day and would almost certainly advise him "to tell the truth." Donaldson then returned to his doomsday prediction: "If the truth doesn't save him, I guess he's out of here."

Donaldson was reflecting the widespread sentiment in Washington at the time that the president was indeed facing a political collapse that could drive him from office in a matter of days. One presidential adviser told Doyle McManus, the Washington bureau chief of the *Los Angeles Times,* "We all thought he might be finished."

As Mike McCurry entered the Crystal Ballroom of the Sheraton Carlton Hotel at 8 a.m., he looked "shaken and downbeat," a White House official who would clearly have preferred not to be the "guest of honor" at a crowded Sperling Breakfast that Friday morning. But McCurry had promised host Godfrey Sperling, Jr., better known as Budge, of the *Chris-*

tian Science Monitor, and the spokesman felt he had no option but to appear and take questions.

The Washington institution known as the Sperling Breakfast started in 1966, when Sperling invited Charles H. Percy, a Republican businessman from Illinois who was running for the Senate, to join him and twenty or so of his print colleagues for an on-the-record conversation about the campaign. Sperling would have preferred a lunch, but he had trouble booking a hotel or a club. It turned out that breakfast seemed easier, non-threatening and non-competitive, and a journalistic tradition was born. Over time, a succession of presidents, candidates, senators, congresspeople, and foreign dignitaries have showed up for scrambled eggs and generally respectful questions. Sperling did not invite television anchors or reporters, fearing the cameras would encourage the visiting politicians to engage in sound-bite discourse. Though he respected a number of television commentators, such as Howard K. Smith and Eric Sevareid, he really preferred old-fashioned newspaper talk. News organizations paid $20 per reporter for the privilege of breakfasting with Sperling and his guest of honor.

Not all Sperling Breakfasts have been newsworthy. Indeed, Sperling would be the first to admit that many have produced only a yawn. But every now and then the relatively relaxed and informal atmosphere has lulled a guest into revealing newsworthy information. For example, in 1993, GOP consultant Ed Rollins boasted that he had given "sitting-it-out money" to black ministers in New Jersey to suppress the Democratic vote. Similarly, in 1995, during the government shutdown, House Speaker Newt Gingrich complained about having to sit in the back of Air Force One during a flight from Israel, resulting in "crybaby" headlines around the country.

On this Friday morning, reporters were especially eager to get behind the screaming headlines about the presidential scandal. What could McCurry tell them? If the White House wanted to make news and yet avoid the hurly-burly of the noon briefing, the Sperling Breakfast would have been the perfect place. Sperling began breakfast with his usual announcement: "The only ground rule here is that we're on the record." What followed was painful. McCurry was trying to be loyal to Clinton and yet put a small but discernible distance between himself and the president. Each question seemed to corner and trouble the usually nimble spokesman, who tried not to go one inch beyond his mandate, plucking lines from White House scripts that the president or his aides had used in recent days.

Q. How was the scandal affecting Clinton?

A. "This president has developed a very rare capacity to focus . . . and to put in a distant place those things that would anger him. He understands there are questions on the mind of the American people and he wants to answer them sooner rather than later."

Q. What about the reported split between the political and legal advisers?

A. "That's not the case," McCurry said, knowing it was the case. "It's more that people know the President needs to address these issues and have answers but at the same time there are legal proceedings going on and he has to give thorough and complete answers. . . . The predominant view of all of us . . . is that we've got to get it done and we've got to get it done right."

Q. But if the president did no wrong, then what has he to hide?

A. "He did no wrong, he says, but there are numerous allegations that require a thoroughly sophisticated and complete review." (Most reporters heard the qualifying "he says" and understood McCurry to be hinting that he knew he might not be getting the whole truth.)

Q. Well, was McCurry being told the whole truth?

A. "I'm very confident and comfortable in what the President has told me to say."

Q. Was McCurry thinking about quitting, as *Newsweek's* Evan Thomas had suggested the night before on television?

A. Obviously irritated, McCurry said he hadn't spoken with Thomas for months. "Obviously it's not so. . . . [The President] is in a tough moment. I think that those of us who work for him think that it's important to help him."

Q. If the allegations proved to be true, did McCurry think the president should resign?

A. "That is so horrible a thought I won't entertain it."

Q. Would McCurry lie to protect Clinton?

A. "Press secretaries can't lie if they want to hold the position."

Q. Would McCurry quit if Clinton asked him to lie for him?

A. "I think you know me well enough to know."
Q. Did McCurry know anything about the Lewinsky entanglement?
A. "These allegations were a total surprise to me and still are, still quite unimaginable."
Q. How come so few Democrats seemed to be rushing to the president's defense?
A. "They are out there in the country wondering if this is a tidal wave that is going to take them away."
Q. So was this a national story?
A. "This is not a Washington-only story."
Q. What, in McCurry's judgment, was a worst case scenario?
A. "It's those horrible things that I refused to contemplate."

McCurry was walking on hot coals. He knew that his comments would ricochet from one Washington newsroom to another, each feeding the scandal frenzy that was already consuming the city. Could Clinton survive? On Friday morning, McCurry seemed less confident about the answer than he had been on Thursday.

That same Friday, The *Washington Post* exploded with twenty-five stories (totaling 22,799 words) about the Lewinsky scandal, more than any other newspaper in the country. On Thursday, it had run eleven stories, which seemed heavy coverage at the time. No angle was ignored or shortchanged. There was a White House story by John Harris. Susan Schmidt and Peter Baker covered Starr's operations. Ruth Marcus and Thomas B. Edsall wrote about Jordan. David Broder explored the concerns of congressional Democrats. Dana Priest and Rene Sanchez profiled Linda Tripp, the "once trusted civil servant at the heart of the scandal." E. J. Dionne, Jr., Richard Cohen, George F. Will, and Broder contributed columns to the paper's op-ed page. There was a long editorial entitled A PRESIDENTIAL DENIAL. The Style section gushed with feature stories—WASHINGTON SINKS ITS TEETH INTO THE CLINTON STORY, for example. Even the Business section (G1) responded to the crisis: Sharon Walsh and Robert O'Harrow, Jr., wrote WHITE HOUSE CRISIS, WALL STREET SHUDDERS.

The *Los Angeles Times* was not far behind. It published twenty stories (16,032 words) about the scandal, having run nine the day before. In a sense, Lewinsky was handled like a home-town girl who made good in Washington. CAPITAL RUSHES TO JUDGMENT, AS PUBLIC HOLDS FIRE, by Doyle McManus and Janet Hook, was the headline of one of three front-page stories. Robert W. Welkos wrote a story about the possibility of American military action against Iraq in the context of the popular movie *Wag the Dog*, a hilarious satire about a president who is caught in an embarrassing situation with a visiting Girl Scout and manufactures a fake war against Albania to distract the nation's attention from the scandal. (Hollywood is an important beat for the *L.A. Times.*) Eleanor Randolph and Jane Hall examined "media coverage," while Howard Rosenberg criticized the press's skimpy treatment of the pope's visit to Cuba.

The New York Times ran twelve stories (8,546 words) about the scandal, as compared with seven the day before. It too covered the waterfront, though not as extensively as *The Washington Post* and the *L.A. Times*. John Broder did the White House story, confusing a dress Clinton might have given Lewinsky as a gift with a different semen-stained dress that later proved to be so crucial in Starr's investigation. David E. Rosenbaum analyzed the "new vigor" in Starr's probe, which, until a few days earlier, had been "seen as flagging." James Barron found the *Wag the Dog* comparison to be simply irresistible. The lead editorial wagged its finger at Clinton—"Tell the full story, Mr. President," it urged. Pam Belluck wrote about the "mood of dismay and concern" among Democrats. Elisabeth Bumiller focused on Isikoff, "the man with the Clinton scoop" who was "scooped again."

The Wall Street Journal was still in its own world, running not a single major story about the scandal on Friday morning. In its front-page "Washington Wire" column, it did top its list of "inside-the-Beltway" stories with the scandal, but kept its report to a skimpy 122 words. "Sex allegations about Clinton stir turmoil among Democrats," it began. The battle between the political and legal wings of the White House was featured in the story, and Pentagon colleagues of Lewinsky quoted her as rejecting opportunities to return to the White House if she wasn't going to be posted near the Oval Office. "I don't feel like I can serve the president if I'm not in the West Wing," she was supposed to have said. Finally, Democratic strategist Bob Beckel was quoted as warning that "the political landscape is littered with the bodies of people who predicted Bill Clinton's demise."

The next news item in the column was devoted to a poll. Co-sponsored by NBC News and the *Journal,* it stated that 79 percent of the American people favored Clinton's domestic program. Pollsters Robert Teeter (a Republican) and Peter Hart (a Democrat) explained that the president's policy initiatives were "so broad that even two-thirds of Republicans and conservatives can live with them."

Clinton's not-so-secret strategy was to co-opt the center of the political spectrum and in this way enlist the support of enough moderates from both major parties to block the opposition of the two extremes. Add economic prosperity at home and peace abroad, according to this strategy, and the odds were that Clinton could survive any scandal. But at the time, judging by the prognostications of many pundits, his presidency seemed to be hanging by a thread, likely to break under the weight of the next whispered rumor.

Forty-eight hours after the scandal broke, political reporters, under immense pressure to advance the story, were desperately searching for new information. Very few of them had reliable sources of their own; most had to rework material that had already appeared in print or on television—or in the new world of the Internet. In this frantic environment, *The Hotline* was an invaluable source of information, rumors, gossip, and eye-catching quotes.

The Hotline became a part of Washington's political and journalistic culture in September 1987, when it was launched as a bipartisan enterprise by two political consultants, Republican Doug Bailey and Democrat Roger Craver. They believed Washington was dominated by an "inside-the-Beltway" mentality, and they wanted to broaden and diversify the conventional wisdom by publishing a daily digest of political quotes from all over the country. They knew from their own experience that they did not have the time to read the *Chicago Tribune* and the *Dallas Morning News*—in addition to *The Washington Post, The New York Times,* and *The Wall Street Journal,* which they routinely read—or watch all the evening newscasts or Sunday morning interview programs. If they could quickly and conveniently find out what the rest of the United States was reading and watching, it would be of interest and value to them—and to anyone else absorbed with the world of politics. *The Hotline,* much to the delight of Bailey and Craver, quickly attracted a devoted audience at the tidy annual sum of $4,800 per subscription, and blossomed into a commercial success. It was then purchased by the National Journal Group, which itself was bought in 1997 by David Bradley, a Washington entrepreneur who expanded his media empire in

2000 by buying *Atlantic* magazine from Mortimer Zuckerman, the real estate magnate who already owned *U.S. News & World Report* and the *New York Daily News.*

At 11:40 a.m. every weekday, *The Hotline* hits the Internet and connects its approximately seven hundred paid subscribers to a thirty-page menu of tasty political tidbits, quotes, and jokes culled from newspapers, magazines, and radio and television programs from around the country. Read one edition and it's easy to see how a political junkie can become addicted. Twenty-five thousand readers, through piracy or group subscriptions, get their political fix from *The Hotline* before going to lunch. ABC News political director Mark Halperin calls and faxes *The Hotline* on an almost daily basis, trying to draw attention to ABC scoops and witticisms. "It's unfathomable to me," he told *The Washington Post*'s Dana Milbank, "how people covered politics before *The Hotline.*" Its 11:40 a.m. release time, he said, is "a major touchstone of my day."

The Hotline operates on the assumption that everyone, from major networks to online magazines and local newspapers, wants to be quoted, read, and recognized. Adam Levine, senior producer of *Hardball with Chris Matthews,* said, "When you're thinking of a line of questioning, *The Hotline* is very much in your mind." Any time Matthews could elicit a quotable quote for *The Hotline,* his interview would immediately be considered a success. Jake Tapper, who writes for *Salon,* an online magazine, joked that he'd throw a party for *Hotline* editors any time. For *Salon* and other new media seeking acceptance and new "eyeballs," the recognition flowing from a *Hotline* mention is crucial; it places *Salon* alongside The *Washington Post* and other mainstream news organizations as a political player.

By Friday, *The Hotline* had become an eagerly awaited "touchstone" for every political reporter covering the presidential scandal. Somewhere in its rich harvest of supercharged quotes, they hoped, was a gem waiting to be reported—again. There was only one problem: by its very nature all of it was not solid news; there was also a great deal of information that was unchecked, unconfirmed, uncertain, and without context.

Take, for example, an item that day: "Matt Drudge reported that there was also a 'DNA situation.' According to Tripp, Lewinsky had saved an item of clothing with Clinton's dried semen on it. Drudge: 'She was bragging to a friend, which she related to Tripp, that "Hey, look at this, look at this and look at those stains—guess what that is."'"

The quote was from conservative pundit Mary Matalin. Was she quoting Drudge accurately, or vamping? Was Matalin pulling a quote from Drudge's Web site on Wednesday, or from his *Today* program appearance on Thursday? Was Matalin on the local NBC affiliate station, WRC, meaning she was heard only in the Washington area; or was she on a network NBC program, meaning she was heard all over the country? No one could tell from the published quote. And yet, the quote was tantalizingly available, tempting reporters under pressure to use it without any confirmation or to raise it with officials and colleagues, thus turning it into a virtual fact, which others, assuming its reliability, might publish or broadcast.

It was not only the journalists who lived in this virtual world of presumed information; it was also the president and his senior advisers, who had to react to the uncontrollable surge of information about the spreading scandal. Political reporter Richard L. Berke and White House reporter James Bennet spent most of Friday trying to penetrate the wall that had quickly been constructed around President Clinton. Their story appeared on the front page of Saturday's *New York Times,* headlined THOSE CLOSEST TO CLINTON ARE LEFT IN THE DARK. What Berke and Bennet learned from "many White House officials" was that the president, "increasingly a picture of isolation," had "shut out his top political aides," who were "so in the dark" that "they spent the last few days staring at the television to stay on top of developments." When questioned by journalists operating under conditions of ferocious competition and time pressures, these aides felt "virtually paralyzed," unable to be helpful because they themselves knew so little and besides were under orders not to talk to the press. Berke and Bennet discovered, however, that a few of the president's political advisers were willing to share their frustration with them, even though they knew it would be reported. "Nobody here knows what's going on," one "high-level White House official" confided. "It's like you're punched in the stomach and the air was knocked out of you. It's a sickening feeling. The president has to say something." Other officials described themselves as "demoralized" and "frustrated." Robert B. Reich, a former secretary of labor in the Clinton administration, told the *Times* reporters that he had known Clinton for thirty years, ever since their days as Rhodes Scholars at Oxford.

"I can't believe he would do these things, including suborning perjury. It seems absurd. Yet, where is all the smoke coming from?"

Where there was smoke, there was Hillary. Mrs. Clinton, recognizing the severity of the crisis suddenly engulfing the White House, entered the president's top-secret deliberations with a trio of lawyers: Bob Bennett, David Kendall, and Bruce Lindsey. (Other lawyers at the White House were excluded from these talks.) "She is strategic, she is savvy, and she is a crisis manager," said one friend of the family. "And she is in battle mode." Did she at the time know the truth about her husband's relationship with Lewinsky? She acted, so far as the public could determine, as if she was still trying to learn the truth, whatever she might privately have suspected. Mrs. Clinton spent much of the day on the phone rallying loyalists to the president's defense or calling former campaign aides for advice and guidance.

At noon, President Clinton took time from his legal defense to meet with members of his cabinet. For a few days, it seemed as if the government of the United States had simply stopped, so great was the impact of the scandal on Washington. When the president entered the Cabinet Room, he paused to check his audience: Secretary of State Madeleine Albright, Secretary of Defense William Cohen, Secretary of the Treasury Robert Rubin, Commerce Secretary William Daley, Education Secretary Richard Riley, Health and Human Services Secretary Donna Shalala, Interior Secretary Bruce Babbitt, and Chief of Staff Erskine Bowles. "I'll be fine," he assured them, trying unsuccessfully to present an encouraging, upbeat picture. "And you will be too, and let's all hang in there." Clinton then looked them in the eye and denied the stories of an improper relationship with an intern.

After an unusually brief meeting, the president left and the cabinet broke unceremoniously into two groups. Cohen and Rubin slipped out of the White House by way of a back door and the others left by way of the front door to face a hungry horde of journalists. Albright, Shalala, Daley, and Riley all said that the president had denied the widespread reports of a sexual relationship with Lewinsky. "The president started out by saying that the allegations are untrue," Albright reported, "that we should stay focused on our jobs and that he will be fine." The journalists were hardly to be satisfied with this pablum. Questions quickly engulfed this courageous remnant of the Clinton cabinet. In a feisty exchange between the secretaries and the journalists, there were many blunt questions but no satisfactory answers. "The president is focused on what he has to do," Albright repeated. "I am focused on what I have to do. The other secretaries are. And I think the American public would be appalled if they thought that we weren't doing our jobs." The allegations, the reporters shouted. What about the allegations? "I believe that the allegations are completely untrue," Albright repeated. "I'll second that, definitely," said Daley, with Riley and Shalala backing him up. The four cabinet members then slowly retreated from the battlefield, neither side victorious. Clinton had lied to his cabinet, the cabinet had carried his lie to the journalists, and they reported it to the public.

Almost as if Hollywood were orchestrating this White House drama, two experienced reporters for *The Washington Post*—John Harris, who covered the White House, and John Goshko, a diplomatic reporter covering the United Nations—discovered on Friday that "Clinton and his senior national security advisers" had "concluded" that the United States would "likely" have to bomb Iraq within a few weeks, unless Iraqi leader Saddam Hussein stopped interfering with the work of UN inspectors. First the United States—and Great Britain, to a much lesser extent—would lead the bombing assault against Iraq, and then they would expand the "no-fly zone" to cover the entire country. Harris and Goshko considered the possibility that Clinton was deliberately trying to manipulate them and the American people by raising the likelihood of war as a distraction from Lewinsky; but the reporters thought the story was too important and Clinton too cautious and responsible in matters of foreign policy to kill it. They had considered the *Wag the Dog* scenario but dismissed it. They submitted their story, and their editors signaled agreement with their news judgment by putting it on the front page.

Richard Cohen's column in *The Washington Post* that day began with a reference to the movie *Wag the Dog*. "It may be time to bomb Albania," he wrote. Cohen was joking, of course. Like other thoughtful columnists, Cohen reached into his history file for a Watergate comparison. Then, he said, it all began with a "mere burglary" but ended with a presidential resignation. Why? Because it wasn't the crime that led to the resignation; it was the cover-up: lies, suborning perjury, and obstruction of justice.

Cohen later recalled that when the scandal broke in his paper on Wednesday morning, he was participating in a panel discussion in New York. Publisher Mort Zuckerman and reporter Matt Cooper joined him on the panel and editor/author Harry Evans served as moderator. "We discussed Monica on the panel, of course," remembered Cohen. "It was a complicated moment, because we all knew so very little, just what we had read in the paper, or heard about it, and we didn't want to suggest anything too serious. I kept pretending to be cautious, but after the panel, I went straight to my office and wrote a column for Thursday's paper." His editor, Meg Greenfield, held the column for a day.

Cohen believed that major scandals generally had their roots in earlier events—that Watergate, for example, really started with the Pentagon Papers case, when the Supreme Court overruled a lower court decision (amounting to prior restraint) that *The New York Times* and other newspapers could not publish a classified history of the Vietnam War. Likewise, the Lewinsky scandal originated with the Gennifer Flowers case in 1992. "The story," he said, "was broken by *The Star* tabloid. I remember when I read the fax distributed in my office, I knew it was true. That night, I went to a dinner in New York with three or four other couples. I thought they'd be absorbed with the Flowers story. They weren't. I was the only one who was. When we turned on the 10 p.m. news, it was all over television. Same at 11 p.m. It was all over the local news. For the first time, the local news decided what was news, not the big boys. The big boys were dinosaurs already. With Monica, that was a monster story."

At 1:27 p.m., the White House's increasingly bedraggled spokesman, who yearned for nothing more than a graceful exit from government service but now found that the scandal had reduced his options, entered a briefing room filled with reporters eager to advance the story. McCurry had only himself to blame for the widespread journalistic belief on Friday that the president was on the edge of resigning in disgrace. His comments at the Sperling Breakfast had fanned the flames of speculation about a Clinton resignation, perhaps within a matter of days.

According to McManus, McCurry "was guilty of sparking saturation coverage and expectations." In his selection of words, McCurry had tried only to be cautious and reasonably candid, but journalists that morning had their ears pitched to the shrill cry of impending disaster. They didn't hear his words, they heard only a melody suggestive of crisis. At the daily briefing, McCurry's mandate was to say nothing in many different ways. For the third day in a row, he could not shed any light on the developing scandal, even as journalistic expectations now reached totally unrealistic levels.

McCurry began: "I don't have anything new to add to this story today."

Reporters erupted with dissatisfaction. They were fed up with the administration's stonewalling. They did not believe that he had nothing new to add to the story. A number of bureau chiefs present at the Sperling Breakfast had transcribed his comments and circulated them among the White House press corps. All of those "horrible things" that he had "refused to contemplate" were on their minds. What "horrible things"? Resignation? Impeachment? For the first time at a White House briefing, McCurry was asked directly whether the president had considered resigning.

"No," he snapped. "That is not a serious question."

But in fact it was a very serious and appropriate question, and it generated widespread speculation over the weekend that the Clinton administration was close to being toppled by a sex scandal. Washington had experienced nothing like this since Watergate.

Helmut Sonnenfeldt, a former State Department and White House expert on the Soviet Union, was a guest scholar at the Brookings Institution in January 1998. Normally, he would be one of a few dozen experts whom reporters would call to explain a foreign policy crisis. In this case, he didn't expect any calls. Lewinsky, though an overwhelming political problem for the Clinton administration, surely did not represent a major moment in foreign affairs. Yet, almost from the moment he entered his office, his phone kept ringing—one foreign (mostly European) correspondent after another wanting a Sonnenfeldt insight into the scandal. Three questions kept coming up: (1) Is President Clinton finished? (2) Is U.S. foreign policy paralyzed? (3) Is the American press crazy for making so much of a president's sex life? Years later, Sonnenfeldt recalled that the West German reporters were convinced that Clinton would resign within a matter of days. No option, they said, sounding for all the world like jaded Washington pundits. Most European reporters worried that the United States as the sole surviving superpower could no longer function in the global arena— that Clinton, too preoccupied with his personal embarrassment and political salvation, simply could not lead the United States. Italians were grateful that American morality did not govern their political elite; everything would come to a sudden halt in Italy if the media focused on the private lives of their public officials. It was similar, Sonnenfeldt thought, to the European reaction to Watergate a quarter of a century earlier.

But no pundit at Brookings had a busier day on Friday than Stephen Hess, a senior fellow and resident media guru who had written more than a dozen books about the press and the presidency. A moderate Republican who had served as a speechwriter for Eisenhower and policy adviser for Nixon, Hess had spent more than a quarter of a century at Brookings. No one was better or quicker at producing an appropriate and riveting sound bite for any political occasion.

On this special day, Hess—who keeps meticulous records—received fifty-five requests for interviews, fifteen of which came from foreign correspondents, and he satisfied every one of them. The first was from Muriel Dobbin of the McClatchy newspapers, the last from Bill Lilly of MSNBC, and in between were calls from the *Detroit News,* the *Pittsburgh Post-Gazette,* the *St. Louis Post-Dispatch,* the *Indianapolis Star,* and many other newspapers, magazines, radio and television stations and networks, interspersed with requests from reporters in Japan, Italy, Canada, Great Britain, Holland, and Ireland. As he later recalled that frantic day, Hess agreed with Sonnenfeldt's conclusions and added two others. First, he said, most reporters were rewriting *The Washington Post* and *The New York Times* and reworking speculation heard on network programs such as *Today, Good Morning America,* and *Nightline.* Very few reporters had independent sourcing for their stories, and they therefore needed quotes from experts to convey the impression of fresh reporting. Second, he said, foreign journalists, usually much more familiar with a parliamentary form of government than an American-style representative form of government, expected Clinton to resign not just because they had heard such speculation from American journalists but also because they expected the parliamentary equivalent of a vote of no confidence. They could see no other realistic option. In any case, during his rush of interviews on Friday, Hess encountered the widespread view among many American and foreign journalists that Clinton's days were numbered.

Washington was the scene of dueling legal and political strategies in which the press played a central role. After Ginsburg opened Friday on ABC's *Good Morning America,* he then said essentially the same thing in four other television interviews that day. He wanted Starr to offer immunity to Lewinsky, but he also criticized Starr for "frightening" his client with unprofessional behavior at the Ritz-Carlton Hotel.

Starr, who considered his conduct above reproach, countered the criticism by issuing a public denial (Ginsburg's comments were "wholly erroneous") and then privately providing *The Washington Post* with a detailed account of his agents' conduct during their apprehension and interrogation of Lewinsky the week before. From the account in the next day's edition of the *Post* by Schmidt and Baker, you might have thought Starr's agents were behaving, for the most part, like Boy Scouts serving milk and cookies to Lewinsky. While waiting for Lewinsky's mother to arrive from New York, they wrote, Lewinsky and the prosecutors and agents "made small talk, watched part of an Ethel Merman movie, 'There's No Business Like Show Business,' then decided to take a walk in the Pentagon City Mall. Lewinsky, Emmick and an FBI agent browsed among the pots and pans at Crate & Barrel, then went to dinner at Mozzarella's Café." The report contained no hint of the pressure Ginsburg had deplored.

Peter Jennings opened *World News Tonight* at 6:30 p.m. with another exclusive by reporter Jackie Judd. "ABC News has new details about what Monica Lewinsky says went on," the anchor teased his audience. Moments later, Jennings turned to the camera. "The White House crisis pretty much dominates the news again tonight," he began. "The president's crisis team has spent the day trying to figure out the best way for him to defend himself against charges of illicit sex and cover-up. Throughout the country, people are sad or angry, frustrated, fed up. There is enormous pressure on Mr. Clinton to explain himself. Today, someone with specific knowledge of what it is that Monica Lewinsky says really took place between her and the president has been talking to ABC's Jackie Judd."

It is a lead-in sentence worth deconstructing. Someone, a single source, "with specific knowledge" of what Lewinsky "says" really took place "between her and the president," has been talking to Judd. Can a single source be trusted? Is the source someone who spoke with either Lewinsky or the president, or is it someone who heard Lewinsky on tape, or who spoke with someone who claimed to have heard Lewinsky on tape? And what constitutes "specific knowledge"? Judd later explained that actually she had had two sources but one put the information off the record, while the other did not. Up to this point, Lewinsky had not herself confided in Starr, his agents or deputies, but she had confided in Tripp, who told everything to Goldberg. Tripp also confided in Starr's deputy, Jackie Bennett, who leaked OIC-serving parts of the story to favored reporters, Judd among them. In those early days, a tight loop composed of Tripp/Goldberg, Ginsburg, Bennett, and the Jones lawyers leaked most of the key elements of the story. Before long, White House officials joined the game and, on occasion, outplayed the rest of the field. Thanks to ABC's internal collaborative approach to sharing information, Judd also got either new nuggets or confirmation of old nuggets from executive producer Dorrance Smith, who spoke regularly with Tripp; Chris Vlasto, who continued his cultivation of Jones's lawyers; and producer Shelley Ross, who kept in close touch with Goldberg.

Judd's report contained five unmistakably important news items: first, that Lewinsky claimed she would "visit the White House for sex with Mr. Clinton in the early evening or early mornings on the weekends, when certain aides who would find her presence disturbing were not at the office"; second, that "Lewinsky says she saved, apparently as a kind of souvenir, a navy blue dress with the President's semen stain on it"; third, that while Clinton and Jordan "never used the word 'lie,' they did say to 'deny' the affair, because there would never be any proof if both parties denied it"; fourth, that "ABC News has obtained documents" confirming Lewinsky's sending "at least seven" packages to the president by way of Betty Currie, the president's personal secretary; and fifth, that Starr and Ginsburg would meet the next day to discuss "cutting a deal and getting Monica Lewinsky to cooperate in this criminal investigation."

The semen-stained dress would eventually prove to be crucial to Starr's case against the president, but at the time the revelation only encouraged many critics to vilify Judd and ABC News. Although the story had been put out by Drudge, and repeated by him on NBC's *Today* the previous day, this was the first time a major news organization was giving it credence. Not only did it reek of cheap salaciousness, it was unconfirmed and based on unnamed sources. Yet here was Judd, a solid, unsensational reporter, leading her Friday story with the semen-stained dress.

"That was a wild day," she later recalled. If it were up to Judd, the dress story probably would not have been reported. When she first informed her New York producers of "everything we had, everything we could offer" the Jennings news program on Friday evening, she mentioned the dress but emphasized "documents"—bills from a courier service—proving that Lewinsky had been sending gifts to the president over a period of time.

When Judd sent the first draft of her television script to New York, she did not include the dress item at all. Why not? I asked. "My discomfort over the subject matter," she replied. "At that stage, only the third day into the Lewinsky scandal, I was still squeamish about putting a story like that on the air. It was all new territory for us." Her producers insisted that she include the dress in a second draft. It could prove to be "the smoking gun," they argued. Later, on reflection, Judd acknowledged that "they were right. It was forensic evidence. It was crucial." She also told me: "I wasn't proud of the fact that I used the word 'semen.' I didn't have to. I could have said 'DNA evidence.' I could have found a better way to report that story."

Did Judd know at the time that Drudge had already reported about the dress? No, Judd swore. "Drudge wasn't even in my universe. I don't think I even had access to the Internet yet." Did she know that Drudge's comment about the semen-stained dress had also appeared in bold type in *The Hotline* on Friday morning? No, she didn't think so, she said.

Complicating the semen-stained-dress story was yet another dress story, persuading many editors and reporters to hesitate before embracing the essence of the Judd report. Donaldson had said on ABC's *Good Morning America* on Thursday that there was a rumor or report to the effect that the president had given a dress to Lewinsky as a gift. He spoke only of a dress, not a semen-stained dress. (The *Times* had also reported a dress story on Thursday.) Anchor Lisa McRee asked the White House correspondent, "How do we know" about the gift? "Well," Donaldson replied, "I guess we don't *know*. We're talking about leaks." The *New York Post* had also published a story on Thursday about a dress—a multicolored peasant dress, it said, plus a pin and a copy of Walt Whitman's *Leaves of Grass*, which Lewinsky allegedly said Clinton had given her. No one was sure at the time whether there was one dress or two and which, if either, was semen-stained.

One dress or two, right or wrong, NBC News had been scooped by ABC News once again. Washington bureau chief Tim Russert claimed later that his reporters had "access to the same information" but could not confirm it and therefore could not broadcast it. Did he feel bad about being scooped again by ABC? "No, not at all," Russert asserted.

The New York Times had also been scooped by ABC. Reporter Don Van Natta, Jr., told me that he had learned about "the dress story" on Thursday and obtained a "wink and nod sort of confirmation," but Joseph Lelyveld chose not to publish it on Thursday or Friday. When ABC's Judd broadcast her dress story on Friday evening, Lelyveld supposedly told a colleague: "We don't have to be first with this story."

"All Monica, All the Time" became the slogan for talk radio and television almost from the moment the story broke on Wednesday. There was for a time very little difference between the talk shows and the news programs, both of which exploited the Lewinsky phenomenon for maximum advantage. Ratings rose dramatically on cable television talk programs, disproving, at least in part, the many polls saying that the American people were turned off by the eruption of scandal coverage. Jack Loftus, senior vice president of Nielsen Media Research, analyzed the polling data. "They [the cable television networks] have benefited enormously by this news coverage of the president's scandal, even though people are sick to death of it." For example, CNN's *Larry King Live*, the network's highest rated program, attracted 300,000 more households in 1998 than in 1997. CNN's *Late Edition* with Wolf Blitzer nearly doubled its audience to 640,000 households per program. The Fox News Channel increased its primetime audience by 540 percent and its daytime audience by 324 percent—deceptive statistics, really, because both audiences remained relatively modest.

Rivera Live! on CNBC was an excellent example of this relatively new genre. Since talk was cheap entertainment and there were plenty of Washington egos satisfied only by frequent exposure to television lights and microphones, such cable programs became nightly jousting matches between pro- and anti-Clinton lawyers, pundits and former prosecutors, each determined to say something so outrageous as to guarantee a return visit. Generally, hosts such as Geraldo Rivera were well briefed on the latest revelations about the president's sex life, but on this Friday evening at 9 p.m., Rivera revealed that he had apparently heard nothing at all about the Judd or Drudge reports about the semen-stained dress.

One guest, Ann Coulter, brought her right-wing legal credentials to the program; she was "balanced" against another guest, Cynthia Alksne, a former prosecutor, who exhibited a far more sympathetic attitude toward Clinton's foibles. Coulter yielded not one inch in her unrelenting assault on the president, accusing him of perjury, suborning perjury, obstructing justice, and "using her [Lewinsky] to service him along with four other interns or staff workers there." She provided no evidence—which "four other interns"? which "staff workers"?—and she was not challenged by Rivera. Coulter echoed Drudge without even pausing to rephrase his copy.

"And now there are rumors, anyway," she continued, "that there's actual DNA evidence beyond the tapes."

A bewildered, uninformed Rivera sputtered: "What do you mean? What—what rumor is that? I—I hadn't heard the DNA evidence."

Coulter countered: "I can't believe, Geraldo, you're not reading the *Drudge Report.*" And, obviously, not watching *Today.*

Alksne joined in the skirmish. "The *Drudge Report* is famous for getting everything wrong."

Wrong or right, the *Drudge Report* was being discussed on CNBC, and its message was being carried across the country.

Rivera, after a commercial break, switched subjects rather than stick with one beyond his knowledge. He disclosed the results of a new *Time* magazine poll, which showed that a solid majority of Americans did not think Clinton should be impeached for lying about an affair—but should be impeached for getting others to lie about it. This attitude would prevail through much of the year.

Then there was a phone interview with Rivera's star attraction: Gennifer Flowers, with whom Clinton was reported to have had a long affair. At the time it was reported, in 1992, he had denied the affair. However, during his Jones deposition the previous Saturday, Clinton admitted to having slept with Flowers on one occasion. For Rivera, Flowers was red meat.

Rivera: "[Are you] actively considering filing a lawsuit against Bill
          Clinton?"
Flowers: "I'm considering it. I'm not saying that that's something
          that I want to do. I just want to enjoy the fact that I have
          been vindicated."
Rivera: "Is this the first time you have mentioned the—publicly,
          the notion that you may sue the president of the United
          States?"
Flowers: "Yes, it is."
Rivera: "And have you considered what you would sue him for?"
Flowers: "I've been advised that certainly defamation. . . . It's really
          not something that I am—am hell-bent to do. But it—it
          has been brought to my attention that it's an option."
Coulter: "If Gennifer's still on the line, I wanted to ask her if she—
          she felt like the entire country believed her."

Flowers: " . . . When the spin doctors went to work on me—you know, they called me a—a lying, money-grubbing, vindictive bimbo and accused me of lying about so many things in my past. . . . It's very hard for me to deal with my family dealing with things like that, like they've had to do."

Rivera: "So, Gennifer . . . you—you claim, to remind people, a twelve-year affair with the president."

Flowers: "Yes, and I have proof of—that the relationship went on actually for fourteen years . . . from 1977, the physical relationship, until 1989."

Rivera: " . . . I remember both a Woody Allen movie and a Marcello Mastroianni movie, they could only, you know, get it on when they were in—in peril. Was he that kind of lover? Did he want to do it in public places or near . . ."

Flowers: "Sometimes, he did, yes. I mean, there was an instance when he wanted to have sex with me in the Governor's Mansion when there—Hillary and fifty people were just a few feet out on the lawn and it was a bathroom that any one could have come in to. Now we—you know, it wasn't always like that, needless to say, because I didn't want to do that . . . I wasn't that big an idiot."

Rivera: "You also told me . . . that you had an abortion and the unborn child was Bill Clinton's."

Flowers: "That's right. Yes, in 1977."

Rivera: "And did Bill Clinton pay for that procedure?"

Flowers: "He did, yes. . . . He gave me two one hundred dollar bills, which is how much it cost back then. . . . And, no—he didn't write me out a check. You know, he was a married man and—and he was at least cautious about that."

Rivera, the talk show host, did his job effectively. He got Flowers, a talkative and controversial guest, to say that she was considering a lawsuit against Clinton, similar to the one Jones had filed against him, and that she had aborted Clinton's child in 1977, a procedure that then cost $200. Still very few reporters picked up and used either "fact," even in a press environment in which almost anything seemed reportable.

There were differences between a cable TV talk show like CNBC's

Rivera Live! and a primetime network news magazine like ABC's *20/20*.
Rivera Live! was a program with a low budget, low ratings, and a low reputation. It appeared five evenings a week, which translated into five hours
of television time, a bonanza in today's world of politics. *20/20* was just the
reverse: it had a huge budget, ratings at least fifteen to twenty times higher,
star anchors and a large staff, at the time one hour a week of network television time, and a reputation commensurate with the quality product of a
network news program. But on this Friday evening, only the truly discern-
ing viewer could have told the difference between "talk" and "news." The
scandal was the single, inescapable, all-consuming focus of the "media."

"These are dark days at the White House," intoned anchor Barbara
Walters, as she opened the program at 10 p.m. "It has been an unbelievable
week. An alleged sex scandal spinning out of control and even more serious accusations of a cover-up." Co-anchor Hugh Downs continued. "We
still haven't heard from the young woman at the center of this storm—
Monica Lewinsky," he announced dramatically. "She's not been seen since
the scandal erupted. But today, new details about her surfaced." Introducing the scandal team of Jackie Judd and Sam Donaldson, Downs said:
"Jackie, let's start with you. You gave a stunning report earlier on *World
News Tonight*. Could you give us the main points on that report?"

Three and a half hours had passed since her report on *WNT*. Judd had
for the moment nothing new to report, but ABC was clearly determined
to milk its "exclusive" for maximum effect. NBC and CBS, like most other
news organizations, were engaged in the embarrassing game of "catch-up
journalism," and ABC enjoyed playing its enviable role of network leader
of scandal coverage. After Judd itemized the main points, Walters interjected: "Boy, Jackie, that's pretty strong stuff, especially with the semen.
That could be forensic evidence." Then Walters raised a key question. "You
have a source very close to Monica Lewinsky," she said. "Do you have any
idea what she might do?" Judd responded: "I honestly have to say I don't."

By late Friday night, many reporters felt that the nation was on the edge of
a dramatic political upheaval—that within a matter of days, perhaps by
Sunday or Monday, Clinton would resign and Gore would become president. All because the president found a young intern irresistible and then
lied about his indiscretion.

CHAPTER II

"BREAKING NEWS"
January 24, 1998

SHE KEPT SEX DRESS
                                        —*New York Daily News*

"IF THERE'S SOMETHING THERE, AND IT LEADS TO HIM HAV-
ING TO STEP OUT OF OFFICE, IT MAY BE TIME TO DO SOME
REPAIR WORK. . . ."
                    —Leon E. Panetta, former White House chief of staff,
                                        in the *San Jose Mercury News*

Though it had surfaced on the Internet and circulated on the *Today* program, it was not until early Saturday morning, after it had been featured on two ABC News shows on Friday evening, that the story of the semen-stained dress finally erupted on the political stage. Tabloids around the world gave it front-page treatment. Talk radio didn't stop talking about it. The more respectable press, including *The New York Times*, tended to be more fastidious, mentioning the dress in their stories but rarely leading with it. But the *New York Daily News* plastered it across the front-page: SHE KEPT SEX DRESS. The *New York Post*, not to be outdone, banner-headlined the story: MONICA'S LOVE DRESS. The *Boston Herald* proclaimed in boldfaced type: SEEKING PROOF: DRESS MAY HOLD TRUTH TO ALLEGED AFFAIR WITH CLINTON. The news agency UPI, crediting Judd's *World News Tonight* account and adding no new sourcing or additional reporting of its own, sent the story out to its subscribers early Saturday morning.

After this initial burst of excitement, the story of the dress slowly fizzled. On Thursday, January 29, CBS's Scott Pelley reported that the FBI had found no "forensic evidence" on any of the clothing taken from Lewinsky's apartment at the Watergate. And, on Friday, January 30, ABC's Jackie Judd, citing "law enforcement sources," said that "Starr so far has come up empty in a search for forensic evidence," noting that Lewinsky's clothes, taken from her apartment by the FBI, had been dry-cleaned.

With these reports, the semen-stained dress lost its allure over the following weeks. Indeed, for months it was cited as an example of journalistic excess and irresponsibility. Critics blasted the press, especially ABC and Judd, for having run with a story that seemed totally baseless . . . until July 29, 1998, when Judd, this time citing "legal sources," reported that, as part of an immunity deal, Lewinsky had given Starr's prosecutors new evidence to support her story of a sexual relationship with the president. Part of the evidence was the semen-stained dress, which, prosecutors learned only then, Lewinsky had given to her mother for safekeeping; her mother had kept it hidden in her New York apartment.

Lewinsky, the central person in the spreading scandal, remained in hiding in her Watergate apartment, reading newspapers, watching television, occasionally catching a glimpse through a curtain of the burgeoning army of television crews outside the building. From time to time, she dissolved into sobs and tears, as she pondered the possibility of prison time as the price of her reckless fling with a president. Her mother, Marcia Lewis, had known about the affair but dismissed its potential impact on the presidency, not to mention on her daughter's life. "What's the big deal?" she asked when confronted a week earlier by Starr's deputies. "So she lied and tried to convince others to lie?" Bill Ginsburg was their contact to the world, but it was a world that had suddenly gone mad. He was only a few blocks away from Starr's office; but throughout the day he was effectively locked into his hotel room, negotiating with the OIC by phone or fax, instead of in person. Both his hotel and Starr's office were besieged by cameras and reporters desperate for even a single frame or word from any of the principals. "We're frozen by the media," he told *The Washington Post.* "There's a thousand people outside my building. There's a thousand people outside his building."

While negotiating privately with Starr, Ginsburg, in time-honored Washington fashion, was continuing to make his case through the media. He happily fielded questions posed by newspaper and magazine reporters. "They're going to have to give her immunity from any prosecution," he told *The Washington Post.* "We're offering him complete cooperation and the complete truth and we're promising him we will not go south on him as apparently Susan McDougal did"—a reference to the Whitewater case.

Ginsburg also accepted invitations to appear the following day on all the major Sunday morning interview programs. This was an unprecedented arrangement, since, as a rule, if a guest agrees to appear on one program, he or she is automatically rejected by the others. Not at this point, when every anchor and producer wanted a piece of Ginsburg so much they dispensed with precedent to book Lewinsky's only spokesman. Maybe, they hoped, he would say something different, more newsworthy, on their program than on the others.

On Friday, *The New York Times* had run twelve stories about the scandal; on Saturday, it ran twenty stories (15,012 words in all), more than any other newspaper in the country. It was as if the *Times* were determined that, beaten at the gate, it would not be beaten at the finish line. The twenty stories included three on the front page. One was a summary of the crisis; another was a piece written by Richard Berke and James Bennet about how those closest to Clinton felt as though they'd been left in the dark; and the third piece was John Broder's—that Lewinsky had offered to tell all in exchange for immunity. The average length of a story was 750 words.

The Washington Post, having run an astronomical number of stories (twenty-five, to be precise) on Friday, ran sixteen stories on Saturday, totaling 17,248 words, or 2,236 more than the *Times.* This number included four on the front page—one by Susan Schmidt and Peter Baker on Lewinsky's rejecting an immunity offer by Starr; another by David Streitfeld and Howard Kurtz on Lucianne Goldberg; a third by John Harris and John Goshko on a pending decision to bomb Iraq; and the fourth by Jeff Leen headlined LEWINSKY: TWO COASTS, TWO LIVES, MANY IMAGES. The *Post* also included three stories in its Style section—one on how the rest of the media stretched its "news hole" to include any and every thing; another on Vernon Jordan, the "fixer-upper"; and the third on "Washington interns," operating "in the shadow of power." The average length of a story was 1,078 words.

The *Los Angeles Times,* publishing twenty stories on Friday, ran thirteen on Saturday, totaling 14,152 words. Five stories appeared on the front page—one by Richard Serrano on the sexual explicitness of the Lewinsky-Tripp tape talk, still another by Serrano on Clinton engaging in "phone sex," a third by David Willman and Richard Cooper on Starr's intensified efforts to nail Lewinsky and her efforts to gain immunity, another by Willman and Cooper on Starr pursuing "criminal charges" against Lewinsky, and the fifth by Jonathan Peterson and Elizabeth Shogren on White House aides debating their best options. The average length of an *L.A. Times* story was 1,088 words.

One characteristic of crisis journalism in newspapers and networks, or "mediathons," is that everyone fastens on to a single story, in this case the Lewinsky scandal, throwing their considerable resources into the coverage while ignoring or downplaying other stories of note. Journalists lose their perspective in a rush to be competitive, thus unwittingly distorting the public's knowledge and appreciation of other issues.

On this Saturday, it was as if Washington was waiting for the other shoe to drop. First came the scandal; next would be Clinton's resignation. The only question was when.

For three days, since the story first disrupted Washington's deceptively routine January, the possibility of a Clinton resignation had dominated the speculation of the pundits, who underestimated the president's resiliency. One after another, from Donaldson to Russert to Imus to Limbaugh, they put their fingers to the wind and concluded—like Dick Morris—that Clinton could survive if he lied about an affair, but that if he was found to have encouraged others to lie as part of a cover-up, then he was engaging in an obvious obstruction of justice and he was, to use the cliché of the day, "toast." Each day provided its own contribution to the widespread belief that he was, in fact, toast. Since belief, image, and perception tend to constitute reality in an age of instant communication, most pundits came to share the expectation that if there was one more big story, one more embarrassing advance in the media's hungry pursuit of Clinton's wildly rumored sexcapades, then he was finished.

Suddenly, on Saturday morning, from the West Coast came the thunderingly candid words of the president's former chief of staff, Leon Panetta, who was then seriously considering a run for the governorship of California. But first he had to address the scandal consuming his old place of employment. Panetta's words carried weight. He was a sympathetic pro adding his dispassionate judgment to the national discussion about Clinton's next move. "This *thing*," he said, unable to find a better word, "has got to be resolved quickly. I'm one of those who believe that when faced with this kind of issue, the president has to go to the people." Speaking to Philip J. Trounstine, political editor of the *San Jose Mercury News,* which ran the bombshell story on the front page of Saturday's edition of the paper, Panetta stressed the importance of speed. "He should do it before the State of the Union," which was scheduled for the following Tuesday, Panetta recommended, because "if he doesn't, people will continue to raise more questions. You can't sidestep an issue this big in terms of the seriousness."

Panetta did not avoid the obvious question of resignation. "If these are baseless charges, it'll be OK," he said cautiously. "On the other hand, if there's something there, and it leads him to having to step out of office, it may be time to do some repair work and that may not have the consequences you would expect." *If there's something there*—Panetta seemed to know intuitively from his own experience with Clinton that there must be "something there." And if so, then it would be better for the Democrats "if Gore became president and you had a new message and new individual up there. The worst scenario is if there's substance to it and it drags on." If Panetta were to run for the governorship, he obviously felt that his chances would be improved by having Gore in the White House rather than Clinton.

Nor did Panetta avoid the other obvious question of Clinton's possible impeachment. A sixteen-year veteran of the House of Representatives, Panetta had participated in brutal political wars on Capitol Hill. He knew the Republican-controlled Congress now smelled blood. If there was a way to get Clinton, congressional lawmakers would exploit it. "This is not going to go away and be lost in the judicial system," Panetta believed. "You're dealing with a Congress that is likely to move against him in the Judiciary Committee. And unless he's got a clear resolution of this matter, Congress itself is going to be paralyzed."

Panetta's candid and controversial comments lit a fire in every newsroom. Everyone wanted a follow-up interview, and for the most part he obliged the media. If someone as prominent as Panetta was openly discussing a Gore presidency—"a new message and new individual"—then reporters assumed that other Democrats of consequence were probably preparing behind closed doors for a Clinton resignation. Reporters who were normally home on weekends were summoned to the office. They worked the phones, digging for the smallest clue or insight into Clinton's thinking. A CNN poll said that Clinton's job approval rating had dropped almost ten points—it was now close to 50 percent. An ABC poll said that fewer than 50 percent of Americans now felt that Clinton had the "honesty" and "integrity" to serve out his term as president.

Everyone seemed to be waiting for a White House announcement.

The problem for ABC's Diane Sawyer was, to quote Lucianne Goldberg, "getting through the scrum of unruly reporters" who crowded the entryway to Goldberg's Upper West Side apartment house. In a series of telephone calls starting Wednesday evening, producer Shelley Ross had arranged a quiet, off the record lunch for the three of them in Goldberg's apartment. Sawyer wanted not only an interview with Goldberg—she wanted the copies of the Tripp tapes that Goldberg was supposed to have in her possession. Goldberg entrusted the awesome responsibility of slipping Sawyer and Ross past the "scrum" to Danny Rivera, her building superintendent. Rivera worshipped Sawyer—"anything for Diane," he said. At the appointed hour, Rivera met Sawyer, the superstar, and Ross, her superfacilitator, at a shoe store at the corner of Broadway and 84th Street. He led them through a maze of tunnels until they emerged in the basement of Goldberg's building. There they boarded an elevator to her apartment, where they arrived safely. Rivera's mission, though impossible on the surface, was completed underground with startling speed. Sawyer and Ross saw not a single reporter, nor did a single reporter see them.

Jonah Goldberg described the lunch as a "banquet" in a "Talk of the Town" piece in the February 9, 1998 issue of *The New Yorker,* a piece Ross described as "adorably written but inaccurate." Actually, Ross said, she ordered six sandwiches from Eats, a very fashionable delicatessen—three turkey sandwiches and three smoked salmon sandwiches, at a cost of $115—and, in a white shopping bag, brought them to Goldberg's apartment. The three women talked, hours passed, and though there were many "juicy tidbits" of gossip and news, there was no deal for either an interview or the tapes.

Sawyer had laid on the charm; she had tried valiantly, calling Goldberg a few times. "One of her great assets," wrote Jonah Goldberg, "is her hypnotic voice. 'Hi, Looocy,' she said. 'Isn't this the most amaaazing story . . .'" They chatted for ten minutes or so, like two old finishing-school chums. Finally, the pitch. 'Hey, Lucy,' Sawyer said. 'I have the greatest idea. Why don't I just run downstairs, get in a cab, zip over there, and listen to the tapes for, say, fifteen minutes or so. Just to say I heard them. That way, I can go on the air and say it's true that these tapes are shocking.'"

At the lunch, they talked about the many news items Goldberg had imparted to Ross and Sawyer in their telephone calls since Wednesday. One concerned the navy blue semen-stained dress. According to Ross, she "passed the story along" to Vlasto, a "personal friend," and presumably Vlasto gave it to Judd. It was, of course, possible that Judd got the dress story from another source, too; she insisted to me that she didn't get it from Goldberg, though, by this circuitous route, she could have gotten it from Vlasto, who'd gotten it from Ross, who'd gotten it from Goldberg, the ultimate leaker.

How did Ross get to Goldberg? Why did Goldberg want to help Sawyer? A few years before, one of Goldberg's clients was detective Mark Fuhrman of O. J. Simpson fame. Goldberg, while hustling his book, persuaded Ross to persuade Sawyer to do a television interview with Fuhrman. Sawyer did two interviews. Goldberg was grateful. When Goldberg had to decide which television anchor to favor, she chose Sawyer. "If I had to help anyone, I'd help Diane," she said. NBC's Tom Brokaw kept sending handwritten notes to Goldberg, urging her to "keep our lines of communication open," but Goldberg extended her favor to Sawyer (not quite in the way Sawyer had hoped) and in return got a turkey sandwich and a smoked salmon sandwich, garnished.

According to an old Chinese proverb, a picture is worth a thousand words. In the Lewinsky scandal, for the first three days, viewers and readers got only one picture of the former intern: the stock photo that appeared on all of her government ID cards. This photo popped up everywhere—on the front page of newspapers and in the lead story of network news shows. It was not a substitute for a thousand words; it was the companion to tens of thousands of words used every hour of every day in every story about the president and the intern. On the fourth day, Saturday, at 6 p.m., CNN took the story to a new dimension. In a "BREAKING NEWS" bulletin, anchored by Judy Woodruff and reported by White House correspondent Wolf Blitzer, CNN showed an actual videotape of a Clinton-Lewinsky embrace in a White House receiving line on November 6, 1996, two days after the president's triumphant reelection. White House staff, friends, and aides had been assembled for the celebration. Along the ropeline, perfectly positioned to shake his hand or hug him, was the young woman with the dark beret suddenly catapulted to national notoriety. Clinton, working this ropeline as professionally as he had so many others in the campaign, gradually moved toward her, shaking hands, holding elbows, patting shoulders, smiling, pointing to familiar and not so familiar faces. Vintage Clinton. When Clinton got to within hugging distance of Lewinsky, he extended his hand, which she shook, but at the same time, she leaned forward on tiptoes and hugged him, her eyes conveying a warm and possessive familiarity.

At last, the American people had more to inflame their imaginations than the unemotional mug shot of their newest *femme fatale*—they actually had the rolling image of the two principals engaged in a quick, polite, public embrace, proof in the context of the moment of a relationship of some kind. Clinton had always been a touchy-feely politician; handshakes and embraces, smiles fake and real, were all natural tools of the trade. This embrace could have been as innocent as hundreds of others in the '96 campaign, but, against the backdrop of the media madness uncorked by the scandal, it seemed decidedly distinctive and suggestive of . . . something more. Despite awkward and tentative White House hints that Lewinsky could have been fantasizing an affair with the president, this videotape, which was then played and replayed thousands of times, conveyed a sense of reality larger than a young woman's fantasy.

CNN's video scoop provided its own insight into contemporary journalism. On November 6, 1996, CNN was assigned to shoot the pool footage for the post-election celebration. When finished with the shooting, CNN fed the video to all of the other networks, meaning every network had the same footage. It was simply a question of which network then exploited its resources to top advantage. In this case, a *Time* reporter who covered the celebration happened to remember the Clinton-Lewinsky embrace not because he knew at the time of a scandalous romance but because it struck him as a terrific representation of an excited aide and a grateful president. *Time* had just hooked up with CNN in a new media-merger, and the mug shot of Lewinsky that he saw on every front page tugged at his professional memory. He had seen that face before. But where? Then he remembered the receiving line, and the embrace, and as a good colleague he mentioned it to a CNN friend, who informed a producer at the CNN library and, late Saturday afternoon after a frantic search, there it was—the young woman with the beret on videotape, the embrace, as large as life.

Did the CNN producer who found the footage continue searching for more footage of other embraces between Clinton and members of his adoring throng? Or, having found the Lewinsky embrace, did he or she stop the search? The question is relevant. If the Lewinsky embrace was only one of a number of other embraces involving the exuberant president, then its significance would be markedly reduced. At the time, one embrace among many would—or could—have injected an element of doubt in journalism's rush to judgment. CNN/US president Rick Kaplan later expressed regret that the video, as shown, lacked context. "Clinton always embraces people and he must have embraced a hundred people just that way at that event." However, on Saturday, competition left little room for context. If CNN had in fact checked for other embraces and found none, it would have had much more justification for running the ten-second video of the Clinton-Lewinsky embrace, endowing it, through the many reruns, with such extraordinary importance.

In Clinton's political life, two moving pictures epitomized the high and low points of his career. The first was his handshake with President Kennedy, which was on ample, profitable display during his first run for the presidency in 1992. The second was his embrace of Lewinsky in 1996.

But the dramatic videotape of the Clinton-Lewinsky embrace was only half of CNN's "BREAKING NEWS" bulletin. The other half was presented by the bearded, highly respected Wolf Blitzer, looking very grim as he delivered his report in front of the White House. Anchor Judy Woodruff began: "The amazing, almost surrealistic events swirling around President Clinton this week are apparently entering another phase." Blitzer, she continued, "has been talking to people close to the president" and "joins us now . . . with an exclusive report."

Blitzer began by quoting "several of [the president's] closest friends and advisers—both in and out of government" as believing that Clinton "almost certainly" had "a sexual relationship" with Lewinsky and "they're talking among themselves about the possibility of a resignation." Always cautious and careful, Blitzer quickly added that "senior White House officials" were "angrily" denying "any talk of resignation." Blitzer said he based his report on talks with "a dozen close Clinton associates," one of whom was supposed to have said: "Things are moving so quickly it's almost getting out of control." Another, described as "one long-time Clinton insider," was supposed to have added: "If he had sex with a 21-year-old intern, any kind of sex, he has to resign." "Any kind of sex," presumably referring to reports of "oral sex." Blitzer's "sources" also disclosed "more lurid details of Mr. Clinton's alleged sex life," including "secretly recorded conversations saying that Mr. Clinton used to engage in late night 'phone sex.'"

Having completed his scripted "exclusive," Blitzer awaited Woodruff's question.

Woodruff: "On what do [these close friends of the president] base their beliefs since the president has denied it?"

Blitzer added as many qualifications as he could squeeze into his response: "*They don't know for sure,* and they were, of course, not present, *if in fact it did occur.* They think that it's *probable;* it's *almost certain* that it occurred *probably for the most part*—and I got different explanations talking to these people—for one, *they say they think* there is a track record. This is *probably* not the first such alleged incident, and they say that the information that they've been gleaning from various sources *appears to be very, very compelling.* . . . I want to point out that *they don't know for sure. They just think it happened,* and as a result, they're beginning amongst themselves *to speculate, to whisper,* as I said, about the *possibility of a resignation,* but the president by all accounts wants to fight" (italics added).

How could such extraordinarily hedged copy be categorized as "BREAKING NEWS"? It lacked the bite and hard edge of a news bulletin. It was essentially speculation; at best, analysis. Yet Blitzer's bulletin was vetted by CNN's top brass for hours—Washington bureau chief Frank Sesno, joined by CEO Tom Johnson and president Rick Kaplan—and they concluded that since this was the first time Blitzer had heard presidential associates use the "R" word, the story deserved bulletin treatment. In addition, they had absolute confidence in Blitzer's integrity. If he thought the story was accurate, then in their view it was accurate. His guidelines, throughout the Lewinsky scandal, were to be "extra cautious." More than a year later, Blitzer recalled the general mood in Washington in January 1998. "There was too much sensationalism, too much trivialization," he told me. "I had to be even-handed and cautious, and to look at the story in a clear, unbiased, unsensational way. I myself, I had to confirm everything I could. No unnamed sources, though that rule definitely loosened up on occasion. I did not want to engage in wild speculation." As he looked back on the January 24, 1998 "exclusive," he believed that he not only got it right, he understated the degree of official White House concern about the president's position. "If I knew then what I know now, what we all know now, I'd have been less cautious about the story, less 'hedged,' as you put it."

Still, in retrospect, there have been doubts about the overuse of "bulletins" during this period. All news organizations, including all-news networks and Internet Web sites, have lately been posting an inordinate number of "bulletins" or "news flashes," as they are sometimes called. The effect has been to dilute the value of a genuine news bulletin. Frank Sesno, CNN's Washington bureau chief, acknowledged that CNN "should never have used" the "BREAKING NEWS" logo to introduce Blitzer's report. It was "a bad mistake." If there was an explanation, he said, it was that it was used as "a convenient production device" that made it easier for CNN to link its reporting of domestic news with its foreign channels. "This was a huge story. The very seriousness of it pushed us over the top. The competitive pressures on us were enormous."

Sesno had also heard "more than one whisper about resignation." One U.S. senator told Sesno that he returned to Washington on Saturday, three days before the scheduled State of the Union address on Tuesday, because he thought he would have "to lead a congressional delegation to the White House to tell the president that he had to resign." A White House official said Clinton had "probably" committed "a grave matter of sin" and ought to consider "resigning." The "noise" that weekend, Sesno recalled, was "so great—it was deafening."

As Blitzer delivered his "BREAKING NEWS" report, top officials inside the White House had a surrealistic experience. They could see him on the lawn and on the tube at the same time. With anger and astonishment, they learned for the first time that a number of their colleagues had been talking to a reporter about a presidential resignation. Infuriated, Emanuel and Begala called Blitzer and vented their fury. Two hours later, during an 8 p.m. CNN update, Blitzer repeated the essence of his story but added that Begala, Emanuel, Lindsey, and Blumenthal by name had all "angrily denied there is any talk of resignation inside the White House."

Compartmentalization was again on conspicuous display at the White House on Saturday evening. While his aides engaged in damage control, calling dozens of reporters, anchors, and columnists to denounce Blitzer's "exclusive" and affirm their belief in the president's denials, Clinton and the first lady hosted a dinner and movie for eighty guests. The movie was *The Apostle,* starring Robert Duvall. It told the story of a "holy roller preacher" who committed a crime, changed his identity, and made a sincere and determined effort to do good, but was caught in the end.

According to a report in *The New Yorker* dated February 9, 1998, nobody raised the embarrassing subject of the president's dalliance with an intern. Only Hillary Clinton, in her welcoming remarks, alluded to the scandal by joking that it had been "such an *un*eventful week at the White House." Duvall remembered the evening as "very cordial . . . relaxed and informal." He said that he sat in the front row between Frank Biondi, chief executive of Universal Studios, and the Clintons. "I didn't look over at them while the film was running," he recalled. "They were kind of sunk back in their chairs, but someone told me they were holding hands and moving their feet in rhythm with the music. The President said afterward that he really responded to the music; he'd been to so many of these churches in the South. I'm told some of his greatest speeches are to black congregations. Over all, I'd say the people at the White House got it—the laughter was spontaneous, and everybody seemed upbeat and appreciative."

One presidential adviser who was present at the screening told a reporter: "A person who hasn't read the papers—a visitor from Mars, say— would never, ever guess there's anything extraordinary going on in his life." Clinton shuttled from a meeting with his lawyers to a practice session on the State of the Union Address to a movie with his wife and friends.

Another presidential adviser had a different take on Clinton's apparently effortless swings from meeting to movie. "Pure bunk," he was quoted as saying more than two years later. He and other colleagues said that "during the Monica Lewinsky scandal Clinton often seemed utterly lost to the world, overcome by a combination of rage toward his opponents and recrimination toward his own weak self."

CHAPTER 12

PEEKABOO

January 25, 1998

"THE PRESIDENT AND LEWINSKY WERE CAUGHT IN AN INTI-
MATE ENCOUNTER IN A PRIVATE AREA OF THE WHITE HOUSE."
—Jackie Judd, ABC News

"SO WHAT DOES PRESIDENT GORE DO?"
—Sam Donaldson, ABC News

"SENIOR DEMOCRATIC LEADERS GO TO THE PRESIDENT—AND
I AGREE WITH SAM: IT COULD BE IN DAYS, NOT IN WEEKS—
AND TELL HIM THIS IS INSUPPORTABLE."
—Bill Kristol, ABC News

Sunday newspapers are usually fat, if not with news then with ads; this Sunday's were obese. *The New York Times* and *The Washington Post*, the daily bibles of scandal coverage during this provocative period of American journalism, seemed to be in competition for the dubious distinction of publishing more stories with more words about the president's affair with an intern than about the Gulf War of 1991.

The January 25, 1998, edition of *The New York Times* published twenty-one different stories, composed of 19,524 words, about the scandal. The longest piece, by Stephen Labaton, Don Van Natta, Jr., and Jill Abramson, ran 2,444 words; it focused on HOW A SINGLE TELEPHONE CALL WAS THE CATALYST FOR A CRISIS. Impressive? Without doubt. But compared with *The Washington Post*'s production on the same day, it seemed only modestly ambitious. The *Post* published twenty-five different stories about the scandal, the same number it ran on Friday, January 23, but the word total on Sunday shot up to a staggering 32,829, an average of 1,313 words per story. One story by Dan Balz ran 5,350 words; it was a clearly constructed review of WASHINGTON'S EXTRAORDINARY WEEK: HOW THE EVENTS UNFOLDED FROM JONES TO LEWINSKY. Another by David

Maraniss ran 3,254 words; it was an elegantly written account of CLINTON: A PAST THAT'S EVER PROLOGUE.

The very heft of both papers reinforced the public's impression of an incomparable political crisis. There was very little interest in any other story—not the substance of the upcoming State of the Union Address, not the military escalation against Iraq, not the delicate negotiations on the Middle East.

Nothing on this Sunday seemed more important than The Scandal, and nowhere was it more obvious than on the morning interview programs, which focused essentially on two words: "resign" and "impeach." When would Clinton resign? When would he be impeached? The possibility that neither might happen was barely broached. The high—or low—point was reached on ABC's *This Week.* Another Judd exclusive in the "ABC News has learned" mode led the broadcast and set the tone for the later interviews and roundtable discussion. She reported: "Several sources have told us that in the spring of 1996, the president and Lewinsky were caught in an intimate encounter in a private area of the White House. It is not clear whether the witnesses were secret service agents or White House staff." Judd highlighted the significance of her report. "Until now," she said, "there had only been circumstantial evidence of an affair and Lewinsky's claims on the tapes." But with this reported sighting, she continued, the president's denial of an affair was "undercut."

This exclusive was to have been aired on an ABC News special on Saturday evening, but anchor Peter Jennings felt the sourcing was shaky. "I wanted to hold it," he said. "I was just not comfortable with the sourcing." Judd and Vlasto agreed to continue digging for additional information. On Sunday morning, they "worked the phones" sufficiently to persuade executive producer Dorrance Smith that their story was solid—indeed, solid enough to be the lead of his program.

Anchors Sam Donaldson and Cokie Roberts, joined by columnist George Will, a regular weekly participant, then interviewed a procession of guests: White House political adviser Paul Begala, Senate majority leader Trent Lott, Lewinsky counsel William Ginsburg, and House Judiciary Committee chair Henry Hyde. The program ended with the usual roundtable discussion: ABC analysts Bill Kristol and George Stephanopoulos adding their "right" and "left" perspectives to a free-for-all with Donaldson, Roberts, and Will.

Begala echoed the White House position—that the president denied the reports of a sexual relationship with Lewinsky and he believed the president; that it was wrong to "shut down the whole country" because the president "made a phone call to somebody"; that the president acknowledged in 1992 causing "pain in my marriage" and "everybody knew what that meant when they voted for him"; and there was "a continuing and troubling ongoing campaign of leaks and lies coming from somewhere." He implied Starr but didn't say so.

Donaldson used the Judd report to puncture Begala's balloon. "If Jackie Judd's report is correct, which we at ABC News believe, or we would not have put it on the air," then was that an example of Starr's "manufacturing evidence," as Begala had implied? Begala refused to bite.

Roberts asked whether "physical evidence" (Judd's semen-stained-dress report of Friday evening) might shake Begala's confidence in the president. Again, he refused to bite.

Donaldson, playing out the string, wondered: "Do you think he's [the president's] going to resign?"

"No," replied Begala, with finality.

Donaldson then turned to Senator Lott, who tried gamely to sound responsible about affairs of state but couldn't quite conceal his partisan delight at the president's foolishness about affairs of the heart. Might this "particular scandal . . . cost the president his job?" Donaldson asked. Lott replied that he didn't "know what the facts are," and "any comment" on his part would be "totally inappropriate." Did Lott think the president would resign? Lott deflected the question with just the proper shrug of self-righteousness. "You're going to spend two-thirds of this show talking about this issue. Shouldn't we talk about the State of the Union and what we are going to do in the Congress this year?" Will raised the question of "moral turpitude." If a president exhibited such depravity, shouldn't he be removed from office? "I think the answer is yes," Lott responded, but he refused to go further.

Wearing a cloak of solemn responsibility as he toured the celebrity-filled studios of Washington, Ginsburg was next on the Donaldson-Roberts list of guests. Roberts wasted no time raising Judd's report. "If that is true," she asked, "that there are other witnesses, alleged witnesses," then doesn't that weaken your case for immunity? Ginsburg acknowledged the obvious: "If they have solid evidence, as Ms. Judd suggested they might, I suppose they are not going to be offering us immunity, or a promise not to prosecute." Might Ginsburg now have to "take a lesser deal"? "Oh, yes," he replied, "given this new information. I have not had a chance to analyze it, but I heard it here first. And if it's true, then I may have to review my negotiating in a different way." The Judd report was being treated as a virtual fact.

Lewinsky's attorney then confirmed, under questioning, that the OIC had shown him the famous talking points (but not given him a copy); that "a week ago" the OIC had informed him of "a dress that might be forensically important in terms of DNA evidence"; and that up to this point he had never heard the Tripp tapes, snippets of which were that day appearing in *Newsweek*.

Roberts then introduced her next guest, Congressman Hyde, noting that his "committee holds the power of beginning impeachment proceedings." Donaldson opened the questioning of the white-haired conservative from Illinois by again raising the Judd report about "corroborating witnesses" who "apparently" saw Clinton and Lewinsky "in an intimate act." Like Lott, Hyde donned the mantle of statesman and attempted to deflect questions about the president's sex life. "It's interesting," he answered, "but again it's an allegation. We don't have any proof of it yet." Will ignored his caution, wondering if Hyde should begin impeachment hearings immediately rather than wait for Starr to produce the evidence. Hyde stressed that the law required Starr to act first. "Impeachment is a political act," Will impatiently lectured the politician. "Isn't impeachment a response to a political problem independent of what professional investigators may turn up?" Hyde reminded the columnist that only the Senate could remove the president from office in any case, and "that means substantial Democratic support. I don't see that happening yet." Roberts picked up Will's argument. "Do you think there is enough evidence to start, if you chose to, to start impeachment hearings?" No, Hyde replied. "I would be loath to start something that I didn't think we could finish." Donaldson thought the crisis would never get to the point of impeachment: "Wouldn't the president resign before that?" Hyde recalled the Nixon example. "When responsible members of his own party would counsel him that he's hurting the party, he's hurting the country, that he would react appropriately to that." Will returned to his high ground. Can't Congress impeach a president for "moral turpitude"? he asked. Hyde replied, "We have elections."

It was then roundtable time. Kristol and Stephanopoulos joined the hanging party.

Roberts:	"Can he survive? Can he recover?"
Stephanopoulos:	"There is one question. Is he telling the truth, the whole truth and nothing but the truth? If he is, he can survive. If he isn't, he can't."
Kristol:	"He cannot survive, because he's not telling the truth. . . . The president of the United States is lying. Everyone knows he's lying. . . . Lies beget lies. Washington is now drowning in deceit, and it can't go on long."
Donaldson:	"If he's not telling the truth, I think his presidency is numbered in days. This isn't going to drag out. We're not going to be here three months from now talking about this. Mr. Clinton, if he's not telling the truth, and the evidence shows that, will resign, perhaps this week."
Will:	"His presidency . . . today is as dead, deader really, than Woodrow Wilson's was after he had a stroke. . . . His moral authority is gone. He will resign when he acquires the moral sense to under-stand . . ."
Stephanopoulos:	"He's like a gut shot confederate soldier; he'll never survive. . . . The idea that he can go to the State of the Union Tuesday night without addressing this before or saying something during the speech is . . . is ludicrous."
Donaldson:	"We're all sort of agreed that if the facts don't bear him out, spinning won't help, and he's going to leave."

A dramatic and deliberate pause preceded the next question. "So what does President Gore do?" Donaldson asked. Everyone laughed.

Kristol:	"I don't think he can survive, because he's not— well, he really isn't telling the truth."
Roberts:	"OK. So he is out. So then what happens?"

Kristol: "What happens is senior Democratic leaders go to the president—and I agree with Sam, it could be in days, not in weeks—and tell him this is insupportable, you can't put the country through this."

Stephanopoulos: "I think if it comes to that, it will happen if he doesn't get out very quickly. And frankly this report this morning, from Jackie Judd—again, all the caveats—if it's true, adds an entirely new element to the case."

Donaldson: "Well, I renew my question. What will President Al Gore do then?" More laughter.

The need for a final commercial break interrupted the flow of the conversation. When Donaldson returned for his concluding comment, he again highlighted the Judd report: "A new report was aired on this broadcast from ABC's Jackie Judd that corroborating witnesses have been found who caught the president and Ms. Lewinsky in an intimate act in the White House."

Wrong in its prognoses, questionable in its reporting, *This Week* on this Sunday was a striking example of journalism gone astray. The commentators were driven by the emotions of the moment to indulge in overheated speculation about Clinton and Congress. No delegation went tromping to the White House to demand the president's resignation, no Clinton-to-Gore handoff happened within days, not even within weeks or months. Moreover, the participants conveyed the impression that they assumed all the accusations against Clinton were true.

More than two years later, Judd, who had quoted "several sources" in her report, stuck to her story but with diminished conviction. She said she still thought there was "probably" a witness to an "intimate encounter." She was also quoted as saying, "I . . . think there might be a potential witness." "Probably" and "potential" do not sound like particularly persuasive underpinnings for a breaking news story. She derived a degree of satisfaction from the grand jury testimony of two sources: one was a Secret Service agent who said that he had seen an "intimate encounter"; the other was Harold Ickes, a high-ranking White House aide, who said on August 5, 1998, six months after Judd's initial report on the "sighting," that he did not remember seeing the president and Lewinsky in an ambiguous situation but could not be absolutely certain. Ickes testified that late in the week the

Lewinsky story first broke, CBS's Scott Pelley had called and asked whether he (Ickes) had seen the president and the intern "in a compromising position." Ickes told Pelley that he had "absolutely no recollection of it," and added, "I was pretty sure I would remember if I had seen them in a compromising position." The prosecutor, eager to confirm the "sighting," which lay at the heart of Judd's January 25, 1998, report, kept pushing Ickes—"Isn't it possible . . . ? Can you exclude . . . ? Might you have forgotten . . . ?" Ickes left himself a small wedge of wiggle room in case of subsequent discovery or revelation. "Anything is possible," he replied. But "I have no recollection whatsoever of this . . . and [I] expressed my amazement to Mr. Pelley and he said that they were thinking about running it. And I said, well, they could do what they wanted, but it would be a denial from me." The prosecutor continued: Did Ickes ever see Clinton and Lewinsky "in the Oval Office study, the Oval Office dining room, the Oval Office itself or this little hallway that leads from the Oval Office to the dining room"? Ickes's answer was typical of other official denials: he denied categorically having seen Lewinsky in those locations, but then added, "You know, I can't rule it out as an absolute, but I have no recollection of seeing her in the Oval or in other places."

There might have been a "sighting" of Clinton and Lewinsky "in a compromising position," and Judd might actually have talked to the person who claimed to have seen them, or to someone who talked to the person who claimed to have seen them, or to someone who saw this person's grand jury testimony; but in all this time the story of the "sighting" has never been confirmed by another journalist or a Starr prosecutor.

Across town, before *Meet the Press* began, when anchors and guests were still exchanging pleasantries and gossip in the greenroom, Russert asked Ginsburg about the report of a semen-stained dress. Nothing to it, Ginsburg replied. Russert, relieved, returned to the subject during his opening interview with the Los Angeles attorney just to be sure. "There are reports," he said, "that there may be some dresses or a dress with DNA evidence." Ginsburg shot back: "That's a salacious comment. . . . I know of no such dress." Later, Russert admitted: "We simply couldn't confirm the dress story. For me the key elements were veracity and legality." Yet, an hour earlier, on ABC, Ginsburg specifically stated that the OIC had informed him of such a dress the week before. Which Ginsburg was telling the truth?

Russert's guests were, in addition to Ginsburg, GOP senator Arlen Specter, Republican of Pennsylvania, an influential member of the Judiciary Committee; presidential apologist James Carville; and roundtable discussants Michael Isikoff of *Newsweek*, legal reporter Stuart Taylor of the *National Journal*, *New York Times* columnist William Safire, and the Internet's inflammatory Matt Drudge. They were no less dramatic than *This Week*'s guests. Russert's inclusion of Drudge provoked criticism of the program. "Our roundtable is an op-ed page," Russert explained later. "And Matt Drudge was a big player—*the* big player—in breaking this story. . . . We can pretend that the seven to ten million Americans who were logging onto him don't have the right to see him—but I don't agree." While acknowledging that "after his appearance, the e-mail and letter response was five to one against him," Russert continued to maintain, "I have had no second thoughts about inviting Drudge onto *Meet the Press*."

Senator Specter, steered to extremes by Russert's question about whether he thought the president would be "forced to resign or face impeachment," as if no other options were even imaginable, guessed that Congress would only "impeach the president" if there were "an open-and-shut case." He added: "And I believe if there is an open-and-shut case, conclusive, that the president will resign. . . . The House is not going to vote impeachment and the Senate's not going to sit on articles unless it's open-and-shut. And if it comes to that, I don't think the president will stay in office."

Carville used his time to lacerate Starr for conducting "a scuzzy investigation" to "get the president," for "these scuzzy, slimy tactics of wiring people up," for leaking "grand jury information," and for "threatening" Lewinsky and her parents. Russert moved Carville to the hot question of "resignation." Echoing Wolf Blitzer's report of Saturday evening, Russert asked Carville about "talk of resignation at the White House." Carville was expecting the question, and he pounced: "There absolutely is not going to be any resignations or any such things as that. But I tell you what there's going to be. There's going to be war. Friends of the president are disgusted by these kind of tactics. And we're going to fight, and we're going to fight very hard, to defend this president."

Taylor, a critic of Clinton, accused "Mr. Carville and others" of using "a classic Clinton non-denial denial strategy," meaning a denial that sounded more definitive and persuasive than it truly was.

Drudge, after criticizing the Washington press corps for not "monitoring the situation close enough," was characteristically irresponsible in his predictions. "There is talk all over this town," he thundered, using the phrase "this town" as if he owned it, "another White House staffer is going to come out from behind the curtains this week. If this is the case—and you couple this with the headline that the *New York Post* has—there are hundreds—hundreds, according to Miss Lewinsky, quoting Clinton— we're in for a huge shock that goes beyond the specific episode. . . . You thought last week was bad, this upcoming week is going to be one of the worst weeks in the history of this country." Drudge's platform for this rhetorical leap of fancy was not *The Jerry Springer Show;* it was *Meet the Press.*

Safire was asked whether he thought Clinton could survive "this crisis without resigning or being impeached." "I think it's too soon to say. I think he's in a fight, in his own words, 'till the last dog dies.' It could be the last dog will die and that would be when Tom Daschle and Dick Gephardt, Ted Kennedy comes to visit him the way Goldwater came to visit Nixon. But that's too long from now."

Though he devoted the first two-thirds of his program to the Lewinsky scandal, Russert showed good journalistic sense as well as historical perspective by concluding with a brief review of the pope's visit to Cuba. "Will these be the final days of Castro?" Russert asked before interviewing two American Catholic cardinals. For those who might have wondered on this Sunday morning whether anything other than Lewinsky existed in our shrinking universe, Russert seemed to be saying yes.

Face the Nation, the only one of the three major Sunday talk shows to have only a half hour of network time, squeezed five guests into its narrow corner of CBS's once proud schedule. Ginsburg led off the parade, followed by Paula Jones's lawyer Jim Fisher, House Judiciary Committee chair Hyde, former independent counsel Joseph diGenova, and finally, though hardly balancing the political ticket, presidential adviser Rahm Emanuel.

Anchor Bob Schieffer, also CBS's chief Washington correspondent, turned to Ginsburg. Holding a sheaf of papers in his hands, he said: "I have here a document that was given to me. An authentic document," Schieffer added. "This is a talking point," he continued. "It's suggestions that we're told [Lewinsky] gave to Linda Tripp. And among other things it said, 'You never saw her go into the Oval Office or come out of the Oval Office. You have never observed the president behaving inappropriately with anybody.' Do you know about this document?"

Ginsburg: "I was shown that document for a brief moment by the
           independent counsel's office."
Schieffer: "Do you believe it to be authentic?"
Ginsburg: "I have not had the privilege of sitting down and picking
           it apart and studying it. . . . I haven't had that opportu-
           nity. I find it rather interesting that you have a copy of
           that and I don't."
Schieffer: "And you—but you were shown it, I guess . . ."
Ginsburg: "I—I was, yes. The independent counsel's office has been
           forthcoming with what they have. They just haven't
           allowed me to hear the tape or take these materials with
           me to analyze them."

Starr's approach was highly irregular. While his staff provided Ginsburg with a "brief moment" to examine the talking points, they arranged (directly and indirectly) for a number of journalists to receive copies, including journalists working for CBS, *The New York Times,* and *The Washington Post.* In Monday's edition of both papers, the stories included transcripts of the talking points as well as leaked speculation that the language was too sophisticated and legalistic for a young woman to have used and that it must have been drafted by someone close to the president, such as Bruce Lindsey or Bob Bennett.

Jim Fisher had little new to add to his comments of the week before, when he was also a guest on Schieffer's program. In fact, the interview would have been a total flop if it had not been for Schieffer's concluding, throwaway question: "What do you make of these talking points?" Fisher, citing the judge's "strict confidentiality order," limited his response to saying that "if it's true" that "talking points like that" were provided and that they came either from the White House or from President Clinton's attorneys, "that would be very disturbing." Most reporters covering this scandal agreed with Fisher's presumption that the talking points had to have been drafted by the White House or by one of Clinton's attorneys; and if true, then the legal draftsmen and their client, Clinton, would have been guilty of obstructing justice. No one could entertain the possibility that the talking points were written by Lewinsky.

In his interview with Congressman Hyde, Schieffer repeatedly used the phrase "impeachable offense or offenses," as though the legal process were close to concluding that Clinton was guilty of such a crime. Hyde, in this interview, tried to sound judicious. When Schieffer asked whether perjury would be considered an "impeachable offense," Hyde answered, "I really don't like to answer 'what if' questions." Pause. "But, certainly, it is serious and would be considered."

"If it came to impeachment hearings," Schieffer persisted, "do you think the Democrats in Congress would let it go that far?"

"Again," Hyde replied, "that's speculating, but I think, as with President Nixon, nobody wants a—long, attenuated hearings that bring out sordid, lurid charges and accusations. So I think Democrats would appropriately make suggestions to the president."

Schieffer picked up the theme. "What you seem to be saying is . . . you think that Democrats would just urge the president to leave rather than go into something like that?"

Hyde retreated. "I can speculate that that might happen, although I hate to speculate."

Joseph diGenova, Schieffer's next guest, had been an independent counsel, and he had developed a reputation as someone who could quickly produce a superb sound bite. Gifted with a deep baritone, diGenova, whether fully informed or ill-informed, always had a response that sounded definitive. Schieffer raised a question about whether Lewinsky might have a tape of Clinton that at the moment was unknown to everyone in the case except the former intern.

DiGenova responded: "That's correct, or there may be witnesses that they don't know about in the White House who saw something." DiGenova seemed determined to talk about "witnesses." But was he simply echoing Judd's report on ABC? Or did he have truly corroborating information that "witnesses" to a "compromising" situation did exist? Later, it turned out that he had "heard" about witnesses but had no confirmation and knew nothing himself. However, that rather large gap in his knowledge did not deter diGenova from speculating about "witnesses" with other reporters later on Sunday and on Monday.

Rahm Emanuel, like Begala and Carville, was an adviser to Clinton with a single responsibility on Sunday morning—to tell the political junkies who watched these talk shows that the president was not going to resign, that Kenneth Starr was on a rampage to "get" Clinton, and that the "media frenzy" was creating "rumor, innuendo and gossip" in place of the older currency of hard news. Schieffer opened with the Blitzer "exclusive," which was still very much in play, despite repeated White House denials. "There are some people in the White House," he said, "who are spinning out scenarios that include the possibility of resignation. . . . What can you tell us about that?" Emanuel shrugged off the question. "That's ridiculous," he exclaimed. "It's not even under consideration and never would be. There—" Schieffer interjected: "There are people talking about it." Emanuel conceded the point but packaged it with the skill of a master spinner. "They may be having private conversations with themselves, but it's not in discussion at the White House because there's no reason for that."

Gloria Borger, a columnist for *U.S. News & World Report* who also worked as a CBS News analyst, suggested that "it's either Ken Starr who has to go or it's the president of the United States who has to go." Emanuel did not respond directly, but seized the occasion to rip into Starr once again, using a rhetorical parallel he must have practiced in front of the mirror. "He started investigating a 24-year-old real estate deal and now he's investigating a 24-year-old young lady, and the only common thread I can find—and I'm not a lawyer—is that they're both 24 years old."

Emanuel then boldly entered the convoluted world of Clintonian definitions. Borger wanted to know what the president meant when he said, "there is no sexual relationship." Emanuel told her that he had gone to see the president immediately after the Lehrer interview and said, "You know, there's some discussions about tense here." Clinton had promised Emanuel that he would clear up the confusion. In his next interview, he pointedly emphasized that "there was no sexual relationship." Emanuel, having told this tale, then leaped to an obvious conclusion: there was no sexual relationship, and the president didn't ask anyone to lie. So, why all the fuss? Schieffer replied, "Perhaps the president has a different definition of what a sexual relationship is. We're talking about oral sex, we're talking about phone sex, things of that nature." Emanuel, without missing a beat, echoed a line Hillary Clinton had used frequently over the years in similarly embarrassing situations: "I think everybody should take a step back, a deep breath, because I think what counts here are—are the facts and getting to the bottom of them."

Schieffer usually ended his weekly gig with a polite and soft-spoken adieu, but on this Sunday he delivered a short commentary.

In recent years, sexual harassment laws have left people so uptight they've hesitated to tell even a slightly off-color joke at the office water cooler. But the stories seeping out of the White House have changed all of that. In our newsroom this week, and from what I can tell in offices all across the country, men and women have been matter-of-factly discussing sexual practices and using euphemisms that up to now were only whispered about in the ladies room or out behind the barn somewhere. And it is all people are talking about. Our office has been so transfixed, we even forgot to do the office pool on the Super Bowl this year. And barriers have come down on screen as well as off. On CNN I heard Judy Woodruff introduce a story with a warning, "We're dealing with a sensitive subject here not suitable for children." And how do you explain this one to the kids? That's what parents around our office have been asking. You know, we keep hearing that President Clinton has been worried about his legacy. Well, if this isn't cleared up, the president who promised to restore idealism may be remembered for little more than presiding over an era when the economy was good but American culture became coarser and its people more cynical.

The Tribune Media Center at 1325 G Street in downtown Washington shares a common entryway and lobby with the Belo Corporation, owner of the *Dallas Morning News* and a dozen or so other newspapers, magazines, radio and television stations. Enter the lobby and walk up a curved flight of stairs to the right, and you enter the modern Belo newsroom, divided into a warren of cubicles for newspaper reporters and editors on one side and a large television studio and radio booth on the other. Walk up a similarly curved flight of stairs to the left, and you enter a newsroom as wide and long as two football fields, filled with large cubicles, one for each of the eighteen reporters working in the Washington bureau of the *Chicago Tribune*. Along the wall are offices for editors and columnists. In the back is a television studio with one camera, a TelePrompTer, a few anchor desks, three tape-editing rooms, and one radio booth as slick and professional as anything at the major networks. In both offices, the marriage of print and electronic journalism is a cause for celebration but also a reason for concern. Celebration, because the marriage makes money—lots of money; concern, because the quality of journalism has begun to fray at the edges. *Tribune* reporters must not only produce copy for their newspaper, but also do radio and television pieces for the increasing number of local stations being acquired by the parent corporation. There are, of course, radio and television reporters, but not enough to fill the needs of the stations. With only twenty-four hours in the day, the newspaper reporters complain about an expanding workload with fewer opportunities for tight and effective editorial control. And they worry about getting things wrong, about competitive pressures, about "quick and dirty news" on their Web site, about the daily rush to produce copy without time to think, reflect, check, confirm.

So it was no surprise that Jim Warren, the *Tribune*'s bureau chief, decided on Wednesday, when the Lewinsky story first hit the front-page of *The Washington Post*, that the *Chicago Tribune* would not compete with the *Post* for exclusives on Clinton's sex life. If "we couldn't independently verify a story," Warren told me, then "we would not run it." "We simply would not put it in the paper." This unusual arrangement lasted until Sunday morning, when a Chicago editor called Warren to ask about Judd's report. Did he—Warren—have "anything at all" on "the reported sighting of the lovemaking couple"? Every station in Chicago had already picked up the report—some of them citing ABC as the source, most ignoring the source and reporting the details as if they were confirmed facts. "What are we going to do?" asked the editor. "We can't avoid mentioning the story—ninety-nine percent of our readers have already heard about it. We've got to deal with it." Warren, under pressure from the home office, broke his own rule: he agreed to publish this story without independent confirmation. "We reached a high-minded compromise," he confessed with a sorry smile. "We reported that ABC had reported the x-y-and-z's of the 'sighting,' but we also wrote that the *Trib* could not confirm the story."

Once it began to report the Lewinsky scandal, the *Tribune* felt that it had no option but to play by the existing rules of sourcing. "We were very poorly sourced at the OIC," Warren explained. "We weren't high on their pecking order. I heard the two key sources over there were Jackie Bennett and Bob Bittman. We did okay. Nobody pressured me to report anything I didn't feel comfortable reporting." He added, "Well, almost anything."

Later, the *Tribune's* senior editor, George de Lama, expressed regret that the paper had compromised its principles. "In retrospect," he told Steven Brill, "I wish we had not published it. . . . It soon became clear to us that there's gonna be all kinds of stuff out there floating around and we should just publish what we know independently."

Nothing is more sacrosanct in American television than coverage of the Super Bowl. Networks battle for the privilege of carrying this premier sporting event. Commercials produce hundreds of millions of dollars. No one—absolutely no one—is allowed to break into this carefully constructed extravaganza: two weeks of interrupted programming. Yet on Super Bowl Sunday, January 25, 1998, even this sacred sporting event proved vulnerable to the hyped bulletin. If anyone needed additional evidence that mainstream news was being forced to adapt its values and style to the economic and technological challenges of cable TV, the Internet, and the twenty-four-hour news cycle, it was provided dramatically by NBC News anchor Tom Brokaw.

At exactly 4:42 p.m., during the colorful spectacle of music, dances, interviews, and sports history, with less than two hours to go before kick-off, Brokaw and White House correspondent Claire Shipman broke into the Super Bowl buildup with a 303-word bulletin, which was, more than anything else, an admission of news bankruptcy on the scandal and an unabashed promo for NBC News programs. Brokaw began with businesslike bluntness: "Here's where we stand in the White House sex scandal." No immunity deal yet between Lewinsky and Starr, he said. Then, quickly, he led into two sound bites from NBC's *Meet the Press,* the first from Ginsburg, saying, "We are dying to tell the story, but we cannot," and the other from Carville promising the president was not going to resign and warning that "there's going to be a war" with Starr. Brokaw then turned to Claire Shipman. "There's an unconfirmed report," the anchor said, "that, at some point, someone caught the president and Ms. Lewinsky in an intimate moment. What do you know about that?" Brokaw obviously had ABC's Judd report in mind. But, denied any new information from his own reporters, Brokaw resorted to vague phrases and words: "an unconfirmed report," "at some point," and "someone." Shipman's answer was revealing in only one respect—its subtle targeting of the OIC as the source of this "sighting" story; but she had nothing new to report. "Sources in Ken Starr's office tell us," she said, "that they are investigating that possibility, but that they haven't confirmed it." Brokaw brought the newsless bulletin to a close by hyping an upcoming *Today* show interview with Mrs. Clinton on Tuesday, the day of the president's State of the Union Address.

"Of course," Brokaw concluded, "NBC News will have continuing coverage of the crisis in the White House. Now back to Greg Gumbel in San Diego and the Super Bowl."

Without doubt, NBC tried—but failed—to generate independent confirmation of the ABC report, leaving it in the embarrassing position of having to echo a rival network's claim before one of the largest audiences ever to gather around the tube. Such a story would not ordinarily merit time on NBC's *Nightly News,* much less justify a breaking news bulletin during Super Bowl coverage, but in the crazy, competitive madness of scandal coverage, NBC felt that it had no choice but to demonstrate that it was on top of every nuance of this developing story.

Brokaw later acknowledged that competitive pressures drove NBC to air a newsless bulletin. "I guess it was because of ABC's report," he conceded. "Our only rationale could be that it's 'out there,' so let's talk about it. I wrestled with the question of whether to include it right up to airtime," he wrote. "What finally prompted my decision to raise it in a carefully worded question to Claire was the pervasive presence of that report [Judd's] on television and radio as well as on the news wires all day Sunday. I felt we should tell our audience it was being investigated, but it was not confirmed. Nothing more." It was another example of the best in journalism succumbing to the pressures of what was "out there."

Brokaw later insisted that NBC had always intended to air a short news report during the Super Bowl broadcast. It was called, he said, a "news update," not a "news bulletin." This fine-tuning in nomenclature was intended to take the sting out of criticism of a newsless bulletin.

On Sunday afternoon, President Clinton practiced his State of the Union message for more than two hours in the White House map room. A dozen or so of his senior aides and advisers crowded into the historic room, watching the president read his one-hour address off a TelePrompTer with all the ease of an accomplished anchorman. Everyone knew that in recent days his popularity had dropped fifteen points, according to White House polls. Clinton had the remarkable ability to soar above the bad news. Every now and then, during the practice session, he would pause to polish a paragraph or scribble a note or joke about the length of the speech. Maybe, he said, smiling, we should tell the American people to "turn to page 33" for the conclusion.

Clinton was obviously determined to convey the impression of being in good spirits. "He's very sharp," one White House aide later told a reporter. "If you ask me how he does it, I have no idea." In the morning he had gone to church, holding his wife's hand for the usual photo-op, and he had invited Jesse Jackson to join him and his family at the White House that evening to watch the Super Bowl. Aides said the president seemed "unusually buoyant," as if the dark clouds of recent days had lifted.

If the president truly succeeded in rising above Judd's report of a "sighting," as his attitude suggested, he may well have been the only one in the White House with such an ability to compartmentalize. Spokesman Mike McCurry was besieged by calls asking for an official reaction to the ABC report. He tried unsuccessfully to extract a particle of helpful information from the lawyers and the politicians. Finally, in frustration, he said, "I have not been able to find anyone at the White House aware of such a report and obviously the president's denial stands." This was not much of a reaction, but it was the best he could do under the circumstances.

At *The Washington Post*, the scandal team of Baker and Schmidt again swung into action, as soon as Judd's report was aired on ABC's *This Week*. Baker worked the lawyers and the White House, his natural beat, and Schmidt worked the OIC, her natural beat. They soon were able to confirm the ABC report, and relying on "sources familiar with the probe," almost certainly prosecutors from Starr's office, they learned a lot more.

For example, the OIC, which did not want to depend exclusively on Lewinsky, had started searching for independent witnesses of any "intimate acts" between the president and the intern. High on Starr's list were the Secret Service agents assigned to protect the president. If anyone knew whether a young intern visited the president at odd hours, it would be these normally tight-lipped agents. "Sources" told the reporters that Starr had heard a "rumor" to the effect that one Secret Service agent had come upon an "intimate act" and informed a senior White House official, who told him to say nothing about it to anyone. Two former top officials—chief of staff Leon Panetta and deputy chief of staff Evelyn Lieberman— quickly issued a statement to the press saying, "Allegations about this report to either of us are completely false." The language of the denial was carefully worded; they seemed to be saying that neither of them was the person to whom a Secret Service agent might have reported a highly embarrassing sighting. Later, a spokeswoman for Lieberman added that "Ms. Lewinsky was not transferred [from the White House to the Pentagon] because of an alleged physical incident."

In this story, Baker and Schmidt made a determined effort to help the reader understand the source of much of this damaging information, fingering "investigators working for prosecutor Kenneth W. Starr" in their lead sentence. But then, as they moved deeper into their story, they retreated behind deliberately obscure phrases to protect their sources. Nineteen times they used variations of "sources" to convey delicate information—"one source," "according to sources familiar with the probe," "a White House official," "a lawyer."

Journalism prizes are given for stories written, not for stories left unwritten.

Yet two reporters in the Washington bureau of *The New York Times* deserve a Pulitzer of their own for deciding late Sunday afternoon to kill rather than publish their story about a possible Clinton-Lewinsky sighting. It was, without doubt, the hottest story of the day. The pressure to publish must have been enormous. Every journalist in Washington was rushing into print or into a studio with largely unverified variations of the original Judd report.

Actually, White House reporter John Broder and investigative reporter Stephen Labaton had been working on the "sighting" story since

Friday evening. Each had reported to their bureau chief. Oreskes in turn had reported to Joseph Lelyveld in New York, who must have yearned for a solid scoop to make up for having been beaten by *The Washington Post* to the Lewinsky scandal.

On Saturday, Broder and Labaton had continued their pursuit of a possible eyewitness, but they were still dissatisfied with their sourcing and ultimately decided to continue working the phones. The story, they thought, could wait another day. Mike Oreskes agreed with their judgment. They had the shape of a story—a sighting perhaps by a Secret Service agent, who might have told a senior official, but might not have. Possibly in the Oval Office or in the narrow corridor just off the Oval Office. Or in the White House movie theater. Possibly, perhaps, maybe. Nothing struck them as really solid. They felt they needed more time, they wanted to talk to more people, and Oreskes did not rush them. "At first, they told me they had an eyewitness who had actually seen them together," Oreskes later recalled. "It seemed true at the time they told me. They are responsible reporters. Anything and everything was in the air, but we didn't know what was true and what wasn't."

On Sunday morning, as Oreskes was preparing to leave his home for work, he caught Judd's report on *This Week*. "Well," he concluded, "we got scooped again." When he reached the office, he called Broder and Labaton. They too had heard about Judd's report, but they thought the sourcing was rather brittle. She had quoted "several sources," but who were they? Were any of them eyewitnesses? How reliable were they in any case? The two men resumed their own legwork, determined that on this day they were going to break a big story about an actual eyewitness to a love scene. Each had—or thought he had—independent sources. Each "cross-checked" with the other, according to Oreskes. "Each thought he knew who the other was calling." In midafternoon, Oreskes informed Lelyveld that Broder and Labaton were in the final stages of finishing their "sighting" story (with three and possibly four excellent sources). An excited Lelyveld planned to run the story on the front page of Monday's paper. By 4 p.m., "when we had our 'page one' meeting," as Oreskes remembered the day, "we were so sure we'd get the story that we set aside four columns. It was to be our lead."

Lelyveld believed that Clinton was so unsteady, so punch-drunk from the pressures of the scandal, that he would have to resign in the face of another bombshell. "I really thought at the time that if this story had run, Clinton would have been gone, finished." Lelyveld underestimated the power of compartmentalization. "I thought we had three good sources, not four—one from the administration, one from Starr's shop, and one who was a former prosecutor. Something about an agent stumbling upon Clinton in the White House theater with Lewinsky. Caught in the act, so to speak."

At 6 p.m., John Broder walked into his bureau chief's office and dropped his own bombshell. "We don't have the story," he said. What? Oreskes asked, obviously surprised and disappointed.

Broder explained that, for one thing, he could not get through to Panetta, who, despite his odd denial, was important to this story. For another thing, Broder and Labaton discovered that they did not really have four knowledgeable sources. They had four different people who seemed either to be echoing the Judd report without any independent confirmation of their own or conveying and then embellishing a rumor they had heard about an agent "stumbling" upon the president with a young woman. Later, they figured out that their four "sources" might all have picked up the rumor from the same person. (The following day, diGenova was widely, though not yet publicly, identified as one of the key sources in spreading the "sighting" story.)

"Nothing was firsthand," Oreskes explained. "Nothing was original. So I called Joe and told him we didn't have the story. We were pulling out. We just didn't have it. Then I hung up and congratulated the two reporters. What they did that day took courage."

What they did was analyze their sourcing. They thought they had four independent sources, but they might actually have had only one source who talked to three other people. And the one real source had not himself seen an embarrassing encounter, nor met an eyewitness, nor spoken with anyone claiming to be an eyewitness. Sourcing can be an art form if taken seriously, and Broder and Labaton took it seriously. "Sometimes," Oreskes reflected, "the story you're proudest of is the story you didn't run."

CHAPTER 13

GOSSIP MASQUERADES AS NEWS

"I DID NOT HAVE SEXUAL RELATIONS WITH THAT WOMAN, MS.
LEWINSKY. I NEVER TOLD ANYBODY TO LIE, NOT A SINGLE
TIME, NEVER. THESE ALLEGATIONS ARE FALSE."
—President Bill Clinton, January 26, 1998

I n October 1998, Oreskes told a group of newspaper executives, "None of us had ever seen a story like this before."

Never before had an independent counsel launched a criminal investigation of a sitting president, charging him with possible perjury, suborning of perjury, and obstruction of justice.

Never before had an independent counsel submitted an impeachment report to the Congress.

Never before had a president been impeached essentially for lying about an affair.

Never before had the media reported so intrusively and exhaustively about the sexual life of a president while in office, "media" being defined as everyone and everything from Koppel to Drudge and from the Internet to a local radio station.

The scandal of January 1998 was an original. It stained the presidency, tarnished the reputation of the press, and cast a long shadow over the entire country.

Sex has always been a good story, but in the coverage of sex there has generally been a distinction between the mainstream and tabloid press. While the tabloids could market fantasy or filth to satisfy the prurient interests of the public, the owners and publishers of the mainstream press have tried to uphold higher standards while delivering the news.

Take the case of Adolph Ochs, who, in October 1896, set up a contest for the best motto to describe the professional ethos of his newly acquired newspaper, *The New York Times*. Day after day, as a promotional gimmick, he ran submissions that provided insights into the public's understanding of the responsibilities of a major newspaper. "News for the Millions, Scandal for None," was one submission. "Free from Filth, Full of News," was another. Finally, there was the official winner: "All the World's News, But Not a School for Scandal," a reference to the Irish dramatist Richard Sheridan's play. D. M. Redfield of New Haven, Connecticut, won $100 for his winning submission, but he had to content himself with the money. Ochs had already made up his mind—the motto was going to be "All the News That's Fit to Print."

The submissions suggested that the readers of the *Times* drew a distinction between "news" and "scandal." Scandal was not appropriate for a serious newspaper.

It took only a few days in January 1998 for journalists to realize that they were in uncharted waters. Faced by a scandalous story involving a president and an intern, a competitive twenty-four-hour-a-day news cycle, and a coldly demanding economic imperative, many found themselves violating just about every rule in the book. There have been many examples, although two have drawn the most attention, perhaps unfairly. One concerned the *Dallas Morning News*, the other *The Wall Street Journal*.

The *Dallas Morning News* is a very good regional newspaper—cautious, proud, respected, with a daily circulation of 500,000 and a Sunday circulation of more than 700,000. Washington reporter David Jackson, who normally covered the Justice Department but also reported about Whitewater, was investigating a story on Sunday, January 25, 1998, about Starr and his zealous compatriots at the OIC. Among his sources was Joseph diGenova, the former independent prosecutor who had appeared on CBS's *Face the Nation* earlier in the day to discuss the Lewinsky scandal and the Judd "sighting." According to Carl Leubsdorf, Jackson's bureau chief, diGenova told Jackson that he knew of a "witness" who had seen

Clinton and Lewinsky in a "compromising situation." A second source, identified by Jackson as someone who had once worked for Starr, also told Jackson that he'd heard there was a "witness." Were diGenova and the "second source" merely parroting Judd's unverified report? Did either source ever see or talk to the "witness"? Did either ever talk to someone, anyone, who had talked to the "witness"? Possibly, though unlikely. Still, Jackson, armed with the word of his two sources and pressured to match Judd's report, wrote a story for Monday's paper. It was to prove to be a very slippery slope for him and his newspaper.

"A federal employee claims to have seen President Clinton and Monica Lewinsky in a 'compromising situation' in the White House, attorneys familiar with the obstruction of justice investigation haunting the administration said Sunday," he wrote. "'There is at least one witness who saw them together in a compromising situation,' a source said, declining to elaborate." Later in his story, Jackson added: "'There are White House people who have seen things,' a source said, declining to elaborate." What "things"? The vagueness of the quote obviously did not deter Jackson, who fleshed out his story with references to the Sunday interview programs.

On Monday, January 26, Jackson continued his pursuit of the "sighting" story. He called Starr's office, which issued a perfunctory no-comment. Jackson then called other sources, including once again diGenova, who added a few fresh details. The witness, he said, had already been in touch with Starr's office. Technically, he was now a "government witness." DiGenova described him as a Secret Service agent, who was prepared to testify that he personally had seen the president and Lewinsky in what he called "a compromising situation." Later in the day, Jackson got confirmation from a second source, whose name and affiliation were never given. He checked again with Starr's office; again, no comment, but, as he later put it, "no sign of a problem" either. He checked with the White House, which expressed deep skepticism about a Secret Service role in the scandal. One official wondered, in fact, whether a Secret Service agent could even have seen an "impropriety." Officially, the Secret Service had no comment.

Jackson wrote another story, leaning very heavily on diGenova's "tips." If diGenova had not been his principal source, Jackson probably would not have written the story. He felt diGenova was a very solid source. So did Leubsdorf, who had worked with diGenova on other stories for years. In the lead sentence of this second story, Jackson reported that Starr had spoken with a Secret Service agent, who was prepared to testify that he had witnessed Clinton and Lewinsky in a "compromising situation." This was explosive stuff, carrying the original Judd story into new terrain. Jackson's story was then reviewed and edited in Washington and sent to Dallas. There it was slapped onto the front page of Tuesday's paper; it also was put on the Internet, which served in this case as a gigantic megaphone for the newspaper. In minutes, the story was picked up by the Associated Press and CNN.

Equally important, Koppel opened Monday's *Nightline* with a reference to a story in "tomorrow's edition of the *Dallas Morning News,* not only citing sources confirming Jackie Judd's report of yesterday, but adding new details." Koppel was, in effect, using a newspaper report to confirm a television report, adding his own authoritative voice to the hot media speculation. He offered no independent confirmation of the newspaper report. More than likely, he had none. "The Dallas paper cites its own sources," he said, "as stating that a secret service agent witnessed the president and Ms. Lewinsky in a compromising situation and that the agent has already been in communication with the office of the independent counsel, Ken Starr." Koppel then quoted one of Lewinsky's lawyers as saying that he knew nothing about an agent/witness. Toward the end of the broadcast, the White House called Koppel to deny and denounce the Dallas story as "false and malicious." Lawyer David Kendall stated, "This is another false political leak for obvious and political reasons on the eve of the State of the Union."

Within an hour, the *Dallas Morning News* took the extraordinary step of retracting and killing Jackson's scoop. In a brief advisory to the press and the public, editor Ralph Langer admitted that "the source for the story, a longtime Washington lawyer familiar with the case, later said the information provided for Tuesday's report was inaccurate." *The* source—in other words, it was not "sources" and "lawyers," who substantiated Jackson's report. It was *the* source. It was diGenova.

A few hours earlier, shortly after Jackson's scoop hit the Internet, someone from Starr's office had called to complain to Leubsdorf that the story was wrongly attributed to the OIC. Much more important, diGenova called Leubsdorf to claim that he was only giving Jackson "a vague tip," which he assumed the reporter would then use to continue his investigation. He hadn't meant for the "tip" to be taken as "fact," he said, just as "something to be looked into." Now, according to Leubsdorf, diGenova was "touting us off the story based on having received additional information."

Moments later, diGenova's wife and law partner, Victoria Toensing, called Leubsdorf and "screaming, very upset," asserted that she had told Jackson, earlier in the evening, "'If Joe is your source, it's wrong. Do not go with that story.'" (Jackson later said that Toensing had told him: "If Joe told you that, he shouldn't have.") Even more than two years later, Toensing recalled her conversation with Jackson in detail. "'Is Joe your source?' I asked. Jackson didn't answer. There was just silence. I said, 'Well, if Joe is your only source, then do not go with it.'"

Hearing Toensing, Leubsdorf felt a sudden, terrible chill. The paper's key source "was getting cold feet." DiGenova conceded, "I was mistaken."

Leubsdorf and Langer then took the courageous if embarrassing step of admitting a major blunder: they pulled Jackson's story. "We had no choice but to pull the story," Leubsdorf told me. "Our source had reneged on it. Besides, we wanted to protect our access to Starr's office." Langer specifically said in the paper's retraction that Starr was not the source for the story, but access to his office was obviously on the publisher's mind, too.

How did Leubsdorf account for diGenova's flipflop? According to a written record of a long Leubsdorf/diGenova/Toensing conversation on Tuesday, January 27, diGenova explained that a Secret Service agent had come to his wife for legal advice. The agent supposedly told her that he had seen or heard about an "ambiguous incident," which later was reported as a "compromising situation," and he wanted to tell Starr about it.

Toensing, a committed anti-Clinton conservative, told editor Steven Brill a somewhat different story. She said she had been approached by a "friend of someone who is a former worker in the White House." It was not clear whether the "someone" was a Secret Service agent or a White House steward. The "someone" knew someone else at the White House who claimed to have seen the president and Lewinsky "in a compromising position." The question for Toensing was whether she should represent this other person, if he/she decided to go to Starr. DiGenova happened to overhear his wife's intriguing conversation. Then, apparently without his wife's knowledge or approval, diGenova told Jackson (and others) that there had been an eyewitness. When Toensing learned about his unauthorized disclosures to reporters, she got very angry, in part, she said, because he didn't know the whole story and confused some of what he did know.

Besides, Toensing never took the case, though she did inform a friend in Starr's office about what she had been told. Toensing told Leubsdorf that the phrase "compromising situation" was inaccurate—she really didn't know, she said, if the alleged witness had actually seen anything himself. "I think there's somebody who saw something, but we don't know what." The story, as related by diGenova and contradicted by his wife, was shaky and unreliable, and it should never have been published.

As Brill put it, "This story of a 'secret service' witness seems to have been a one-source story from a fifth-hand source: diGenova (1) heard his wife (2) talking to a friend (3) of someone (4) who had talked to someone (5) who said he'd seen Lewinsky with Clinton."

Leubsdorf was under heavy pressure from Dallas to "out" his source. After all, it was argued, diGenova had "shafted" both him and the paper. Leubsdorf was angry and disappointed, but in principle he refused to "out" diGenova. "That was a bad idea," he told me. "You don't 'out' sources." First, because no source would then trust the paper to keep a confidence. Second, in this particular case, because "Starr's people might conclude that the paper was unreliable, and they'd stop dealing with us." Like most Washington reporters covering the scandal, Leubsdorf and Jackson were dependent upon Starr's guidance and leaks.

On Wednesday, January 28, the *Dallas Morning News* ran another story about the alleged sighting. Using vague language and trying to suggest that now they had the true story, Leubsdorf and Jackson wrote in their lead sentence that "an intermediary for one or more witnesses" of "an ambiguous incident" had talked with Starr about "possible cooperation" and that the "witness or witnesses" included "one or more current or former secret service agents," who were described as "frightened and worried" about being subpoenaed. The lead sentence, to put it charitably, was confusing. The reporters quoted "two sources," presumably diGenova and Toensing. At one point, they even quoted diGenova by name as saying, "In essence, your story is correct."

That afternoon, the usually shy Ralph Langer faced two hundred of his reporters and editors in the grand ballroom of the Hyatt Regency Hotel in downtown Dallas. He fielded their questions, walking among them with a hand-held microphone. On a speakerphone hooked to the public address system came Carl Leubsdorf's voice from the Washington bureau. Both Langer and Leubsdorf tried to explain how the usually dignified *Dallas*

Morning News managed to stumble into this embarrassing mess. It was not a very easy task. A few editors thought things were so bad some heads should roll. Others felt Leubsdorf ought to assume responsibility and quit or be sacked. Langer tried to ease the roiling tension between Dallas and Washington. There was "miscommunication," he said. Too much reliance on one source. Some confusion about whether there had ever been a second source. Worse, he continued, their one sure source had called in a "panic" late Monday night and inexplicably "bailed out" on them. Never in his explanation did Langer mention Jackson, perhaps because he'd earlier been informed that Jackson knew there were problems with his sourcing well before he filed his story (Toensing had told him not to go with the story). Leubsdorf protected Jackson, who continued to cover the story. Leubsdorf, according to Toensing, "covered up" for Jackson.

That evening on CNN, Jim Warren of the *Chicago Tribune*, speaking for many of his Washington colleagues, criticized the *Dallas Morning News* for setting "a troubling new standard" in American journalism. CBS's Dan Rather asked Mike McCurry: "What is the biggest error, the single biggest mistake you believe has been reported in this case so far?" McCurry replied: "Well, obviously, it has to be the *Dallas Morning News* story that was retracted, because I think that's the only case that I'm aware of in which a news organization has just had to flat-out say, 'What we told our readers simply was not true, and it was based on erroneous information that we had from a single source.'" *The New York Times* devoted a long story to the Dallas debacle under the headline: RETRACTING A RETRACTION, SELF-DEFENSE AND REVELATION. Reporter Janny Scott wrote: "The *Dallas Morning News*, the newspaper that made news by becoming the first news gathering organization to officially retract a front-page story on the White House sex scandal, went itself one better yesterday and retracted the retraction. Sort of."

The sad spectacle of the best in American journalism rushing after the "sighting" story continued a week later with the cautious and dignified *Wall Street Journal*. Editors at the *Journal* wanted their scoop, too, and found it in yet another version of the original ABC News report. According to Alan Murray, the Washington bureau chief, two of his best investigative reporters came to him on the morning of February 4 with a well-sourced report to the effect that White House steward Bayani Nelvis had told the grand jury that he had seen Clinton and Lewinsky alone in a study near the Oval Office, and that later, after they'd left, he'd found tissues with "lipstick and other stains" on them. The reporters, Brian Duffy and Glenn Simpson, told Murray that they had not talked to Nelvis, or to his lawyer, but they had talked to other sources who confidentally told them that Nelvis, upset and worried, had informed the Secret Service about his discovery. Murray, donning his hat as bureau chief, did not have to remind Duffy and Simpson about the acute embarrassment suffered by the *Dallas Morning News.* His reporters had to be right. Duffy and Simpson assured Murray that their story was right. Murray then called managing editor Paul Steiger and others in New York and told them about the Duffy/Simpson scoop.

Over the next few hours, there were more calls. The obvious questions were raised, the obvious risks were considered. These were serious editorial deliberations, forcing a number of lunch dates to be delayed in New York and Washington. Finally, after 1 p.m., a puff of white smoke arose from the roof of 1025 Connecticut Avenue, a few blocks from the White House. The decision was that if the story was right (and given the quality of the reporters, everyone assumed that it was), and if the White House was informed and had a chance to respond, then there was no journalistic reason to hold it up.

At the *Journal,* the decision to go with the story meant more than just publishing it in the morning's newspaper. It also meant putting it out on the Dow Jones wire, which is normally the place for the latest financial news but also includes hard news with potential relevance to the markets. It meant putting it on the *Journal*'s Web site. And it now meant putting it out on CNBC, an NBC-owned cable network devoted during the day to financial news and during the evening to politics.

As Murray explained the background of the new WSJ/CNBC agreement, which went into operation in mid-January 1998, just as the Lewinsky story broke, the *Journal* had been looking for a television connection for years. First, in 1997, it entered into a joint venture with ITT for the $200 million purchase of Channel 31 in New York. "Big plans, big eyes," Murray called it. Within six months, the venture fell apart. Then the *Journal* entered into negotiations with CNN for the purchase of CNNfi, its financial cable network. This effort also failed. Finally, the *Journal* approached General Electric. The idea here was that the *Journal* and CNBC would share assets—the *Journal* providing CNBC with its editorial smarts and CNBC providing the *Journal* with the reach of cable television. Both thought they had discovered nirvana when Monica Lewinsky burst upon the scene. The immediate upshot was that dark rings began to form under Murray's eyes. His responsibilities, already considerable, enlarged to include two appearances a day on CNBC, which moved a camera into the *Journal*'s newsroom for his convenience. Murray's first appearance every weekday was at 6:15 a.m., his second at 2:15 p.m.

From then on, any story generated by the Washington bureau had to consider four different outlets, each with its own culture and urgent requirements: the newspaper itself, the Dow Jones ticker, the Internet Web site, and CNBC.

By 2 p.m., the Duffy-Simpson story had been written, edited, and sent to New York. Having decided to go with the story, everyone in the bureau suddenly felt a surge of competitive anxiety. Who else might have the story? Nelvis had appeared before the grand jury on Tuesday, and though he seemed to attract very little press attention, a smart reporter, hearing so much talk about a possible sighting, might have wondered why a steward was being subpoenaed to testify. Of all his competitors, Murray seemed to worry more about ABC, which he thought had a direct pipeline to Starr's office, than he did about *The Washington Post* or *The New York Times*.

At 4 p.m., Murray made a controversial decision, which he later admitted was a "mistake." He asked Simpson to call Joe Lockhart, the deputy press secretary at the White House, tell him about the Nelvis story, and ask for an official comment. Although Lockhart promised a quick response, Murray decided not to wait for one. "I didn't expect a comment," Murray explained. "The White House had taken the position that it was not commenting," he told Steven Brill later. "So, I figured, why wait?" Simpson was surprised. "When I told Murray that Joe was going to get right back to me," he said, "Alan told me it was too late. He'd already pushed the button." Within seconds, the Nelvis story was on *The Wall Street Journal*'s Web site. Within minutes, it was the heart of Murray's "exclusive" report on CNBC. Months later, Murray acknowleged the competitive pressure: he wanted to beat ABC to the gold ring. He also wanted to impress his new video master. "Yes, it was in my mind that we could impress them [CNBC] with this." One *Journal* colleague sourly observed:

"They got too excited and Alan rushed to get on television." By the time the story was ready for its newspaper deadline later in the evening, it had been significantly softened by new information. No longer was it reported that Nelvis had told the grand jury about the sighting and the soiled tissues; now it was said that he told only the Secret Service about it.

Still, the *Journal* paid a heavy price for Murray's managerial and editorial impatience. The White House immediately denounced the story, questioning the *Journal's* integrity. McCurry referred to the whole story as "the sleaziest episode in the history of American journalism." Nelvis's lawyer leaped on the White House's bandwagon, describing the story as "absolutely false and irresponsible." Worse, by the following Monday, February 9, the *Journal* felt the need to publish a prominent retraction, which said in part: "White House steward Bayani Nelvis told a grand jury he didn't see President Clinton alone with Monica Lewinsky, contrary to a report in *The Wall Street Journal* last week." Stieger added: "We deeply regret our erroneous report of Mr. Nelvis's testimony."

Brill raised a fascinating question. "Could it be," he asked, "that Judd's report . . . about a 'witness' catching the president in the act, and the *Dallas Morning News's* dead-wrong, one-sourced, fifth-hand report . . . about a secret service agent being ready to testify, and this report about Nelvis testifying or, as it later became, about Nelvis telling a secret service agent what he had seen, are all different versions of the same story?" For an answer, Brill turned back to Victoria Toensing, whose conversation with a friend about a possible witness, overheard by her husband, became the basis of a bad story in the Dallas newspaper. "Yes, I'm sure it's all the same story," she said.

It is logical that there might have been a witness, but it has never been proven. More than three years later, journalistic accounts of the "sighting" still remain highly suspect.

Leusbdorf and Murray, two of the most experienced and respected bureau chiefs in Washington, offered their own conclusions:

Leubsdorf: "Things have changed enormously. It is so much more
difficult now to retain full control over what gets into the
newspaper, now that gossip masquerades as news, when
so much of it is around. In the '92 campaign, when the
Flowers story broke, we had confirmation from a source
in Dallas, and we ran it on page one. Six months later,

the *New York Post* ran a story about an affair between President Bush and an aide. I questioned whether we should publish it. But we did, and it ran on page one. Then, in Maine, with [Israeli prime minister Yitzhak] Rabin at his side, CNN asked Bush about the affair. He was angry. I didn't think we should run that either, but we did, on page one. Why? Because it was out there."

Murray: "There is so much more competition, so many more people involved in the process of news gathering and distribution. Competition has always been the rule of the day. Now it is so much more intense, so much more unavoidable. It is not only different in degree; it is different in kind."

CHAPTER 14

NEEDED—A FEW GOOD MEN
AND WOMEN

A WOULD-BE SATIRIST, A HIRED BUFFOON,
A MONTHLY SCRIBBLER OF SOME LOW LAMPOON,
CONDEMNED TO DRUDGE, THE MEANEST OF THE MEAN,
AND FURNISH FALSEHOODS FOR A MAGAZINE.
　　　　　　　　　　　　　　　　　　　—Lord Byron (1809)

The Lewinsky scandal did not, on its own, smash the standards of American journalism. It merely accelerated a disturbing trend that had been apparent for several decades. Standards continue to exist, though now they are observed more in slogans than in practice. The trend is rooted in two basic factors that have gradually but inexorably changed the core values of modern-day journalism. One is the new technological revolution that started with the explosion of cable television in the late 1970s and continued through the rise of the Internet in the late 1990s; the other is the radical change in the economic ownership and management of a deregulated business. Both the new technology and the new, looser economic underpinning have transformed the news business from one tied to public trust to one linked to titillation and profit.

When publisher Jay Harris resigned from the *San Jose Mercury News* on March 10, 2001, shocking the world of journalism, he explained his motivation by turning to the shifting balance between the financial and editorial sides of the business. "Much greater priority is given today to the business aspects of our enterprise," he wrote, "than is given to fulfilling our 'public trust.' I fear as well that we no longer sense the same level of 'moral obligation' to 'excel in all that we do' and that our founders' commitment to publishing 'high quality newspapers' is no longer the powerful drive in the company [Knight-Ridder] that it once was."

For more than twenty years, we have been the beneficiaries—or the victims—of a vast technological revolution that has transformed the way we get and process information. In the late 1970s, most Americans watched one of three evening newscasts on ABC, CBS, and NBC. That's where they got their information about the United States and the rest of the world. Now they have the same three networks, though fewer than 40 percent of Americans have been watching evening newscasts. They also have five cable news networks (CNN, CNBC, C-SPAN, Fox, and MSNBC); ten (at last count) weekly news magazines on ABC, CBS, and NBC in primetime; a half-dozen cable business news networks; and a growing number of hugely profitable sports news networks, each with a corresponding Web site featuring constantly updated news reports. And the number of these networks keeps growing exponentially.

Take CNN, for example. At the Republican and Democratic Party conventions in the summer of 2000, the signs on the brightly lit skybox studios indicated that Cable News Network is now much more than just CNN; it is also a cluster of CNN offspring, such as CNN Headline News, CNN International, CNNfn, CNN en Español, two radio networks, seven Web sites, and a syndicated news service called CNN Newsource. In addition, there is CNN Airport Network, the Better Health Network, the College Television Network, CNN/SI, and much more. CNN brought a small army of 450 people to each convention and spent $20 million on its political coverage.

NBC and Fox tried and, with mixed results, succeeded in emulating CNN. By acquiring cable operations, NBC widened its reach and established CNBC and MSNBC. Fox set up a cable news network that achieved considerable recognition during the 2000 political season.

A few years ago, some observers, examining CNN's growth, predicted a universe of at least five hundred channels. Although this prediction proved to be wildly inflated, it did point people in the right direction. There has been a mammoth increase in cable channels, and the public has responded with enthusiasm. In market terms, this has been called "fractionalization." Where once there was a handful of news sources, there are now hundreds, each struggling to compete for a smaller share of an increasingly distracted audience. The guessing game of how to hold or increase audience share has become a profit-driven obsession. Ratings charts show that the most popular and profitable offerings on cable television are—aside from wrestling matches—talk shows. In our celebrity culture, talk has proven to be the cheapest form of information and entertainment. These shows have managed to befuddle viewers into believing that whatever they see or hear can be equated with news.

Perhaps even more significant than the expansion of cable has been the sudden emergence of the Internet as a major force in national and global communications. Once the exclusive resource of the Pentagon, the Internet has now blossomed into a ubiquitous asset in industry, universities, journalism, and private homes. Every newspaper, network, or magazine has its own Web site. On the operating assumption that the Internet will become a very profitable extension of its business, each news organization goes to great lengths to highlight its Web site's contribution to expanded coverage. The Republican and Democratic conventions in 2000 were called the "first Internet conventions," testing the new technology on a proven political event. Thirty-six different Internet companies covered the conventions, and traditional news organizations highlighted their own Web site coverage, too.

For example, on August 2, 2000, during the Republican National Convention in Philadelphia, *The Washington Post* listed its "On the Web" coverage, hour by hour, on page C7, clearly to publicize its aggressive Web site coverage and to attract a bigger audience. For example: "**11 a.m. EDT: On The Job Live:** Post columnist Kenneth Bredemeier answers questions on workplace politics; **Noon EDT: The Grapevine** with **Michael Franz** is an interactive discussion about all things bottled and corked; **1 p.m. EDT Schools & Kids:** *Post* 'Family Almanac' Columnist Marguerite Kelly takes your questions on parenting," and so on and so on, until 5 p.m., when "washingtonpost.com," host of the Web site, featured a conversation with Terry McAuliffe, chair of the Democratic National Convention Committee. Despite this daily output of appealing subject matter, research conducted by the Vanishing Voter project of the Shorenstein Center on the Press, Politics and Public Policy at Harvard University showed that this costly Internet effort attracted comparatively few hits.

Of those polled about their viewing habits during the Republican convention, 25 percent said that they had used the Internet on a convention day, but only 34 percent of them remembered coming upon any convention coverage. When asked how much time they actually spent reading convention coverage on the Internet, 66 percent answered, "just a few seconds." Most of them stumbled upon convention coverage "inadvertently." Only 16 percent of those who used the Internet said they had deliberately set out to seek information about the convention.

Nevertheless, in recent years, more and more Americans have entered the Internet age in their quest for news. In 1995, only 4 percent of Internet users searched for news. Three years later, the number had jumped to 13 percent. By 2000, it was 23 percent of the adult population who said they went online for news at least three days a week. Yet, for many people, it was news that had not inspired confidence in its essential reliability. TV critic Tom Shales of *The Washington Post* described Internet news as "glorified gossip and rampant rumormongering." Shales believed that "plain old unadorned television" still provided the most reliable, solid information about the 2000 campaign.

In December 1962, William Paley, who created CBS, outlined his ambitious plans for the news department to a small group of CBS correspondents. One of them, Charles Collingwood, cautioned that his plans could be costly. Paley responded: "You guys cover the news. I've got Jack Benny to make money for me." Those were the days when news was assumed to be a loss leader—serious, imposing, important, but never profitable. Benny and the other CBS entertainers were supposed to make the profit, and they did so handsomely. The reporters served two other functions: one was to cover the news, and the other was to provide Paley with respectability and legitimacy. "My jewels in the crown," he called the correspondents.

Thirty-six years later, in 1998, one of Paley's successors, Michael H. Jordan, disavowed such an idealistic vision. "Yes, we want to hold on to journalistic and other standards," he asserted coolly. "But I don't aspire to that Paleyesque role. This is a business."

The post-Paley generation of network leaders discovered that news could not only buy respectability—it could also make unimaginable profits. But there was a price: when news began to live by the rules of any other profitable enterprise, it lost its soul to the demands of the marketplace. News became a big, big business, no longer controlled by powerful families but by media moguls who placed a higher value on their profits than on their contributions to society.

Networks became so profitable in the deregulated Reagan years of the 1980s that General Electric acquired NBC, Loews bought CBS, and CapCities picked up ABC. By the mid-1990s, as one megacorporation after another expanded its technological horizons, pushing profits into the stratosphere, Disney purchased ABC (for $19 billion), Time Warner acquired CNN, Westinghouse bought CBS, Fox was created, and other conglomerates rushed forward to wire the world with satellites, faxes, cellular phones, and cable television.

In February 1996, Congress passed the Telecommunications Act, which reduced or eliminated existing governmental regulations affecting radio, television, and telephone operations. One immediate effect was a dramatic increase in the rate of megamedia mergers, including buyouts of modest-sized companies in local markets. Everyone participated, everyone made money; it was a mad scramble, and soon it seemed as if there were no limits to the media to be merged and the money to be made. Westinghouse/CBS bought Infinity Broadcasting's empire of radio stations. Rupert Murdoch's News Corporation, which bought and built Fox, acquired New World Communications Group. Viacom purchased half of the UPN-TV network. Tele-Communications Inc. (TCI) bought one-third ownership of Cablevision, making it one of the largest cable operations in the country. Westinghouse/CBS expanded its radio empire by purchasing American Radio Systems. Then AT&T, wanting to get into the action, bought TCI for $45 billion. And, as one century and millennium blended into another, Viacom acquired CBS, and America Online (AOL) bought Time Warner. Now, for the first time, an Internet giant owned a media Goliath.

How profitable could this megamedia revolution be? Let us take NBC as one example. In 1996, NBC produced three hours of television news a day. Two years later, using its newly acquired and developed cable subdivisions of CNBC, MSNBC, and others as markets, NBC produced and fielded the equivalent of twenty-seven hours of news every day. While it is true that the additional twenty-four hours of news were not filled with the same professionally polished programming of yesteryear, they provided at least twelve more minutes per hour for commercials that the network never had before. Put quality to one side; quantity was now the exploitable asset. One minute could be sold for $25,000 in advertisements, or $100,000, or $1 million, depending on the program, the time, and the expected size of the audience. For the first time in its history, television news made so much money that it came to be considered a "profit center." In this brave new world, NBC has begun to manufacture news in much the same way that GE manufactures light bulbs.

Both the new technology and the new profit-driven economy have—not surprisingly—transformed the ethics, values, and standards of journalism. One example of the "new news" that has emerged from this modern marriage of technology and profit was on embarrassing display on election night 2000. It was a disaster waiting to happen. After the 1988 election, the networks, under financial pressure from corporate bigwigs to slash unnecessary expenses, decided to eliminate their own polling operations. Each network, according to this calculation, would save $5–10 million per election cycle. Except the networks still needed polling data to make their projection calls. To satisfy this need and still save money, the networks, joined by the Associated Press, pooled their resources and established the Voter News Service (VNS) in 1990. The VNS would become the single source of polling data for all the networks and the AP. If the source was right, everyone was right; if the source was wrong, then everyone was wrong. The system, as structured, worked reasonably well in 1992 and 1996.

Then the networks cut VNS's budget, just as the corporate owners had cut theirs. Insiders at VNS worried about quality loss and warned of a possible disaster, but they were ignored. Network bookkeepers worried only about profit loss and ignored VNS's warnings. On election night 2000, VNS's enfeebled operation in Florida led the networks twice to make faulty calls, misleading the public and creating a political crisis unparalleled in American history. The networks apologized, but they lost their credibility. Imagine for a moment that Florida is again the scene of a close, bitter struggle in the 2004 presidential election, and the networks again "project" a winner. Who will believe them? And if the networks are not to be believed, then who or what will replace them and assume the awesome responsibility of calling an election?

Other historic factors have also played important roles in changing the relationship between the reporter on the one side and the government and the public on the other. Vietnam and Watergate jarred the nation's psyche.

The United States had never lost a war before. No president had ever resigned in disgrace before. The war and the scandal served as wake-up calls for journalists who had previously given the benefit of the doubt to politicians and presidents who professed to be telling them the truth. Now many journalists began to assume that politicians were lying to them and the public. They approached official pronouncements with deep skepticism. They distrusted government. Soon this attitude spread from one newsroom to another, radically changing the relationship between reporter and politician—and nowhere more so than in the White House press room. There in the 1990s scandal replaced budgets and diplomacy as the story of choice.

In addition, with the end of the Cold War, newsrooms faced what appeared at first glance to be a news vacuum. Encouraged by polls indicating that the American people had lost interest in the world, reporters and editors began to shortchange foreign news. When the Berlin Wall collapsed in November 1989, ABC reporters instinctively hurried to capture this moment of history; but very few Americans watched the drama. One result was that with the exception of CNN, most networks and newspapers substantially cut and/or trimmed their foreign bureaus and slashed their budgets. When a major earthquake hit Taiwan on September 21, 1999, *Nightline*'s Ted Koppel called producer Tom Bettag, wondering whether they should not be doing a story about it. Do we have a reporter in Taiwan? Koppel asked. No, he was told. Do we have one in Hong Kong? No, he was told. Do we have one in Beijing? No. Well then, what about Tokyo? Yes, but the reporter is on vacation. How about Moscow? No, no one there either. That week, ABC News did not have a single correspondent anywhere in Asia or Russia who could cover a major news story. CBS, once an international powerhouse, has been reduced to a pale shadow of its former self. It once maintained more than a dozen full-time foreign bureaus; now it had four. NBC had gone "lite" even earlier.

The Cold War had provided a sharp focus for the news: the threat of nuclear annihilation. Without the Cold War, journalism seemed to lose its rudder and a kind of anarchy set in. There was some good reporting: the coverage of health care, education, and the environment increased in direct proportion to the number of women moving into positions of greater authority in the newsrooms. But there was some awful reporting, too: the coverage of gossip and scandal not only came to dominate network and newspaper reporting but also moved to marginalize most other news stories.

How was the Lewinsky scandal covered? The journalists claimed that, under the circumstances, they did quite well, thank you. The president did in fact have an affair with Lewinsky, he did lie about it, the dress did have a semen stain, and so on. In fact, a small number of reporters with good sources did a good job, but many did poorly. In the process, they ended up confirming the politicians' and the public's low esteem for the media as spoiled and disgruntled scribes engaged in an endless game of "gotcha."

Moreover, imagine for a moment that Ann McDaniel's original concern about Lewinsky proved to be right—that the intern, who confessed to Tripp that she'd been lying all her life, was actually imagining or exaggerating her relationship with the president. Much would then have been published and broadcast based on an utterly false assumption. How deep into the scandal would the truth have surfaced and the madness stopped? In this sense, we were all lucky that Lewinsky was telling the truth to Tripp.

Coverage of the Lewinsky scandal heightened and dramatized four evolving tendencies in contemporary journalism:

"OUT THERE"

In January 1992, after a tabloid broke the story of Clinton's affair with Gennifer Flowers (she claimed they had had a twelve-year-long affair; he denied it for years and later admitted under oath to one weak moment), NPR's *All Things Considered* at its Friday morning editorial meeting discussed using the story. A number of producers pushed for broadcasting it. Executive producer Ellen Weiss and anchor Linda Wertheimer had their doubts. "The *Times* ran one hundred words inside somewhere," Weiss observed. "Why should we? Just because some paper in Florida did?" Well, it was argued, because it was "out there." Weiss recalled there was "lots of back and forth," but "I was not persuaded." Her final decision, as framed, is a classic line from another era of journalism: that doesn't mean, she responded finally, that it has to be "in here."

In the ensuing six years, the distinction between "out there" and "in here" vanished in the crush of competition. The wall that used to separate tabloid from traditional news was breached and in some places shattered. During the O. J. Simpson trial in 1995, reporter David Margolick of *The*

New York Times used the tabloid *National Enquirer* as his sole source for an alleged prison confession by Simpson to his friend, former football player and cleric Roosevelt Greer. "I did feel a little skittish," Margolick said, "but the *Enquirer* had broken a few stories." During the Lewinsky scandal, every network and newspaper used gossipmonger Matt Drudge, though they rarely cited him as their source.

Once the Lewinsky story was "out there," once it was reported by a network (ABC) and a newspaper (*The Washington Post*), it fueled a prairie fire of copy-cat journalism. Many reporters felt they had to get into the act. They had no option. Competition was fierce. A "semen-stained dress" was a major story, even though very few journalists had reliable sources or hard information about it. A White House steward was widely identified by name as someone who had actually seen the president and Lewinsky in a "compromising position." Was there confirmation? No. Were there denials? Yes. Did the denials discourage reporters from returning to the same stories? No.

RUSH TO JUDGMENT

For a long time, during hot and cold wars, presidents and reporters were reading essentially from the same sheet of music. In the 1940s, the Nazis were a common enemy. Patriotism bound the press to the cause of "unconditional surrender." On December 7, 1941, the date that would "live in infamy," Edward R. Murrow dined with President Franklin Roosevelt at the White House. No reporter had yet been briefed on the devastating dimensions of the Japanese attack on Pearl Harbor. By dessert time, the president had told the noted CBS correspondent everything—how many lives were lost, how many planes destroyed, how many ships sunk. And he imposed no ground rules. As Murrow walked back to his hotel, he considered doing a broadcast; the news, after all, was sensational, vitally important, and he had it from a superb source. There is little doubt that the modern equivalent of Murrow would have rushed to a studio and broadcast his exclusive, assuming, quite properly, that in the absence of any inhibiting ground rules, the president might have wanted him to disclose the extent of the catastrophe. Let the news first come from a reporter and later be confirmed by the president. Possibly that might have been Roosevelt's strategy. But what did Murrow do? He returned to his hotel and retired. He decided that the news could wait until the next day. Better than now? Worse? Certainly different, and, in my judgment, wrong. The news should have been reported.

Then, for more than four decades, during the tense period of the Cold War, the Communists became the common enemy. Relations between presidents and reporters were at times strained, especially during the Vietnam War; but there were rules, and the rules were generally respected. Ben Bradlee and John Kennedy were good friends, each benefiting from their friendship, each protecting the other. Walter Cronkite occasionally dined with Lyndon Johnson. Often the president would express opinions about the war or race relations that, if broadcast by the anchor considered "the most trusted man in America," would have been front-page news. But Cronkite, like Murrow, did not rush to a microphone. "It was clearly private," as he later wrote, "and it should remain such."

The election of Richard Nixon marked the beginning of the end of this era of relative goodwill between president and reporter. Nixon was paranoid about the press, imagining every reporter to be a member of some insidious enemy camp. During the height of the Watergate scandal, he even produced an "enemies list," consisting of many prominent politicians, writers, and journalists. I was proud to be included in this distinguished company. Nixon's vice president, Spiro Agnew, prior to his forced resignation on corruption charges, delivered a series of speeches attacking the credibility and integrity of the mainstream media. Nixon was determined to undermine the press, but in the end he failed. The people had a right to know the truth about their president's actions, and they ultimately learned the truth. *The Washington Post*'s reporting of the Watergate scandal led to Nixon's resignation. The *Post*, the press, and the American people won—a journalistic triumph of historic proportions.

But there was a downside of equally historic proportions. Watergate fostered a climate of skepticism and cynicism about the political process, affecting not only the public but the press. Ben Bradlee, executive editor of *The Washington Post* during that scandal, wrote that "journalism was forever changed by the assumption—by most journalists—that after Watergate officials generally and instinctively lied when confronted by embarrassing events." He admitted he was among those journalists. "I found it easier to cope with Washington by assuming no one ever told me the complete truth." While researching a book, Thomas Patterson, a Harvard professor, asked reporters why they consistently portrayed presidential candidates as liars. "Because," he was told, "they *are* liars." Martin Tolchin, a former *New York Times* reporter who now publishes *The Hill*, a weekly newspaper on Capitol Hill, said that "public officials and those in authority are per se dishonest, incompetent, untrustworthy and more interested in their careers than in the problems of their constituencies." Tom Brazaitis, Washington bureau chief of the *Cleveland Plain Dealer*, is even blunter. "Hell, we're the cheerleaders of cynicism."

By January 1998, unless a president could prove he was telling the truth, reporters assumed he was lying, dissembling, cutting corners for the purpose of political salvation. They operated on a presumption of presidential guilt. Many simply assumed that Clinton was lying, as were those aides speaking on his behalf. The Lewinsky story "felt" right; the reporters didn't need facts to confirm their instincts—indeed, on occasion, facts seemed to get in their way.

Cynicism about government was half the problem; a loss of respect for presidents and politicians was the other half. During the Ford administration, reporters joked about whether the president could walk and chew gum at the same time. During the Reagan administration, reporters ridiculed the president's apparently limited command of fact and detail. During the Bush administration, there were jokes about the president's mangled syntax. By the 1988 presidential campaign, reporters had shifted from joking to poking into the private lives of candidates. Paul Taylor, then a reporter for *The Washington Post* and now a crusader for media responsibility, asked Senator Gary Hart at a news conference whether he had ever committed adultery. Within twenty-four hours, Hart pulled out of the race. He felt that if the story of his alleged infidelities ran, he could no longer raise money and his family life would be shattered. When Bill Clinton entered the Oval Office, there were few journalistic constraints. Everything was considered fair game, from the trivial to the towering, from underwear to impeachment.

The faint traces of respect for presidential candidates still visible from earlier administrations had vanished by the late 1990s. Reporters rushed to judgment about Clinton, and he gave them ample reason. In this age of contrived images, Clinton always wanted to be seen as one of the boys— not as an aloof leader like France's Charles de Gaulle, who refused to wear glasses in public though he was clinically blind, but rather as an ordinary

baby boomer not above disclosing in Oprahesque fashion the most intimate details of his private life.

BLURRING THE LINES

For a long time, reporters were observers; they were not the observed,
they were not celebrities. Now many of them have become both the
observers and the observed, emerging as instantly recognizable celebrities.
No longer will the new technology or the new economics allow them to be
flies on the wall of history. Because reporters live and work in a world of
television, they have come to live by the standards of television. If they
command air time, they are seen as special emissaries to power and wealth,
no longer able to be objective.

Television, more than any other tool of modern communication, facil-
itates the blurring of the line between journalism and politics. A government official leaves his or her White House or congressional job and
becomes a commentator or columnist. So what? one may ask. One answer
is that the public, after a while, has difficulty distinguishing who's who
among the Washington power elite. Who's the reporter? Who's the official? Who's telling the truth? Who's shaving the truth? Indeed, in these
slippery times, what is the truth? In a democracy, the truth-teller holds the
key to the kingdom. The journalist used to be the truth-teller. But now?

Former *Washington Post* editor Russ Wiggins was one of the first to
spot the problem. "Journalists belong in the audience," he'd often tell his
reporters, "not on the stage." At the time, in the early 1970s, many journalists would have agreed with Wiggins—that is, until they saw their real-life
colleagues, Bob Woodward and Carl Bernstein, portrayed in the movie *All
the President's Men* by Hollywood stars Robert Redford and Dustin Hoff-
man. Suddenly, the honorable but hardly lucrative craft of journalism
opened new horizons; instead of a pat on the back for a story well done,
journalists began to search for a pot of gold at the end of the rainbow. The
placement of a good story on the front page used to be regarded as the
highest form of reward; now a good story can also be seen as a stepping
stone to an occasional or regular television appearance, maybe a book, even
a movie. Reporters now appear regularly in movies, sometimes simply
playing the role of a reporter, at other times playing themselves.

Ben Bradlee, in his memoir, *A Good Life*, points out that coverage of the Nixon scandal converted the reporter into a star. "Watergate," in his words, "marked the final passage of journalists into the best seats in the establishment." Once in the best seats, journalists were expected to produce more than just good, clean copy; now they were also expected to deliver their opinions, and their opinions carried weight in a universe shared with celebrities and politicians spouting controversial, crisscrossing insights, right or wrong. The upshot is that many journalists have become too big for their britches. For those who want to offer commentaries on television, deliver speeches for hefty fees, even appear in the movies, the once glorious if somewhat mundane pursuit of the truth now seems too humble a calling. The temptation to perform, to pontificate, to rise above the story has clearly become irresistible; and as the editorial walls separating straight reporting from commentary, political participants from political observers, crumble in a heap, journalism takes another large step toward becoming a business like any other—but it is the only business in America protected by the First Amendment.

Journalism, largely because of the lure of money and glamour, has become an attractive alternative to politics. Susan Molinari, a rising GOP congressional star from Staten Island, leaped directly from politics to an anchor's chair at CBS. After a year, the ratings, which she was expected to boost, did not rise, and she went down in television history as a flop. Bill Bradley, a respected Democratic senator from New Jersey, left Capitol Hill partly to prepare for his presidential run in 2000. He needed frequent exposure on television to be considered a live option, so he became a "liberal commentator" on CBS. His pieces were well written and sensible, but his voice was flat, and he too was dropped. But many other politicians take to playing reporters and commentators with ease. Superficial similarities abound. Both enjoy the publicity, both love television, both play to the crowds, both happily give their opinions on anything from Bosnia to baseball.

At the 2000 party conventions in Philadelphia and Los Angeles, there were now so many ex-politicos acting as pundits that authentic journalists suddenly seemed like an extinct species. Turn on the television, and there they were. Former White House spokesman Mike McCurry and former Newt Gingrich spokesman Tony Blankley served as political analysts on CNN. Former White House aides David Gergen and George Stephanopoulos appeared regularly on ABC's *Nightline* and elsewhere as well. Former Clinton adviser Paul Begala, former Reagan speechwriter Peggy Noonan, and former Iran-contra expert Oliver North provided commentary for MSNBC. Former White House staffers Lanny Davis, Bill Kristol, Newt Gingrich, and Tony Snow were regulars on Fox. Bill Press, once chair of the California Democratic Party, and Mary Matalin, a GOP operative, represented "left" and "right" on CNN's *Crossfire*. And so on.

There is probably no more damaging example of the back-and-forth government-journalism confusion than the role John Ellis played on election night 2000 on the Fox News Channel's decision desk in New York. Ellis spent eleven years (1978–89) working for the Election Unit of NBC News, and he wrote a superb political column for the *Boston Globe* for five years, quitting in the summer of 1999 because, as he explained, his cousin, George W. Bush, was running for president and he could no longer be objective about the campaign. Ellis and Bush are very close cousins.

On election night 2000, Ellis ran a four-person team of political experts whose job was to check Voter News Service data and recommend a call for the Fox network. One would have imagined that Ellis and Bush would have built a firewall between them on that night, especially when it was clear by as early as 1:14 p.m. in the afternoon that the election was going to be extraordinarily tight. But according to Ellis, they spoke to each other six times that night—Ellis calling Bush and Bush calling Ellis. Once, Florida governor Jeb Bush called Ellis. "Both gave us very valuable information about what precincts in what counties had not yet reported, what the absentee counts looked like in New Mexico and Arizona, and, in the case of Florida, exactly which precincts had yet to report and how those precincts had voted in Jeb's prior gubernatorial races," Ellis later wrote. "These conversations helped me better understand the data that were appearing on our screens." Ellis did not report on what he had told George and Jeb Bush, if anything, during those telephone calls. At 2:16 a.m. on Wednesday morning, Fox News Channel was the first network to project Bush the winner of the presidential race. Within minutes, the other networks on hair-trigger alert followed Fox and created the impression that Bush had won the election. Had Ellis crossed the line?

David Broder, dean of political columnists in Washington, has been watching the turnstile between politics and journalism with increasing unease. On November 19, 1988, he expressed his alarm at the National Press Club. "We damn well better make it clear we are not part of the government," he declaimed, "and not part of a Washington insider's clique where politicians, publicists and journalists are easily interchangeable parts. Once we lose our distinctive identity, it will not be long before we lose our freedom." He spotted a "new hybrid creature" slipping suspiciously between the two worlds of politics and journalism—an "androgynous political insider . . . blurring the lines between journalism on one side, and politics and government on the other." Speaking from an ethical podium of unblemished accomplishment, Broder added: "We all know them. The journalists who go into government and become State Department or White House officials, and then come back as editors or columnists. . . . One day he or she is a public official or political operative; the next, a journalist or television commentator. Then they slip into the phone booth and emerge in their original guise." More likely, in recent years, the politician emerges as a media pundit and, loving his or her new role, sticks to it.

SOURCING—OR THE LACK THEREOF

On this story, who were the sources?

Every reporter knows that good sources have always been crucial to good journalism. A good source can provide the journalist with a key fact, an insight, even with the whole story. A bad source can lead the journalist to present an incomplete, distorted, or biased story. All too frequently, many journalists covering this story had neither good nor bad sources; they simply had what was already "out there"—what had been published by *The Washington Post* or *Newsweek*, broadcast by ABC or discussed on talk radio or television.

There were at the time five different categories of sources who knew parts or all of the story. They talked to reporters—some enthusiastically, most quite reluctantly. They were:

1. **Office of the Independent Counsel, led by Kenneth Starr.** Starr later acknowledged that on occasion he himself spoke to reporters—basically, he told Steven Brill, to correct inaccuracies— but the bulk of the OIC briefing was left to his deputies, principally Jackie Bennett. Bennett employed the self-protective "deep background" rule, meaning his comments could not be ascribed to the OIC, to "officials" in the OIC, or to Starr. Reporters used his

information and said it came from "sources"—free-floating "sources" linked to no institution. Bennett was particularly busy in those days leading up to the breaking of the story and immediately thereafter. He fenced with reporters, asking how much they knew, who their sources were, what they had heard—and they told him, hoping in exchange to get confirmation or more information from him. One of his OIC colleagues explained, "Jackie was constantly talking to the press. That was his job. He bargained with them, he argued with them, he briefed them. What he was trying to do, more times than not, was stop the disinformation about us. But if he could get someone not to publish or broadcast something, he had to give some information back to that reporter, as a form of compensation. Jackie didn't like the press, but he was very good at dealing with them." Bennett's negotiation with Isikoff on January 15, before the story broke, was the most dramatic example of this technique.

2. **White House, Department of Justice.** White House officials were most loyal to the president, but on this story even a few of them, moved by conscience, disgust, or disagreement, wandered off the official reservation. Every now and then, when desperate, the White House would employ a cynical, preemptive tactic known as "inoculation"—seeding the public with damaging anti-Clinton information before its political opponents could release or leak the same or even more damaging information. In this way, the public impact would be softened, because the public would already have been "inoculated" to the bad news. Even though some reporters were aware they were being manipulated, they went along with the game, believing they had no option if they were to be competitive on a hot story.

Not all sources working for the executive branch blindly followed White House orders, however. Attorney General Janet Reno was in a most awkward position: she worked for the administration, yet found herself investigating its shortcomings. She met with the press on a regular basis, saying very little, but she knew that a number of her top advisers were saying much more in "deep background" conversations with reporters like Daniel Klaidman of *Newsweek*, who covered the Justice Department.

3. **Lewinsky, Tripp, and Goldberg.** As a rule, during this period, Monica Lewinsky did not talk to the press. Ginsburg thought it wiser for him to do her talking. Linda Tripp, who spoke with a few selected journalists, was ultimately the single most important source of information about the Lewinsky scandal. She had listened to Lewinsky's confidences for months and then surreptitiously taped their conversations. She then shared Lewinsky's confidences—and the tapes—with Lucianne Goldberg, as well as with lawyers for the OIC and Jones. Goldberg, who knew everything Tripp knew, was an enthusiastic leaker. She shared her information widely, with the *New York Post* or anyone who would listen.

4. **Lawyers.** Every principal in the scandal had at least one lawyer; each of them had associates and assistants. The president had many lawyers: David Kendall and Bob Bennett, the two principal ones, spoke with reporters on a regular basis—"on the record" and "off the record," though these ground rules were often misunderstood. A succession of Tripp lawyers spoke with reporters, and Paula Jones's official lawyers, also eager to influence public opinion, were happy to leak information to reporters, especially if they seemed sympathetic. A small, determined group of behind-the-scenes attorneys, known as the "elves," worked closely with Goldberg seeding information wherever they thought it would be most harmful to Clinton.

5. **The Internet.** If Isikoff's exclusive had been published on January 18, 1998, it would have been the "source" for hundreds, perhaps even thousands, of other stories in newspapers, networks, and magazines. But when his exclusive was "spiked" and Drudge published the rough outlines of his story, it was suddenly the *Drudge Report* that became the source of news leads and information about the brewing scandal. Because Drudge was a new and unreliable source, some reporters felt the need to check the information, and that took time. Other reporters used Drudge unashamedly. Why? Because he was "out there."

More than two and a half years after she helped break the Lewinsky story, Susan Schmidt returned to her "sources." On August 18, 2000, the same day *The Washington Post* banner-headlined its lead report GORE DEBUTS AS HIS "OWN MAN" from the Democratic National Convention in Los Angeles, it ran a related story in the lower left-hand corner of the front page entitled NEW GRAND JURY PROBE SET FOR LEWINSKY CASE. Schmidt shared the byline with David A. Vise, but in one major respect the story read like those she had written in the early days of the scandal that led to the impeachment of a president.

"Independent counsel Robert W. Ray has impaneled a new federal grand jury to consider evidence on whether President Clinton should be indicted on criminal charges arising from the Monica S. Lewinsky investigation after Clinton leaves office, *sources* said yesterday."

A new and major development, deeply embarrassing to Bill Clinton but, more important, to Al Gore on the day he was to accept the Democratic presidential nomination, splattered across the political landscape. The Republicans had been so careful at their convention not to mention the scandal, the intern, or the impeachment, alluding to such topics only tangentially on the assumption apparently that a direct assault would have been politically counterproductive. Yet, on the fourth and most important day of the Democratic convention, here again was the scandal to beat all presidential scandals beating on Gore's door. It was, for a time, a very big story, in large part because few reporters knew the motivation of the story's source. Was the Office of the Independent Counsel again playing politics? Was the White House playing its old game of inoculation? Was the Bush campaign playing hardball in the middle of the Democratic convention? Who was running off at the mouth this time anyhow? And for what purpose?

Schmidt's use of the word "sources" was misleading. Its very vagueness suggested mystery and gravitas. If this had been a *Washington Post* exclusive, similar in its secrecy and explosiveness to other stories leaked by the OIC and published in January 1998, then there might have been an excuse—namely, the need to protect *Post* access to the OIC at the height of a hot story. But this was not a Schmidt exclusive. It began as an Associated Press story, written by reporter Pete Yost. Within twenty-four hours, everyone was to learn that Judge Richard D. Cudahy, appointed by President Carter, a Democrat, in 1979, had "inadvertently" advised Yost about the impaneling of the grand jury. It was an innocent mistake on the judge's part. It was not part of a deliberate plot to advance anyone's political agenda. More candid and careful sourcing by Schmidt and Vise and other reporters could have spared Gore, Clinton, and the OIC a few anxious hours, but it would have denied the pundits an evening of exciting speculation.

Sources? They come in many shapes and sizes: sources who know the full story and share it honestly with a reporter; who know the whole story but share only part of it and thereby convey an incomplete picture; who know only part of the story but suggest they know all of it; who know only part of the story and candidly convey only part of it, leaving the reporter to get the rest from others; who know none of the basic details of the story but, for political or psychological reasons, cannot acknowledge the truth and end up telling the reporter only what they have read in the papers that morning or heard on talk radio on the drive to work or spotted on a Web site of dubious reliability (or overheard their spouse telling a client); who consciously spin a story for political or selfish advantage; who enjoy the "game" of politics and will say anything to a reporter in order to get mentioned in the paper or on a talk show; who hide behind the loosest formulation of "sources" for the time-honored purpose of "leaking" a politically charged story. So, which "sources" were we talking about? When a reporter of Susan Schmidt's experience and commitment uses the word "sources" without any amplification, she really is not doing the reader any favor.

In the early days of the Lewinsky scandal, when only a handful of reporters, lawyers, and officials had any substantive information, most newspapers and networks were competitively pressured into copying from their colleagues or, worse, concocting aspects of the scandal to satisfy the public's appetite for what Lucianne Goldberg called "juicy tidbits." Many reporters felt the need to persuade their editors or producers that they too had "sources." None wanted to admit that they had no sources.

But for a serious newspaper, this was a serious problem, demanding an explanation; and on March 15, 1998, managing editor Robert Kaiser of *The Washington Post* wrote a thoughtful explanation. "'I'm sick of this sourceless news,'" he quoted one reader as having told the paper's ombudsman. Summing up the whole problem, Kaiser quickly added: "He's not alone." Kaiser explained that "trust" defined the essential relationship between a paper and its readers. Every now and then (and he provided examples), the paper had to protect its sources while providing vital information to the public. The ideal since Watergate was two solid sources, but the ideal had variations. Sometimes, Kaiser wrote, a reporter might actually get an "authentic, classified or confidential document." That was often good enough for the paper. At other times, a story might be based on only "a single human source." At still other times, two or three other sources might be needed.

But during the Lewinsky scandal, many readers lost confidence in the *Post*'s editorial judgment. So many stories were published with apparently inadequate sourcing that readers came to the conclusion that the paper must have been protecting or covering up for somebody. Kaiser argued: "We do not print unconfirmed stories just because they are juicy, or just to beat our competition. . . . We realize many readers are infuriated by anonymous sourcing. Many journalists are, too. But we also think our readers should know that sometimes granting anonymity to sources is the only way to acquire publishable information on matters of interest and importance to them. So, if we have confidence in our information, we will print it."

Kaiser concluded by acknowledging that there was "insufficient room for dialogue between journalists and their readers," and he "resolved to do better." But more than two years later, Schmidt and her editors were still citing only "sources" on a story with less than explosive impact. In the interests of a "better . . . dialogue," why?

In one of their books about Watergate, Woodward and Bernstein related a conversation with Ben Bradlee about their sources. Although Bradlee understood the need to keep promises of anonymity to sources, he wanted to be certain that his reporters were not relying on "people who have . . . [a] big ax to grind on the front page of *The Washington Post*." Getting the story was important, but making sure the sources were reliable and honest was even more important. The two reporters wrote that their talk "satisfied Bradlee's reportorial instincts and responsibilities as an editor."

In journalism, it has often been said that the first casualty of war is truth. For more than thirteen days in January 1998, Washington was a battlefield. Lying there, as one of the first casualties of this conflict, was sourcing. Many reporters used flimsy, questionable sources; some struck secret deals with government officials to get a jump on a story. This practice lowered journalistic standards and, even worse, damaged the public's trust in its newspapers and networks. Questions arose: Where were these "juicy" details, allegations, rumors, gossip coming from? Who benefited from these leaks? Readers and viewers were left to wonder.

What, then, is the essential obligation of journalism? For much of the twentieth century, an unresolved argument between the philosopher John Dewey and the journalist Walter Lippmann echoed through the corridors of journalism. The argument, simplified, could be framed: Should the press try to educate the public, or should it cater to the public taste? Should it go highbrow, or lowbrow?

Lippmann envisaged journalists as members of an elite corps of specially trained observers—for example, political or diplomatic experts who not only reported on matters of public policy but also provided editorial guidelines for elevating the quality of public policy, for making government better. Dewey objected to any form of journalistic elitism, believing that the best newspapers had only to reflect the public's interest to be fulfilling their fundamental responsibilities to society. Journalistic legitimacy, in his view, was the natural consequence of tapping into the people—it was a bottom-up process. Lippmann saw journalistic legitimacy as a top-down process—elite journalists who knew how to organize and explain what the public needed. Never before have American journalists been better prepared for this task. They are the best educated and best paid professionals in the business, more powerful as an institution than at any other time in American history.

Journalism is among the most analyzed and self-analyzed professions in America. Dozens of academic and media experts direct their fire at any infraction of journalistic ethics or practice as soon as one is spotted on the near horizon. Yet there is something profoundly wrong here. For, while there has been more self-flagellation and anguished navel-gazing, more scholarship and analysis, more foundation support, more unabashed care for the media than at any other time in American history—in other words, more pressure and encouragement to clean up its act—the effect on the practice of journalism has been negligible. Indeed, though some journalists have argued that the relentless criticism of the press is a sign of strength and self-confidence, there is overwhelming evidence that standards have continued to fall. All of this well-intended criticism has apparently fallen on deaf ears; or journalists have heard the criticism but can do little to nothing to improve their ways.

In September 1993, Dan Rather of CBS delivered a remarkably candid keynote address to the annual meeting of the Radio and Television News Directors of America. He based his address on Edward R. Murrow's 1958 speech to the same organization. At that time, the legendary newsman had chastised the industry for failing to utilize "this weapon of television" in the battle against "ignorance, intolerance and indifference." Of television then, Murrow used words now familiar to many: "This instrument can teach, it can illuminate; yes, it can even inspire. But it can do so only to the extent that humans are determined to use it to those ends. Otherwise it is merely wires and lights in a box."

Rather looked the 1993 news directors in the eye. "We've all gone Hollywood," he charged; "we've all succumbed to the Hollywoodization of the news, because we were afraid not to." Fear was one of Rather's central themes. "Just to cover our rears, we give the best slots to gossip and prurience." Corporate executives and sponsors "got us putting more and more fuzz and wuzz on the air, cop-shop stuff, so as to compete, not with other news programs, but with entertainment programs (including those posing as news programs) for dead bodies, mayhem and lurid tales." The "post-Murrow generation of owners and managers," Rather continued, "aren't venal—they're afraid. They've got education and taste and good sense, they care about their country, but you'd never know it from the things that fear makes them do—from the things that fear makes them make us do."

Rather has been a $7 million anchorman, the heart and soul of CBS News, and yet he acknowledged then and has acknowledged since that fear of ratings and bottom-line "slippage" has forced him and his colleagues to do infotainment rather than hard news. He quoted one news director as ordering his staff to do more stories on Madonna and her sex life than on a papal visit to America. Rather begged his audience to put together "a few good men and women with the courage of their convictions to turn [the news industry] around." A question cries out for an answer: why hasn't Rather, or Brokaw, or Jennings led the charge?

Rather spoke his words in 1993. Sandra Mims Rowe, editor of *The Oregonian* and former president of the American Society of Newspaper Editors (ASNE), spoke her words in April 1998, at an ASNE meeting in Washington, D.C. She too looked her colleagues in the eye and pleaded with them to take the "high road." She said bluntly: "Other media that do not share newspaper standards are recasting the definitions of news. But we do not have to be pulled along. . . . New media will not adopt our standards. . . . The high road is there if we will just take it. The notion that readers have created the demand for lowest common denominator journalism is false. We are doing that ourselves. We can and must stop." Rowe was lustily applauded. Her logic was unassailable—newspapers did not have to go the route of cable talk shows. Her message was resonant and powerful. But there have been few takers. Many of her colleagues realized that they were under pressure to expand tabloid-style coverage of the news, and they could do little if anything to break the momentum. Even three years later, when Jay Harris resigned from the *San Jose Mercury News*, they couldn't stop the drive toward further tabloidization.

Between Rather's appeal in 1993 and Harris's heralded resignation in 2001, eight years of journalism passed into history. They marked a steady decline in journalistic quality and values. "We can and must stop," cried Rowe. But the situation has only worsened. Is the battle irreversible? Are the news directors, the corporate managers, the journalists in fact powerless to change their course for the better? The incentives in the news business, as currently arranged, run in the direction of a further maximization of corporate profits and minimization of interest in the public welfare.

Yet I want to believe that journalism can change for the better—and must change for the better. The evidence at the moment, while depressing, is only the accumulated result of many individual decisions by network presidents, anchors, reporters, editors, producers, writers, and commentators. If they were to change their ways, the evidence would also change. Rather was right. It would take just a few good men and women, of courage.

NOTES

INTRODUCTION

6 *Many years later, my friend R. W. Apple:* R. W. Apple, Jr., Interview, March 14, 2000; *Media Studies Journal* (Winter 2000), p. 63.

9 New York Times *columnist Frank Rich labeled*: Frank Rich, *New York Times Magazine,* October 29, 2000, pp. 58–60.

CHAPTER I

11 *"Maytag repairman"*: Mark Jurkowitz, "In D.C., No News Is Bad News," *Boston Globe,* July 3, 1997, p. E1.

12 *The president, of course, denied*: Richard Berke and John Broder, "A Mellow Clinton at Ease in His Role," *The New York Times,* December 7, 1997, p. 1.

12 *His staff was planning a January 1998*: William J. Clinton, *State of the Union Address,* reprinted in *The Washington Post,* January 28, 1998, p. A24.

13 *"This is a story that is a classic"*: Paul Begala, "Fashioning the White House," *Harvard International Journal of Press/Politics,* vol. 3, no. 3 (Summer 1998), p. 7.

16 *"Look,"* Downie told me: Leonard Downie, Interview, April 2, 1999.

16 *discovered that the Resolution Trust Corporation*: Susan Schmidt, Michael Isikoff and Howard Schneider, "U.S. Is Asked to Probe Failed Arkansas S&L; RTC Questions Thrift's Mid-'80s Check Flow," *The Washington Post,* October 31, 1993, p. A1.

17 *David Hale, a former municipal judge*: Michael Isikoff, Howard Schneider, and Susan Schmidt, "Clintons' Former Real Estate Firm Probed; Federal Inquiries Focus on Financial Activities of Other Arkansans," *The Washington Post,* November 2, 1993, p. A1.

17 *Webster Hubbell, associate attorney general*: Susan Schmidt, "Regulators Say They Were Unaware of Clinton Law Firm's S&L Ties," *The Washington Post,* November 3, 1993, p. A4.

17 *Justice Department was sending a three-man team*: Michael Isikoff and Susan Schmidt, "U.S. Steps Up Investigations in Arkansas; Justice Dept. Names 3 As Prosecution Team," *The Washington Post*, November 10, 1993, p. A1.

17 *the House Banking Committee would investigate*: Jeff Gerth, "House Panel to Examine Arkansas S&L Failure," *The New York Times*, November 10, 1993, p. D2.

17 *Enter David Gergen*: David Gergen, Interview, December 20, 1999; Michael Isikoff, *Uncovering Clinton: A Reporter's Story* (New York: Crown, 1999), p. 35.

18 *Downie pointed out*: Isikoff, *Uncovering Clinton*, p. 35.

18 *"overdoing it a bit"*: Ibid., p. 36.

18 *Downie, when questioned*: Downie, Interview, April 2, 1999.

18 *Clinton had also made an unwelcome*: Isikoff, *Uncovering Clinton*, pp. 29–30.

19 *"very lawyerlike"*: Downie, Interview, April 2, 1999.

20 *Ann Devroy*: Downie, Interview, April 2, 1999.

20 *"It's not rocket science"*: David Gergen, Interview, December 20, 1999.

22 *"could have the thing"*: Kenneth Starr, *Larry King Live*, CNN, October 18, 1999.

22 *In Texas back in 1993*: Maria Recio, "Starr's Lieutenant Built Reputation on Texas Court Cases," *Fort Worth Star-Telegram*, May 16, 1998, p. 33; www.salon.com, July 17, 1998, Maria Recio, 8:15 a.m.

22 *CNN's Bob Franken, an Arkansas native*: Bob Franken, Interview, December 21, 1999.

23 *Ewing spoke "freely"*: Dan E. Moldea, Affidavit filed August 24, 1998, U.S. District Court, District of Columbia; Moldea.com, pp. 3, 5, 6, 9.

CHAPTER 2

26 *"sexual investigative reporting"*: Jeffrey Toobin, *A Vast Conspiracy* (New York: Random House, 2000), p. 31.

27 *"I was part"*: Isikoff, *Uncovering Clinton*, p. ix.

27 *"the bizarre characters"*: Ibid., p. 9.

27 *"That was something"*: Michael Isikoff, Brown Bag Lunch Seminar, Shorenstein Center for the Press, Politics and Public Policy, Harvard University, April 21, 1998.

28 *"didn't have much use"*: The following incident, with quotes, comes from Isikoff, *Uncovering Clinton*, pp. 11–17; it has also been confirmed to me by other participants.

31 *"He was helpful"*: Downie, Interview, April 2, 1999; Isikoff, *Uncovering Clinton*, p. 96.

32 *White House officials were pleased*: Bob Woodward, *Shadow* (New York: Simon & Schuster, 1999), p. 283.

32 *"What do you do"*: Isikoff, *Uncovering Clinton*, p. 356.

33 *Their existence was not known*: Don Van Natta, Jr. and Jill Abramson, "Starr Said to Have Received Tip on Affair Before Call by Tripp," *The New York Times*, October 4, 1998, p. A1.

33 *"There are lots of us"*: Isikoff, *Uncovering Clinton*, p. 182.

33 *"About six times"*: Gil Davis, Interview, September 27, 2000.

33 *Clinton backers strongly opposed*: Ruth Marcus, "Republican Draws Criticism, Praise," *The Washington Post*, August 6, 1994, p. A1; Ruth Marcus and Howard Schneider, "White House Supports Starr," *The Washington Post*, August 9, 1994, p. A1.

34 *"He pulled me to him"*: Isikoff, *Uncovering Clinton*, pp. 107–8, 119–21.

34 *"told me everything"*: Ibid., pp. 122–23.

34 *"disheveled—her face"*: "Twist in Jones v. Clinton," *Newsweek*, August 11, 1997, p. 30.

34 *"I can tell you"*: Grand jury testimony of Linda Tripp in Toobin, *A Vast Conspiracy*, p. 112.

35 *"You're barking up"*: Isikoff, *Uncovering Clinton*, p. 129.

35 *Intrigued, Isikoff kept calling*: Ibid., pp. 134–37.

36 *"If word were to leak"*: Ibid., p. 142.

36 *"All we've really got"*: Ibid., p. 158.

37 *"When I heard"*: Lucianne Goldberg, www.slate.com, March 30, 1999.

37 *"Wait a minute"*: Isikoff, *Uncovering Clinton*, pp. 204–5.

37 *Tripp and Goldberg kept providing*: Ibid., pp. 220–21.

37 *They told him of a hurriedly arranged*: Ibid., pp. 229–30.

37 *"I realized I was"*: Ibid., pp. 233–34.

38 *Thomas was disturbed*: Evan Thomas, Interview, January 4, 1999.

39 *"tape-recording a woman"*: Del Quentin Wilbur, "Tripp Loses Court Ruling," *Baltimore Sun*, December 15, 1999, p. 1A.

39 *"the woman who was"*: Neil A. Lewis, "Immunity Ruling Makes Tripp More Likely to Stand Trial," *The New York Times*, December 15, 1999, p. A20.

39 *she told the startling story*: Isikoff, *Uncovering Clinton*, p. 266–67, and Toobin, *A Vast Conspiracy*, pp. 187–88.

40 *"I don't exist"*: Isikoff, *Uncovering Clinton*, p. 382.

40 *The caller stated that*: Ibid., p. 286.

40 *" Do you know anything"*: Ibid.

40 *"every single day"*: Lucianne Goldberg, Interview, March 30, 1999.

40 *"I definitely did tell"*: Lucianne Goldberg, Interview, January 3, 2000.

40 *"Everything that had happened"*: Isikoff, *Uncovering Clinton*, p. 286.

41 *"This was [no longer] about sex"*: Ibid., p. 287.

41 *"completely changed the way"*: Ann McDaniel, Interview, October 2, 1999.

41 *Isikoff called Willie Blacklow*: Isikoff, *Uncovering Clinton*, pp. 290–91.

42 *Isikoff called again*: Ibid., pp. 292–93.

43 *"We were running"*: McDaniel, Interview, Oct 2, 1999.

43 *By the time he placed*: Toobin, *A Vast Conspiracy*, p. 200.

43 *"Breaking. Pay close attention"*: Ibid.

43 *"We need to meet"*: Isikoff, *Uncovering Clinton*, p. 293.

44 *"The credibility of the magazine"*: Ibid., p. 310.

45   *Next, Isikoff called Betty Currie*: Ibid., pp. 296–97.
45   *"Betty/POTUS"*: Ibid.
45   *"I know what you guys"*: Ibid., pp. 297–98.
45   *"We'd have been thrilled"*: Stephen Bates, Interview, July 21, 1999.
46   *Bennett, sensing soft turf*: Isikoff, *Uncovering Clinton*, pp. 298–300.
46   *"Look, you guys"*: One OIC prosecutor at the meeting confirmed Isikoff's account.
47   *"We can take the heat"*: Isikoff, *Uncovering Clinton*, p. 299.
47   *Isikoff set a deadline*: Ibid., pp. 298–300.
48   *After his encounter*: Ibid., pp. 301–2.
48   *"The entire situation"*: Ibid.
48   *"I suspect, although"*: McDaniel, Interview, October 2, 1999.
48   *Then he called Goldberg*: Isikoff, *Uncovering Clinton*, pp. 302–3.
48   *"That at any rate"*: Ibid.
49   *Bennett overstated his case*: Toobin, *A Vast Conspiracy*, pp. 200–201.
49   *"A seriously complicating factor"*: Steven Brill, "Pressgate," *Brill's Content* (August 1998), p. 127.
49   *Holder promised to contact*: Isikoff, *Uncovering Clinton*, pp. 304–5; Woodward, *Shadow*, p. 372.

Chapter 3

50   *"Something about perjury"*: Viveca Novak, Interview, January 6, 2000.
50   *As fierce competitors*: Ibid.
51   *The panel formally reviewed*: Toobin, *A Vast Conspiracy*, pp. 200–202; Isikoff, *Uncovering Clinton*, pp. 312–13; Woodward, *Shadow*, p. 375.
52   *"just in case"*: Isikoff, *Uncovering Clinton*, p. 310.
52   *"especially interest the OIC"*: Affidavit by Stephen Bates delivered to Maryland judge Diane O. Leasure of the Howard County Circuit Court, December 8, 1999
53   *Bennett promised to get copies*: Bennett declined repeated attempts to be interviewed for this book or even to answer submitted questions.
53   *activating Tripp's immunity*: Or so Moody and Tripp thought, until a Maryland judge ruled nearly two years later that the immunity had not taken effect until three weeks after their agreement, when it was confirmed by a federal judge.
53   *"I nearly jumped"*: Isikoff, *Uncovering Clinton*, p. 311.
53   *Davis had a farewell lunch*: Lanny Davis, *Truth to Tell* (New York: The Free Press, 1999), pp. 18–19.
54   *At 12:30 p.m., Monica Lewinsky*: Andrew Morton, *Monica's Story* (New York: St. Martin's Press, 1999), pp. 175–91.
54   *"I just felt an intense"*: Ibid., p. 176.
54   *"nearly hysterical with tears"*: Isikoff, *Uncovering Clinton*, p. 314.
55   *needed some "gray hair"*: Ibid., p. 315.

55 *"You're twenty-four years old"*: Morton, *Monica's Story*, p. 184.

55 *handed over sixteen audiotapes*: According to the Bates affidavit, "four of the 16 tapes appeared to be blank, and two others were distorted."

56 *"Mr. President, I find your explanation"*: Woodward, *Shadow*, p. 374.

56 *"totally improbable that the president"*: Ibid., p. 373.

56 *"Betty Currie had invited"*: Ibid., p. 370.

56 *Bennett had received a copy*: Isikoff, *Uncovering Clinton*, p. 317.

56 *"The first sign of trouble"*: Ibid., pp. 317–18.

57 *"something linking Ken Starr"*: Deborah Orin, Interview, January 27, 2000.

57 *"Under normal circumstances"*: Isikoff, *Uncovering Clinton*, p. 318.

57 *"This was making"*: Brill, "Pressgate," *Brill's Content*, p. 128.

58 *"Don't worry," she said*: Isikoff, *Uncovering Clinton*, p. 318.

58 *"Friday night, Spikey called"*: Brill, "Pressgate," *Brill's Content*, p. 128.

58 *"Hear anything about the president"*: Davis, *Truth to Tell*, p. 17.

59 *and Davis wanted to be helpful*: Ibid., p. 19.

59 *"Any chance you could"*: Ibid., p. 20.

61 *"Monica's in some kind"*: Toobin, *A Vast Conspiracy*, p. 236.

61 *Don't worry, Ginsburg said*: Jeffrey Toobin, "Secret War in Starr's Office," *The New Yorker*, November 15, 1999, p. 68.

61 *he called Emmick and said*: Morton, *Monica's Story*, pp. 188–89; Woodward, *Shadow*, pp. 375–76.

61 *Emmick was unhappy*: Woodward, *Shadow*, p. 376.

62 *delivered the key*: In Post-Kastigar Hearing Memorandum in the Circuit Court for Howard County, Case No. 13-K-99-038397, *State of Maryland v. Linda R. Tripp*, December 14, 1999, p. 18, prosecutor Stephen Montanarelli outlined George T. Conway III's central role in helping Moody obtain December 22, 1997, tape from Jackie Bennett and Udolf on the night of January 16, 1998, and then deliver the tape to the *Newsweek* bureau in Washington.

62 *"We loaded up"*: Isikoff, *Uncovering Clinton*, p. 321.

62 *"I heard Monica's voice"*: Evan Thomas, Interview, January 4, 1999.

62 *"Within five or ten"*: Brill, "Pressgate," *Brill's Content*, p. 128.

62 *"Astonishing," Klaidman said*: Daniel Klaidman, Interview, February 17, 2000.

62 *"an elaborate fictional world"*: Isikoff, *Uncovering Clinton*, pp. 322–23.

63 *"We felt the tape"*: Klaidman, Interview, February 17, 2000.

64 *"I had to fight"*: Brill, "Pressgate," *Brill's Content*, p. 128.

CHAPTER 4

65 *"like in the next few hours"*: Isikoff, *Uncovering Clinton*, p. 324.

66 *McDaniel was sympathetic*: McDaniel, Interview, October 2, 1999.

66 *"So I hear you got"*: Isikoff, *Uncovering Clinton*, p. 324.

66 *"in a bind"*: Ibid., pp. 324–25.

67 *Podesta promised Isikoff that he would check*: Marvin Kalb, The Rise of the "New News," Discussion Paper D-34, Harvard University, October 1998, p. 6.

67 *"a very weird phone call"*: Michael Isikoff, Interview, January 12, 2000.

67 *"I talked to Isikoff"*: Isikoff, *Uncovering Clinton*, p. 325.

68 *"the laughingstock of the world"*: Toobin, *A Vast Conspiracy*, p. 217.

68 *(Bennett was astonished)*: Woodward, *Shadow*, p. 382.

71 *Perhaps Smith was allowing*: Much later, Smith told Isikoff that had nothing to do with his thinking—Isikoff, *Uncovering Clinton*, p. 328.

72 *"Can we really accuse"*: Ibid.

72 *"You can talk"*: Ibid., p. 329.

73 *"I kept thinking"*: Ibid.

73 *"It was so free"*: Klaidman, Interview, February 17, 2000.

73 *"I favored publication"*: Thomas, Interview, January 4, 1999.

73 *"I was persistent"*: Novak, Interview, January 6, 2000.

74 *"I couldn't believe"*: Brill, "Pressgate," *Brill's Content*, p. 128.

74 *"Mike and I were pretty"*: Klaidman, Interview, February 17, 2000.

74 *"If we were"*: Isikoff, *Uncovering Clinton*, p. 334.

75 *A prosecutor, he angrily told Bennett*: Ibid.

75 *"You know this"*: Ibid.

75 *"So what if"*: Ibid., p. 335.

75 *"We are already players"*: Klaidman, Interview, February 17, 2000.

75 *"There are times"*: Isikoff, *Uncovering Clinton*, p. 335.

75 *"Eighty percent just wasn't good enough"*: McDaniel, Interview, October 2, 1999.

75 *"We think you've done"*: Isikoff, *Uncovering Clinton*, p. 337.

76 *"uneasiness about what"*: Brill, "Pressgate," *Brill's Content*, p. 129.

76 *Isikoff was drained*: Isikoff, *Uncovering Clinton*, p. 337–38.

76 *"At the end of six hours"*: Ibid.

77 *"CBS News has learned"*: CBS Evening News Transcript, January 17, 1998, p. 1.

77 *"That chickenshit," she sobbed*: Isikoff, *Uncovering Clinton*, p. 336.

78 *developed an acute distaste for Clinton*: Chris Vlasto, Interview, January 13, 1999.

78 *"Though Chris had the lean"*: Jim McDougal and Curtis Wilkie, *Arkansas Mischief* (New York: Henry Holt, 1998), pp. 258–59.

79 *"Not only was I despondent"*: Ibid., p. 291.

79 *"It was a most infuriating"*: Vlasto, Interview, March 30, 2000.

79 *"Yes, I took Paula Jones's"*: Vlasto, Interview, January 19, 1999.

79 *Matt Drudge called Isikoff*: Isikoff, *Uncovering Clinton*, p. 338.

80 *the disgruntled lawyer called Conway*: Toobin, *A Vast Conspiracy*, p. 230.

CHAPTER 5

82 *"This is going to be ugly"*: Isikoff, *Uncovering Clinton*, p. 340.

82 *"Maybe it could [still] be contained"*: Ibid., p. 341.

82 *"if Kristol wants to go"*: Ibid., p. 340.

83 "It's what we had feared": McDaniel, Interview, October 2, 1999.

84 *he began to acquire a modest following*: David McClintick, "Town Crier for the New Age," *Brill's Content* (November 1998), p. 115.

84 *"a cheap Sanyo television"*: Ibid., p. 114.

85 *Drudge, always on the prowl*: Isikoff, *Uncovering Clinton*, pp. 144–47.

85 *"OK, I'll give you this"*: McClintick, "Town Crier for the New Age," *Brill's Content*, pp. 115–16.

86 *White House officials logged*: Ibid.

86 *"I don't think I had"*: Jackie Judd, Interview, January 7, 1999.

86 *White House correspondent John Broder*: John Broder, Interview, January 10, 2000.

86 *"I was basically in the dark"*: Wolf Blitzer, Interview, September 17, 1999.

87 *"didn't believe it"*: David Shuster, Interview, April 16, 1999; Jim Warren, Interview, October 4, 1999.

87 *"If that's the kind of story"*: Doyle McManus, Interview, January 5, 1999.

87 *the* Post *invested $85 million*: *The Washington Post*, February 3, 2000, p. E1.

87 *"So many people already"*: Paul Sperry, "Is the Washington Post Website Site Imploding?" WorldNetDaily.com, March 14, 2000.

88 *"We do box it off"*: *NBC-Mutual News* Transcript, January 19, 1998.

89 *"absolute nonsense—absolute reckless"*: Peter Baker, "Battle Looms Over Scope of Clinton Trial Inquiry," *The Washington Post*, January 19, 1998, p. A1.

89 *"We think it would be highly relevant"*: *Face the Nation* Transcript, January 18, 1998.

90 *"What we're attempting to prove"*: *Meet the Press* Transcript, January 18, 1998.

90 *"We hadn't confirmed"*: Tim Russert, Interview, June 29, 1999.

91 *"The only way you can respond"*: Toobin, *A Vast Conspiracy*, p. 233.

91 *"What worse can come out"*: ABC's *This Week* Transcript, January 18, 1998.

91 *"Drudge, this better not be true"*: McClintick, "Town Crier for the New Age," *Brill's Content*, pp. 115–19.

91 *"phone was ringing off the hook"*: Isikoff, *Uncovering Clinton*, p. 341.

92 *"in a very quick manner"*: *The Starr Report: The Official Report of the Independent Counsel's Investigation of the President*, Referral to the U.S. House of Representatives by the Office of the Independent Counsel, September 9, 1998.

94 *CBS's evening news program*: Normally an evening news broadcast begins at 6:30 p.m., but on Sunday the serious part of CBS's "primetime" schedule gets underway at 7 p.m. with *60 Minutes*, which, because it has been a longtime moneymaker for CBS, cannot be monkeyed with. So the evening news is unceremoniously slipped to 6 p.m., allowing affiliated local stations to run their hugely profitable half-hour news programs of fires, traffic, weather, and sports at 6:30 p.m., a more desirable time for advertisers. However, if the anchor for the Sunday evening news was a genuine star, such as Rather, the network would be unlikely to run the risk of ruffling his feathers and changing the time.

95 *in a state of near hysteria*: Toobin, "The Secret War in Starr's Office," *The New Yorker*, p. 68.

95 *Ginsburg was appalled*: Toobin, *A Vast Conspiracy*, p. 265.

CHAPTER 6

98 *"a former White House aide"*: Isikoff's piece about Kathleen Willey and the presidential "grope."

98 *"long-running tryst"*: Baker, "Battle Looms Over Scope of Clinton Trial Inquiry," *The Washington Post*, January 19, 1998, p. A1.

99 *"Some of the president's intimates"*: John Harris, "Jones Case Tests Political Paradox," *The Washington Post*, January 19, 1998, p. A1.

99 *"I was almost too tired"*: Isikoff, *Uncovering Clinton*, pp. 342–43.

99 *"You need to talk"*: Ibid., p. 343.

99 *"I'm committed to making"*: *CNN Morning News* Transcript, January 20, 1998.

100 *"three or four of us"*: Susan Schmidt, Interview, January 12, 1999.

100 *"far and wide"*: Schmidt, Interviews, January 12–13, 1999.

101 *"A very strange witness"*: Vlasto, Interview, January 13, 1999.

101 *Weisskopf was on the phone*: Davis, *Truth to Tell*, p. 21.

103 *"confused reality with the movie"*: *Equal Time*, CNBC News Transcript, January 19, 1998.

103 *Lewinsky, Ginsburg, and Speights*: Toobin, *A Vast Conspiracy*, p. 267.

104 *"This thing just fell"*: Howard Kurtz, "Clinton Scoop So Hot It Melted," *The Washington Post*, January 22, 1998, p. C1.

105 *"She wasn't strong"*: Solomon Wisenberg, Interview, December 8, 1999.

105 *"Come on, we're leaving"*: Morton, *Monica's Story*, p. 197.

106 *"The press is overstepping"*: Louis D. Brandeis and Samuel D. Warren, "The Right to Privacy," *Harvard Law Review*, IV, December 15, 1890, p. 196.

CHAPTER 7

110 *"We share nothing"*: Schmidt, Interview, January 12, 1999.

110 *"We don't cooperate"*: McDaniel, Interview, October 2, 1999.

110 *"I wanted to give him"*: Downie, Interview, April 2, 1999.

110 *Vlasto was furiously working*: Vlasto, Interview, March 31, 2000.

111 *without checking with senior editors*: Vlasto, Interview, March 30, 2000.

111 *"That was one of the key"*: Vlasto, Interview, January 13, 1999.

112 *"people who would know"*: Judd, Interview, January 7, 1999.

112 *"We had access to the same information"*: Russert, Interview, June 29, 1999.

112 *She knew she had a big story*: Schmidt, Interview, January 12, 1999.

113 *"When we get close to publication"*: Downie, Interview, April 2, 1999.

113 *a "key piece of information"*: Schmidt, Interview, March 30, 2000.

113 *"At first, it all seemed so fanciful"*: Peter Baker, Interview, April 6, 2000.

113 *"If the president of the United States"*: Susan Schmidt, Peter Baker, Toni Locy, "Clinton Accused of Urging Aide to Lie," *The Washington Post*, January 21, 1998, p. A1.

114 *"behaving strangely"*: McManus, Interview, January 5, 1999.

114 *"vague intimations of genuine"*: David Willman, Interview, March 25, 2000.

114 *"Boss," he said glumly*: Ibid.

115 *"Firewalls were smashing"*: McManus, Interview, January 5, 1999.

116 *"the same old-fashioned poppycock"*: Mike McCurry, Interview, April 4, 2000.

116 *The pressure on the OIC for answers*: Solomon Wisenberg interviews, December 8, 15, 1999.

118 *"Monica's in town"*: Carl Cannon, Interview, July 27, 1999.

119 *"nailed it from an impeccable source"*: Judd, Interview, October 29, 1998.

119 *"everything came together"*: Vlasto, Interview, January 5, 1999.

119 *his reporters still treated the information*: McManus, Interview, April 17, 2000.

120 *"Isikoff's got something"*: Toni Locy, Interview, April 17, 2000.

120 *"Can you take a conference call"*: McCurry, Interview, December 30, 1998.

121 *Joining ABC chairman Roone Arledge*: Judd, Interview, January 7, 1999.

121 *"I was very frustrated"*: Brill, "Pressgate," *Brill's Content*, p. 130.

121 *"Are you seated"*: Davis, *Truth to Tell*, pp. 21–22.

121 *"This could be the worst"*: Ibid., pp. 22–23.

121 *Davis called Podesta immediately*: Ibid., p. 24.

122 *"the basic facts right"*: Ibid., p. 24.

123 *At 10:30 p.m., Baker called Lanny Davis*: Ibid, p. 24.

124 *"Jesus! Jesus! Jesus!"*: Woodward, *Shadow*, p. 387

124 *"Have you heard the latest"*: Ibid., p. 387.

124 *Clinton spoke once again with Lindsey*: Judd, Interview, January 7, 1999.

124 *Frustrated by* Nightline*'s decision*: Judd, Interview, April 17, 2000.

Chapter 8

126 *"It's breaking! It's breaking!"*: Brill, "Pressgate," *Brill's Content*, p. 123. This was confirmed in separate conversations with Lucianne and Jonah Goldberg.

126 *"A totally new phenomenon"*: Joseph Lelyveld, Interview, April 19, 2000.

127 *"Here was everything we'd done"*: Jonah Goldberg, Interview, January 3, 2000.

127 *"For five years"*: Brill, "Pressgate," *Brill's Content*, p. 128.

127 *"I wanted to keep"*: George Lardner, Jr., "The Presidential Scandal's Producer and Publicist," *The Washington Post*, November 17, 1998, p. A1.

127 *"My mom was the only one"*: Jonah Goldberg, Interview, January 3, 2000.

127 *"They felt themselves adrift"*: Michael Oreskes, Interview, December 29, 1998.

129 *"we would all have been dead"*: Toni Locy, Interview, April 17, 2000.

129 *according to one reliable study*: Tom Rosenstiel and Bill Kovach, *Warp Speed* (New York: The Century Foundation, 1999), p. 107.

130 *Judd also used the Ginsburg*: A year later, Judd justified her use of the vague word "sources," saying, "It was the best I could do under the circumstances." The OIC would not allow her to be any more specific. Next time, she promised, she would use the term "legal sources" as a way of both protecting her sources and advancing her story—Judd, Interview, January 7, 1999.

130 *72 percent of all of its statements*: Rosenstiel and Kovach, *Warp Speed*, pp. 114–15.

131 *"I don't know anything"*: *Good Morning America*, ABC News Transcript #98012101-j01, January 21, 1998.

131 *President Clinton was awakened*: Woodward, *Shadow*, p. 388.

132 *"There's an air of unreality"*: John F. Harris, "FBI Taped Aide's Allegations," *The Washington Post*, January 22, 1998, p. A1.

132 *"Once the story broke"*: Morton, *Monica's Story*, p. 199.

132 *"What? Are you mad?"*: Evelyn Lieberman, Interview, December 14, 1999.

132 *The VOA treated*: Eight months later, GOP senator Jesse Helms, chair of the Foreign Relations Committee, summoned Lieberman to produce a file of VOA broadcasts on the Lewinsky scandal, assuming apparently that he could catch her in an attempt to cover up for the president and launch a round of embarrassing hearings. There had been no cover-up, so there were no hearings.

132 *"outraged by these allegations"*: Davis, *Truth to Tell*, p. 25.

133 *"I'm going to make it clear"*: Woodward, *Shadow*, p. 388.

133 *"The usual atmosphere and routine"*: Davis, *Truth to Tell*, pp. 25–26.

133 *"The atmosphere of intellectual"*: Ibid., p. 27.

133 *"I still didn't grasp how big"*: Jill Abramson, Interview, January 18, 2000.

134 *"From the moment Ken Starr"*: Oreskes Address, *Ahead of the Times*, vol. 6, no. 6 (November–December 1998), p.10.

135 *"something in the air"*: Frank Sesno, Interview, September 29, 1999.

135 *"there was no question"*: Blitzer, Interview, September 17, 1999.

135 *"Like the* Times, *we were playing"*: David Mazzarella, Interview, July 21, 1999.

135 *"When I opened my door"*: Les Crystal, Interview, February 17, 2000.

136 *"We just got creamed by ABC"*: Lisa Myers, Interview, March 28, 2000.

137 *"slip-sliding his way"*: Howard Kurtz, *Spin Cycle* (New York: The Free Press, 1998), pp. xiv–xvi.

138 *"the political story of a generation"*: Susan Schmidt and Michael Weisskopf, *Truth At Any Cost* (New York: HarperCollins, 2000), p. 307.

138 *McCurry was asked 128 questions*: Kalb, The Rise of the "New News," pp. 8–9.

139 *"a garment with Clinton's"*: *Drudge Report*, Transcript 18:42 UTC, January 21, 1998.

140 *"Everyone was calling"*: Crystal, Interview, February 17, 2000.

140 *"Is that true?"*: *NewsHour with Jim Lehrer*, Transcript #6047, January 21, 1998.

140 *"We went wild"*: Isikoff, *Uncovering Clinton*, p. 347.

140 *"Did you notice he used"*: Davis, *Truth to Tell*, p. 28.

140 *"How can he stand there"*: McDaniel, Interview, October 2, 1999.

140 *"Well, that was a disaster"*: Woodward, *Shadow*, p. 390.

140 *"Look, you used the present tense"*: Ibid.

141 *"I'll never forget it"*: Crystal, Interview, February 17, 2000.

141 *"Certainly I believe they're false"*: John F. Harris, "FBI Taped Aide's Allegations," *The Washington Post*, January 22, 1998, p. A1.

142 *"The next three years"*: *ABC Special Report*, Transcript #98012104-j14, January 21, 1998.

143 *"key close aides"*: Russert, Interview, June 29, 1999.

144 *"What do you know"*: Isikoff, *Uncovering Clinton*, p. 348.

144 *"Now I know what was wrong"*: McDaniel, Interview, October 2, 1999.

145 *"to modify comments she had made"*: Michael Isikoff, "Diary of a Scandal," *Newsweek*, January 21, 1998.

146 *"We had a ton"*: Isikoff, *Uncovering Clinton*, p. 346.

146 *"You poor son of a bitch"*: Toobin, *A Vast Conspiracy*, p. 243.

147 *"We have had a complicated relationship"*: Tom Bettag, Interview, December 30, 1998.

147 *"Forty-seven times"*: Ann Lewis, Interview, January 4, 1999.

148 *"It was clearly an important"*: *ABC Nightline*, Transcript #98012101-j07, January 21, 1998.

Chapter 9

150 *"a media gossip page"*: *Today*, NBC News Transcript, January 22, 1998.

151 *All told*, Newsweek *reporters and editors*: In fact, Isikoff had been under contract to MSNBC since January 1997, paid by appearance, meaning he could appear on any NBC station or cable as a political commentator so long as he was imparting information that had already been reported to or in *Newsweek*.

155 *"I worked at the White House"*: *New York Times*, January 26, 1998, p. A13.

155 *"And ABC News reported"*: *New York Times*, January 24, 1998, p. A10.

155 *"She was in love"*: *New York Times*, January 25, 1998, p. A16.

155 *"Two members of the Cabinet"*: *New York Times*, January 26, 1998, p. A1.

155 *"But confidantes of Mr. Clinton"*: *New York Times*, January 25, 1998, p. A16.

156 *"Lewinsky's sworn affidavit"*: Ibid.

157 *"three times in an hour"*: *The New Yorker*, February 9, 1998, p. 29.

158 *"a central figure"*: *New York Daily News*, April 30, 2000, p. 43.

158 *"only the vaguest sourcing"*: Robert Kaiser, Interview, January 6, 1999.

158 *"misquoted me—I'd disregard"*: Schmidt, Interview, January 12, 1999.

158 *Schmidt shed no light*: It is interesting and perhaps revealing that in their book, Schmidt and Weisskopf provided very little information on how reporters learned about the Lewinsky story in the days leading up to her own exclusive in *The Washington Post* on January 21, 1998. She knew, of course, but she didn't disclose anything about her role.

159 *"Yes, it's true"*: Downie, Interview, April 2, 1999.

159 *Its front page is designed*: The lead story on the right is often a news feature, occasionally timely and often interesting; the "off-lead" story on the left is generally a long take-out on a major theme, such as the impact of illegal immigration on the Texas economy—the kind of story that is clipped for later reference. Between the lead story on the right and the off-lead on the left are the remaining four columns. The two nearer the off-lead are bracketed and headlined: "What's News." One is labeled "Business/Finance"; the other is "Worldwide," but also includes news from or about the United States. Moving then from left to right, another news feature story occupies a middle column, and finally a column of "Trends," composed of short news items (the closest the *Journal* comes to business gossip), completes the layout of the front page.

160 *"We didn't do O. J."*: Alan Murray, Interview, May 18, 2000.

163 *"Like the Times"*: Mazzarella, Interview, July 21, 1999.

164 *"to tell people who was reporting"*: Letter from David Mazzarella to Marvin Kalb, July 22, 1999.

165 *"I gave him a story"*: Lucianne Goldberg, Interview, May 9, 2000.

165 *"journalistic rule about two sources"*: Marc Kalech, Interview, May 22, 2000.

167 *"evasive, untruthful, unsure"*: Davis, *Truth to Tell*, pp. 30–32.

167 *the battles were "robust"*: John F. Harris, "Clinton Advisers Disagree About How to Respond," *The Washington Post*, January 23, 1998, p. A1.

168 *"The pressure is immense"*: Davis, *Truth to Tell*, p. 33.

168 *"the old classroom whisper game"*: Ibid., p. 35.

170 *"Escandalo sexual, eh?"*: ABCNEWS.com, Tom Nagorski, January 30, 1998.

170 *"First we heard that Brokaw"*: Brill, "Pressgate," *Brill's Content*, p. 135.

171 *"I've got it here"*: ABCNEWS.com, Tom Nagorski, January 30, 1998.

171 *"The emphasis of style"*: Schmidt and Weisskopf, *Truth At Any Cost*, p. 2.

171 *Finally, someone in the jostling*: Tim Kiska, "Media Quits Cuba for Hot Story Back Home," *Detroit News*, January 3, 1998, p. E1.

171 *"as promptly as we possibly can"*: Susan Schmidt and Peter Baker, "Judge Delays Lewinsky Deposition," *The Washington Post*, January 23, 1998, p. A1.

172 *McCurry's briefing was live*: During the day, NBC ran five "Updates" and five "Special Reports"—ten interruptions of its normal programming.

172 *"struck by the strangeness"*: Kiska, "Media Quits Cuba for Hot Story Back Home," *Detroit News*, January 23, 1998, p. E1.

174 *"May I have your attention?"*: Ruth Marcus, "Jordan Gives Beleaguered President His Presence," *The Washington Post*, January 23, 1998, p. A1.

175 *By year's end*: Media Monitor, vol. XIII, no. 1 (January–February 1999) p. I-b.

175 *"It was impossible for one person"*: Judd, Interview, May 23, 2000.

176 *The "document contain[ed] talking points"*: Isikoff's "Diary," published Wednesday evening on *Newsweek*'s Web site, was first to report extensively on the talking points in the mainstream press.

178 *68 percent of such speculation*: Committee of Concerned Journalists, "The Clinton Crisis and the Press" (February 1998). This relatively short report was released to the press and put on the Web site of the Committee of Concerned Journalists under the auspices of the Project for Excellence in Journalism. Kalb, The Rise of the "New News," p. 26.

178 *"The president has denied"*: David Shribman, "Gore Defends President Emphatically," *Boston Globe,* January 23, 1998, p. A23.

179 *"I wish [Starr] would call me"*: Schmidt and Baker, "Judge Delays Lewinsky Deposition," *The Washington Post,* January 23, 1998, p. A1.

180 *"It may . . . ultimately come down"*: ABC *Nightline* Transcript #98012201–j07, January 22, 1998.

CHAPTER 10

187 *"Devastated, concerned, upset"*: ABC News Transcript #98012301–j01, January 23, 1998.

189 *"What do you think the White House"*: Ibid.

190 *"too honest"*: Judd, Interview, May 23, 2000.

190 *"several messages from the president"*: ABC News Transcript #98012308–j01, January 23, 1998.

190 *"We all thought"*: Doyle McManus faxed letter to Marvin Kalb, dated January 25, 1999.

190 *"shaken and downbeat"*: McManus, Interview, January 5, 1999.

191 *The Washington institution*: Francis X. Clines, "At Breakfast with Godfrey (Budge) Sperling Jr.," *The New York Times,* January 10, 1996, p. C1.

196 *"It's unfathomable to me"*: Dana Milbank, "Trying to Ring the Hotline's Chimes," *The Washington Post,* May 18, 2000, p. C1.

196 *"Matt Drudge reported"*: Mary Matalin, WRC-TV, Washington, D. C., January 22, 1998.

197 *"Nobody here knows"*: Richard Berke and James Bennet, "Those Closest to Clinton Are Left in the Dark," *The New York Times,* January 24, 1998, p. A1.

198 *"She is strategic"*: Ibid.

198 *"I'll be fine"*: John Broder, "Ex-Intern Offered to Tell of Clinton Affair in Exchange for Immunity, Lawyers Report," *The New York Times,* January 24, 1998, p. A1.

198 *"The president started out"*: Susan Schmidt and Peter Baker, "Ex-Intern Rejected Immunity Offer in Probe," *The Washington Post,* January 24, 1998, p. A1.

199 *"Clinton and his senior"*: John Harris and John Goshko, "Decision to Strike Iraq Nears," *The Washington Post,* January 24, 1998, p. A1.

199 *"It may be time"*: Richard Cohen, "But Is It a Matter for the Law?" *The Washington Post,* January 23, 1998, p. A27.

199 *"We discussed Monica"*: Richard Cohen, Interview, June 8, 2000.

200 *"was guilty of sparking"*: McManus, Interview, January 5, 1999.

200 *"I don't have anything new"*: Broder, "Ex-Intern Offered to Tell . . . ," *The New York Times*, January 24, 1998, p. A1.

201 *Helmut Sonnenfeldt, a former*: Helmut Sonnenfeldt, Interview, July 5, 2000.

201 *But no pundit at Brookings*: Stephen Hess, Interview, July 10, 2000.

203 *"made small talk"*: Susan Schmidt and Peter Baker, "Lewinsky Immunity Talks with Starr Show Little Progress," *The Washington Post*, January 25, 1998, p. A1.

203 *"ABC News has new details"*: ABC News Transcript #98012301-j04, January 23, 1998.

204 *"That was a wild day"*: Judd, Interview, January 7, 1999.

205 *"My discomfort over the subject matter"*: Judd, Interview, May 23, 2000.

205 *"At that stage, only"*: Lawrence K. Grossman, "The Press and the Dress," *Columbia Journalism Review* (November–December 1998), p. 34.

205 *"they were right"*: Judd, Interview, January 7, 1999.

205 *"Drudge wasn't even"*: Judd, Interview, May 23, 2000.

205 *"I guess we don't"*: Lawrence K. Grossman, a former president of both PBS and NBC, wrote in the *Columbia Journalism Review* (November–December 1998): "Donaldson's revelation on GMA is a text-book example of an unsourced, unsubstantiated, pseudo-fact, disseminated by a reporter playing catch-up, that simply feeds the public's distrust of the news media" (p. 36).

205 *"access to the same information"*: Russert, Interview, June 29, 1999.

205 *a "wink and nod sort"*: Don Van Natta, Jr., Interview, January 10, 2000.

206 *because both audiences remained relatively modest*: Its primetime audience was 147,000 households and its daytime audience only 72,000 households. On an average day, NBC attracted a viewing audience forty-two times larger, for example.

206 *"using her [Lewinsky] to service"*: *Rivera Live!* CNBC Transcript, January 23, 1998, 9 p.m.

209 *"These are dark days"*: ABC News Transcript #98012302-j11, January 23, 1998.

CHAPTER 11

211 *"What's the big deal?"*: Dan Balz, "Washington's Extraordinary Week," *The Washington Post*, January 25, 1998, p. A1.

211 *"We're frozen by the media"*: Baker and Schmidt, "Lewinsky Immunity Talks with Starr Show Little Progress," *The Washington Post*, January 25, 1998, p. A1.

211 *"They're going to have to give her"*: Ibid.

214 *"He should do it"*: Philip J. Trounstine, "Panetta Shows No Fear of Taint from Clinton," *San Jose Mercury News*, January 24, 1998, p. 1.

215 *"getting through the scrum"*: Lucianne Goldberg, Interview, May 9, 2000.

215 *"adorably written but inaccurate"*: Shelley Ross, Interview, May 9, 2000.

217 *"CNN's video scoop"*: Much later Saturday evening, NBC found its footage of the embrace and ran it. The other networks were badly scooped.

218 *"Clinton always embraces"*: Brill, "Pressgate," *Brill's Content,* p. 138.

218 *However, on Saturday, competition*: CNN was under fierce competitive pressures from two relatively new cable television channels—MSNBC and Fox—which registered their highest ever ratings that evening.

218 *"The amazing, almost surrealistic"*: CNN Transcript #98012402V00, January 24, 1998, 6 p.m. EST.

219 *"There was too much sensationalism"*: Blitzer, Interview, September 17, 1999.

220 *"If I knew then"*: Blitzer, Interview, July 21, 2000.

220 *"should never have used"*: Frank Sesno, Interview, September 28, 1999.

220 *"more than one whisper"*: Ibid.

220 *"angrily denied there is any talk"*: Blitzer files, January 24, 1998, 8 p.m. script.

221 *"such an* un*eventful week"*: Jonah Goldberg, in "The Talk of the Town," *The New Yorker,* February 9, 1998, p. 29.

221 *"A person who hasn't read"*: R. W. Apple, Jr., and Adam Nagourney, "Surreal Air Envelops Capital as Some Change the Subject," *The New York Times,* January 26, 1998, p. A1.

221 *"Pure bunk"*: John Harris, "The Last Chance Presidency," *The Washington Post Magazine,* September 10, 2000.

Chapter 12

223 *The January 25, 1998, edition*: On a comparable day during the Gulf War, January 21, 1991, four days after the United States began bombing Iraq, *The Washington Post* ran twenty stories with 20,354 words. The next two days saw an increase in the number of stories and words, but in this period of comparable coverage *The Washington Post* actually published more words about the scandal than about the war. On January 22, 1991, the *Post* ran twenty-six stories with 22,994 words, and on January 23, it ran twenty-seven stories with 24,530 words about the bombing of Iraq.

223 *"Several sources have told us"*: ABC News Transcript #98012502-j12, January 25, 1998.

223 *"I wanted to hold it"*: Brill, "Pressgate," *Brill's Content,* p. 140.

223 *"worked the phones"*: Judd, Interview, July 25, 2000.

224 *to "shut down the whole"*: ABC News Transcript #98012503-j12, January 25, 1998.

224 *"particular scandal . . . cost"*: ABC News Transcript #98012504-j12, January 25, 1998.

224 *"If that is true"*: ABC News Transcript #98012505-j12, January 25, 1998.

225 *his "committee holds the power"*: ABC News Transcript #98012506-j12, January 25, 1998.

226 *"Can he survive?"*: ABC News Transcript #98012507-j12, January 25, 1998.

227 *More than two years later*: Judd, Interview, July 25, 2000.

227 *"I . . . think there might be a potential witness"*: Brill, "Pressgate," *Brill's Content*, p. 140.

227 *he had seen an "intimate encounter"*: The Starr Report: The Official Report of the Independent Counsel's Investigation of the President, pp. 70–72.

228 *"There are reports"*: Meet the Press, NBC News Transcript, January 25, 1998.

228 *"We simply couldn't confirm"*: Russert, Interview, June 29, 1999.

229 *"Our roundtable"*: Ibid.

230 *"I have here a document"*: Face the Nation, CBS News Transcript, January 25, 1998.

232 *Later, it turned out that he had "heard"*: Dallas Morning News, January 27, 1998, p. A1.

235 *If "we couldn't independently verify"*: Jim Warren, Interview, October 4, 1999.

236 *"In retrospect"*: "Pressgate," Brill, *Brill's Content*, pp. 141–42.

236 *"Here's where we stand"*: NBC News Special Report, NBC News Transcript, January 25, 1998, 4:42 p.m.

237 *"I guess it was because"*: Brill, "Pressgate," *Brill's Content*, p. 141.

237 *"I wrestled with the question"*: Letter from Tom Brokaw to Marvin Kalb, October 13, 1998.

238 *a "news update"*: In the days immediately following the breaking of the scandal story, NBC ran twenty-eight "Special Reports" or "News Updates," almost twice the combined total of its broadcast competitors and even more than CNN, the champion of "Breaking News."

238 *"He's very sharp"*: Alison Mitchell, "President Preparing Message on Policy," *The New York Times*, January 26, 1998, p. A1.

238 *"unusually buoyant"*: Richard Berke, "White House Acts to Contain Furor as Concern Grows," *The New York Times*, January 26, 1998, p. A1.

238 *"I have not been able"*: Peter Baker and Susan Schmidt, "Starr Seeks to Confirm Allegations: Did Secret Service See 'Intimate Acts'?" *The Washington Post*, January 26, 1998, p. A1.

238 *"sources familiar with the probe"*: Ibid.

240 *"At first, they told me"*: Oreskes, Interview, December 29, 1998.

240 *"Well, we got scooped"*: Oreskes, Interview, July 24, 2000.

241 *"I really thought at the time"*: Lelyveld, Interview, May 25, 2000.

241 *"Nothing was firsthand"*: Oreskes, Interview, December 29, 1998.

CHAPTER 13

242 *"None of us had ever seen"*: Oreskes, Ahead of the Times, vol. 6, no. 6 (November–December 1998), p. 10.

243 *"News for the Millions"*: Susan E. Tifft and Alex S. Jones, *The Trust* (Boston: Little, Brown, 1999), pp. 45–46.

244 *"A federal employee claims"*: David Jackson, "Source Reports Employee Saw Clinton, Intern," *Dallas Morning News*, January 26, 1998, p. 1A.

245 *in a "compromising situation"*: Carl Leubsdorf, Interview, January 8, 1999.

245 *"tomorrow's edition of the* Dallas*"*: *Nightline,* ABC News Transcript, January 26, 1998.

245 *"a vague tip"*: Joseph diGenova, Interview, August 10, 2000.

246 *"touting us off"*: Letter from Leubsdorf to Marvin Kalb, October 6, 1998.

246 *"Is Joe your source?"*: Victoria Toensing, Interview, August 10, 2000.

246 *"was getting cold feet"*: Leubsdorf, Interview, January 8, 1999.

246 *a "friend of someone"*: Brill, "Pressgate," *Brill's Content,* pp. 142–43.

247 *"This story of a 'secret service'"*: Ibid., p. 143.

248 *Leubsdorf protected Jackson*: Months later, Leubsdorf was still defending the paper's witness story. He pointed to an April 1998 *Time* report that Starr was convinced there was a witness and to the later testimony by Secret Service agents Gary Byrne and John Muskett, released on October 2, 1998, by the House Judiciary Committee, alleging that Harold Ickes "interrupted" Clinton and Lewinsky in "very unusual circumstances," apparently "proving" that there had in fact been a witness and it was Ickes. Letter from Leubsdorf to Marvin Kalb, October 6, 1998.

248 *"a troubling new standard"*: Jim Schutze and Christine Biederman, "Poop on the Scoop," *Dallas Observer,* February 5, 1998, p. 1; Janny Scott, "Rules in Flux," *The New York Times,* January 27, 1998, p. A13.

249 *"lipstick and other stains"*: Murray, Interview, December 30, 1998.

249 *As Murray explained*: Ibid.

250 *At 4 p.m., Murray made*: Ibid.

250 *"The White House had taken"*: Brill, "Pressgate," *Brill's Content,* p. 146.

250 *"When I told Murray"*: Ibid.

251 *"Could it be"*: Ibid.

251 *"Things have changed"*: Leubsdorf, Interview, January 8, 1999.

252 *"There is so much more competition"*: Murray, Interview, December 30, 1998.

CHAPTER 14

253 *"Much greater priority"*: David Shaw, "Dispute over Newspaper Chain Profit Goals Gets Public Airing," *Los Angeles Times,* March 21, 2001, p.15.

255 *For example, on August 2, 2000*: Every day, on the television page of *The Washington Post,* editors place a large ad promoting washingtonpost.com and listing what a reader can find by dipping into its many informational delights.

255 *Despite this daily output*: www.vanishingvoter.com, August 13, 2000, p. 2.

256 *In 1995, only 4 percent*: "Internet Sapping Broadcast News Audience," Pew Research Center, June 11, 2000.

256 *"glorified gossip"*: Tom Shales, "For The Networks, Reality Checks In," *The Washington Post,* December 31, 2000, p. G1.

256 *"Yes, we want to hold"*: Ken Auletta, "The Invisible Manager," *The New Yorker,* July 27, 1998, p. 42.

257 *One immediate effect was a dramatic increase*: See Dean Alger, *Megamedia* (Lanham, Md.: Rowman & Littlefield Publishers, 1999), pp. 5–11.

259 *That week, ABC News did not have*: Between 1997 to 1999, Disney had cut $25 million a year from the ABC News budget.

260 *"The* Times *ran one hundred"*: Ellen Weiss, Interview, September 2, 2000.

261 *"I did feel a little skittish"*: David Margolick, Interview, September 1, 2000.

262 *"It was clearly private"*: Walter Cronkite, *A Reporter's Life* (New York: Ballantine Books, 1996), p. 235.

262 *"journalism was forever changed"*: Ben Bradlee, *A Good Life* (New York: Simon & Schuster, 1995), p. 406.

263 *"public officials and those in authority"*: Kalb, The Rise of the "New News," p. 12.

263 *"Hell, we're the cheerleaders"*: Ibid.

265 *"Watergate," in his words*: Bradlee, *A Good Life*, p. 207.

265 *protected by the First Amendment*: Would the American people now support "freedom of the press," as written in the First Amendment? In 1991, the American Society of Newspaper Editors commissioned a poll and found that the answer was no. In 1997, the First Amendment Center at Vanderbilt University commissioned another poll. Do you think the press has "too much freedom"? Thirty-eight percent said yes. In 1999, in answer to the same question, 53 percent said yes.

265 *ex-politicos acting as pundits*: Howard Kurtz, "Leaving Wonkville, Entering Punditopolis," *The Washington Post*, August 21, 2000, p. C8.

266 *"Both gave us"*: "A Hard Day's Night: John Ellis' Firsthand Account of Election Night," *Inside Magazine*, December 12, 2000, p. 9.

268 *"Jackie was constantly talking"*: Wisenberg, Interview, December 8, 1999.

269 *A succession . . . were happy to leak information*: For example, Conway and Porter leaked stories to Drudge and Kristol at the beginning of the reporting of the scandal. Once upon a time, lawyers avoided journalists—that was the legal custom. Leaving the courthouse, for example, they would walk past the journalists and cameras, ignoring their questions; now, like politicians, they walk directly to the cameras, lay out their case, attack their opponents, and answer questions. As long as they think that by talking to the press they can advance their cases or causes, they are ready to do so.

271 *"I'm sick of this sourceless news'"*: Robert Kaiser, "More About Our Sources and Methods," *The Washington Post*, March 15, 1998, p. C1.

272 *the conclusion that the paper must have been protecting*: It was; it was protecting its excellent access to Starr's OIC.

272 *"people who have . . . [a] big ax"*: Bob Woodward and Carl Bernstein, *All the President's Men* (New York: Simon & Schuster, 1974), p. 146.

INDEX

ABOUT THE AUTHOR

One Scandalous Story is Marvin Kalb's tenth book. Seven others are works of non-fiction, focusing on Russia, China, Vietnam, and American foreign and domestic policy; two are novels set in Vietnam and the Middle East.

During a thirty-year career at CBS News and NBC News, Kalb won many awards for excellence in diplomatic reporting. He hosted documentaries and *Meet the Press*. As Moscow correspondent, he covered the Cuban missile crisis in 1962, and as chief diplomatic correspondent, he covered many Soviet-American summit meetings during the Cold War.

In 1987, Kalb became founding director of the Shorenstein Center on the Press, Politics and Public Policy at Harvard's Kennedy School of Government, a position he held until 1999, when he accepted the post of executive director of the Washington office of the Shorenstein Center. He was also the Edward R. Murrow Professor of Press and Public Policy. To honor his work, Harvard established the Marvin Kalb professorship in international communication.

Kalb has lectured extensively throughout the country. He appears regularly on radio and television, including PBS's *NewsHour with Jim Lehrer*, and he hosts *The Kalb Report* at the National Press Club in Washington, DC.

He is married and lives in Chevy Chase, Maryland.